Understanding the Consumer

A European Perspective

Understanding the Consumer

A European Perspective

BERNARD DUBOIS

An imprint of **Pearson Education**

Harlow, England · London · New York · Reading, Massachusetts · San Francisco · Toronto · Don Mills, Ontario · Sydney
Tokyo · Singapore · Hong Kong · Seoul · Taipei · Cape Town · Madrid · Mexico City · Amsterdam · Munich · Paris · Milan

Pearson Education Limited

Edinburgh Gate
Harlow
Essex CM20 2JE
United Kingdom

and Associated Companies throughout the world

Visit us on the World Wide Web at
www.pearsoneduc.com

First published in Great Britain in 2000

ISBN 0–136–16368–8

British Library Cataloguing in Publication Data
A CIP catalogue record for this book can be obtained from the British Library.

10 9 8 7 6 5 4 3 2 1
05   04   03   02   01   00

Typeset by 3 in Sabon
Printed in Great Britain by Henry Ling Ltd at the Dorset Press, Dorchester, Dorset.

Contents

Foreword

I am pleased to see an English translation of Professor Bernard Dubois's text on *Consumer Behavior*. I have long admired his research into the complex task of explaining, predicting, and influencing customer value drivers. The English edition promises to open a whole range of new ideas, stories, and experiences normally not accessible to uni-lingual managers and students.

Consumer behavior is the keystone of marketing planning. As Drucker observed, 'the customer is the business.' Companies are increasingly shedding their stereotypes about customers and moving toward a more sophisticated micro-segmentation of the customers making up their market. But segments not only need to be discovered; they need to be profiled and measured. One of Professor Dubois' talents is to bring quantification into the search for understanding consumer dynamics. Consumer insight comes not only from observation, empathy, and theory, but from careful data-based analysis.

Professor Dubois eschews a single doctrinaire approach to understanding consumers, as is the learning of 'school-based' theorists, such as Freudians, Gestaltists, Maslowians, Interactionists, and Behaviourists. All of these systems throw only partial light on the complex behaviour of consumers. What Professor Dubois offers is a comprehensive and systematic discussion of major elements that contribute to understanding different aspects of consumer behaviour.

This book is valuable in its abundant use of European examples and cases. To date, most consumer behavior texts have been written by Americans with the advantages as well as limitations of American frames of reference. The field of consumer behavior will increasingly benefit from texts written by authors from other regions of the world. Their approaches and examples will contribute greatly to both widening and deepening the concepts needed to forge a richer theory of consumer behaviour.

Philip Kotler
July 2000

Preface

By opening this book and reading these words, you are engaging into consumption. It does not take long to realise the ubiquitous nature of consumption. We are always, even when we sleep, consuming something. Since the day we are born until we die, we spend most of our life acquiring, receiving, and using a tremendous variety of products and services, from the most trivial (a glass of water) to the most significant (a home).

The second amazing aspect of consumption has to do with what is at stake. In a supermarket, a consumer places in her trolley a pack of detergent, almost without thinking about it. From this act (and the underlying decision or habit), repeated by millions of other consumers, at other places and times, depends the fate of a brand, of a factory, of a company employing hundreds or perhaps thousands of people.

"Everyone lives by selling something" said Robert Louis Stevenson. In order to grow, or just continue to exist, any organisation, whether large or small, public or private, domestic or multinational, critically depends upon the regularity and quality of the flow of exchange relationships with its markets, audiences, or publics. These relationships will be successful only if managers are able to understand demand and make adequate decisions on the basis of such understanding. In that sense, managers have no choice but to develop assumptions about market response. The only problem left is the validity of these assumptions.

There are only two ways of increasing the confidence that one has in his or her hypotheses regarding consumer behaviour. The first consists in relying extensively on one's observations and intuition. Over the years, marketing managers develop considerable experience about their markets and consumers which allows them to make what they believe are the most appropriate decisions (even though they sometimes have to admit they are just lucky); but, as the Chinese maxim says, "experience is a comb for the bald", underscoring its nontransferable nature. And it is true that we do not have to travel far away from home to discover that consumers do not always behave like we thought they would or should, based on our local knowledge. So, the second route open to us is to confront our ideas to those who have already explored and studied the subject. This is the approach adopted in this book.

The primary objective of *Understanding the Consumer* is to provide a concise and structured account of the essentials of what is currently known about consumer behaviour. Although the book is primarily intended for those, managers or students, who have a professional interest in this area, we hope it will also be of interest to all those who want to better understand the consumer who lives in every one of us.

Bernard Dubois
Jouy-en-Josas, France, July 2000

Acknowledgements

As far as I can remember, I have always been interested in consumers and consumption behaviour. In the late 60's, when this interest had turned into a "professional passion", consumer research was still in its infancy. Very few courses were given on the topic and, in business schools, consumer behaviour was, at best, considered a stepchild of marketing. Very few social scientists expressed an interest for what appeared to them as a rather mercantile domain.

Over the last thirty years, this field has literally exploded to the point where consumer research is now a fully mature discipline with its own associations (such as the Association for Consumer Research) and journals (such as the Journal of Consumer Research). Every year hundreds of studies are conducted and their results reported in journals or at congresses held all over the world. Since the content of this book is based on what I consider to be the most influential of these works, my first debt is owned to all researchers who have contributed to a better understanding of consumer behaviour.

On a more local level, I would also like to express my deep gratitude to Groupe HEC, Jouy-en-Josas, France, where I have had the pleasure of teaching and researching consumer behaviour for the last twenty-five years, as well as to my present and former colleagues in the marketing department. Among them, I would like to pay a special tribute to my friend Gilles Laurent with whom virtually all my research on the luxury market (some of it reported in this book) has been conducted.

On a more personal note, my original and overriding gratitude is to my wife, Michèle, and my two children, David and Caroline, to whom this book is dedicated.

Introduction

1898. In a modest workshop located in Billancourt, then a small village about three kilometres west of Paris, a 22-year-old engineer was building his first cars. This man was Louis Renault. He was both artist and craftsman. Having conceived the idea, he drew up the plans and assembled all the vehicles himself. By 1900 he had sold 179 of them. The relationship Louis Renault had with his customers could not have been more direct; he knew each of his customers personally and they could watch their car being made – even help in choosing the leather for the seats and the wood stain for the panelling. There was no need at this stage for customer motivation studies or market surveys.

A century later, Renault, the second largest French industrial group, is a major player in the global car industry with a turnover roughly equivalent to the French national budget for defence or agriculture. A network of 20 000 dealers distributes Renault products across 150 countries. With about two million vehicles being sold each year, half of which are exported, it is obviously no longer possible for the head office to maintain a direct relationship with each client, let alone with prospective purchasers. A central marketing department of several hundred people analyses a flood of quantitative and qualitative studies conducted on a variety of markets all over the world. Researching and understanding the consumer has become a necessity.

Even if not all car makers have experienced such explosive growth (only around fifteen Rolls-Royces and a hundred Ferraris are sold in France each year), the story of Renault illustrates the difficulties experienced by all companies which grow such that they lose direct contact with their markets. Basic but vital questions must be asked. Who are my customers? What do they want? How do I win them over? All the major decisions made by the company, whether highly strategic ones such as choosing to diversify or very operational ones such as managing promotional tactics, are dependent upon the answers to these questions. Like Sherlock Holmes, marketing analysts have to follow the clues revealed by the customers, while trying to understand their innermost attitudes and the most trivial aspects of their behaviour. Let us follow the Martin family in their search for a new car.*

192

Coming out of the Mercedes showroom on the Champs Elysées, Mr Martin and his family stared in complete astonishment at the order they had just signed. They were

---

*The following text is adapted from the Martin case study, developed by B. Dubois with the collaboration of a major European car maker.

all surprised that they had been capable of making a unanimous decision in such a short space of time. It was 4 December 1993.

There are are three people in the Martin family: Mr Martin, Mrs Martin and their son Gregory, who is 16 years old. Mr Martin, who is almost 50, is the deputy director of the technical department of a small mechanical construction company. He works in the company's head office, based in Paris. His boss described him as 'level-headed, courteous and most conscientious in his work'. Mrs Martin is the same age, does not work but is an accomplished homemaker. She enjoys an active social life; friends are always calling round, they chat about a variety of subjects: the children's education, their holiday plans, outings and so on. Gregory still goes to school. He has not definitely decided what he would like to do in the future but is considering a career in engineering. The Martins live in a small house in the residential area of Rueil-Malmaison, in greater Paris, which they had built five years ago. They get on well with their three or four closest neighbours; often when Mr Martin gets back from work, or when he is doing the gardening, he chats to one of his neighbours. They discuss their jobs and hobbies; sometimes they talk 'cars', especially when one of the families is thinking of buying a new car. The Martins are comfortably off without being ostentatious; they like to think of themselves as being upper middle class. It was about nine months before the Martin family actually bought it that they first considered the idea of buying a new car. That was on the day that Mr Martin, who uses the family car to get to work, arrived at the office very late because the car broke down. A few months before he had already had to replace the silencer and for the first time had asked himself about future maintenance costs. That evening he said to his family, 'We bought the Ford Sierra in 1986 when we were still in Marseilles and it's already done over 100 000km. The motor goes all right but I am worried about the clutch. The tyres have only been changed once and three of them are now in quite bad condition. The bodywork has got a few scratches and even a few spots of rust have appeared. The car could do another 30 to 40 000km but we would run the risk of having to do more repairs. I think it's more sensible to start thinking about buying a new car.'

Gregory was enthusiastic from the beginning. Fascinated by technology, he was pretty interested in cars. When Mr Martin told him he still had quite a lot of confidence in Ford, Gregory acquiesced but remarked that, with the exception of the recently launched Mondeo, Ford wasn't updating its models very often. Mrs Martin was much more reserved. She said she 'liked the Sierra very much' and felt it could go on for another few years. According to her it was much more urgent and of far more use to re-do the kitchen; she had also read articles on new kitchen layouts in several women's magazines and had been impressed by the benefits they offered. The previous year the Martins had planned to spend their holidays in America but had finally decided against it. Mrs Martin suggested that they make the trip this year, inspired by one of her friends who had just returned from an enjoyable visit to the United States.

The family therefore dropped the subject of a new car for a time. Mr Martin had been struck by the importance his wife attached to an American holiday, which he had not been aware of. He was also irritated by the idea that his wife believed he could not afford to give his family all these things at once. On several occasions Gregory and his father discussed the acquisition of a new car. They reckoned their plan was both quite reasonable and timely. The more Mr Martin thought about it, the more convinced he became; Gregory was a continual source of encouragement. Mrs Martin, however, held her ground and Gregory and his father were forced to ask themselves what they could do to convince her.

Several months passed. One day in June 1993, Mr and Mrs Martin went to dinner at the Vidals' house. During the evening, the Martin family learned that the Vidals had just bought the latest Ford Mondeo – with air conditioning and anti-lock brakes. They expounded enthusiastically and at length about its features to the Martins, who listened with great interest. When they were leaving their friends' house, the Martins had a lot of trouble getting the Sierra to start. On the way back, Gregory and Mr Martin noticed that Mrs Martin was unusually quiet.

A week later, during dinner and without the subject having been mentioned, Mrs Martin said she had 'reconsidered about the car'. She had revised her opinion and now gave her agreement – as long as 'the colour of the new car is not too showy'. Mr Martin and Gregory were over the moon and accepted enthusiastically. Now it was a question of which make and model to choose. The Martins had never for a moment thought of buying a second-hand car; for them, on principle, 'we buy only new and pay in full'. They had already excluded the idea of buying a less powerful or less comfortable model. 'A car,' Mr Martin explained, 'is like a career: as one goes up in the world, one becomes more exacting.' The Martins had noticed that many of their friends were staying faithful to a given car maker; similarly, they considered whether it wouldn't also be best to continue to patronise Ford. However, Gregory was encouraging his parents to try something new. Mrs Martin started to read the car adverts in different magazines bought by the family. Each time she made her judgement on the aesthetics and the colour of the vehicle, on one occasion even cutting out a picture of a Japanese car which she particularly liked. Mr Martin did not know exactly how much he was going to spend on buying a new car. He had mentioned one day that a trade-in of FF15 000 seemed to him to be very reasonable. By consulting the price of new cars in the edition of *Autocar* that Gregory had lent him, he saw the cost of the Mondeo 2000 Ghia: FF142 000. He also looked at the price of a Scorpio 2000 Ghia: FF164 000. 'That is far more than I want to pay,' declared Mr Martin.

One evening on the way to the post box, Mr Martin met one of his neighbours, Mr Dupont, and was happy to have a chat with him. The conversation turned quickly to cars, because Mr Dupont's brother-in-law had just bought a new car from 'Central Auto' in Nanterre, one of the largest of the greater Paris garages. During the conversation Mr Martin shared his thoughts with Mr Dupont, who suggested that he go and have a look round 'Central Auto'; 'they have a large number of new vehicles and offer good trade-in terms. In particular, they sell a lot of Fords, so they must be agents,' When he got home he told his wife what his friend had told him and they decided to go to 'Central Auto' on Saturday. Gregory, who had already planned to go out with his school friends that day, said that he couldn't go along with his parents.

'Central Auto' was situated on a little road joining the supply road for Nanterre. The garage looked like a vast hangar where dozens of new and second-hand cars of all different makes, both French and foreign, were on show. Going towards the reception office as directed by the sign, the first impression that Mr and Mrs Martin had was that the establishment was dirty and badly run. When Mr and Mrs Martin went into the reception area, they saw it was actually a small part of the garage that had been turned into an office; the salesman – or rather a person who looked like a salesman – was busy on the telephone. The seats were all dusty, one was covered in a pile of brochures. The salesman, who was in shirt sleeves, was obviously annoyed: he was almost shouting into the receiver and waving his arms around. A small ventilator was valiantly trying to draw in some fresh air. Feeling rather uneasy, Mr and Mrs Martin had to wait a good ten minutes for the salesman to finish on the telephone before he spoke to them at all.

'What are you after then?'

Mr Martin: 'I would be interested in buying a Mondeo.'

'You've come on the right day. One has just come in. It's at the back of the garage. Come with me, I'll show it to you,' said the salesman.

The Martins examined the vehicle carefully. It was a red 200i GLX with a sun-roof. Mrs Martin declared straight away that she didn't like the colour. They opened the doors and got into the car. Mr Martin tried to make the reclining seat work but it was a bit stiff so he did not force it. Then he lifted the bonnet up and examined the engine. At this point the salesman joined him.

'So, what do you think? It's a beautiful car, isn't it?'

Mr Martin: 'It's not exactly the colour we wanted.'

Salesman: 'What colour had you in mind?'

Mr Martin: 'We would have preferred something a bit less garish and which doesn't show up the dirt so much.'

Salesman: 'D'you mean something like this?' (He showed him a dark blue Mondeo in the Ford brochure he was carrying.) 'Yes,' he continued, without waiting for Mr Martin's reply, 'this colour's nice as well. I sold one like this three weeks ago and the buyer's very pleased with it.'

Mr Martin: 'How much will it cost me if I part-exchange my Sierra?'

Salesman: 'Is that the car you came in, the one parked outside reception?'

Mr and Mrs Martin nodded their heads.

Salesman: 'What year was it made in?'

Mr Martin: '1986. It's got about 100 000 kilometres on the clock.'

The salesman approached the Martins' car and quickly examined it. He commented on the scratches, rust spots and the condition of the tyres and then, after a moment of hesitation, declared: 'Yeah, well, if it's OK we could give you ten thousand for it. All right?'

Mr Martin: 'Well … before we decide I'll have to test drive it, and we haven't settled on the colour yet.'

Salesman: 'You know, I've only got this one at the moment (he waved towards the red Mondeo), but you shouldn't attach too much importance to colour! Mondeos are going like hot cakes at the moment.'

Mrs Martin: 'Oh no, there's no way I'd want a *red* car!'

Salesman: 'In that case ... Just order now and I'll try to get one for you a bit quicker.'

Mr Martin: 'Listen, we'll have to think about it. We'll come back later.'

Salesman: 'Whatever. Here, take my card. You'll have to excuse me, I've got other customers waiting.'

On the way home Mr and Mrs Martin agreed that 'Central Auto' employed unfriendly and pushy salesmen. Mrs Martin particularly noticed that he ran the Sierra down and said it was worth less than it really was. They agreed that they would never set foot in there again.

The 'Central Auto' episode had 'cooled the Martins down' and the topic of a new car disappeared from family discussions. Gregory tried hard to rekindle interest in the subject in conversation from time to time, but his efforts were in vain and he didn't force the issue. Moreover, Mr Martin declared that he was no longer bored with the Sierra; they even decided to go on holiday to Italy in it. After their holiday Mr Martin, who had just received a substantial pay rise, overheard two of his colleagues in conversation in the company restaurant:

Mr Laurent: (assistant after-sales service manager): 'I saw on the television that the Renault Safrane is selling well.'

Mr Janvier (foreman, known in the company for knowing everything about cars. His workmates have even nicknamed him 'the Expert'): 'Yes, they're already selling at a rate of 3000 a month and they've stepped up production to reduce delivery time. You know, last time I bought a Renault 21, they told me three weeks to a month, and I ended up having to wait two and a half months. Dealers are all the same: once they've got the cheque they don't want to know you any more, you're only a number. Before you buy they promise you the world; and you don't ask much of them – only that they stick to their word. If you happen to come across a good dealer then everything's different, but it's pot luck! It's best to go straight to the manufacturers' showrooms really, it's less risky.'

That very evening, after the family had just watched a programme about cars, Mr Martin, taking advantage of the situation, reported what he had heard during the day. As the subject had been brought up again, the Martins decided to go to the biggest showrooms in Paris – which had just been mentioned on the programme – the following Saturday. Mr Martin parked his Sierra in the street next to the Mercedes showroom, where they started their visit.

Several models were displayed in the showroom, which the Martins found attractive and well decorated. These included a 200 diesel, a 320 CE coupé, the old 190 and several of the new class C models, which seemed to be attracting the most attention. The Martins first of all made for the C180 Elegance, which captured their imagination straight away. Mrs Martin immediately declared, 'What a beautiful car; it reminds me of a picture of a car I cut out of a magazine.' She then opened the front left-hand door and sat herself in the passenger seat: she was visibly impressed by the car's comfort and interior; she noticed the generous seats, the wood finish on the dashboard, and the wide armrests and windscreen. Gregory had already lifted up the bonnet. Mr Martin, who was inspecting the dashboard meticulously, found it a bit small and not really worthy of the car but said that this was not a reason to reject it. Although not wishing to admit it, Mr Martin had been equally impressed by the car's aesthetics, size and prestige. He wondered if he hadn't always dreamed, in his heart of hearts, of owning a Mercedes. He then remembered that recently, at the factory, he had met a client who had just bought one of these cars; he hadn't known then it was a C Series but, looking at this one, he recognised the line and the car's general look.

The Martins hadn't noticed that an elegant young woman had discreetly approached them and Mr Martin was somewhat surprised when she started up a conversation.

'Hello, Sir. Can I help you in any way?'

Mr Martin found himself wondering if a woman would really have the necessary technical knowledge to be able to sell a car. A little suspicious, he asked question after question about the vehicle's performance, its petrol consumption, its price, the guarantee and the Mercedes after-sales service. He also asked for an explanation, backed up by practical demonstration, of the position and management of each of the features on the dashboard – the lights, airbag, windscreen wipers, switches for the electric windows, etc. As the saleswoman spoke, Mr Martin's fears disappeared.

When Mrs Martin brought up the question of delivery time, the saleswoman suggested to the family that they follow her to the office, where she could give them some more detailed information. After checking the price (FF140 000 with an additional FF10 000 for the Elegance series) and choice of colour (the Martins opted for dark blue, the colour of the car on show), the saleswoman replied that around three weeks seemed to be the average delivery time, as long as they didn't choose any of the optional extras (leather seats, for example), in which case they would have to wait ten weeks. She then suggested that Mr Martin should give the car a test drive and immediately opened her appointments book. Mr Martin hesitated – to him arranging an appointment and having his name written in a book was making a commitment. He went back to his wife and son, saw the enthusiasm on their faces and realised they would be disappointed if he didn't concede. He made an appointment for the following week and the saleswoman suggested that he also brought his car in so that its part-exchange value could be evaluated during the test drive. Mr Martin agreed. The saleswoman then handed the Martins a brochure on the C Series and took her leave of them. Looking at the time, the Martins realised that they had spent more time in the Mercedes showroom than they had intended to. It was already late so, deciding not to visit the other showrooms, they got back into the family Sierra and returned to Rueil.

The day of the test drive, Mr Martin turned up as arranged at the showroom. A mechanic in white overalls was waiting for him in the garage. He suggested he take the wheel and they went for a quick spin round the block. While Mr Martin was driving the mechanic explained how to work the vehicle's different functions. On the way back, Mr Martin told the mechanic how surprised he was at its manoeuvrability and the sheer pleasure of driving it. He then remembered what the saleswoman had said about the suspension. Back in the showroom, Mr Martin met up with the saleswoman, who was accompanied by the part-exchange negotiator. After consulting his file, he said that he'd take the Sierra for FF10 000. Mr Martin asked why this price was less than the one he had looked up a couple of days before. The negotiator explained that those prices were applicable only to second-hand vehicles in impeccable condition. He added that Mr Martin's car was in less than perfect condition and that FF10 000 was the most he could offer him. Mr Martin didn't press any further and said he'd have to think about it; he'd let him know in about ten days' time.

Since visiting the showroom Mrs Martin had thought a lot about the car. She had already found out about the price of alarms. Gregory had been talking about learning to drive as soon as he was old enough. The Martins discussed buying the Mercedes over and over again, and realised that they were all of the same opinion. As Christmas was coming up, the family's present was naturally decided. Taking into account the delivery time, the Martins calculated that the car would be delivered just before the end of the year and so they decided to go along to the Mercedes showroom to sign the order form. They chose the first available Saturday. It was 4 December 1993.

*   *   *

How should we interpret the Martins' purchase? Their behaviour can be analysed according to the three key questions which comprise a purchasing decision: **Who buys? How? Why?**

The first question refers to the consumer's identity. It is fundamental to the targeting of advertisements and communication strategies. In the Martins' case, it is clear that 'the consumer' does not correspond to a single individual but to a family; it will therefore be necessary to refer to a **decision-making unit,** in which different members may exercise a greater or lesser influence on the decisions taken. Mr Martin clearly plays an important role. Living in Rueil but commuting to Paris, he will be the principal user of the car and it is therefore no surprise that when his Sierra breaks down he is the first to suggest buying a new car. When he learns that he has recently been promoted at work, with a substantial pay rise, it is also he who reopens the subject for discussion within the family. Finally, with his status as husband and father, it is towards him that the other members look when the time for taking a concrete decision comes: the visit to the garage, filling in the appointments book and signing the order form.

Although less obvious, Mrs Martin's role is none the less significant. Apparently a lesser user of the family car, from the beginning she feels a lot less enthusiasm for her husband's plans than she would for things that really matter to her: her kitchen or a holiday, for example. She does not work and has quite an active social life; naturally, the advice of her friends and how she appears to them is important to her. Dinner with the Vidals will have had a strong impact on the reconsideration of her point of view. And Gregory, like a lot of adolescents, is interested in cars and favourably disposed towards anything new. So he joyfully welcomes his father's plans and, when the chance arises, willingly serves as his ally. However, his outings with his school friends often stop him directly participating in any purchasing decisions.

How did the Martins make their decision? Nine months passed between the idea and its fulfilment. What happened can be described as a form of **purchasing process** comprising several stages and decisions. First of all an incident awakens a need; there then follows an information acquisition period, which is sometimes very active and sometimes slow. Gradually the different decisions which make up the purchase are taken: the type of car, the make, the model, the colour, the place and the moment. Once all these decisions have been made, the Martins feel a sense of happiness tinged with the relief which is characteristic of the feelings that follow an important purchase. Of course, not every member of the family goes through every stage of the process in the same way, and it is therefore important to understand individual roles as well as interactions.

Why a Mercedes? In order to reply to this question the **explanatory factors** which have played a part in everyone's motivations must be examined. Mr Martin is a staid character, not one to take risks in life, and so it follows that he prefers makes of car known for their safety features and in which he can place his trust. Security prompts him to take the advice of people he regards as experts, to buy a new rather than a second-hand car, and stops him getting into debt. All the same, a test drive seems to him to be a logical stage in the process of making a purchase. Mrs Martin, who is inexperienced when it comes to technical matters, is a lot more sensitive to the external and internal aesthetics of the vehicle – from both her own point of view and that of her friends. The preoccupations of form, comfort and colour are foremost in her mind. Lastly Gregory, the future engineer, is concerned mostly with the technical details. The time which separates him from his driving licence also explains his greater interest in the engine than the dashboard.

The **decision-making unit,** the **purchasing/consumption process** and **explanatory factors** make up the three key areas of consumer behaviour analysis. For clarity of expression, they will be discussed in this book in reverse order. To start with, therefore, the isolated acts which are mainly relevant to the individual will be looked at as well as the variables which allow us to examine them. In the second part of the book, we shall look at the purchasing and consumption process as well as the decision-making unit.

Part 1

The factors explaining purchase and consumption

Purchase and consumption are particular facets of human behaviour. In order to explain them one can, therefore, benefit from the many theories and studies found in the field of the social sciences. Social scientists, considered here in the broadest sense of the word, have provided a number of perspectives which may prove useful in the analysis of consumer behaviour. Asked to explain the Martins' decisions, a group consisting of an economist, a psychologist, a social psychologist, a sociologist and an anthropologist would probably behave like the five blind men of popular fable who were asked to describe an elephant and did so according to the part of the animal they had touched! Thus an economist would be quick to explain that Mr Martin bought a Mercedes 180 and not a Ford Scorpio 2000 because he found the latter too expensive in terms of his income. A psychologist would probably highlight the role played by the Mercedes brand name and its ability to boost Mr Martin's self-esteem. The social psychologist would certainly notice the impact of interpersonal relationships: friends, colleagues, neighbours and salespeople. A sociologist would say that by ordering their car in a luxurious showroom on the Champs Elysées, rather than at 'Central Auto', where they felt they had been badly treated, the Martins have expressed the concern for respect which is so characteristic of the upper middle class. Finally, an anthropologist would explain that the Martins' deep financial and emotional involvement in the purchase of their car is largely due to the dominant role played by materialistic values in Western civilisation.

Generally speaking, it is possible to structure the various factors which have been put forward to understand consumer behaviour as shown in Figure 1, where they are represented as three concentric circles. In most cases, purchase and consumption reflect individual characteristics such as motivations, perceptions, past experience and attitudes; it is therefore logical to use them as a starting point for our exploration of consumer behaviour. At a second level, it is equally clear that in the case of many purchases, consumers are influenced by their immediate environment: their family, friends, neighbours or colleagues. At a third and final level, consumption patterns derive their meanings from the broader sociocultural context in which they take place. In the first part of this book, one or more chapters will be devoted to each of these levels in turn. As in photography, we will therefore use different lenses: starting with a 'close-up' of the individual, we shall finish with a 'wide-angle' view of society.

Figure 1 The three levels of explanation of buying and consumption behaviour

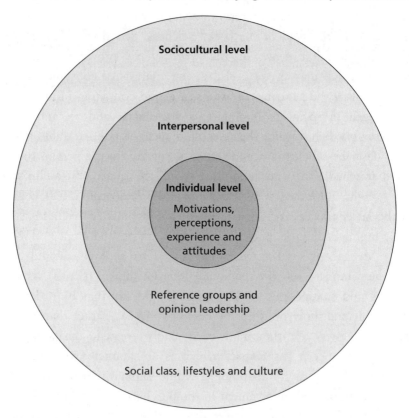

1

Motivation, involvement and personality

Learning objectives

After reading this chapter, you will:

1 understand the essentials of the contributions made by economists to an analysis of consumer behaviour but also their limits and conditions of application;

2 be familiar with the method of conjoint analysis, one of the most widely used methods in marketing research for the measuring of consumer utility (i.e. value) from an assessment of preferences in a choice situation;

3 be able to put into perspective the theoretical underpinnings of motivation theory as well as the various approaches and tools which have been used in marketing for detecting and interpreting consumer needs;

4 understand the concept of involvement and the various ways in which it is used in current marketing practice;

5 be familiar with the concept and theories of personality and the issues associated with its use for understanding and predicting consumer behaviour;

6 have identified the role played by additional personal characteristics – such as gender identity, chronological and cognitive age, and the self-concept – in shedding light on several aspects of consumer purchase and consumption activities.

Key words

consumption	needs	cognitive dissonance
utility	motivation	involvement
income	motivational research	personality
purchasing power	drive	self-concept
price	want	gender identity
elasticity	homeostasis	chronological and
conjoint analysis	laddering	cognitive age

Every year, on average, each Western European spends about 8000 Euros on goods and services.[1] But this average figure is rather misleading since the expenditure per capita varies from less than 2000 Euros in Portugal to more than 14 000 in Switzerland. Figure 1.1 illustrates some of the facets of European consumption, while Table 1.1 details the division of spending in each of the European Union member states (plus Norway and Switzerland) and Table 1.2 indicates the level of penetration of household goods across Europe.[2] With its 340 million individuals, the European Community has become the world's foremost consumer market.

Figure 1.1   Consumption in Europe

- On average, Western Europeans spend about 20 per cent of their income on food, but the Portuguese, the Irish and the Greeks spend as much as one-third, while the Germans and the Dutch spend about 15 per cent.

- On average, European households spend 77 Euros per week for buying food (61 in the UK, 115 in Luxembourg).

- In all Western European countries, except Denmark, white collars and professionals spend more per capita than any other social group.

- The French are the greatest shoe buyers in Europe: 6 pairs per person compared with 4 for the English and 2.5 for the Italians.

- In Europe, 76 per cent of food purchases are made in supermarkets, 11 per cent in hypermarkets, 5 per cent in hard-discounters, 4 per cent in proximity stores and 2 per cent in specialised shops.

- 70 per cent of Europeans watch the news on TV every day. This percentage is highest in Italy (82 per cent) and lowest in Portugal (52 per cent). 44 per cent of them listen to the news on radio (71 per cent in Denmark, 23 per cent in Italy).

- The average European reading time is 40 minutes per day. There are 315 newpapers in Germany, 117 in Greece, 102 in Spain, 86 in the Netherlands, 79 in France, 76 in Italy, 47 in Denmark, 33 in Belgium, 24 in Portugal, 7 in Ireland and 5 in Luxembourg.

Sources: G. Mermet, *Euroscopie* (Larousse, 1991), A. Tordjman, *Trends in Europe* (Food Marketing Institute, 1995), and *Marketing Bulletin* (Europanel, 1996).

What accounts for such figures as those displayed in the figure and these tables? And why do we consume what we consume? One of the first areas to have been examined in consumer studies concerns the investigation of the **reasons** which prompt an individual to buy and consume one product rather than another, in what quantity, when and where. Considered from this perspective, economists were the first group to attempt to reply to this question, and so the first section of this chapter will be devoted to their approach.[3]

The shortcomings of the economists' model have directed investigation towards the social sciences, which offer explanations in terms of **needs** and **motivation**. More recently, marketing research has sought to understand the role of the **involvement** a consumer has with a product. The second part of this chapter will discuss these findings.

Table 1.1 The division of spending in European states

% of Total household budget	Food drinks tobacco	Clothing and footwear	Housing and household fuels	Household goods and services	Health	Transport and communi- cations	Leisure	Others
Austria	20.4	9.3	18.8	8.3	6.0	18.2	8.2	10.8
Belgium	21.9	7.7	16.5	11.3	12.6	13.0	4.8	12.3
Denmark	20.2	5.3	27.8	6.1	2.2	14.9	10.4	13.0
Finland	22.2	4.6	21.2	5.9	4.9	13.7	9.1	18.4
France	18.6	6.0	21.1	7.5	10.3	15.9	7.5	13.0
Germany, East (1992)	25.0	4.5	15.8	11.7	5.9	20.1	7.8	9.2
Germany, West	16.8	7.8	22.5	9.2	5.2	17.0	10.4	10.9
Greece	37.4	8.2	13.0	8.0	4.1	15.7	5.9	7.8
Ireland	35.6	7.1	12.3	7.2	4.2	12.9	12.5	8.2
Italy	19.6	9.8	15.8	9.6	7.0	12.5	9.0	16.7
Luxembourg	18.6	5.9	20.0	11.3	7.7	20.1	4.5	11.9
Netherlands	14.7	6.8	18.0	6.9	13.2	13.2	10.1	17.1
Norway	25.3	6.2	19.3	6.4	5.6	13.0	8.7	15.6
Portugal (1986)	32.7	9.2	7.8	5.4	2.6	12.3	5.3	24.7
Spain	21.0	8.9	13.0	6.9	4.6	16.4	7.0	22.2
Sweden	18.6	6.2	29.6	6.6	2.0	15.5	9.5	11.9
Switzerland	25.0	4.0	19.3	4.5	12.7	11.2	9.9	13.4
United Kingdom	21.1	5.5	16.2	6.1	1.5	9.8	10.2	29.7

Source: Based on *1995 European Marketing Data and Statistics*, Euromonitor, London.

Finally, the integration of the reasons which incite an individual to buy a certain product or brand in the wider context of personal reactions is considered. This is referred to as **personality**. We will look at this approach in the third and final section of this chapter.

Table 1.2 Percentage of homes owning each durable

Durable	GB	B	NL	Dw*	F	DK	I	IRL	E	De*	P	GR	Total EU 11
	per cent	per cent	per cent	per cent		per cent		per cent		per cent		per cent	per cent
Colour TV	94	93	97	97	90	97	92	95	95	88	84	80	93
Still camera	81	78	86	83	78	88	76	56	61	86	50	64	76
Radio-clock	65	70	64	80	66	57	46	56	43	56	48	44	60
Electric drill	73	67	72	69	55	70	53	47	37	70	38	17	58
Video recorder	71	47	56	59	42	47	36	48	50	18	34	41	49
Electric deep fryer	36	84	44	39	30	5	22	50	26	9	28	25	31
2 cars+	29	23	12	26	30	17	41	19	13	14	12	8	26
PC/home computer	29	18	27	21	14	23	19	13	12	6	10	9	18
2nd home	6	8	3	6	11	16	17	3	15	9	5	19	10
Video camera	5	7	7	12	10	5	6	4	5	1	5	2	7

* Dw = West Germany; De = East Germany
Source: Eurobarometer 34 (Oct. 1990)/INRA Europe.

Homo economicus

If one excludes philosophers and other observers who have made passing remarks on aspects of human nature related to buying and consuming, economists – and more specifically classical microeconomists – were the first 'school' to study purchasing behaviour in some depth. Not only did they put forward a model of purchasing behaviour, but they also used their model to develop a complete theory of demand.

The economists' model can be better understood if viewed within the historical context – the eighteenth century – in which it was born. In those days, economists' attention was concentrated on the most basic foodstuffs such as wheat, salt, wine, etc., and, since all these goods were in scarce supply considering population needs, production was deemed more important than consumption. As a result, in an economy centred around allocation of limited resources, consumer behaviour was initially analysed in a **choice** context: that is, a context in which consumers would have to decide what to buy (and how much) to satisfy their ever-present and basically unlimited needs. Consequently, economists made **preference** the central variable of their analysis: what we buy and consume should reflect our priorities.

Once this basic premise is accepted, the theory is then built upon three key hypotheses concerning less the origin of the consumer's preferences (which do not really interest economists) than the conditions necessary to give rise to a purchase. The first hypothesis says that the consumer can express preferences for every product or combination of products which might satisfy his or her needs. Suppose that Mr Davies has to choose between shopping basket A, comprising three kilograms of potatoes and two classical records, and shopping basket B, comprising a litre of milk and a copy of this book. According to classical microeconomic theory, Mr Davies must be able to say whether he prefers A to B, B to A, or whether he is indifferent between the two. Of course, this presupposes that Mr Davies is fully aware of (a) the nature of his needs and (b) the combination of products which will satisfy him. This is referred to as the condition of 'transparency'.

According to the second hypothesis, the structure of preferences must be transitive. For example, if Mr Davies prefers Frank Sinatra to Mozart, and Mozart to the Beatles, he must prefer Frank Sinatra to the Beatles.

Finally, the third hypothesis states that more is always preferable to less. Mr Davies will prefer two kilograms to one kilogram of sugar, and three kilograms to two. It follows that he seeks to maximise **utility**, that is, the satisfaction brought by the quantitative consumption of products. Behind this theory is the idea that humans are essentially driven by concerns for their well-being and self-interest, a concept which originated in the work of the physiocrats.[4]

Although these three axioms assist us to understand what consumers **prefer**, they do not necessarily tell us what they **do**. They omit two essential factors: the **price** of the various products (the economist is interested only in goods which are limited in quantity and are therefore sold in a market) and the available **income**. Both factors will limit what consumers are **able** to do.

The simultaneous consideration of preferences and constraints attached to price and income results in the theory of the **maximisation of marginal utility**: a consumer will divide his or her purchases between different items according to the incremental satisfaction brought by the consumption of one additional unit of a product, given its price.[5] A state of equilibrium is reached when all products and services acquired have the same utility in relation to their price and the consumer, therefore, has no reason to favour the purchase of one product over another.

There has been much criticism of the microeconomic theory of consumer behaviour.[6] These criticisms have often led economists either to further their investigations or to explore new hypotheses. In the following section, the principal of these objections and criticisms are highlighted. The development of one of the most significant contributions to the evolution of economic thought on consumption, the hypothesis developed by Lancaster, is also discussed.

Consumer = Homo economicus?

The first criticism of the theory is directed at the transparency condition – the hypothesis that the consumer has perfect knowledge of his or her needs and the products likely to satisfy them. Such an assumption is hardly realistic. For example, the grocery department of a supermarket, such as Sainsbury's in the UK or ICA's in Sweden, will have more than five thousand products, while a department store like C&A or Marks & Spencer will stock more than 300 000 items. How is it possible for a consumer to know them all? Research in the social sciences shows that an individual's knowledge of him or herself and of his or her environment is far from perfect (we explore in detail perceptual phenomena in Chapter 2), and that there is a limit to the amount of information a human being can retain (memory is discussed in Chapter 3). Should the economic theory therefore be rejected? Not necessarily. There are situations where the condition of transparency is less problematic (for example in the purchase of basic foodstuffs such as salt, milk and bread, where only a few variants are usually available),[7] while adjustment of the basic model – by use of appropriate stochastic (that is, probabilistic) properties – allows for incomplete or uncertain knowledge.[8]

The second hypothesis (the transitivity of preferences) has also been the subject of much discussion and research.[9] Work on information processing (which is presented in detail in Chapter 8) has shown that beyond a certain limit, which depends on cognitive capability and the number of items to be processed, the individual can no longer ascertain the transitivity of his or her choices.[10] If you take a list of seven objects – for example seven countries you would like to visit – and rank order them according to your preferences, at first in a group of seven together and then in twos, you will almost certainly find inconsistencies in the two classifications.

The third hypothesis (the maximisation of satisfaction), which is at the heart of the economic model, is also found to be at odds with the observation of everyday purchasing behaviour.[11] Generally, consumers are unable to 'optimise' their purchasing behaviour but content themselves with a 'satisfactory' level obtained on the key characteristics of the product sought (for example performance, durability, price, etc.).[12] This can be observed when after a certain time spent shopping the consumer decides to make the purchase, even if he or she knows that by continuing to look around a better or cheaper product would be found. Again, the conclusion is not to reject the economic model outright but to discover situations in which it represents an acceptable approximation to reality. Generally speaking, it appears that the maximisation of satisfaction hypothesis is less problematic when applied to a professional buyer (business-to-business marketing) or in the case of the purchase of capital goods (such as land or a house).

Other criticisms of the theory include:

1 The approach is individual, that is, the decision-making unit is confined to the isolated consumer,[13] and social influence is disregarded.[14]

2 Analysis is static because behaviour is not related to either memory or future intentions.

3 The consumer is assumed not to have any influence on price; it is deemed to be imposed on him or her.

4 The behaviour analysed is deterministic and choices are definitive.

5 The consumer is assumed to derive his or her satisfaction directly from the consumption of the product.[15]

By taking into account these criticisms, or at least some of them, Lancaster has developed an original and very interesting model.

The Lancaster approach

Lancaster's hypothesis is simple: it is not the product itself which brings satisfaction but the attributes which characterise it.[16] For example, it is not the toothpaste itself which brings consumer satisfaction (or disappointment), but the fact that using toothpaste provides improved breath, protection against cavities, whiter teeth, etc. Therefore individuals do not base their decisions on a product itself but on the configuration of its characteristics. Moreover, Lancaster claims that it is possible to classify all products into subsets, thus allowing separate analysis (where the products in the same subset possess the same characteristics).

Suppose that in the toothpaste market two characteristics prevail – the prevention of cavities and the whitening of teeth – and that there are three leading brands: A, B and C. Every brand 'delivers', by its own characteristics, more or less of each benefit. A brand which contains fluoride, for example, gives greater protection against decay than a brand which does not. However, every brand is also offered at a specific price. If one supposes that consumers look for the most 'efficient' brand (the one giving the highest value for money), individual consumers will divide their purchases according to the utility bought by each penny invested in each brand.[17]

Lancaster's theory represents a progression against the classical approach in that it takes into account a product's attributes and helps to predict the market share of each brand, brand loyalty, and sensitivity to price and positioning, all of which are inadequately explained by the original model.[18] However, there are a number of limitations:

1 The assumption of homogeneous subsets is debatable,[19] just as the search for maximum efficiency supposes perfect background information and easily measurable attributes.

2 The possibility of alternating the purchase of several brands only applies to commonplace products which are bought on a regular basis; it would be impossible for household furnishings, for example.

3 The quest for maximum satisfaction in consumption is again assumed.

4 The consumer is still analysed at an individual, static and deterministic level.

5 The prices are always assumed to be certain and indisputable.

However, in its initial[20] as well as later versions,[21] the Lancaster approach has given rise to concrete commercial applications and has been used to explain purchasing behaviour related to products as diverse as cars and breakfast cereals. In the latter case, it has been possible to predict the amount that consumers would be willing to spend based on the dietary composition (vitamins, nutritional supplements, etc.).

What, in the end, is the contribution of the economic perspective? Generally speaking, marketing people and consumer researchers have rejected the economic model as the most appropriate approach for explaining consumer behaviour. They acknowledge the basic premise of the original framework (consumption is the ultimate aim of production) but criticise its simplistic hypotheses and its normative arguments. While it is true that a considerable number of improvements have enhanced the original model, the theory's key axioms – in particular the maximisation of satisfaction – cannot form the central explanation of consumer behaviour. As a result, the contribution of microeconomists is usually reduced to a minimum in consumer behaviour textbooks, and many lecturers even choose to ignore it altogether in their lectures. In our opinion, such a disregard is regrettable. Most sales and market share forecasting tools currently used in marketing research – including (as we see later) conjoint analysis, one of the most widely used methods for measuring consumer preferences – still rely heavily on the economic model.

More generally, it can be said that economists have contributed to a better understanding of purchasing behaviour by introducing three essential concepts, frequently used in business studies: income, price and utility.

Income

Because of its impact on purchasing power, income is a major determining factor in the level of consumption. Consider the case of France. Table 1.3 compares the growth of consumption (in volume) with that of real income (with inflation eliminated). Examined over a long period, the link is striking and therefore very useful for predictive purposes. The slackening in consumer growth which has been noticeable in the 1990s appears to originate in three tightly linked factors: the levelling in purchasing power, the rise in unemployment and increasing taxes.

Like in many other European countries in the late 1990s, the growth of **purchasing power** in France has stayed below between 1 and 2 per cent per year, markedly lower than in previous decades. As the French are also saving more (13 per cent of gross disposable income, that is after tax and social contributions, compared with 10–11 per cent at the end of the 1980s) and have less access to credit, growth in consumption is affected. Clearly, the disparity between segments of consumers is considerable. The 10 per cent which make up the wealthiest households own half of property, while the 10 per cent of poorest households own only 0.1 per cent. The wealthiest French people naturally form the basis of demand for a number of markets: luxury property, exotic holidays and high-class restaurants and hotels. At the same time, in a recession, certain markets (clothing, alcoholic drinks) are more deeply affected than others (health, telecommunications, non-alcoholic drinks).

In the mid-1990s, the number of unemployed broke through the three million barrier and exceeded 10 per cent of the active population. There are numerous studies which document the impact of **unemployment** on consumption. The unemployed reduce spending on clothes, food, motoring and holidays; only spending related to children remains relatively unaffected.[22] More importantly, the experience of insecurity can lead the unemployed to develop a cautious – even pessimistic – attitude to their lives, which can affect their consumption habits for a prolonged period, particularly if they do not find work quickly.[23]

The level of **taxes** (including social contributions) has grown from 25 per cent of Gross Domestic Product (GDP) in 1950 to more than 46 per cent in 1999. This change is largely due to the growth in social contributions, which are themselves derived from the increase in public spending. This ultimately results in a redistribution of income by the government.

To measure the impact of income on different product categories, economists have developed the notion of **income elasticity of demand**, which provides a measure of relative variation in income and demand. An elasticity of 1 means that demand and income are growing – or decreasing – at exactly the same rate; a higher elasticity conveys a higher than proportional impact, while with a lower rate the opposite is true. The Institut National de la Statistique et des Études

Table 1.3 Growth of consumption and income in France

| | Average annual rate in percentage | | | | |
	1949–59	1959–69	1969–73	1973–81	1981–85
Consumption in volume	4.5	5.5	5.6	3.4	1.6
Real income	4.5	5.5	6.5	3.0	0.9

Source: Institut National de la Statistique et des Études Économiques, *Données de la Compatibilité Nationale*. Read: between 1949 and 1959 consumption grew annually in volume by an average of 4.5 per cent.

Économiques (INSEE) has thus calculated that elasticity corresponding to food, clothing and leisure was 0.40, 0.74 and 1.18 respectively in France at the end of the 1980s. In other words, when income doubles, leisure demand grows even more rapidly but proportionately less in the other two categories. These results are in line with German economist Ernst Engel's findings in the nineteenth century; he observed that when income increases, the proportion spent on food products tends to diminish, while that spent on leisure increases. Past results must be used with caution, however, as long-term elasticity sometimes differs from short-term elasticity. The difference between the two elasticities can currently be observed in the case of products like cigarettes. When the price of tobacco increases significantly, some smokers react to the increase by stopping smoking; however, most of them will resume smoking after a period of time has elapsed.

Price

In 1997, the inflation rate was 1.6 per cent in the EU as a whole (from a low 1.1 per cent in Austria to a high 5.2 per cent in Greece). Even if double-digit inflation seems to have disappeared in Western Europe (the 1995 inflation rate was 27.8 per cent in Poland, 28.2 per cent in Hungary, 78.9 per cent in Turkey and 315 per cent in Russia), the impact of inflation on consumption remains. In 1991, for example, the price of non-tropical fresh fruit increased by 16 per cent because of an extremely cold spring, leading to a drop in consumption of 12.6 per cent. In the same way as for income, economists have measured **price elasticity of demand** to compare relative variation. For example, INSEE has calculated the following price elasticities: (a) meat, 0.50; (b) alcohol, 0.84; and (c) books, newspapers and magazines, 1.17. In other words, demand has reacted a great deal more to the successive rises in newspaper prices than to rises in drinks' prices. Such estimates are useful to marketers like tobacco firms, which want to predict the impact of a tax increase on cigarette consumption. However, it seems fair to say that while price is central to economic policy, in marketing, it is often secondary to other factors, notably promotion. Many factors other than price will affect demand. As Nagle nicely puts is: 'Economic theory is just that – theory … Marketers are still left with the problem of how to price products.'[24]

Utility

Finally the notion of utility, so dear to economists, remains at the heart of sales and market share predictive models based on panel diaries, which have been recently developed thanks to the rapid development of scanner data.[25] The modern use of the concept of utility will be illustrated using a method which has seen much success in commercial research: **conjoint analysis**.

A tour operator has decided to revise his offers on flight-only deals from Copenhagen to San Francisco. He knows that his customers prefer quick flights. But how many of them will be prepared to pay extra for them? Conjoint analysis helps him to find out. Following the Lancaster model, this method assumes that the consumer attaches a certain value (utility) to each characteristic such as duration or route (non-stop; direct without changing aeroplane; one stop without changing airport; one stop with a change of airport), and that the customer will choose the flight which offers the best 'global utility' while at the same time taking price into account. Rather than attempting to measure the utility of each criterion directly, which would involve asking theoretical questions like, 'How much more would you be prepared to pay for ...', conjoint analysis seeks to identify these utilities from the customer's preferences chosen from the product's different 'profiles'.[26]

For this example, the customer has been invited to indicate his or her order of preferences for sixteen 'packages'. The results, arranged in descending order of preference, are as follows:

1	non-stop flight	4500 DKK
2	non-stop flight	5000 DKK
3	direct flight	4500 DKK
4	direct flight	5000 DKK
5	1 stop airport only flight	4500 DKK
6	non-stop flight	5500 DKK
7	direct flight	5500 DKK
8	1 stop airport only flight	5000 DKK
9	1 stop airport only flight	5500 DKK
10	non-stop flight	6000 DKK
11	1 stop with change flight	4500 DKK
12	direct flight	6000 DKK
13	1 stop airport only flight	6000 DKK
14	1 stop with change flight	5000 DKK
15	1 stop with change flight	5500 DKK
16	1 stop with change flight	6000 DKK

These results show the traveller's priorities. On comparing the second and third choices, for example, it becomes apparent that the consumer will pay 500 DKK for a non-stop flight (without stopover) rather than take a direct flight (with stopover, but same flight). Obviously, other features such as frequency (daily, twice weekly, weekly, etc.), ticket conditions, the possibility of open return, etc. can play a part in the analysis. Let us assume that the above results were provided by a representative sample of customers. The travellers' responses are then fed into a computer program which derives from preference rank orders the corresponding 'utility' attached to each level of each characteristic; then, for each package, the result is obtained by addition of the corresponding utility figures (or, in some cases, by multiplication).[27] This is the aim of conjoint analysis. The results appear as follows:

Attribute		Utility	Utility difference (max–min)
Price	6,000	0.1399 ⎫	
	5,500	0.5408 ⎪	0.8257
	5,000	0.7530 ⎬	
	4,500	0.9656 ⎭	
Type of flight	Non-stop	1.0000 ⎫	
	Direct	0.8070 ⎪	1.0000
	1 stop without change	0.5924 ⎬	
	1 stop with change	0.0000 ⎭	

Percentage of correct comparisons: 87.9 per cent

These figures, which are sometimes presented as 'utility curves', prove extremely interesting for our tour operator. First, they show the 'best' results possible as no other set of numbers would be closer to original preference rank orders (87.9 per cent of two by two comparisons were correctly recovered here). The other figures reveal:

- the relative importance of each criterion (as measured by utility difference);
- the relative importance of each level of each criterion (in this case, price and type of flight).

To make comparison easier, the utility coefficients are expressed in the range of 0 to 1, 1 being the maximum utility (satisfaction) and 0 indicating total absence of value. Here, all things being equal, we can conclude that a non-stop flight is most likely to satisfy customers, while a flight involving a change of airport will be universally rejected. As our tour operator has foreseen, the type of flight will have a strong impact on choice as it brings about the maximum utility difference (equal to 1 in this case). In comparison, price appears slightly less important, with a utility difference of 0.8257. The utility coefficients relating to specific levels allow us to calculate the perceived value attached to each package. So a non-stop flight sold for DKK 4500 'is worth' 1.9656 (1.0000 + 0.9656), almost twice the value of a flight sold for DKK 5500 with a stop not involving a change of airport (0.5924 + 0.5408). Our tour operator can, therefore, plan his promotions accordingly. For example, he would conclude here that a reduction of DKK 500 on a starting price of DKK 6000 (utility increase of 0.5408 − 0.1399 = 0.4009) would compensate for the replacement of a direct flight with a flight including a stop without a change of airport (utility difference of −0.2146) but would not be sufficient to make those who wanted a 'stop without change' might accept a 'stop with change' flight (utility drop of 0.5924).

Clearly, not all travellers will attach the same importance to the different criteria and levels. The business client, for example, will be more concerned about the duration of the flight than the price, while the reverse will be true for holidaymakers. Of course, there is nothing to prevent the comparing of results obtained by conjoint analysis and their application to different groups of clientele; this is an excellent basis for market segmentation. A recent study has shown that in the USA alone, at least one conjoint analysis is carried out each day. Their aims can be extremely varied: test for new product concepts, comparative analyses of offers, fixing of price points, brand positioning, or research into method of communication. Conjoint analysis has truly taken its place in the commercial world.[28]

More than any other, the economists' heritage reflects the 'rational' approach, which has had a profound influence on researchers adopting a cognitive orientation in the analysis of consumer decisions.[29] The cognitive approach emphasises the way in which an individual acquires, processes and uses the available information. It seeks to understand how choice of products and brands operates according to an evaluation which takes into account the characteristics of the offer. The economic tradition has also encouraged a positivist approach to the exploration of purchasing behaviour and consumption. This approach assumes the existence of the observer's and observed independent reality, and relies mainly on experimentation and surveys. This is in contrast to the interpretive approach, which focuses on an in-depth understanding of consumers' experiences and is to a large extent based on research related to motivation and involvement.

Motivation and involvement

Everyone can draw up a list of things that they want and which they would make special efforts to get. It is thus possible to say that, from time to time, we are all 'motivated'. **Motivation** refers to the process which causes people to behave in the way in which they do.

The social sciences have coined numerous terms such as needs, wants, desires, drives, motives and instincts to describe the same basic idea. Although their meanings are not identical, all these words refer to the existence of a force within an individual which pushes him or her in a particular direction and stimulates behaviour with a predetermined objective. Accordingly, explaining consumer behaviour involves the identification of these forces, their number, their strength and their direction, as well as the mechanisms which underlie them. What are these mechanisms?

A **homeostatic** vision of human beings has often been put forward: when relaxed, the individual is in a state of equilibrium and is not disposed to action. However, if this fragile equilibrium is disturbed by an internal or external stimulus, it is broken and gives rise to a **need**. Tension will arise from this unpleasant state. The individual will then display behaviour which is aimed at satisfying the newly formed need. For example, a small child may be angry if he or she cannot reach the toy he or she has just seen and cry or shout for an adult's help. Once the objective has been attained, the tension is assuaged and equilibrium returns.

The best example of this mechanism at work is found in the **biological** motivations linked to the physical needs of the body. Hunger, for instance, can be explained as a process whereby the blood degenerates more and more until the appetite is stimulated. Once the necessary calorific level has been reinstated, motivation will slacken. The American psychologists Nisbett and Kanouse conducted an experiment where the impact of this process was measured in a commercial context. Two equivalent groups of consumers who had been 'deprived' of food for two and five hours respectively were sent to a supermarket with a shopping list. Nisbett and Kanouse found that impulse buys (items not mentioned on the list) were three times more likely to be made by the more hungry group.[30] The homeostatic principle is not limited to physiological needs; certain social motivations (for example, the need to dress according to fashion) appear to obey mechanisms of a similar nature.

The forces that drive human beings are many. All motivational researchers may agree on the idea of the underlying internal needs of the human being, but they differ when it comes to identifying their nature and dynamics, and their many views enrich the analysis of purchasing behaviour all the more.[31] In fact, some researchers have endeavoured to concentrate on one particular force, while others have put forward systems of classification. We examine their work in this order.

The Freudian theory of motivation

In contrast to the conscious and rational homo economicus, Sigmund Freud was probably one of the first psychologists to investigate the role played by subconscious motivations (inextricably linked, he claimed, to sexual needs), which were not directly observable but detectable through the inference of analysis.[32]

According to Freud, a young child is motivated by her instinctive needs, which she tries to satisfy by different methods, such as cries and gesticulations. She quickly, and painfully, learns that she cannot obtain immediate satisfaction. A state of frustration will therefore lead her to use more subtle mechanisms to obtain gratification. As she grows up, she becomes more sophisticated. One part of the psyche, the 'id', remains the source of her motives and drives. The id operates on the pleasure principle. It directs a person's energy towards immediate gratification, with maximum pleasure and minimal pain. A second element, the 'superego', internalises the constraining and moralising influence of society. The superego becomes the person's conscience, telling her to behave in socially acceptable ways. Finally, a third part, the 'ego', referees the conflict between the id and the superego. It operates according to the reality principle: looking for gratifying but socially acceptable solutions, thus avoiding any feelings of guilt or shame.

The guilt or shame that an individual experiences with regard to his or her desires, particularly sexual desires, leads to their subconscious repression. These desires are thus denied or expressed through processes such as **projection**, which identifies one's own desires with those of others; **identification**, which involves the imitation of people one admires (for example, using Lux soap, the 'soap of the stars'); or **sublimation**, which allows the displacement or discharge of the energy of a primitive impulse into a socially acceptable area (for example, sport).

Even though many aspects of Freudian theory remain controversial, Freud's influence on marketing and advertising has been considerable, as much in ideas as in methods. In the commercial arena, the most important aspect has been the discovery of the significance of the **symbolic** in addition to the purely functional aspect of consumption. Obviously, products are not bought solely for what they do but also for the meaning expressed by their form, colour or name. How else can you explain that toilet paper sells better if it is of a pastel colour?[33] Figure 1.2 illustrates the use of sexual symbolism in contemporary Spanish advertising. In the advertisement, everything – from the picture to the snake-bottle – suggests virility.

One of the most committed disciples of the Freudian theory of motivation was Ernest Dichter, who devoted more than twenty years of his life to the interpretation of purchasing situations and choice of product in terms of subconscious motivation.[34] Dichter developed a method known as **motivational research**, which involves interviewing a limited number of potential buyers in depth in order to uncover the deep-seated motives which led them to buy and consume a product.[35] Various **projective** and **creative** techniques are also used to reduce the individual's defence mechanisms, including focus groups, word association, sentence completion tests, story telling, Chinese portraits (asking if you were a flower, an animal, etc.), interpretation of images (with or without speech 'bubbles' to fill in), role playing and collages.[36] All these methods still occupy prime position in commercial research today. Figure 1.3 shows some projective tools used in a recent study on gift giving. In this study, participants were asked to comment freely on the two pictures. From their stories, an in-depth analysis revealed the 'dark side' of the gift: as Martial said almost two thousand years ago, 'gifts are hooks'.

Motivational research has revealed some interesting, and sometimes unexpected, results about what goes on in a consumer's mind as he or she makes a purchase. However, Dichter's methods have often been criticised for lacking scientific rigour and many of his results have to be considered as anecdotal as they do not have the same status as research-based scientific inference making.[37] Figure 1.4 summarises some of Dichter's consumer motivations for several types of product.

Figure 1.2　Example of sexual appeal in advertising

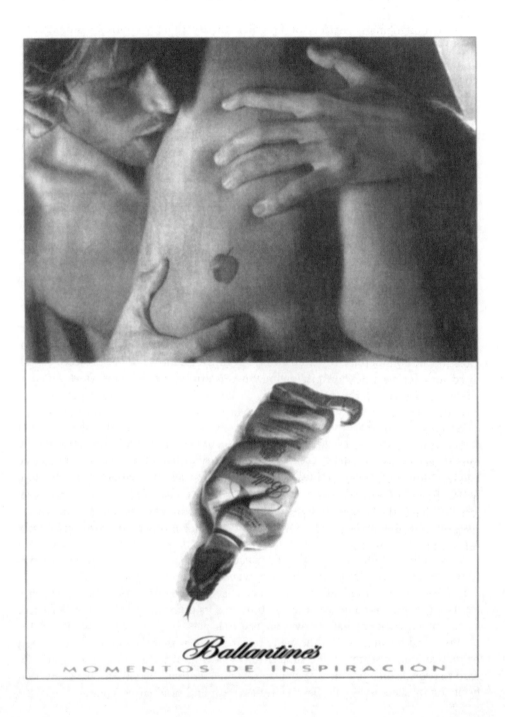

Figure 1.3   Two projective tools

A

B

Source: J. Sherry *et al.*, 'The Dark Side of the Gift', *Journal of Business Research*, 1992, no. 26, pp. 10–12.

While retaining the idea of subconscious motivation, several disciples of Freud have studied instincts other than sexual ones. Adler, for example, has stressed the importance of the inferiority complex, which derives from the state of dependence which characterises early childhood,[38] while Horney has emphasised the role played by anxiety.[39] All these extensions of the Freudian approach are interesting because they throw a sometimes unexpected light on consumer behaviour. Motivational studies have thus shown that certain buyers of powerful and sporty cars are compensating for feelings of inferiority that they experience or have experienced within the family. Similarly, the consumer will often buy well-known brands to reduce the sense of risk that they feel when making their purchases.[40]

At the same time, motivation research has become the target for criticism: at times for its too powerful influence, at other times for its doubtful worth. Vance Packard, for example, claimed that motivation research acts as a supreme instrument for manipulating the masses,[41] while many researchers fear that the interpretations given by motivational researchers are subjective. Today, motivational studies are generally used to provide an exploratory perspective, when working hypotheses have not been firmly established and could benefit from a fresh and original viewpoint.

Figure 1.4　Some consumer motivations, according to Dichter

Furs　The value of furs is linked to the fact that they were originally trophies a hunter would bring back to his loved one in the tribe. The more dangerous and difficult to kill the animal, the more valuable the fur. The hunter of today has exchanged his club for a wallet, but the fundamental significance remains the same. Because of its value, a fur proves that its buyer has succeeded financially because of his or her ability to make money. Leopard and mink are no warmer than cat or rabbit fur, but their value is greater because of their rarity. Fur also suggests the sexual powers of the hunter, and studies have shown that the public often attaches connotations of vice to both the giver and recipient of mink coats.

Spaghetti　For many consumers, spaghetti evokes a warm and friendly environment. Children in particular find it fun to eat because it is slippery and escapes easily from the fork. It is also considered to be a cheap dish which one would serve only very occasionally to guests. To elevate its status, it can be associated with elaborate sauces, beautifully set tables and appropriate wine.

Leather goods　Like iron, steel and bronze, leather is one of the basic materials whose symbolism is widely associated with the history of mankind. Historically, leather was the material of nomads, outside people who took their possessions wherever they went. Leather protected them, their belongings and their animals, and was also the symbol which linked them together and established the relationship of ownership and domestication. This would explain the modern-day link between leather and the world of travel (luggage, car seats, etc.) as well as its role as protector of important possessions (the leather wallet).

Cigarettes　Smoking allows escape from an unpleasant or tedious task, a little like a child fed up with his homework submits to a few moments daydreaming. Smoking is a form of self-reward, appreciated more if it is frequently applied. Smoking the first cigarette of the day anticipates the gratification it will bring, while the last of the evening draws a full day to a close. The cigarette is a modern timepiece which marks the hours passing, both at work and at home. In assuaging impatience, it also allows time to pass more quickly and this is why in certain situations where the idea of filling time is particularly acute (on railway stations, in prison, a father waiting for his wife to give birth), smoking is often resorted to. Smoking is an oral, sensual pleasure, and the use of tobacco and chewing-gum have substitution at their heart. Cigarettes also fulfil a social role by acting as a sort of companion or friend (a comforting glow in the dark), as well as serving as an interpersonal exchange system. They give the smoker a personality while demonstrating his or her rapport with other smokers. A cigarette case, for example, suggests a certain distance and individuality. Finally, smoke's magical and mysterious character confers on the cigarette an intangible and surreal quality which transcends that of the individual. Lots of smokers like to watch the furls of smoke which drift towards the sky in intricate patterns, taking their worries and thoughts with them.

Asparagus　Asparagus bears phallic connotations. Sexual virility is often attributed to asparagus. The way in which it is eaten is also revealing. In many countries it is held by the fingers and dipped in a white sauce before being placed in the mouth.

Fashion　Clothes have a double function. Hiding nudity, they differentiate us, but we can also employ them to make us look like others. When we choose a tie or hat, we hope that no one else will have one exactly the same. However, if we are sure that no one else has bought a similar one before, we will hesitate before buying it, uncertain now of our own taste. Seeing someone else wearing the same tie as us worries us and reassures us at the same time. Just like ancient armour, modern clothes protect us and allow us to express ourselves and our rank in society.

▶

> **Rugs and carpets** A rug is woven with emotion. The individual will buy it all the more readily if a variety of colours, types and materials are available, making its uniqueness more likely. A carpet will form the link between the various household objects and furnishings. It harmonises the contents of a house by offering continuity and colour. By insulating the floor, it gives the human who walks on it a feeling of elevation and protection. Because it is a non-essential item, it confers a feeling of luxury and status. Once it has been laid, a carpet is difficult to change and so it reinforces the idea of continuity. It will often be bought by a family and assumes a collaboration between husband and wife, and sometimes children as well.

Source: Adapted from Ernest Dichter, *Handbook of Consumer Motivations*, New York: McGraw-Hill, 1954. This book is based on more than 2500 motivation studies carried out by the Institute for Motivational Research founded by Dichter. Dichter's interpretations are, of course, open to debate. For a contemporary criticism, see J. J. Durgee, 'Interpreting Dichter's Interpretations: An Analysis of Consumption Symbolism in the Handbook of Consumer Motivations', *Marketing and Semiotics: Selected Papers from the Copenhagen Symposium*, Hanne Hartvig Larsen, David G. Mick and Christian Alsted (eds) (Copenhagen, Handelshöjskolensforlag, 1991).

Apart from theories which were centred around specific factors, other researchers endeavoured to draw up lists of the most important human motivations – or at least attempted to group them into categories. For example, somewhat arbitrary distinctions are often made between biogenic (innate) and psychogenic/sociogenic (learned) needs as well as between utilitarian and hedonic needs. Establishing lists of needs has long been a favourite pastime of psychologists, and the number of classifications is quite impressive. It is important to understand that every classification has an arbitrary element to it and it is pointless to try to find the 'best' list; what is most appropriate depends on the particular aim. For the purposes of illustration, two examples will be given below: the Murray classification and Maslow's pyramid.

The Murray classification

Towards the end of the 1930s, psychologist Henry Murray put forward a list of 28 needs, from which the following fundamental eleven have been extracted:[42]

1 *The need to acquire* The need to possess; to seize, to steal objects; to haggle and play; to work for money or for nature's goods.

2 *The need to accomplish* The need to overcome obstacles, to exercise responsibility; to fight to achieve something difficult in the best time and fashion possible.

3 *The need to exhibit* The need to attract attention of others; to excite, to amuse, to move, to shock, to frighten; to dramatise.

4 *The need to dominate* The need to influence or control others; to persuade, to forbid, to lay down the law; to guide and direct; to organise a group.

5 *The need for affiliation* The need to create friendships and to belong to associations; to live with others; to contribute one's collaboration and conversation; to love.

6 *The need to play* The need to relax, to have fun, to seek entertainment: to take time off; to laugh, to joke, to avoid stress.

7 *The need for order*   The need to harmonise, to organise, to tidy objects; to be clean and neat; to be precise and scrupulous.

8 *The need for recognition*   The need to draw favours and elicit compliments, to command respect; for one's actions to be valued; to seek distinction, social prestige and honour.

9 *The need for deference*   The need to admire and to follow a superior freely; to co-operate with a leader; to serve.

10 *The need for autonomy*   The need to resist influence and coercion; to defy authority and to seek liberty; to fight for one's independence.

11 *The need for aggression*   The need to attack and injure; to kill; to do wrong; to accuse, to blame or to ridicule others, to punish and chastise.

Such lists[43] are useful because they guide explanation of the consumption of products and services (for example, a link has been found between the need to accomplish and the intention to buy skis, lawnmowers and boats,[44] while another study showed that working women who were high on achievement motivation were more likely to choose businesslike clothing[45]) or even help to analyse the structure of a market. In this way, in a motivational study carried out on hi-fi purchasers for Bang and Olufsen,[46] a preliminary list of potential buyers' needs was established as shown in Figure 1.5.

Figure 1.5   A list of hi-fi purchasers' possible needs

need for identity	need for recreation
need for conformity	need for affection
need for pleasure	need for variety
need for entertainment	need for comfort
need for relaxation	need for aesthetics
need for social approval	need for music
need for personal interest	need for economy
need to spend	need for freedom
need for novelty	need for accomplishment
need for curiosity	need for pride
need for power	need for prestige
need to belong	need for success
need for distinction	need for individuality
need to conform	need to imitate others
need to acquire	need for independence
need for musical cultivation	need to explain equipment to others
need to collect	need to update: the perfection of one's auditory sensitivity
need for leadership	need for interest in sound reproduction
need to dominate	need to play the technical expert
need for exhibition	need to escape in music
need to be sociable	need for love of music
need for perfection in the technical aspects of the apparatus	need to express richness and culture

Source: C. Dussart, *op. cit.*

These needs and benefits were then used as a basis for identifying, through a technique known as cluster analysis, four types of consumer (as shown in Figure 1.6):

1 the technical experts (15 per cent), primarily interested in the sound reproduction.

2 the musicians (20 per cent), mindful of the music's reproduction;

3 the snobs (20 per cent), sensitive to social status; and

4 general users (45 per cent), who had no specific demands.

Figure 1.6 Segments and types of need

1 Technical experts:
  a) need to update the perfection of one's auditory sensitivity
  b) need for interest in sound reproduction
  c) need for novelty, for updating and perfecting existing equipment
  d) need for accomplishment, success, pride in possessing a perfect hi-fi
  e) need to be identified as an expert in sound reproduction and hi-fi knowledge
  f) need to explain equipment to others
  g) need for continual improvement (buying a more and more desirable hi-fi)

2 Musicians:
  a) need to listen to music
  b) need for love of music
  c) need for musical cultivation
  d) need for relaxation
  e) need for entertainment, pleasure
  f) need for intimacy
  g) need to escape in music

3 Snobs:
  a) need to spend
  b) need to collect, acquire
  c) need for prestige, superiority, power
  d) need for exhibition, pride
  e) need for social approval, to conform
  f) need for aesthetics
  g) need for comfort
  h) need for variety (in their furnishings)

4 General users:
  a) need for economy
  b) need to listen to music in general
  c) need for pleasure, entertainment
  d) need for relaxation, recreation
  e) need to imitate others (in relation to wealth)
  f) need for comfort
  g) need to conform

A selection of specific needs corresponded to each type (see Figure 1.6).

In the end, differing advertising arguments were used to reach each of the target groups (the first three segments): (a) the prestige and reputation of B & O equipment (snobs); (b) the quality of reproduction of great pieces of classical music (musicians); (c) the technological superiority of the components of the system (technical experts).

The Maslow pyramid

Abraham Maslow extended previous work by putting forward both a list and a hierarchical ordering of fundamental needs. His theory is based on three hypotheses:[47]

1 An individual has many needs, which are not of equal importance and can therefore be placed in hierarchical order.
2 An individual will first seek to satisfy the need which is most important to him or her.
3 A need ceases to exist (at least for a period) when it has been satisfied and the individual will then seek to satisfy the next, higher-order need.

According to Maslow, needs can be classified in the following increasing order of importance (see Figure 1.7):

1 physiological needs
2 security needs
3 belonging needs
4 esteem needs
5 accomplishment needs.

Therefore, according to Maslow's theory, it would be pointless to inform someone who was dying of hunger (a first-level need) of the latest do-it-yourself techniques, even if they would allow him to impress others (a fourth-level need) or make him more easily accepted in his group of friends (a third-level need).

In Southern Europe, an unpublished study on packet soups carried out by Nestlé uncovered the principal reasons why some housewives were opposed to this type of product. All these reasons can be clearly linked to the Maslow model and relate to physiology (packet soup = a light food, not very nutritious), security (packet soup = mysterious, artificial, chemical food), belonging (packet soup = a dish for one, breaking up the unity of the family), esteem (packet soup = a dish which can be prepared instantly, which is not particularly praiseworthy) and accomplishment (packet soup = a processed and impersonal dish).

Some advertising agencies have developed methods to systematically link the attributes of products to needs expressed by consumers. Grey Advertising, for example, has thought up the 'Benefit Chain', which seeks to reveal any product's functional, practical and emotional advantages. So a light hairspray has for its

Figure 1.7   Maslow's hierarchy of needs

advantages: (a) ease of hairstyling (functional); (b) reduction of time spent arranging hair (convenience); and (c) allowing more time for other, more worthy activities (emotional).[48] A similar approach is known as the 'means–end chain model'.[49] The idea is to interview consumers on what they have bought and at the same time ask them for their reasons. Certain factors then become evident which are explored further (following a so-called '**laddering**' approach) by additional questioning. More and more abstract levels will emerge as consumers 'climb the ladder' of the explanations, from product characteristics (physical or symbolic attributes) to desired benefits (functional or psychological), and finally to abstract values underlying these benefits. For example, a light ale may be drunk because of its low alcohol level (product characteristic), which avoids drunkenness (benefit sought), which would draw disapproval from one's circle of friends (social value).[50]

Laddering and the means–end model are not without problems, however. They assume that respondents can articulate their thought processes in a logical and hierarchical fashion.[51] Over the years, 'softer' approaches – where consumers are allowed to go back and forth – have been developed.[52] It would, however, appear that the laddering technique remains inappropriate for certain products such as luxury goods, given consumers' unwillingness to reveal some aspects of their behaviour.[53]

Motivational conflicts

In the preceding discussion, we identified several categories of needs. It is not necessarily true that one type of behaviour corresponds to a single type of need and vice versa. Specific behaviours which at first glance appear identical can reveal very different motivations. For example, affiliation to a political party may involve a desire to belong to a group, a need for power, or even the need to protect oneself against future uncertainties. Conversely, widely different acts can be provoked by the same motivation. For example, the need for accomplishment can manifest itself in a number of ways depending on the individual and their sociocultural environment: some learn a musical instrument, others take up DIY or gardening. Moreover, an individual can experience a number of different desires and needs at the same time, and they may be contradictory or impossible to satisfy simultaneously. For example, one may want to buy a present which is both original and fashionable (and therefore already possessed by many), or one may desperately try to reconcile superior quality and affordability. This is where psychologists' interest in motivation dynamics and their related mechanisms, in particular **attitudinal change** (discussed in more detail in Chapter 4), **aggression** and **management of conflicts**, stems from.

It has often been observed that when an individual's desires cannot immediately be satisfied, he or she will adapt their convictions in order to make them compatible with the desires. The **theory of cognitive dissonance**, which assumes that people have a basic need for consistency in their lives, accounts for this.[54] A state of dissonance is experienced when people are faced with conflicting beliefs or sets of behaviour. In such a case, cognitive dissonance theory predicts that the individual will try to reduce the tension resulting from the conflict, for example by refusing to accept a belief which they perceive as incompatible with their behavior. Thus, studies have shown that heavy smokers are less inclined than others to believe that smoking can lead to lung cancer.[55] This raises an issue for health education campaigns and their targets: the people they are aimed at often think these campaigns are for others.[56]

In other circumstances, it is the obstacle itself which is the object of a real or symbolic attack. The amateur gardener will kick his lawnmower, which has just broken down, and the busy businessman will hammer on the door of the lift which fails to work. When the obstacle itself cannot be overcome, a weaker or more accessible 'scapegoat' may be used.[57] Accordingly, a number of consumer associations decided to boycott Shell products in Europe because of the *Amoco Cadiz* oil slick, even though the company was not involved in the catastrophe.[58]

To facilitate analysis, motivational psychologists have identified three cases of conflict of needs:[59]

1 the conflict opposing at least two equally strong appeals (sometimes called an approach–approach conflict);
2 the ambivalence of a situation which presents both factors of attraction and repulsion (approach–avoidance);
3 the choice between two or more threats (avoidance–avoidance).

In the first case, the conflict is quickly resolved. Unlike the famous Buridan donkey, a starving man will not hesitate for long between two different plates of food. The conflict is here said to be unstable. Translated into a commercial situation where products are very similar, it might lead to (and therefore explain) frequent brand switching.

Conversely, the second situation brings a state of semi-permanent tension, expressed through hesitation and changes of mind with regard to the objective, and a powerful desire to get close to something from which one has just distanced one-self. Purchasing decisions involving durable goods such as furniture or expensive electronic goods are often made this way. From a distance, the attraction of the object and the satisfaction which it would bring predominates; while it is being approached – for example by visiting shops, studying brochures and questioning sales assistants – anxiety grows with the perception of possible risks and potential mistakes. Sometimes, this perception can be so great that the consumer will abandon the purchase, knowing very well that desire for the object could resurface at any moment. Studies carried out on house buying thus reveal a constant swaying between dream and reality.[60] Marketers very often position products to solve approach–avoidance conflicts, for example a 'light' sugarless dessert.

Finally, when individuals have to 'choose' between two evils or two poles of repulsion (for example, two different types of surgery), it has often been observed that they will seek to minimise the overall risk. They will therefore favour the solution which, if things must turn out unfavourably, guarantees a certain level of safety. Of course, marketers can help them understand the benefits attached to the option perceived as the less risky one (or even try to change this perception).

Involvement

The approach based on motivation has recently been expanded by work carried out on the related concept of **involvement**. While motivation describes an internal force linked to a human need, involvement is based on the relationship between the consumer and a particular product category .

While the first theoretical works on involvement go back a long way,[61] its use in commercial research has developed steadily over the course of the last fifteen years or so to the point where certain analysts have made it one of the key concepts to analyse purchasing behaviour.[62] Marketing practitioners are not to be outdone; certain advertising agencies like FCB systematically refer to the notion of involvement in their message elaboration procedures.[63]

Although the concept of involvement may not always be precisely defined and separated from its antecedents and its consequences,[64] it seems that today there is a consensus on the following definition: 'Involvement is a state of motivation, stimulation or interest which cannot be observed. It is stimulated by an object or a specific situation and brings certain types of behaviour: certain forms of search activities, information processing and decision making.'[65] Involvement, therefore, refers to an individual's state with regard to a domain of interest, the type and intensity of which can evolve according to circumstances. Some draw a distinction between **affective** or emotional involvement and **cognitive** involvement.[66] In the first case, one would therefore link an individual's involvement with his or her deep ego and with the anxiety to express it when making purchases. A study on luxury goods used this concept to reveal that female consumers often like to allocate themselves a territory of their own, or a 'secret garden', which they describe as 'their own luxury'. Whether it be perfume, beauty products, shoes or scarves, affective involvement will refer to the pleasure and emotions that purchase and consumption of these products bring.[67] Conversely there are cases where interest in a particular activity, such as reading classified adverts, is explained by necessity: for example, when one is looking for a job. In this case, involvement would be more of a cognitive nature and one would even then talk of 'rational' involvement. Involvement then primarily refers to a motivation to process information.[68]

Other researchers establish a distinction between **enduring** (sometimes called ego) and **situational** involvement.[69] A person's enduring (that is more or less permanent) involvement in a certain type of product can often be explained by his or her previous experience or system of values.[70] To explain temporary involvement, the specific characteristics of a product might be considered (its complexity, technical nature, length of use, etc.) or equally, the context of the purchase (self-purchase versus gift) may be.

The relationship between enduring and situational involvement is a complex one. While a young mother who happens to be a professional photographer will be meticulous when it comes to taking photos of her new-born child, for a mother who is not a photographer, similar portraits will not succeed in procuring a long-lasting interest in photography. More generally, it would appear that involvement is stronger and more permanent in consumption than in purchasing activities, the former being the *raison d'être* of the latter.

Subtleties such as these obviously hold some influence over the choice of method for measuring involvement. Beyond a simple measure of 'perceived importance', multi-item (but still unidimensional) scales have been developed. Zaichowsky, for example, has created the scale shown in Figure 1.8.

Others have pointed out that the reasons two different people may have for being involved in a certain type of product may not be the same. Laurent and Kapferer prefer to talk about multidimensional 'involvement profiles'; they distinguish as many as five facets of involvement: personal interest in the product category (its significance for or importance to the individual); the negative consequences that a bad choice can bring; the perceived probability of an erroneous decision; the value of the (symbolic) signs that the consumer attributes to the product; and finally, the hedonistic value of the product, that is its emotional potential and its capacity to give pleasure. It is possible that the number of facets or their complexity differ according to the nature of the product category. For example, with luxury products, the sources of pleasure are many and can include the atmosphere of their sales outlets as well as the consumption of the product. Table 1.4 shows involvement scores recorded by several products in France, demonstrating that neither the global levels nor the components of involvement are the same. Purchasing a vacuum cleaner, for example, affords neither pleasure nor status. At the same time, the purchase is considered quite risky as a bad choice will 'commit' the consumer for several years. When total scores are considered, it appears that the level of involvement in dresses or perfumes is far superior to that of batteries or pasta.

Figure 1.8   Personal involvement inventory

```
                  Important. . . . . . . . . . . . . . . . . Unimportant*
         Of no concern to me. . . . . . . . . . . . . . . . Of concern to me
                 Irrelevant. . . . . . . . . . . . . . . . Relevant
          Means a lot to me. . . . . . . . . . . . . . . . Means nothing to me
                   Useless. . . . . . . . . . . . . . . . Useful
                  Valuable. . . . . . . . . . . . . . . . Worthless*
                   Trivial. . . . . . . . . . . . . . . . Fundamental
                 Beneficial. . . . . . . . . . . . . . . . Not beneficial*
             Matters to me. . . . . . . . . . . . . . . . Doesn't matter*
             Uninterested. . . . . . . . . . . . . . . . Interested
               Significant. . . . . . . . . . . . . . . . Insignificant*
                     Vital. . . . . . . . . . . . . . . . Superfluous*
                    Boring. . . . . . . . . . . . . . . . Interesting
                Unexciting. . . . . . . . . . . . . . . . Exciting
                 Appealing. . . . . . . . . . . . . . . . Unappealing*
                  Mundane. . . . . . . . . . . . . . . . Fascinating
                 Essential. . . . . . . . . . . . . . . . Non essential*
             Undesirable. . . . . . . . . . . . . . . . Desirable
                   Wanted. . . . . . . . . . . . . . . . Unwanted*
               Not needed. . . . . . . . . . . . . . . . Needed
```

Note: Scores (reversed for asterisked items) total between 20 (minimum involvement) and 140 (maximum involvement).
Source: J. Zaichowsky, 'Measuring the Involvement Construct', *Journal of Consumer Research,* December 1985, pp. 341–52. For a revision, see E. F. McQuarrie and J. M. Munson, 'A Revised Product Involvement Inventory: Improved Usability and Validity', *Advances in Consumer Research,* 1992, pp. 108–15.

An individual's involvement directly affects his or her behaviour. For example, an involved consumer will take the trouble to find out about the product and evaluate the available information more critically.[71] In a similar way, disappointment with the product is more significant for the involved customer,[72] while a link between the level of involvement and innovative behaviour as well as opinion leadership has been established in fields such as cars[73] and fashion.[74]

Table 1.4 Average involvement scores for various types of product

Type of product	Interest	Pleasure	Sign	Imporisk*	Proberr**
Clothes	123	147	166	129	99
Perfume	120	154	164	116	97
Pasta	69	73	74	56	80
Batteries	36	39	59	65	98
Champagne	75	128	123	123	119
Vacuum Cleaners	108	94	78	130	111

* Imporisk: Importance of perceived risk
** Proberr: Perceived probability of making an erroneous choice
Source: G. Laurent and J. N. Kapferer, 'Measuring Consumer Involvement Profiles', *Journal of Marketing Research*, February 1985, pp. 41–53.

Clearly, these findings can be put to use by any company wishing to better understand its most valuable clients. Strategically, a business will use the idea of involvement to segment its market and position its products. A new 'light' cheese, for example, will be better received by consumers concerned with diet than by those who are not.

Tactically speaking, the development of products and brands, particularly the development of their advertising, directly benefits from comprehension of the dominant mode of involvement. For example, when one finds that the level of enjoyment with champagne is greater than the level of interest, communication based on contexts of consumption has a greater chance of attracting the consumer than a descriptive history of the product. At the same time, champagne's ability to portray personal values can vary tremendously from one culture to another, and the approach used in one country may have to be adapted to suit another. For example, and even though cross-cultural research is difficult, given the complexity of measurement instruments (culture is discussed at length in Chapter 7), researchers have found that involvement in soft drinks tends to be higher in China than in Canada or Sweden. Similarly, Mexicans appear much less involved with going to the movies than the Chinese or the French.[75]

There are many strategies available for companies wishing to increase the level of involvement in the products or services they sell. One tactic is to ask celebrities to endorse the product (this issue will be discussed more fully in Chapter 5); another consists in bonding with consumers so as to maintain a long-lasting relationship. In the United States, one perfume manufacturer ingeniously exploited the customers' deep involvement in its products. By launching a competition where consumers were asked to divulge their personal memories or dreams connected with using the product, the company rewarded them with a special book as a gift for each bottle purchased![76]

Personality and self-image

In the preceding section of this chapter, we have seen that motivation is made up of specific internal forces, while involvement is concerned with specific domains of interest. If an individual tends to react in a similar way across products and domains, it becomes possible to suggest that the motives for a purchase or the permanent involvement in a certain type of product rest on the same stable pattern characterising the consumer. Debate on personality has evolved along these lines. At the centre of this debate are the following two questions:

- Is it possible to measure the consumer's personality?
- What influence does personality exercise on purchasing and consumer behaviour?

A brief history of personality

Personality is most often defined as the collection of an individual's stable and co-ordinated reactions to their environment.[77] The fundamental hypothesis says that a person's behaviour, attitudes and opinions are influenced to some extent by a central and integrated ego. Definition of the ego and its variations has always been a troublesome issue. Cattell divides the history of personality into three periods.[78] The first (from ancient times to the middle of the nineteenth century) is literary and philosophical, and its identification of personality patterns is due more to the intuition of writers on the subject than to empirical investigation. Hippocrates, for example, classified human beings into four 'humours' according to the nature of their temperament: the 'sanguine' type is warm and active; the 'phlegmatic' type slow and detached, the 'melancholic' depressive and the 'choleric' impulsive. These ideas were not submitted to rigorous tests and are, therefore, difficult to substantiate. The second period (up until the Second World War) is characterised by more structured observations and elaborate theorisation. The contributions of Freud, Horney, Reisman and Erikson (detailed below) are included in this period. The third and final period, which encompasses current trends, is experimental and quantitative and is based on the concept of **traits.**

Personality according to Freud

Freud not only postulated the three key components of personality mentioned above (the id, the ego and the superego) but also sought to explain the development of the psyche. In the first year of life, a baby mainly derives pleasure from oral stimulation (the oral stage). At two years, the child becomes primarily concerned with controlling the elimination process (the anal stage). Then, up until five years of age, interest is centred around the sexual organs (the phallic stage), which becomes the genital stage at adolescence. According to Freud, the basic personality is acquired in childhood and the transition to each stage is marked by a crisis (weaning, learning about cleanliness, etc.) which is either easily or painfully overcome, depending on the child's own defence mechanisms. For example, according to Freud, a child who does not overcome the oral stage successfully will become an adult very dependent on others. Similarly, the way in which a child resolves his or her relationship with the parent of the opposite sex during the phallic stage will later affect his or her attitude to figures of authority, for example employers, teachers and superiors.

In commercial research, the psychoanalytical approach to personality has influenced consumer classification. For example, a European marketing research group called IPSOS has developed the so-called TRIPSY classification system based upon seven types:[79]

1 oral

2 anal

3 phallic-narcissistic

4 phobic

5 hysterical

6 paranoid

7 introverted

It is sometimes possible to relate character type to the consumption of certain products. For example, 'oral' people are more attracted to rich, fatty, substantial food products than to diet foods.

Horney and the CAD test

Although in agreement with Freud on the importance of the subconscious and childhood in the formation of personality, Karen Horney considers that traditional psychoanalysis overestimates the role of biological drives and underestimates that of the social environment.[80] She prefers to emphasise the anxiety which stems from the state of dependence in which the child learns about the world. She goes on to claim that there are three ways of dealing with this anxiety:

1 going **towards** others on a current of affection and affiliation;

2 turning **against** others by developing an appetite for power and domination;

3 turning **away** from others by taking refuge in isolation and constructing an air of indifference.

A particular type of personality corresponds to each strategy: the complacent (sometimes called the accommodating), the aggressive and the detached. Such an approach allows an understanding of how interpersonal context influences purchasing decisions. A corresponding measurement instrument (the CAD test) has been developed and it has been discovered that the consumption of certain products and the choice of certain brands are linked to Horney's personality types. The aggressive type will use more body lotion, brand name deodorant and will be more likely to use an ordinary razor. He or she will also be more likely to buy 'signature goods'.[81] The complacent (or accommodating) type will have a preference for soap and likes drinking wine, while the detached type will prefer tea. For other products though (cigarettes, shirts, toothpaste, beer), it is not really possible to establish a link.[82]

Reisman's lonely crowd

In a more historical and sociological context, David Reisman recognises an evolutionary scheme within Western society which points to the identification of three types of behaviour: **orientation towards tradition**, which was dominant in ancient times but has since declined; **orientation towards oneself**, which is anchored in individual values and **orientation towards others**, most characteristic in modern society.[83] Today, these three basic personality types coexist and, according to Reisman, purchasing and consumer behaviour is greatly affected by the consumer's dominant orientation. Traditionalists are more inclined to drink, eat and dress in conformity with society. Introverts are primarily concerned with their own well-being, while extroverts make purchases which will enhance their status and prestige. His approach, which has influenced research on national stereotypes and lifestyle, has also been subjected to more direct tests.[84] It has been shown, for example, that ego-centred housewives who are less dependent on social environment will accept new products more readily,[85] and that they are more responsive to advertising which addresses them directly.[86] A link between the audience's personality type and the chosen style of communication can therefore be posited.

Erik Erikson

Although Erikson's work belongs to psychoanalytical thought, he believes that the personality is formed not only in childhood but emerges throughout the entire course of life. Eight major crises trace its development:

1 The **trust/distrust** opposition, which appears at birth and whose resolution depends on the mother's behaviour.

2 The **autonomy/doubt** opposition, which appears around two years of age and involves the parental attitude to the child's first discoveries.

3 The **initiative/guilt** dilemma, resolved according to the reward/punishment system that is in place.

4 The **perseverance/inferiority** opposition, which is particularly noticeable in school life.

5 The **identity crisis**, which is characteristic of the adolescent on the threshold of two worlds.

6 The **intimacy/isolation** debate, which comes into play at the beginning of a couple's relationship.

7 The **reproductive/withdrawal** dilemma at the heart of the debate about the creation of a family or a self-centred life.

8 Finally, the **integrity/despair** opposition, which is most prominent in old age and is affected by physical and mental health.

It may at first seem that Erikson's theory offers few immediate uses to marketing, except perhaps the analysis of ritual behaviour (the organisation of surprise parties by teenagers, for example, is part of the rites of passage to adult life).[87] However, his indirect influence is profound and aids a better understanding of purchasing and consumption contexts during each stage of life.[88]

The traits-based approach

After the Second World War, and under the influence of studies on the selection of conscripts, a new approach which endeavoured to use existing theories (rather than develop new ones) appeared and resulted in the development of batteries of tests. In the same spirit as the list of needs, these tests were constructed from inventories of personality traits with variable contents and of varying size. From then on, there was to be less concern with classifying types and more emphasis on discovering aspects which would be of use to describe individuals. Guilford, for example, proposed the use of the following ten traits to measure personality:

1 sociable–timid
2 dominant–submissive
3 action-oriented–reflection-oriented
4 friendly–hostile
5 stable–nervous
6 hard–sensitive
7 serious–frivolous
8 quick–slow
9 tolerant–suspicious
10 masculine–feminine[89]

Eysenck's system is reduced to two traits:

1 extroverted–introverted
2 ethnocentric–neurotic[90]

Others have developed ways of measuring particular traits, for example authority[91] or anxiety.[92] Easier to implement, these instruments have, as we shall see, frequently been used in commercial research – particularly such tests as the Edwards Preference Schedule[93] (created in accordance with Murray's findings) or the Gordon Personal Profile (GPP, shown in Figure 1.9).

Figure 1.9 The Gordon Personal Profile test: an example of a personality test used in commercial research

The Gordon Personal Profile test seeks to measure the following four personality traits: ascendancy, responsibility, emotional stability and sociability. The subject is required to indicate which one of four statements are most (M) and least (L) like him or her:

M L	M L	M L
a good mixer socially	a person who can be relied upon	free from worry or care
lacking in self-confidence	easily upset when things go wrong	lacks a sense of responsibility
is tough in any work undertaken	not too sure of own opinions	not interested in mixing with the opposite sex
tends to be somewhat emotional	prefers to be around other people	skilful in handling other

M L	M L	M L
is interested in being with other people	finds it easy to influence other people	finds it easy to be friendly with others
is free from anxieties and tensions	gets the job done in the face of any obstacle	prefers to let others take the lead in group activity
is a reliable person	limits social relations to a select few	seems to have a worrying nature
takes the lead in group discussion	tends to be a rather nervous person	sticks to a job despite any difficulty

▶

M L	M L	M L
is somewhat jumpy and nervous	doesn't make friends very readily	able to sway other people's opinions
has strong influence on others	takes an active part in group affairs	lacks interest in joining group activities
does not like social gatherings	keeps at routine duties until completed	quite a nervous person
is a very persistent and steady worker	not too well-balanced emotionally	very persistent in any task undertaken

M L	M L	M L
finds it easy to make new acquaintances	assured in relationships with others	calm and easygoing in manner
does not stick to the same task for too long	feelings are rather easily hurt	cannot stick to the task at hand
is easily managed by other people	follows well-developed work habits	enjoys having lots of people around
maintains self-control even when frustrated	would rather keep to a small group of friends	not too confident of own abilities

M L	M L	M L
likes to make important decisions without help	becomes irritated somewhat readily	can be relied upon entirely
does not mix easily with new people	capable of handling any situation	doesn't care for the company of most people
inclined to be tense or highly strung	does not like to converse with strangers	finds it rather difficult to relax
takes a job through despite difficulties	thorough in any work performed	takes an active part in group discussion

M L	M L	M L
not too interested in mixing socially with people	prefers not to argue with people	doesn't give up easily on a problem
doesn't take responsibilities seriously	unable to keep a fixed schedule	inclined to be somewhat nervous in manner
steady and composed at all times	a calm and unexcitable person	lacking in self-assurance
takes the lead in group activities	inclined to be highly sociable	prefers to pass the time in the company of others

Note: On each trait, a maximum of 36 points may be obtained. The reader interested in calculating his or her own score on, let's say sociability, should proceed as follows. After completing the whole scale, he or she would count as 1 point an M for items 1, 6 to 10, 12, 13, 17, 19, 20, 22 to 24, 28 to 30, 32, 34 to 39, 41, 42, 44, 48 to 50, 52, 53, 57, 59, 60, 63, 65, ,67, 68, 72 and as 1 point an L for all other items (assuming items are numbered from top to bottom starting from the left column, so that, for example, the top item of the right column becomes item 49).
Source: L. V. Gordon, Gordon Personal Profile, Answer Sheet 1968 Edition.

Personality and consumption

More than a hundred published studies have been conducted on the relationships between personality and purchasing behaviour.[94] Such studies explore a double-sided issue. On the one hand, one must understand the link between personality and product use as well as exposure to the media; on the other, one would like to 'predict' purchasing behaviour by knowing the personality type of the buyer. Let's consider these two issues in turn.

When a company launches an advertising campaign in the media, it takes considerable pains to target the right consumer group. In many countries the target is primarily defined according to socio-demographic criteria, as available from audience studies, and the media mix is established on this basis. Cleaning products and cooking recipes will typically be found in women's magazines. This may appear logical, but is it sufficient? If it were also possible to characterise magazine readers by their need to accomplish household (or culinary) tasks, matching the message with the medium would be all the more precise. Concrete results which might feed this hope are few and far between, however; a limited number are currently available. For example, it has been shown that innovative individuals are more likely to subscribe to cable television than others;[95] and that men's preferences in magazines are linked to their need for order.[96] Some companies have gone as far as redefining their clientele on the basis of personality types. As a case in point, one regional bank has categorised its clientele according to a double-sided personality criterion: self-control (+ or −), and control over others (+ or −). Four segments of customers have thus been identified: the excitable (++), the level-headed (+−), the receptive (−+) and the demonstrative (−−). Specific advertising messages have been developed for each group.

The second problem, that of predicting purchasing behaviour by personality type, goes back further. In 1959, the American psychologist Franklin Evans began his quest to find out if Chevrolet and Ford owners had different personalities.[97] Using the Edwards EPPS scale, he discovered that with the exception of one or two variables, the profile differences were almost non-existent. This study provoked a controversy that subsequent articles used as a point of reference: the method Evans chose was criticised,[98] and the choice of car models was deemed inappropriate as the two makes were very similar. Afterwards, it was shown that if brand was not influenced by personality, then the type of car (for example a standard or convertible car) could be.[99]

In other studies, significant but weak links have been found between the consumer's personality and the act of smoking,[100] choosing a push-button rather than a dial telephone,[101] and even the consumption of chewing gum and vitamins.[102] Similarly, it has been shown that an individual's preference for words rather than images will lead him or her to prefer games which contain such elements and vice versa.[103]

On the whole, researchers have found the link between personality and purchasing disappointing. Is this really surprising? Is it really logical to expect personality, a rather abstract and generic concept, to predict a phenomenon as specific and local as brand purchase, especially when one considers that a personality trait can manifest itself in extremely diverse, even opposing ways? Let us take an example. In a fit of snobbery and desire to stand out from the crowd, an individual may buy a Mercedes. But if his or her group of friends already own this type of car, he or she could have satisfied this aspiration for differentiation equally well by buying a second-hand VW 'Beetle'! Identical behaviour can, conversely, express very different traits: depending on the individual, going to church every Sunday can correspond to obeying very individual motives (nurturing a personal faith) or may be connected with preoccupations of a social nature (meeting friends). Furthermore, the absence of prespecified hypotheses has led many researchers to apply tests developed by psychologists (often with a clinical perspective) to samples of 'ordinary' consumers. It is not certain that the traits which lead individuals to the wards of psychiatric hospitals are the same ones which lead them to buy a washing machine or pair of shoes![104] Finally, consumer researchers have not hesitated to shorten or modify the original tests when they found them difficult to use. The effects of such adjustments are difficult to estimate, even when a certain consistency can be observed in the results.[105]

In the end, one could argue that inconsistency of empirical results is due to methodological inadequacies and not to the inefficiency of the personality concept. The idea that, over the years, an individual constructs a coherent mode of response to his or her environment seems plausible and there is no reason why purchasing behaviour should be an exception. However, using a generic instrument to explain a very specific act is hardly appropriate. To resolve this difficulty, it seems necessary either to adapt the selected instruments to a consumption context or to widen the range of observed behaviour. Consumption or purchasing style (for example, impulsive vs. reflective) is probably better explained by personality than the acquisition of a particular brand in a particular store at a particular time.

Certain studies, for example, have shown that better results are obtained when predicting opinion leadership for electrical goods as a product category rather than for any particular item.[106] In the same vein, it has been found that personality can be associated more easily with generic benefits (for example durability, price, performance) than with specific products.[107] Moreover, it has been shown that by developing a test measuring accomplishment in a specific consumption-related context (that is by taking into account aspects which have do with the consumption of products, the purchasing process or media exposure) one can confidently predict the purchase of 'green' products (organic fertiliser, lead-free petrol).[108]

Following a somewhat different approach, researchers have sought to measure the **cognitive style** of an individual, that is his or her mode of collecting and processing information. Individuals with a complex cognitive style are capable of comprehending a greater range of concepts (differentiation), of establishing finer distinctions (discrimination) and of combining them according to more elaborate rules (integration). Different modes of complexity can also be distinguished: depending, for example, on the capacity for dealing with ambiguous information, or on the tendency to minimise or to draw attention to differences. It has been found that people with a lower level of tolerance for ambiguity were more faithful to brands, that impulsive individuals were more attracted to risk and that the more discriminating consumers remembered comparative advertising more easily.[109] Similarly, it was found that consumers who did not easily accept ambiguous information evaluated fewer alternatives when they were choosing a bank.[110]

The self-concept

Finally, one has to decide which type of personality one really wishes to measure. In the traditional approach, 'objective' instruments were used and any attempt to give the self an image other than reality was considered 'biased'. However, it may be that purchasing behaviour is influenced more by the perceived than by the 'real' self. Several studies have found a link between the image that the consumer holds of him or herself (the '**self-concept**') and the products that he or she buys[111] or the stores he or she visits.[112] For example, for many of us, the brand of cigarettes, beer or cars that we prefer are those that match our personal image.[113] Inversely, it may happen that we buy and consume products or services to hide an aspect of ourselves which we do not like.

The self-concept approach is an interesting extension of research on personality which has generated a number of recent studies. Instead of approaching a person from an angle inferred by the researcher, the link between purchase and personality 'as perceived' is explored.[114] Although the self concept involves a variety of complex images – what one believes oneself to be (the actual self), what one would like to be (the ideal self), what one appears to be to others (the self to others) and what one would like to be to others (the ideal self to others) – it is an area which deserves further exploration.[115.] A discrepancy between the real self and the ideal self could, for example, lead to a compensatory purchase. Thus, although she will never be a film star, a shop assistant can acquire a star's attributes through product purchases: perfume by Liz Taylor, jewellery by Catherine Deneuve, make-up by Cindy Crawford, and so on. In many cases, the discrepancy will be triggered by a **social comparison** process, according to which people evaluate their own worth (often called **self-esteem**) by comparing themselves with either their immediate social environment or advertising stereotypes.[116.] Self-esteem, sometimes aggravated to the point of vanity, has proven to be an important variable to explain consumer behaviour.[117] For example, people with high self-esteem tend to accept innovations more easily,[118] while people low in self-esteem prefer ready-to-eat food products to those which require complex recipes. Advertising often tries to change attitudes towards products by boosting the target audience's self-esteem (for example, by using themes such as 'L'Oreal, because I'm worth it').[119]

Which aspect of the self will have the strongest influence on a particular product purchase largely depends upon the role identities assumed by the consumer. The theory of **symbolic interactionism** holds that people spend a large part of their life as if they were actors on stage in a theatre. Depending upon the situation, they try to understand what is expected from them (that is, their role script) and in many cases make efforts to behave accordingly. In fact, they continuously interpret their own identity by 'negotiating ' the meanings attached to a particular context.[120]

The 'self to others' (that is, how we think we appear to other people) also plays an important part in explaining purchase and consumption, especially for conspicuous products. For example, many women like to go shopping with their friends to get feedback on 'how they look' before buying a dress or a cosmetic item.

Obviously, certain consumers are more **self-conscious** than others and their product choices will be influenced accordingly,

It has even been suggested that the various objects that one owns can be considered an extension of oneself.[121] In an attempt to verify this claim, researchers studied the reactions of consumers who are victims of theft, loss or destruction and found they considered it to be a violation of their identity. They have also analysed the phenomenon of 'attachment' to an object (for example, collecting or seeking to acquire objects or mascots).[122] In some cases, celebrity fan clubs for example, consumers become so involved in an activity that they become fanatical enthusiasts, ready to try to convince the rest of their world.[123] More generally, it has been shown that taking possession of an object confers on it a value far superior to that which it had before ownership. This 'appropriation effect' explains the considerable discrepancies in price that are initially proposed by the buyer and the seller when a second-hand car is being purchased.

Research has shown that many elements come together to comprise the self-concept. Among them, three appear particularly important: body image, gender identity and membership of an age group. These are now discussed in more detail.

Body image

A person's physical appearance is obviously a key component of his or her self-concept. The way people feel about their body is perhaps more important than the way they 'really' are and many advertising efforts exploit consumers' subjective evaluations of their physical self. For certain products such as soap, shampoo or deodorant, it is essential to understand body image and be aware that international studies reveal strong cultural variations also exist. For example, Procter and Gamble measured the following hygiene habits in Europe. Number of showers per week: 4.4 in Germany, 3.7 in the UK, 4.7 in Spain, 4.4 in France and 3.8 in Italy; the corresponding percentages for using a deodorant are 76, 86, 75, 52 and 72; the numbers of toothbrushes used per year are (respectively) 2, 1.4, 0.8, 1.2 and 1.2; while the corresponding numbers of tubes of toothpaste are 4.9, 2.9, 4.5, 3.9 and 3.3.[124] At the same time, consumers who are more satisfied with their bodies tend to use more grooming products.[125]

Of course, advertising and the media strongly influence ideals of beauty and one study showed that women expressed less satisfaction with their body after being exposed, even for a short time, to advertisements depicting attractive models.[126] Naturally, these ideals change over time[127] and specific periods are often described by a particular 'look', like the 'New Look' Christian Dior launched in the post-war Europe of the late 1940s, or the contemporary fashion of body piercing. Critics have often complained about the widespread portrayal of excessively thin women as role models in advertisements or even toys such as the Barbie doll. As a result, many female consumers seem to be preoccupied with their weight, even though the percentage of people (of both sexes) 'officially' classified as 'obese' remains relatively limited (6 per cent in France, 9 per cent in the Netherlands, 14 per cent in the UK and 18 per cent in Germany, according to European statistics). Such a concern nevertheless provides a tremendous marketing opportunity for an ever-increasing number of products and services, from 'diet' food to liposuction and other forms of cosmetic surgery. Unfortunately, consumers obsessed with their weight may fall victim to eating disorders or body mutilations.

Gender identity

In modern society, gender identity is seen as being as much a psychological as a biological construct. Evidently, belonging to one of the two sexes exercises a profound influence on consumption, and products which target one sex rather than the other (beauty creams and toiletries as well as clothes and games) abound. Factors concerning the evolution of men's and women's roles are also important. For example, in Europe the number of women in work grew from less than one-third in 1960 (33.6 per cent in Germany but 29.6 per cent in the UK, 28.2 per cent in France, 16.8 per cent in Spain, 16.1 per cent in the Netherlands and 12.7 per cent in Portugal) to almost two-thirds 35 years later (74.9 per cent in Sweden, 61.3 per cent in Germany, 65.4 per cent in the UK, 61.9 per cent in Portugal, 60 per cent in France, 58.9 per cent in the Netherlands and 43.7 per cent in Italy) and this has had a considerable impact on many different markets. In France, for instance, women's publishing was traditionally dominated by weekly magazines such as *Femmes d'Aujourd'hui* (4 500 000 readers in the 1970s) and *Elle* (2 500 000) or monthly publications such as *Modes et Travaux* (7 000 000) and *Marie Claire* (4 000 000). The 1980s saw the introduction of new titles which were particularly aimed at 'active' women. *Prima*, which was launched in 1982 after three years of market research studies and a thorough investigation of market needs (through market tests and direct marketing), quickly established itself as the number one magazine; in contrast, others (*Marie-France*, for example) disappeared. In a similar fashion, *Femme Actuelle* made an astonishing impact on the world of weeklies. As far as advertising is concerned, certain studies have shown that women attach a greater importance to television advertising than do men. They pay more attention to the arguments put forward and remember them more easily.[128]

At the same time, **gender identity** – the feeling of one's masculinity or femininity – is influenced by society's expectations of each sex.[129] It is determined more by culture than by biology and evolves quickly.[130] In Anglo-Saxon cultures, for example, men normally avoid close physical contact with each other, while hugging is the norm in Latin countries (Chapter 7 provides additional discussion of role expectations across cultures). Moreover, gender identity is in turn conveyed by advertising and the products represented, which are often sex-typed.[131] Traditionally, advertising is somewhat conservative and tends to reproduce expected roles. More recently, however, it has become more frequent to see men performing household tasks – at least in adverts – while women seem to play a more and more important role in traditionally masculine decisions. In the United States, for example, it has been estimated that 40 per cent of condom purchases are made by women.[132] However, not all women are participants in the gender revolution and a specialised researcher has recently split the female market into four segments based on the following different identities:

1 'housewives' who do not have and do not intend to have a career;

2 women currently out of work but who would like to have a job;

3 'career women' to whom a professional career is everything;

4 women who work solely out of necessity.[133]

Research also reveals that sex-role orientation can influence several stages of the decision-making process (see Chapter 9 for a more complete discussion of the buying process). For example, one study showed that females tend to process advertising messages more completely and pay more attention to detail, while males have a better recall of overall themes.[134] Another showed that, depending upon their **sex-role orientation**,[135] household members could exert more or less influence over the purchase of consumer durables.[136]

Chronological and cognitive age

Although age may appear as a rather unambiguous variable, it is necessary to distinguish between real and cognitive age. Real (chronological) age is perhaps, out of all the demographic factors, the one which most influences purchasing behaviour. Because of the various phenomena which age brings (biological changes, social status, etc.), a whole set of behavioural traits, values and symbols which characterise the different stages of life are associated with age. Consumption of clothes, games, medicines, drinks and cosmetics, among other things, is modified by age. Even within a given category distinctions exist. The Fisher-Price range sold in Europe, for example, comprises the 'Musical Mobile' for birth to twelve months, the 'Snoopy Sniffer' for two to six years, the 'Alphaprobe' spaceship designed for four- to nine-year-olds, and a wooden aeroplane which requires assembly, aimed at older children of six years and upwards.

Studies have also shown that capacity for the understanding and processing of commercial information, particularly advertising, evolves with time. Three- to four-year-old children can already differentiate advertising from its programme context.[137] By comparison, older people appear more vulnerable to seduction by advertising, particularly in areas which they do not feel familiar with.[138]

In the European Union, an analysis of age structure has revealed four major tendencies over the last ten years – a consequence of the birth rate and longer life expectancy:

- The 15–25-year-olds, who in the early 1990s numbered 50 million, are now 44 million. Manufacturers of products for young people (motorbikes, records, clothes, etc.) must anticipate the consequences of today's overcapacity.

- The number of 25–55-year-olds has increased from 140 to 180 million. The furniture, household goods and sports markets benefit from this increase.

- The 55–65-year-olds have increased from 39 to 50 million, mainly due to the number of 50–60-year-olds increasing steadily from 1985. Free from the constraints of bringing up a family, this group will have more and more time and money to spend on entertainment, travel and leisure.

- Finally, the 65 years and over age group, who represent 31 million people in 2000, will increase to 40 million in 2050. This market poses considerable interest for cruises, rest homes, and health products and services.

Beyond statistics, marketing managers must understand that new trends are emerging and developing. Two such phenomena are the 'kids' generation' and the 'granny boom', discussed in more detail below.

The kids' generation. In France alone, the 9–13-year-old group (the kids' market) numbers more than 4 million. They have their own interests, language, style and behaviour. They are the ones responsible for making fashions and pop and film stars popular. Their opinions and their subsequent influence on 45 per cent of the family budget have made them a target for many different industries (food, records, clothes and electronic games). Wearing jeans (Levi 501s), trainers (Adidas) and a sweatshirt (Benetton), and with a Walkman clamped to their ears, they are happy but realistic.

'Never to be unemployed' is more important for 37 per cent than 'to be able to do what I like' (31 per cent) or 'to earn a lot of money' (27 per cent). They receive an average 40 francs per month pocket money, which represents a national budget of more than two billion francs. Such a valuable market is an advertising target. To convince them of the value of an item of clothing, for example, there are three prerequisites: comfort, simplicity and the brand names (or labels) of which they are so fond.

Granny power. In Europe, the 65-plus segment represents between one-eighth and one-sixth of the population (from a low of 11.5 per cent in Ireland to a high of 17.5 per cent in Sweden) and is expected to grow in the future (16 per cent in Ireland, but 21.8 per cent in Belgium and 21.6 per cent in Finland by 2010). A growing group who have a guaranteed income at their disposal, and are more inclined to spend than save, the 'grandmas and grandads' are the market of the future! According to a study carried out in Western Europe, the 50 years and over age group are a powerful consumer group (making up 34 per cent of the coffee market, 36 per cent of the champagne market, 40 per cent of the mineral water market and 37 per cent of the travel market). Their desires and expectations, particularly when it comes to health and leisure, have led manufacturers to develop specially adapted products and services: retirement homes, specialist magazines, radio stations, anti-ageing creams, etc. Several European telecom companies have recently launched a digital telephone with large pads aimed especially at this group.

Several broad results emerge from the many studies conducted on the elderly. Compared with the rest of the population, older people have difficulty in assimilating all the information available in a shop or sales outlet; they make more mistakes when it comes to price and rely more on their own experiences, family and friends when choosing products; they use credit facilities less, are more inclined to shop around, are reasonably faithful to brands and shops, and are less likely to be dissatisfied with their purchases.[139] Some conclusions have obvious implications for public policy on consumerism. For example, it has been found that older people have a fair amount of difficulty in understanding the nutritional information on food products, when it would be of particular interest to them.[140]

At the same time, the age that one feels oneself to be does not necessarily correspond to the age that one really is, and it seems that the age one gives oneself (cognitive age) has more influence on consumption than biological age.[141] Therefore, the many products ostensibly aimed at young people (Coca-Cola, Wrigley's chewing gum, the Peugeot 205 Junior) attract consumers who are beyond the advertising's target group. Some of these products are youthful symbols and may be consumed by those who wish to appear younger (interestingly, one in five buyers of the Renault Twingo is over 50).

Cognitive age is based on the following four components: the age that one feels inside, the age that one appears to be by one's physical appearance, the age that comes across through one's actions, and the age that corresponds to one's interests.[142] Measured in this way, cognitive age is always lower than real age – on average by five to fifteen years in adults, particularly older adults. Biological age, professional activity, marital status and income are also factors which influence perception of one's age. One feels older if one is inactive, rich and married.[143]

In general, a younger cognitive age brings a greater self-confidence and a more active social life. This in turn has consequences for consumption, for example a greater interest in fashion and more diverse cultural activities.[144] It has been shown that people who are cognitively young wish to dress better and spend more time shopping.[145] The implications for advertising are straightforward. Knowing that the older people are, the more they wish to feel young, and that the younger they feel, the more fashionable they want to be, it would be advisable for manufacturers of clothes for older women to use models who are typically youthful in their catalogues. In this area, as in many others, individuals make purchases in accordance with projected self-images rather than actual images!

Finally, the expansion of research into self-concept invites a re-examination of the meaning of causal relationships: does one buy products because of one's self-image or does one receive this image from the products bought? The question is relevant because it draws attention to the indirect nature of the personality-purchase relationship, which is conveyed by the self-concept.[146] It has thus been possible to show that drinkers of a particular brand of beer see themselves differently from non-drinkers, even if both see the brand in the same way.[147] Conversely, some products which are highly visible and have the capacity and versatility for customisation (T-shirts, jewellery) contribute to the image that one forms of oneself through their symbolism. Ultimately, it is the status of purchasing and consumption of a product which becomes an ingredient of the personality attributed to it.

Notes

[1] Eurostat Statistics.

[2] Y. Marbeau, J. Quatresooz and D. Vancrayenest, 'Harmonisation of Demographics in Europe', *Marketing and Research Today*, March 1992, pp. 33–47.

[3] In fact, economists were more interested in making predictions about consumer purchases than in explaining the processes leading to purchase decisions. In developing their predictions, however, they had to make assumptions about what drives consumption. To that extent, they can be considered as precursors in consumer analysis. For a complete description of the economic theory of the consumer, the reader is referred to any textbook on microeconomics, for example M. Henderson and R. E. Quandt, *Microeconomic Theory* (McGraw-Hill, 1958) or, for a less advanced text, E. Mansfield, *Microeconomics* (Norton, 1970).

[4] See A. Smith, *An Inquiry into the Nature and the Causes of the Wealth of Nations*, 1796 (The Modern Library, 1937) and J. Bentham, *An Introduction to the Principles of Morals and Legislation*, 1780 (Clarendon Press, 1907).

[5] A. Marshall, *Principles of Economics*, 1890 (Macmillan, 1927).

[6] Veblen was one of the first to recognise the limits of the consumer's rational vision. See T. Veblen, *The Theory of the Business Enterprise*, 1904 (Kelley Bookseller, 1965).

[7] J. F. Bernard-Bechariès, *Le Choix de Consommation: Rationalité et Réalité du Comportement du Consommateur*, (Editions d'Organisation, 1980).

[8] R. D. Luce and M. Raiffa, *Games and Decisions: Introduction and Critical Survey* (J. Wiley, 1978).

[9] A. Tversky, 'Intransitivity of Preferences', *Psychological Review*, 1969, Vol. 76, pp. 31–48.

[10] J. Bettman, *An Information Processing Theory of Consumer Choice* (Wiley, 1979).

[11] See E. Mueller, 'A Study of Purchase Decision' in L. Clark (ed.), *Consumer Behavior*, Vol. 1 (New York University, 1954), pp. 36–87.

[12] See H. A. Simon, *Models of Man* (Wiley, 1957).

[13] See R. Ferber, 'Family Decision Making and Economic Behaviour' in B. Sheldon (ed.), *Family Economic Behaviour: Problems and prospects* (Lippincott, 1973).

[14] Duesenberry has claimed, since 1949, that the economic theory takes the social dimension of consumption into account. See J. S. Duesenberry, *Income, Saving and the Theory of Consumer Behavior* (Boston, 1949).

[15] This, therefore, ignores the phenomenon of 'conspicuous consumption'. See R. Mason, *Conspicuous Consumption*, (St Martin's Press, 1981).

[16] For a complete description of the theory, see K. Lancaster, *Consumer Demand: A New Approach* (Columbia University Press, 1971).

[17] See L. Geitsfeld, 'Consumer Decision Making: the Technical Efficiency Approach', *Journal of Consumer Research*, June 1977, pp. 48–56.

[18] B. T. Ratchford, 'The New Economic Theory of Consumer Behavior: an Interpretative Essay', *Journal of Consumer Research*, September 1975, pp. 65–78.

[19] For the idea of market segmentation based on product benefits, see R. J. Haley, 'Benefit Segmentation: A Decision-oriented Tool', *Journal of Marketing*, July 1968, pp. 93–6 and, from the same author, 'Benefit Segmentation: 20 Years Later', *Journal of Consumer Marketing*, 1988, pp. 5–13. See also M. Wedel and C. Kistemaker, 'Consumer Benefit Segmentation Using Clusterwise Linear Regression, *International Journal of Research in Marketing*, 1989, 6, pp. 45–60.

[20] E. Ryans, 'Estimating Consumer Preference for a New Durable Brand in an Established Product Class', *Journal of Marketing Research*, 1974, pp. 434–43.

[21] See G. Ladd and M. Zobber, 'Model of Consumer Reaction to Product Characteristics', *Journal of Consumer Research*, March 1977, pp. 89–101. Also see work on the Rosen model: S. Rosen, 'Hedonic Prices and Implicit Markets: Product Differentiation in Pure Competition', *Journal of Political Economy*, 1974, 82, pp. 34–55, and for empirical tests, M. Agarwal and B. T. Ratchford 'Estimating Demand Functions for Product Characteristics: the Case of

Automobiles', *Journal of Consumer Research*, December 1980, pp. 249–62; K. Morgan *et al.*, 'Hedonic Index for Breakfast Cereals', *Journal of Consumer Research*, June 1979, pp. 67–75; B. Wierenga, 'Empirical Test of the Lancaster Characteristics Model', *International Journal of Research in Marketing*, 1984, 1(4), 263–94; and A. Verbruggen and E. Gijsbrechts, 'Estimating the Sales Potential of a New Heating System', *International Journal of Research in Marketing*, 1988, 5, pp. 289–302.

[22] D. W. Tiffany, J. R. Cowan and P. M. Tiffany, *The Unemployed: A Psychological Portrait* (Prentice Hall, 1970).

[23] See surveys regularly carried out by the University of Michigan Research Center on the evolution of the 'consumer sentiment'.

[24] T. Nagle, 'Economic Foundations of Pricing', *Journal of Business*, 1984, pp. 522–3.

[25] G. Allenby, 'A Unified Approach to Identifying, Estimating and Testing Demand Structures with Aggregate Scanner Data', *Marketing Science*, 1989, pp. 265–80.

[26] For a specific example, see J. Weiner, 'Forecasting Demand: Consumer Electronics Marketer Uses a Conjoint Approach to Configure its New Product and Set the Right Price', *Marketing Research*, Summer 1994, pp. 6–11.

[27] For an excellent non-technical description of how conjoint analysis works, see R. J. Dolan, *Conjoint Analysis: A Manager's Guide*, Harvard Business School case 590–059, 1990.

[28] See D. R. Wittinck, M. Viens and W. Burhenne, 'Commercial Uses of Conjoint Analysis in Europe: Results and Critical Reflections', *International Journal of Research in Marketing*, January 1994, pp. 41–52.

[29] See G. Stigler, 'The Economics of Information', *Journal of Political Economy*, June 1961, 69, pp. 213–25.

[30] R. Nisbett and D. Kanouse, 'Food Deprivation and Supermarket Shopping Behavior', *Journal of Personality and Social Psychology*, 1969, pp. 289–94.

[31] See C. N. Cofer and M. H. Appley, *Motivation: Theory and Research* (Wiley, 1964) and B. Weiner, *Theories of Motivation: From Mechanism to Cognition* (Markham Publishing Co., 1972).

[32] For a general introduction to Freudian theory, see S. Freud, *The Basic Writings of Sigmund Freud* (A. Brill, 1938) and S. Freud, *The Ego and the Id* (Hogarth Press, 1927).

[33] S. Levy, 'Symbols for Sale', *Harvard Business Review*, July–August 1959, pp. 117–24.

[34] E. Dichter, *A Strategy of Desire* (Doubleday, 1960) and *Motivation and Human Behaviour* (McGraw-Hill, 1962).

[35] G. McClelland, *Studies in Motivation* (Appleton-Century-Crofts, 1955), No. 5, 2150–2.

[36] For an example of a recent study employing collages, among other techniques, see R. Belk, G. Ger and S. Askergaard, 'Consumer Desire in Three Cultures', *Advances in Consumer Research*, 1997, pp. 24–8.

[37] J. J. Durgee, 'Interpreting Dichter's Interpretations: An Analysis of Consumption Symbolism in the Handbook of Consumer Motivations', in H. Hartvig Larsen, D. G. Mick and C. Alsted (eds), *Marketing and Semiotics, Selected Papers from the Copenhagen Symposium*, (Copenhagen, HandelshöjskolensForlag, 1991).

[38] A. Adler, *Understanding Human Nature* (Greenberg, 1927).

[39] K. Horney, *Our Inner Conflicts* (Norton & Co., 1945) and *The Neurotic Personality of Our Time* (W.W. Norton, 1937).

[40] T. Roselius, 'Risk Reduction Methods', *Journal of Marketing*, January 1971, pp. 56–61.

[41] V. Packard, *The Hidden Persuaders* (Pocket Books, 1957) and, from the same author, *The Waste Makers* (David Mckay, 1960).

[42] H. Murray, *Motivation and Emotions* (Prentice Hall, 1964).

[43] For other lists, see Cofer and Appley, *op. cit.* For classification of needs based on the origin of motivation (cognitive and affective), see W. J. McGuire, 'Psychological Motives and Communication Gratification' in J. G. Bulmier and E. Katz (eds), *The Uses of Mass Communication: Current Perspectives on Gratification Research*, Vol. 3 (Sage, 1974).

44 D. M. Gardner, 'An Exploratory Investigation of Achievement Motivation Effects on Consumer Behavior', *ACR Proceedings*, 1972, pp. 20–3 and E. L. Landon, 'Role of Need for Achievement in the Perception of Products', *APA Proceedings*, 1972.

45 M. K. Ericksen and J. M. Sirgy, 'Achievement Motivation and Clothing Preferences of White-Collar Working Women', *The Psychology of Fashion*, M. R. Solomon (ed.) (Lexington Books, 1985), pp. 357–69.

46 See C. Dussart, *Comportement du Consommateur et Stratégie Marketing* (McGraw-Hill, 1982), pp. 104–13.

47 A. Maslow, *Motivation and Personality* (Harper, 1954).

48 S. Young and B. Feigin, 'Using the Benefit Chain for Improved Strategy Formulation', *Journal of Marketing*, July 1975, pp. 72–4.

49 J. Gutman, 'A Means–End Chain Model Based on Consumer Categorization Process', *Journal of Marketing*, Spring 1982, pp. 60–72. Also see P. Valette-Florence and B. Rappacchi, 'Improvements in Means–End Chain Analysis', *Journal of Advertising Research*, February–March 1991, pp. 30–45. See also F. ter Hofstede, A. Audenaert, J. B. E. M. Steenkamp and M. Wedel, 'An Investigation into the Association Pattern Technique as a Quantitative Approach to Measuring Means–Ends Chains', *International Journal of Research in Marketing*, February 1998, pp. 37–50; and R. Pieters, H. Baumgartner and D. Allen, 'A Means–End Chain Approach to Consumer Goal Structures', *International Journal of Research in Marketing*, 1995, pp. 227–44.

50 See T. J. Reynolds and J. Gutman, 'Laddering Theory, Method, Analysis, and Interpetation', *Journal of Advertising*, February/March 1988, pp. 11–34; T. J. Reynolds and D. B. Whitlark, 'Applying Laddering Data to Communications Strategy and Advertsing Practice', *Journal of Advertising Research*, July/August 1995, pp. 9–17.

51 See the 1995 special issue of the *International Journal of Research in Marketing*, and in particular K. Grunert and S. C. Grunert, 'Measuring Subjective Meaning Structures by the Laddering Method: Theoretical Considerations and Methodological Problems', *International Journal of Research in Marketing*, 1995, pp. 209–25.

52 G. Botschen and E. Thaler, 'Hard versus Soft Laddering: Implications for Appropriate Use', in I. Balderjahn, C. Mennicken and E. Venette (eds), (Schäffer-Poeschel Verlag and Macmillan Press, 1998).

53 R. Mason, 'Measuring the Demand for Status Goods: An Evaluation of Means–End Chains and Laddering', *European Advances for Consumer Research*, 1995, pp. 78–82.

54 L. Festinger, *A Theory of Cognitive Dissonance* (Stanford University Press, 1957).

55 See W. J. McGuire, 'The Current Status of Cognitive Consistency Theories' in J. B. Cohen (ed.), *Behavioral Science Foundations of Consumer Behavior* (Free Press, 1972).

56 For more on how people perceive the causes of behaviour, see E. E. Jones *et al.*, *Attribution: Perceiving the Causes of Behavior* (General Learning Press, 1972).

57 J. Dollard *et al.*, *Frustration and Regression* (Yale University Press, 1939).

58 Shell was again the target of strong public criticism when the company, this time correctly identified, considered sinking one of its platforms at sea rather than recycling it on land.

59 See K. Lewin, *The Conceptual Representation and the Measurement of Psychological Forces* (Duke University Press, 1938) also see N. E. Miller, 'Experimental Studies of Conflict' in J. McHunt (ed.) *Personality and the Behavior Orders* (Ronald Press, 1984).

60 See L. Marchand, *Le Marketing des Biens Immobiliers* (Le Moniteur, 1984).

61 M. Sherif and H. Cantril, *The Psychology of Ego-Involvement* (Wiley, 1947) and M. Sherif and C. L. Hovland, *Social Judgement: Assimilation and Contrast Effects in Communication and Attitude Change* (Yale University Press, 1961).

62 H. Assael, *Consumer Behavior and Marketing Action* (Kent, 1981).

63 R. Vaughn, 'How Advertising Works: A Planning Model', *Journal of Advertising Research*, October 1980, pp. 27–33.

64 J. B. Cohen, 'Involvement and You: 1000 Great Ideas', *Advances in Consumer Research* (ACR,

1983), pp. 325–8 and J. H. Antil, 'Conceptualization and Operationalization of Involvement', *Advances in Consumer Research* (ACR, 1984), pp. 203–9.

65 M. Rothschild, 'Perspectives on Involvement: Current Problems and Future Directions', *Advances in Consumer Research* (ACR, 1984), p. 217. For other definitions and approaches, see J. Antil, 'Conceptualization and Operationalization of Involvement', *Advances in Consumer Research* 1984, pp. 203–9; and P. H. Bloch, 'Involvement Beyond the Purchase: Conceptual Issues and Empirical Investigations', *Advances in Consumer Research*, 1981, pp. 61–5.

66 C. Park and B. Mittal, 'A Theory of Involvement in Consumer Behavior: Problems and Issues', *Research in Consumer Behavior* (JAI Press, 1985), pp. 201–35; also see C. Park and S. Young, 'Consumer Response to Television Commercials: The Impact of Involvement and Background Music on Brand Attitude Formation', *Journal of Marketing Research*, 1986, No. 23, pp. 11–24.

67 B. Dubois, F. Enel and G. Laurent, 'L'Autre Face du Marché du Luxe: Ruses et Excursionnisme'. Working Paper (HEC, 1993).

68 See A. Mitchell, 'Involvement: A Potentially Important Mediator of Consumer Behavior', *Advances in Consumer Research,* 1979, pp. 191–6; see also R. Celsi and J. C. Olson, 'The Role of Involvement in Attention and Comprehension Processes', *Journal of Consumer Research,* September 1988, pp. 210–24.

69 M. Houston and M. Rothschild, 'Conceptual and Methodological Perspectives on Involvement' in S. Jain (ed.), *Research Frontiers in Marketing: Dialogue and Directions* (AMA, 1978), pp. 184–7. See also M. L. Richins, P. H. Bloch and E. F. McQuarrie, 'How Enduring and Situational Involvement Combine to Create Involvement Responses', *Journal of Consumer Psychology*, 1992, pp. 143–53.

70 J. Lastovicka and D. Gardner, 'Components of Involvement', in J. Maloney and B. Silverman (eds), *Attitude Research Plays for High Stakes* (AMA, 1979), pp. 53–73.

71 W. Clarke and R. Belk, 'The Effects of Product Involvement and Taste Definition on Anticipated Consumer Effort', *Advances in Consumer Research* (ACR, 1979) pp. 313–18. Also see R. Celsi and J. Olson, 'The Role of Involvement in Attention and Comprehension Processes'. *Journal of Consumer Research*, September 1988, pp. 210–24.

72 G. Day, *Buyer Attitudes and Brand Choice Behavior* (Free Press, 1970).

73 L. Feldman and G. Armstrong, 'Identifying Buyers of a Major Automative Innovation', *Journal of Marketing*, 1975, pp. 47–53.

74 D. Tigert *et al.*, 'Fashion Involvement in Buyer Behavior', *Advances in Consumer Research* (ACR, 1974), pp. 46–52.

75 J. L. Zaichkowsky and J. H. Sood, 'A Global Look at Consumers' Involvement and Use of Products', *International Marketing Review*, 1989, 6, pp. 20–34.

76 L. Freeman, 'Fragrance Sniffs Out Daring Adventures', *Advertising Age*, 6 November 1989, p. 47. For additional discussion of involvement in luxury goods, see B. Dubois, J. N. Kapferer and G. Laurent, 'Implication et Produits de Luxe', 1ere journee régionale, 'Études et Rencontres, IAE Aix-en-Provence, 27 March 1993. For a recent study on the 'deep' involvement that some consumers have with their brands, see S. Fournier, 'Consumers and Their Brands: Developing Relationship Theory in Consumer Research', *Journal of Consumer Research,* March 1998, pp. 343–73. See also D. Mick and C. Buhl, 'A Meaning-Based Model of Advertising Experiences', *Journal of Consumer Research*, December 1992, pp. 317–38.

77 E. Hilgard, *Introduction to Psychology* (Harcourt, Brace & World, 1967).

78 R. B. Cattell, *The Scientific Analysis of Personality*, (Penguin Books, 1965). Also see C. S. Hall and G. Lindzey, *Theories of Personality,* 2nd edition (Wiley, 1970).

79 M. C. Degrese and T. Picault, 'Comment Quantifier des Profils Psychologiques', in *Au-Dela du Quantitatif: Approches Qualitatives et Non-Metriques*, seminaire IREP, May 1976, pp. 69–80.

80 K. Horney, *Our Inner Conflicts* (Norton, 1945).

81 M. Johnson *et al.*, 'Profiles of Signature Goods Consumers and Avoiders', *Journal of Retailing*, Winter 1991, pp. 19–38.

[82] J. B. Cohen, 'An Interpersonal Orientation in the Study of Consumer Behaviour', *Journal of Marketing Research*, August 1967, pp. 270–8. For other findings see J. Kernan, 'The CAD Instrument in Behavioral Diagnosis', Proceedings of the 2nd Annual Conference of the ACR, 1971, pp. 307–12. The CAD test is analysed in detail in J. P. Noerager, 'An Assessment of CAD: A Personality Instrument Developed Specifically for Marketing Research', *Journal of Marketing Research*, February 1979, pp. 53–9 and P. Tyagi, 'Validation of the CAD Instrument: A Replication', *Advances in Consumer Research*, 1983, pp. 112–14.

[83] D. Reisman, N. Glazer and R. Denney, *The Lonely Crowd*, abridged (Doubleday, 1956).

[84] See the section on the VALS system in Chapter 6 – 'The value-based approach'.

[85] J. H. Donnelly, 'Social Character and Acceptance of New Products', *Journal of Marketing Research*, February 1970, pp. 111–13.

[86] H. Kassarjian, 'Social Character and Differential Preference for Mass Communication', *Journal of Marketing Research*, May 1965, pp. 146–53.

[87] See for example D. R. Rook, 'The Ritual Dimension of Consumer Behavior', *Journal of Consumer Research*, December 1985, pp. 251–64.

[88] See the section on the family life cycle in Chapter 9.

[89] J. P. Guilford, *Personality* (McGraw-Hill, 1959).

[90] H. J. Eysenck, *The Structure of Human Personality* (McThuen, 1960).

[91–99] T. W. Adorno *et al.*, *The Authoritarian Personality* (Harper & Row, 1950).

[92] J. A. Taylor, 'A Personality Scale of Manifest Anxiety'. *Journal of Abnormal and Social Psychology*, 1953, pp. 285–90.

[93] A. L. Edwards, *Edwards Personal Preference Schedule* (Psychological Corporation, 1957).

[94] See W. D. Wells and A. D. Beard, 'Personality and Consumer Behavior' in S. Ward and T. Robertson, *Consumer Behavior: Theoretical Sources* (Prentice Hall, 1973); H. Kassarjian and M. J. Sheffet, 'Personality and Consumer Behavior: An Update' in H. Kassarjian and T. Robertson (eds), *Perspectives in Consumer Behavior*, 4th edition (Scott, Foresman, 1991); and G. Foxall and R. Goldsmith, 'Personality and Consumer Research: Another Look', *Journal of the Market Research Society*, 1988, Vol. 30, pp. 111–26.

[95] L. E. Boone, 'The Search for the Consumer Innovator', *Journal of Business*, April 1979, pp. 135–40.

[96] A. Koponen, 'Personality Characteristics of Purchasers', *Journal of Advertising Research*, September 1960, pp. 6–12.

[97] F. B. Evans, 'Psychological and Objective Factors in the Prediction of Brand Choice', *Journal of Business*, October 1959, pp. 340–69.

[98] R. Horton, 'The Edwards Personal Preference Schedule and Consumer Personality Research', *Journal of Marketing Research*, August 1974, pp. 335–7.

[99] R. Westall, 'Psychological Factors in Predicting Consumer Choice', *Journal of Marketing Research*, April 1962, pp. 34–40.

[100] Koponen, *op. cit.*

[101] T. S. Robertson, 'Determinants of Innovative Behavior', American Marketing Association Educators' Summer Conference Proceedings, 1967, pp. 328–32.

[102] W. T. Tucker and J. J. Painter, 'Personality and Product Use', *Journal of Applied Psychology*, 1961, pp. 325–29.

[103] M. Holbrook *et al.*, 'Play as a Consumption Experience: The Roles of Emotions, Performance and Personality in the Enjoyment of Games', *Journal of Consumer Research*, September 1984, pp. 728–39.

[104] H. H. Kassarjan, 'Personality and Consumer Behavior: A Review', *Journal of Marketing Research*, 1971, pp. 409–18.

[105] K. Villani and Y. Wind, 'On the Usage of Modified Personality Trait Measures in Consumer Research', *Journal of Consumer Research*, December 1975, pp. 223–8

[106] T. S. Robertson and J. H. Myers, 'Personality Correlates of Opinion Leadership and Innovative Buying Behavior', *Journal of Marketing Research*, May 1969, pp. 164–8.

[107] M. Alpert, 'Personality and the Determinants of Product Choice', *Journal of Marketing Research*, February 1972, pp. 89–92.

[108] G. Brooker, 'The Self-Actualizing Socially Conscious Consumer', *Journal of Consumer Research*, September 1976, pp. 107–12.

[109] C. Pinson, N. K. Malhotra and A. K. Jain, 'Cognitive Differentiation in Consumer Product Judgments', *Journal of Economic Psychology*, 1984, 5, pp. 353–69. See also R. Batra and M. L. Ray, 'Operationalizing Involvement as Depth and Quality of Cognitive Responses', *Advances in Consumer Research*, 1983, pp. 309–13.

[110] A. K. Jain *et al.*, 'A New Approach to Market Segmentation Strategy: A Banking Appication', *Proceedings*, 7th Senanque International Seminar, 1980.

[111] See S. Onkvisit and J. Shaw, 'Self-Concept and Image Congruence: Some Research and Managerial Implications', *The Journal of Consumer Marketing*, Winter 1987, pp; 13–24; and A. Birdwell, 'Influence of Image Congruence on Choice', *American Marketing Association Winter Conference Proceedings*, 1964, pp. 290–303.

[112] R. J. Dornoff and R. L. Tatham, 'Congruence Between Personal Image and Store Image', *Journal of the Market Research Society*, 1972, 14, pp. 45–52.

[113] See I. Dolich, 'Congruence Relationships between Self-Images and Product Brands', *Journal of Marketing Research*, February 1969, pp. 880–5; R. Ackoff and J. Emsch, 'Advertising Research at Anaheuser-Busch (1968–1974)', *Sloan Management Review*, Spring 1975, pp. 1–45; and A. E. Bidwell, 'Influence of Image Congruence on Choice'; *Proceedings AMA Winter Conference*, 1964, pp. 290–303.

[114] Several scales have been developed for measuring the self-concept. See for example N. Malhotra, 'A Scale to Measure Self-Concepts, Person Concepts, and Product Concepts', *Journal of Marketing Research*, November 1981, pp. 456–64.

[115] For an overview of research in this area, see J. Sirgy, 'Self Concept in Consumer Behaviour: A Critical Review', *Journal of Consumer Research*, December 1982, pp. 287–300.

[116] See M. Richins, 'Social Comparison and the Idealized Images of Advertising', *Journal of Consumer Research*, June 1991, pp. 71–83; see also M. C. Martin and P. Kennedy, 'Advertising and Social Comparison: Consequences for Female Pre-adolescents', *Psychology and Marketing*,

[117] R. Netemeyer. S. Burton and D. R. Lichtenstein, 'Trait Aspects of Vanity: Measurement and Relevance to Consumer Behavior', *Journal of Consumer Research*, March 1995, pp. 612–26.

[118] R. F. Baumeister, D. Tice and D. Hitton, 'Self-Presentational Motivations and Personality Differences in Self-Esteem', *Journal of Personality*, September 1989, pp. 547–75.

[119] J. F. Durgee, 'Self-Esteem Advertising', *Journal of Advertising*, 1986, 14, pp. 4–21.

[120] G. H. Mead, *Mind, Self and Society* (University of Chicago Press, 1934). For a presentation of symbolic interactionsim in a consumer behaviour context, see M. Solomon, 'The Role of Products as Social Stimuli: A Symbolic Interactionism Perspective', *Journal of Consumer Research*, December 1983, pp. 319–29.

[121] See R. Belk, 'Possessions and the Extended Self', *Journal of Consumer Research*, September 1988, pp. 159–68. For discussion of this idea, see J. Cohen, 'An Over-Extended Self', *Journal of Consumer Research*, June 1989, pp. 125–8; and R. Belk, 'Extended Self and Extending Paradigmatic Perspective', *Journal of Consumer Research*, June 1989, 129–32.

[122] A. D. Ball and L. H. Tasaki, 'The Role and Measurement of Attachment in Consumer Behaviour', *Journal of Consumer Psychology*, 1992, pp. 155–72.

[123] See for example R. P. Hill and H. Robinson, 'Fanatic Consumer Behavior: Athletics as a Consumption Experience', *Psychology and Marketing*, Summer 1991, pp. 79–100.

[124] Reported in G. Mermet, *Francoscopie* (Larousse, 1996), p. 53.

[125] D. Rook, 'Body Cathexis and Market Segmentation', in *The Psychology of Fashion*, ed. M. R. Solomon (Lexington Books, 1985), pp. 233–41.

[126] P. N. Myers Jr and F. A. Biocca, 'The Elastic Body Image: The Effect of Television Advertising and Programming on Body Image Distortions in Young Women', *Journal of Communication*, Summer 1992, pp. 108–33.

[127] M. Fay and C. Price, 'Female Body-shape in Print Advertisements and the Increase in Anorexia Nervosa', *European Journal of Marketing*, 1994, pp. 12–28.

[128] J. Meyers-Levy, 'Exploring Differences in Males' and Females' Processing Strategies', *Journal of Consumer Research*, June 1991, pp. 63–70; also see B. Schmitt *et al.*, 'Sex Typing and Consumer Behavior: A Test of Gender Schema Theory', *Journal of Consumer Research*, June 1988, pp. 122–8.

[129] J. Meyers-Levy, 'The Influence of Sex Roles on Judgment', *Journal of Consumer Research*, March 1988, pp. 522–30.

[130] See J. A. Costa (ed.), *Gender Issues and Consumer Behavior* (Sage, 1994) and also *Gender, Marketing and Consumer Behavior* (Association for Consumer Research, 1996).

[131] K. Debevec and E. Iyer, 'Sex Roles and Consumer Perceptions of Promotions, Products and Self: What Do We Know and Where Should We Be Headed', *Advances in Consumer Research*, 1986, pp. 210–14. See also B. H. Schmitt, F. Leclerc and L. Dubé-Rious, 'Sex Typing and Consumer Behavior: A Test of Gender Schema Theory', *Journal of Consumer Research*, June 1988, pp. 122–7.

[132] B. Cutler, 'Condom Mania', *American Demographics*, June 1989, p. 17.

[133] R. Bartos, 'Marketing to Women: The Quiet Revolution', *Marketing Insights*, June 1989, p. 61. Also see, by the same author, *Marketing to Women around the World* (Harvard Business School Press, 1989) for a comparison of women's roles in ten different countries and its marketing and advertising implications.

[134] J. Meyers-Levy and D. Maheswaran, 'Exploring Differences in Males' and Females' Processing Strategies', *Journal of Consumer Research*, June 1981, pp. 63–70.

[135] J. Scanzoni, 'Changing Sex Roles and Emerging Directions in Family Decision-Making', *Journal of Consumer Research*, December 1977, pp. 185–8.

[136] B. Dubois and R. Z. Marchetti, 'The Influence Triangle: A New Methodology for Identifying the Influence Process in Family Buying Decisions', in M. Baker (ed.), *Perspectives on Marketing Management*, Vol. 3 (Wiley, 1993), pp. 400–11.

[137] J. Rossiter and T. S. Robertson, 'Canonical Analysis of Developmental, Social and Experimental Factors in Children's Comprehension of Television Advertising', *Journal of Genetic Psychology*, 1976, 19, pp. 317–27. See also D. L. Roedder, 'Understanding and Overcoming Children's Processing Deficits', *Advances in Consumer Research*, 1982, 9, pp. 148–52.

[138] L. Phillips and B. Sternthal, 'Age Differences in Information Processing: A Perspective on the Aged Consumer', *Journal of Marketing Research*, 1977, pp. 444–57 and I. Ross, 'Information Processing and the Older Consumer: Marketing and Public Policy Implications', *Advances for Consumer Research*, 1982, pp. 36–9.

[139] See M. Abrams, 'A Survey of the Elderly Shopper', 1985, Age Concern Research Unit, Mitcham, Surrey; W. O. Bearden and J. Barry Mason, 'Elderly Use of In-store Information Sources and Dimensions of Product Satisfaction/Dissatisfaction', *Journal of Retailing*, 1979, 55, pp. 79–101; K. L. Bernhardt and T. C. Kinnear, 'Profiling the Senior Citizen Market', *Advances in Consumer Research*, 2, pp. 449–52; C. Cole and M. Houston, 'Encoding and Media Effects on Consumer Learning Deficiencies in the Elderly', *Journal of Marketing Research*, February 1987, 24, pp. 55–63; R. Desphande and S. Krishman, 'Correlates of Deficient Information Environments: The Case of the Elderly', *Advances in Consumer Research*, 9, pp. 515–19; D. J. Roedder-John and C. Cole, 'Age Differences in Information Processing: Understanding Deficits in Young and Elderly Consumers', *Journal of Consumer Research*, December 1986, pp. 297–315; I. Ross; 'Information Processing and the Older Consumer: Marketing and Public Policy Implications', *Advances in Consumer Research*, 1981, 10, pp. 253–8; and C. Schewe, *The Elderly Market: Selected Readings*, 1985.

[140] C. Cole and G. Gaeth, 'Cognitive and Age Related Differences in the Ability to Use Nutritional Information in a Complex Environment', *Journal of Marketing Research*, May 1990, pp. 175–84.

[141] R. E. Wilkes, 'A Structured Modelling Approach to the Measurement and Meaning of Cognitive Age, *Journal of Consumer Research*, September 1992, pp. 292–301.

[142] R. Kastenbaum *et al.*, 'The Ages of Me: Toward Personal and Interpersonal Definitions of Functional Ageing', *Ageing and Human Development*, 1972, 2, pp. 197–211.

[143] B. Barak and L. Schiffman, 'Cognitive Age: A Nonchronological Age Variable', *Advances in Consumer Research*, 1981, pp. 602–6.

[144] B. Barak and D. Rahtz, 'Cognitive Age and Youthfulness: Demographic and Psychographic Dimensions', in *Advances in Health Care Research*. Also see C. Chua *et al.*, 'The Antecedents of Cognitive Age', *Advances for Consumer Research*, 1990, pp. 880–5.

[145] R. E. Wilkes, 'A Structural Modeling Approach to the Measurement and Meaning of Cognitive Age', *Journal of Consumer Research*, September 1992, pp. 292–301.

[146] C. Cole and G. Gaeth, 'Cognitive and Age Related Differences in the Ability to Use Nutritional Information in a Complex Environment', *Journal of Marketing Research*, May 1990, pp. 175–84.

[147] Wilkes, *op. cit.*

2

Perception and images

Learning objectives

In this chapter, you will learn that:

1 perception is a process consisting of two major stages: **sensation** and **interpretation**;

2 the intensity of a stimulus or the difference between two stimuli must reach a minimum **absolute** or **relative threshold** to be registered by sensory organs;

3 depending upon their characteristics as well as those of the receiver, only a small proportion of stimuli are able to attract **attention**;

4 raw sensory inputs are organised and given meaning according to certain principles, such as those provided by **Gestalt** psychology;

5 interpretation is a complex process, obeying many rules such as those suggested by **semiology** (also called **semiotics**), the discipline dedicated to the study of signs and symbols;

6 consumers form **images** of products and brands available in their environment and different methods (surveys, projective tests, grids, observation) are available to detect and measure them;

7 to undertand and build upon consumer product and brand images, marketers often find it useful to organise a market on the basis of **perceptual maps** on which they base their **positioning** decisions.

Key words

perception	blind test	categorisation
cognitive psychology	attention	typicality
sensation	selective exposure	symbolism
absolute threshold	Gestalt psychology	semiology
psychophysics	figure-and-ground	semiotics
sensory adaptation	grouping	brand images
subliminal advertising	closure	positioning
relative threshold	stimulus ambiguity	perceptual maps
Weber's law	projective tests	consideration sets

If a consumer's motivation, involvement and personality, as analysed in Chapter 1, often lead to a purchase act, it must not be concluded that such person-related factors are sufficient to understand purchasing behaviour. The reason is very simple: what consumers buy does not depend only upon their needs but also on the nature of the products and services available in their environment. The perceptual mechanism controls the relationship between the individual and the surrounding world, and all the information he or she has about this environment is necessarily acquired through perception. Consequently, perception is an omnipresent factor in buying and consumption behaviour.

How do we perceive the world around us? Do we all perceive the same object in the same way? Which factors influence perception? What effect does it have on our minds and our behaviour? This chapter deals principally with these questions. It draws extensively on results and insights obtained from the scientific discipline most concerned with these topics, the domain of **cognitive psychology** or the psychology of perception.[1]

The first 'discovery' made about perception is amazing. When we shut our eyes for a few seconds and then re-open them, we instantly perceive our environment again. But this impression of immediacy is indeed deceptive. In reality, perception is a **process** that can be broken down into two distinct phases:

1 **sensation**, the physiological mechanism by which our sensory organs take in external stimuli; and

2 **interpretation**, which allows us to organise this information and to give it meaning.

Directly complementary, sensation and interpretation are our two doors onto the world. Let us look at them, one at a time.

Sensation

Beyond the physiological description of the organs of the five senses (sight, hearing, smell, taste, touch), whose functioning is innate and for the most part automatic,[2] basic research on sensation has demonstrated the **differential** nature of sensory processes. Even though it may sometimes appear counterintuitive, we notice only differences, deviations or discrepancies. Plunged into a completely dark room we do not see anything at all. This has nothing to do with darkness *per se*, it is due to the fact that the environment around us is suddenly undifferentiated; we find it just as difficult to pick out white objects on a white background. In the same way, if forced to listen to a continuous whistle, we end up not hearing it – not registering its existence – so long as it does not change in pitch or volume. In fact the differentiation of our environment affects not only our sensations but also our mental balance; a person who is blindfolded and has his or her ears covered up for a long period of time loses touch with their environment and, progressively, loses sanity too.[3] In many European countries, 'relaxation centres' have recently opened, offering a wide variety of anti-stress devices for overworked people. Some of them include 'relaxation tanks' where the clients are completely immersed in water for several hours. However, before being isolated, clients are asked to touch both the tank and the surface of the water so that they do not hallucinate.

In consumer research, the idea of sensation as differentiation has led to two major areas of investigation relating respectively to **thresholds** and **selective exposure**. Both have been extremely fruitful in terms of commercial applications.

Thresholds

Since sensation is primarily a matter of differentiation, a question naturally arises: above what intensity of stimulus do we begin to perceive something? There are two answers to this question depending on whether one is seeking to measure an absolute threshold (with a complete absence of stimulus as a reference point) or a relative one (with reference to the difference bewteen two stimuli). Research done in **psychophysics** on **absolute thresholds** has reached a double conclusion:

1 There exists for each sense, a minimum threshold, situated relatively low – for example, under normal conditions a human being is capable of detecting (a) a candle flame at a distance of 50 km on a dark night (sight), (b) the ticking of a watch placed at a distance of 6 metres in complete silence (hearing), and (c) a single drop of perfume that has evaporated in a three-room apartment (smell).[4]

2 Humans are capable of adjusting such thresholds depending on the circumstances. When placed in a dark room, even if we don't see anything to start with, our eyes soon adjust and we become able to distinguish first shapes and then the objects themselves. In fact, human beings have a tremendous faculty for **sensory adaptation**.[5]

Such results have numerous implications for communication in general and advertising in particular. In order to maintain interest, some change must be perceived from time to time by the audience; for example, a university lecturer must be careful to adjust his teaching styles over the duration of a course in order to maintain the interest of students and keep them engaged in study. Similarly, widely diffused TV spots for the same product or brand must be rejuvenated frequently so as to keep their audience. In other cases, the marketer wants the change to go unnoticed (for example when there is a price increase or a reduction in the volume of the product) and will bring as much continuity as possible by making very gradual modifications.

The relatively large number of studies done on absolute thresholds have fuelled a strange controversy in advertising, on the effects of **subliminal messages**. The controversy started in September 1957 when, in a cinema in New Jersey, and while the public were watching a film, two messages were projected at 1/3000th of a second, well below the threshold of visual perception (which is about 1/25th of a second).

The first one was saying 'Drink Coca-Cola' and the other 'Eat popcorn'. A 52 per cent rise in sales of popcorn and an 18 per cent rise in sales of Coke were subsequently recorded. These results provoked many negative reactions, mainly from an ethical standpoint, and led some authors to write about new forms of 'hidden persuasion'.[6] However, no researcher has ever been able fully to replicate such results. Furthermore, the specific conditions under which the experiment was conducted have not been completely established and serious doubt rests over its scientific value. From time to time, however, journalists and theorists of hidden manipulation have contributed to a revival of this debate. For example, at the time of the French presidential election in 1988 some voters got very upset because a subliminal image of candidate François Mitterand had been inserted, on several occasions, in the evening news programme of a major TV channel. However, it hardly seems plausible that a consumer can be conditioned in this way to buy a product, for a number of reasons.

To start with, it has not yet been established that something received subliminally has a long impact on an individual's psyche, even though experiments have shown that, when subjected to a subliminal stimulus, human beings have a tendency to remember it and to use it – for example, appearing in spontaneous ideas that come into their mind.[7] But simply remembering an image or a name, often out of context and without the benefit of any further supporting information, seems quite incapable of producing purchasing behaviour on its own. In fact, very few experts now believe that subliminal effects can be useful for advertising purposes.[8] On the other hand, the use of subliminal messages continues to be the subject of speculation and suspicion.[9] In 1990 in Europe, a radio station was condemned in court for having insinuated that a large supermarket chain was broadcasting the following message (below the level of auditory perception): 'I feel good about myself, I never steal, I am honest', so as to reduce shoplifting in its stores.

Studies perfomed on **relative** (also called differential) **thresholds** are of more importance. They have led to one of the few laws that exist in psychophysics: Weber's law. According to Weber's law, the increase in intensity of a stimulus which is necessary to produce a sensation is proportional to the initial intensity of the stimulus. 'K', known as Weber's constant, measures this proportion. In other words:

$$\frac{\Delta I}{I} = K$$

where I = initial intensity of the stimulus
     DI = increased intensity
     K = Weber's constant (which depends upon which sense is being measured)

In our everyday lives, we have many opportunities to verify Weber's law: for example, the difference between one hour and two hours seems great, but the difference between one year and three hundred and sixty-four days seems negligible. Also, it would appear that we become less and less sensitive to identical rises and falls in the price of petrol or cigarettes when they keep occurring. In the United States, the Hershey chocolate bar underwent fifteen slight reductions in size without the consumer remarking upon it.

The measurement of differential thresholds plays an important role in commercial research, especially as far as products and packagings are concerned. In particular it provides the foundation for the marketing research technique known as 'blind testing'. This method consists of a consumer trying several products which have been rendered anonymous, then measuring the just noticeable differences (JND) in sensation experienced by the tester. Results obtained from blind tests reveal an individual's capacity for differentiation. By and large, manufacturers tend to overestimate consumer differentiation abilities, especially with regard to food products. Allison and Uhl, two marketing researchers, have shown that an average American consumer, for example, is totally incapable of detecting differences in taste between ordinary beers even if his favourite beer is included in the selection. In contrast, when the lids and labels are put back on, the individual finds strong differences in flavour between the beers.[10] These results, observed for many other products, all over the world, clearly show that the raw sensory data alone are seldom sufficient to produce a consistent response. For most people, the support of the **brand image** and all the meanings associated with it (often related to its history, values, personality, etc.) is necessary. Such a conclusion underlines the importance of branding, packaging and imagery in influencing consumers' perceptions of a given product or service.

The way prices are perceived provides another rich area for study. According to Weber's law, a reduction of say 10 Euros on a product worth 100 Euros should be perceived in the same way as a reduction of 100 Euros on an article worth 1000 Euros. Such an hypothesis of a constant relative error can be tested through an investigation of consumers' knowledge of prices. Questioned some time ago at the exit of a supermarket, a sample of 300 shoppers were asked to give the prices of 16 different products available for sale that day and chosen for their different unitary value and frequency of purchase (from mineral water to dishwasher).[11] Empirical evidence showed that the average relative error was always positive (revealing a systematic overestimation of prices) and varied from 16 to 84 per cent. This result would tend to invalidate Weber's law. However, for half the products, relative errors fell between 25 and 35 per cent, a rather narrow range. Furthermore, there was no significant relationship between the magnitude of the relative error and the price level, the frequency of purchase or type of product (food, maintenance, household equipment, bodycare and leisure).

More generally, Gabor and Granger have shown, from a study of 640 housewives, that the knowledge of prices is (a) inversely correlated to social class; (b) weaker for branded goods; and (c) weaker for products bought frequently. Such results have important managerial implications. For example, they support the view that well-known brands are better protected than lesser-known ones from competitive aggressive pricing. Concerning thresholds, Gabor and Granger have also found that, for every product, there exists an **acceptable price range** (that is, the difference between the maximum price that a consumer would pay and the minimum price below which a consumer would have serious doubts about the product's quality), which, for a given person, also depends upon the amount of income available. Acceptable price ranges tend to be smaller among lower income households primarily because the lowering of the upper limit acts as a deterrent.[12]

In conclusion, it seems that Weber's law must be used with care. On the one hand, it provides a useful reference point and in particular explains the success of price discounts expressed as percentages (for example, sale prices offering 50 per cent off). On the other hand, it appears that below a certain price threshold, the reduction is perceived as greater when it is expressed as a percentage rather than as an absolute value but that the opposite is true for high prices. Weber's law primarily applies between these two extremes.

Selective exposure

The process of sensory adaptation demonstrates that sensation does not work in a mechanical way on a passive organism; quite to the contrary, the individual participates directly in what he feels. Such an active role played by the subject is not limited to sensory adaptation but in fact strongly influences the number and nature of stimuli attended to in the first place. Sensation is therefore highly dependent upon **attention**, a process through which an individual focuses on certain stimuli rather than others.[13]

The number of stimuli which an individual is capable of perceiving is astronomical. It has been estimated that each day, in industrial countries, a person takes in 800 words, 2000 pictures and 20 000 visual stimuli relating to 500 brands. On the advertising front alone, on average a consumer is exposed to several hundred messages each day (from 300 to 1000 according to experts).[14] Less than a dozen of them will have any influence on his or her behaviour. Selective attention works like a merciless guillotine which few adverts escape, and marketers talk about 'advertising clutter'. Bearing in mind the amount of money at stake, it is essential for advertising practitioners to understand this mechanism. Two major sets of factors have been put forward: the first concerning the **stimulus** itself, the second concerning the **individual**.

Why are certain stimuli more easily picked up than others? The many studies dealing with this subject highlight seven key variables:

1 Size

All other things being equal, an advert has more chance of being noticed if it fills a larger space (either visually or in terms of sound). Thus, at special gift-giving periods such as Christmas, perfume advertisers buy large blocks of advertising time to make sure their adverts get noticed. Other techniques include 'broken ads', in which the message is split into two parts – an introduction and a (usually) brief conclusion separated by other commercials – so as to increase artificially the total duration; and 'time compression', in which the speaking rate is accelerated by 20 or 30 per cent to give the impression of a more dense and informative message.[15] The effect of size, however, is seldom in proportion. For print media, a number of specialists believe in the 'law of the squared root': to double attention, you have to quadruple the size of the message.[16] However it's all relative; the smaller format of *Readers Digest* is not at a disadvantage in relation to a full page in a daily newspaper.[17]

2   Colour

All other things being equal, colour is more attractive than black and white. Often considered more exciting, it is also both more subtle and more evocative. Among the various colours, red is often considered as having the highest attention value, but this may vary among cultures. In Western societies, the use of colour is particularly noticeable for conspicuous products such as clothing or interior decorations.[18]

3   Intensity

Have you noticed that many of Haydn's symphonies open with a 'da da' played fortissimo? People have said that this was how he captured the attention of his audience at the start of a concert. Today, a number of radio advertisements work on exactly the same principle.

4   Movement

A moving poster, like one of those of rolling placards often displayed at airports or at sports venues for example, draws attention more than a static poster does. It is the same for pivoting panel adverts, vehicle-mounted advertising boards and intermittent flashing signs. Because movement attracts attention, advertising specialists often try to incorporate it even in static images. For example, a close-up photograph of a glass bursting into pieces suggests movement. Animation can also be obtained through visual effects. Cinema is entirely based on the *phi* phenomenon, an impression of movement created by a rapid succession of images.

5   Contrast

The law of contrast explains many of the preceding effects. A black-and-white advert in a colour magazine can make more of an impact than one in colour may. By causing a visual break, this contrasting message will surprise people and consequently get their attention. A few years ago, a European wool company transmitted a TV advert which simply consisted of a blank screen and 15 seconds of total silence. Only the name of the company was mentioned at the end. It is not known whether this advert increased sales but many people still remember it years later. Similarly, in the early 1990s, Audi, the German car manufacturer, put out an advert in which the first five seconds had absolutely no pictures. Contrasting with the hubbub of the usual adverts, this TV spot got very good attention ratings. Another way of playing with contrast effects is to use advertising clichés as part of the message itself or to mock advertising stereotypes. For example, the message of a recent spot for Ovaltine, a malt-based drink, was entirely built on the idea that a mere eight seconds (that is, the actual duration of the advertising spot) was too short to detail the merits of the product.[19]

6 Position

The same stimulus will not catch the same level of attention depending upon its particular position. Publishers sometimes call the right-hand page the 'beautiful page' in order to express its higher attention value. In many books, new chapters always start on the beautiful page. Similarly, all magazines charge a higher advertising rate for their back cover because messages displayed on that page can be noticed even without opening the magazine. The specific position of an object on a page also has an influence. A few years ago, the marketing staff of a European mail-order house wanted to assess the impact of the various pages of their catalogue. By testing different pages in which the position of various objects had been systematically rotated, they found that whatever object was positioned at the top left was more likely to be noticed first and therefore better remembered. Of course, such effects are influenced by prevailing cultural norms regarding reading habits. In a classic case, a pharmaceutical lab got into trouble in the Middle East when using an advert developed in Europe. Its idea was to tell a story using three consecutive pictures: the first one, on the left, featured a woman not feeling well; in the second, in the middle, she was taking a tablet; in the last one, on the right, the woman – now obviously relieved – was smiling. Unfortunately, the pharmaceutical lab (and its advertising agency) had forgotten that in the Middle East this cartoon would be read from right to left and so the tablet appeared to make the woman ill!

In a store, the position of an object on the shelf largely determines its capacity to attract consumers' attention. In a jewellery shop, for example, the articles which have a low turnover (such as clocks and other 'bulky' objects) are usually placed at the bottom of the display window, while watches and jewellery enjoy the best positions. On television, it would seem that advertising messages directly inserted into the programmes (as in sponsored shows) have a greater impact than adverts regrouped at the end (or at the beginning) together with other commercials.[20] Also, research conducted in Amsterdam by Initiative Media has shown that an advert is remembered better when it is placed first in a series, no matter how many other adverts come after it. In the Netherlands you thus have to pay 10 per cent more to get this 'pole position'.[21]

7 Novelty

Finally, the inclusion of unusual or incongruous objects or messages – by virtue of their nature, size, colour or any other characteristic (for example upside-down messages in print media or the insertion of commercial messages in a movie, a technique known as product placement) – also facilitates attention but sometimes at the expense of understanding.[22] This is the essence of 'shock tactics' in advertising, for example the well-known Benetton street posters showing a priest kissing a nun or displaying a human body part 'HIV infected'. Getting attention in this way is not without risk however. Benetton lost market share and had to close several retail outlets in Europe due to the irritation that had resulted from such provoking adverts. In fact, such messages had very little to do with the products sold by the textile company. There is an important message here: attracting attention is a real challenge and will probably become even more difficult in the future as consumers continue to be bombarded with an increasing number of adverts; however, advertising stimuli should primarily help reinforce the brand name or the product positioning, otherwise the message can be self-defeating. More generally speaking, it would seem that using novelty in order to benefit from a surprise effect is more important for products which otherwise do not arouse much consumer interest.

Regardless of its characteristics, a given stimulus will not be picked up on by everyone to the same degree. There are four principle determinants of **voluntary attention** (also called **perceptual vigilance**[23]).

1 Perceptual abilities

Not all individuals have the same capacity for sensory adaptation. The 'noses' employed in the perfume industry can recognise subtle differences in fragrance which are unrecognisable to the uninitiated. Their assistance is obviously critical in developing new perfumes. Even at birth, newborn babies do not all have the same perceptual abilities, and specialists talk of the 'competencies of the newborn'. The main marketing implication is that products and especially services aimed at 'connoisseurs' have to be managed differently to products and services aimed at the general public. For example, in Lisbon there is a special place (Instituto do Porto) entirely dedicated to port wines. Given the very wide choice available and the nature of target consumers, the Instituto do Porto makes sure that its salespeople are extremely knowledgeable in oenology.

2 Needs and motivation

A person who is hungry notices advertising for food products more rapidly than other people. In the United States, the televised campaign 'Are you hungry?' which was broadcast late at night by Burger King was so successful that it forced the hamburger chain to stay open later. In marketing, a number of studies have shown that consumers pay more attention to information regarding attributes which are relevant to them. For example, consumers most concerned about decay prevention in a toothpaste might be especially attentive to information about the product feature fluoride, while those seeking flavour might be more attracted to features such a minty taste.[24] Scientific experiments have also shown that a poor child 'sees' a coin as being larger than a rich child does.[25] Conversely, there is little chance of a confirmed smoker paying attention to a public information slot on lung disease.[26] Perceptual vigilance then acts as a defence mechanism: to a large extent, a consumer does not see any more than he or she 'wants to see'.

3 Involvement and hobbies

As explained in Chapter 1, a person's level of involvement directly affects what they concentrate on, especially in situations perceived as highly risky. The more consumers feel that there are risks associated with a purchase that they are contemplating, the more attention they will pay to the information available – especially if this information is quickly recognised as providing a solution to their problem. The perceived risk can either be (a) physical (fearing for one's health), as for example with pharmaceutical products; (b) financial (fear of losing money), especially when buying something expensive; or (c) psychological (fear of ridicule), for example when buying ostentatious products such as clothing or cosmetics.[27]

Also a person's hobbies (another aspect of personal involvement) may regulate what he or she concentrates on.[28] If you are very interested in cars, you will normally pay more attention to the adverts concerning cars when you read a magazine or a newspaper.[29] In the same way, a handyman has more chance of noticing a poster for a drill than somebody not interested in DIY. Contrary to motivation, which is a temporary phenomenon, hobbies and other centres of interest are more enduring and therefore easier to identify. In direct marketing, it is thus possible to increase the amount of attention given to a message by focusing its diffusion on a target group of individuals with favourable predispositions. A file of addresses from people who have spontaneously written in for information has a much higher response rate than an address file made up from the telephone directory.

4   Attitudes and expectations

If what we believe is based upon what we perceive, the opposite is also true. In general a person has more chance of noticing a message which fits in with his or her own belief system. Psychologists call this phenomenon **cognitive consistency**.[30] Thus, we usually recognise our favourite brands more quickly than other brands;[31] in fact the process appears to assist us to achieve a perceptual balance between our perceptions and our preconceptions. This also means that when we receive conflicting information, we attempt to restore consistency. For example, when we hear a friend denigrate our latest purchase, we either like our purchase a little less or our friend.[32] This process can be illustrated by the two diagrams in Figure 2.1, showing the two ways in which the conflict may be solved.

In summary, it appears that under the influence of factors linked to the stimulus or to the individual, one's attention is either bestowed voluntarily or provoked. In the first case the individual is often actively seeking information, while in the second he or she is 'confronted' by the stimulus. Contrary to the characteristics of the stimuli, many of the factors that determine what a person pays attention to are not within the control of the marketer. The best marketing managers can hope for is to identify the segments of the audience most likely to pay attention. Sometimes, perceptual defences are so strong that they create a real barrier to introducing any new products, as well as providing strong protection for the well-established brands. This is how certain brand names end up becoming part of the everyday language (for example, Hoover, Sellotape, Walkman, etc.) and thus almost unassailable.

Figure 2.1 Cognitive consistency

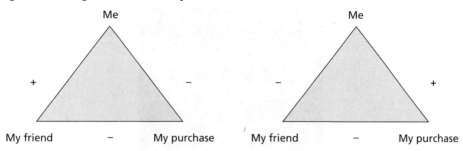

Interpretation

People do not just 'choose' the stimuli they take in but also organise and interpret them. Understanding the mechanisms according to which sensory inputs are structured and given meaning offers many rewards for those concerned with communication effectiveness. A particular type of packaging, a brand name, a label or a price – depending on how they are recognised – induce different behaviour. Are there principles which govern the ways in which we structure our perceptions? A whole research domain known as **Gestalt psychology** (the psychology of the form) responds affirmatively to this question.

Figure and ground

We have a tendency to organise all our perceptions into two major patterns: the **figure**, the central element, which captures most of our attention, and the **background**, which is left rather undifferentiated. This principle, on which rests the effect of contrast, is widely used in advertising, for example in order to communicate the prestigious nature of a product. Consider the Lancaster advert shown in Figure 2.2. Sheathed in light, the product emerges in its full majesty. The advert clearly conveys the idea that the product is sufficient on its own and has no need of any 'proof' of legitimacy that could be conferred by external surrounding visual elements. The figure-and-ground principle can also be used in the opposite way. In some pictures, for example the famous picture of the goblet and the two profiles (Figure 2.3), the viewer can choose which part of the image will be the figure and which will be the background. Indeed, it is possible to go back and forth between the two as you choose. The resulting cognitive processes will favour an **assimilation** between the object and its context. The advertisement for Roquefort cheese (Figure 2.4) makes the most of this principle. Here the cheese, with its rugged texture, is almost lost in the Causses countryside, and the use of the same shades as for the countryside reinforces the genuinely rural nature of the product. Advertisers regularly use this principle, for example when they display upmarket products surrounded by objects evoking class and distinction (crystal glasses, expensive furniture, precious jewellery).

Figure 2.2   The figure-and-ground principle

Figure 2.3   The goblet and the two profiles

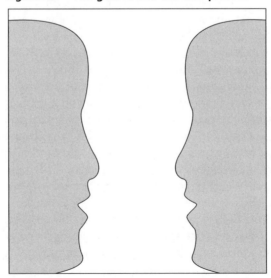

Figure 2.4   The assimilation principle

Grouping

When there are many distinct stimuli which are not immediately recognisable as an object, we make out the object by relating the stimuli to each other according to their physical proximity to each other, their similarities and any continuity that may exist. So Figures 2.5 and 2.6 are more easily interpreted as rows than as columns. The Orlane advertisement (Figure 2.7) also works in this way. The arrangement of the objects makes us think of two battalions of armed forces that are put into readiness for active service, which is consistent with the slogan of the advertisement (Orlane 'mobilises' for your beauty).

Closure

We do not only sort and group objects; if necessary, we actually complete them. Look at Figure 2.8. Although it is not all drawn in, everybody will have recognised the letter 'A'. This explains why we usually have no problem reading a neon sign

Figure 2.5 Proximity grouping effects   **Figure 2.6 Similarity grouping effects**

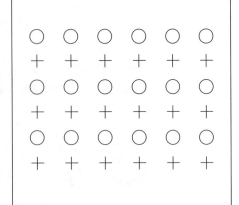

Figure 2.7 The grouping principle in advertising

Figure 2.8　Closure effects

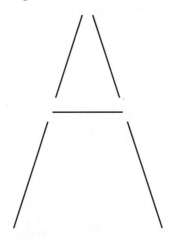

even though a few letters may be missing. But we also use symbols when interpreting images on the basis of associations built around them. For example, when the picture of a cowboy smoking a cigarette is displayed, many people all over the world immediately think of Marlboro cigarettes – even though the name may not be mentioned in the picture. Inversely, just hearing the Marlboro name or seeing the Marlboro logo may be enough to bring into our mind images of the Far West. Several psychological studies have shown that the fact that you have 'completed/made sense of' a message helps you to remember it.[33] The Zeigarnik effect (as it is called) is regularly used in advertising communications.[34] Let us look at the Orly advertisement (Figure 2.9), which went out at a time when the only colour considered suitable for men's underwear was white. By 'dressing' the man, we get used to the idea that T-shirts and underpants can be coloured.

Stimulus ambiguity

A stimulus is said to be ambiguous when it does not correspond to a shape/form which is immediately recognisable or when it can be 'read' in several different ways. Human beings tend to interpret ambiguous stimuli in order to make them coherent. This interpretation is often aligned with the expectations of the audience. Look at Figure 2.10. What do you see? One can either read it as the letter 'B' or the number '13'. The first solution is perhaps more plausible; but is this due to the fact that we have seen the letter 'A' before and have become accustomed to seeing letters used as examples? If Figure 2.8 had been a '12', what would we have seen?[35]

The process through which we interpret ambiguity is the foundation for the research instruments known as **projective tests** (discussed later in this chapter), which are widely used in psychology to reveal one's personality and in commercial research to understand attitudes towards products and brands. Equally this

Figure 2.9   The closure effect in advertising

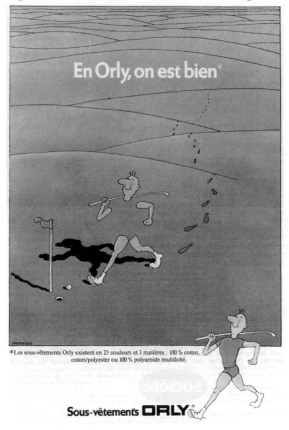

Figure 2.10   Stimulus ambiguity

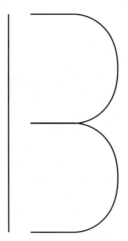

mechanism can be used in advertising; an ambiguous stimulus may capture the audience's attention and prepare them for a message positioned as a 'solution to an enigma'. This is the essence of 'teasing campaigns', which are often used for new product launches. In France, a successful example of a 'teasing' approach is the now famous 1981 'Myriam' campaign orchestrated by Avenir, a poster company. The object of the campaign was to convince potential advertisers that Avenir could respect very tight deadlines in terms of advertising programming. The campaign was in three stages. The first poster showed Myriam, an attractive young woman in a bikini, announcing that in two days' time she would take off her bikini top. Two days later, Myriam, now topless, announced she would remove her bikini bottom in the next poster. In the final poster, again appeared exactly two days later, Myriam – now completely naked (but seen from behind) – concluded: 'Avenir keeps their promises'. More than ten years later, an English brewery used a very similar approach with a series of posters showing a man (times are changing!) in various stages of undress. The stimulus ambiguity principle can also be used in relation to product characteristics but, again, ambiguity has to be manipulated with care. A few years ago, the Pepsi-Cola company decided to launch a new colourless cola drink called Crystal Pepsi in the USA. This product failed miserably. People were so used to traditional cola drinks that they simply did not accept the idea that a cola drink could be anything but brown.[36] But numerous studies show that 'bizarre' stimuli (for example, a bear smoking a pipe, a rabbit reading a newspaper or a laughing cow) have far greater powers of attraction than ordinary ones.[37] In the UK, a Saatchi & Saatchi campaign promoting male contraception obtained very high attention ratings with the aid of an image showing a concerned man with a swollen abdomen, rather like a pregnant woman's. The slogan was 'wouldn't you be more careful if it was you?'

In interpreting ambiguous or incomplete stimuli the consumer also uses **categorisation principles** to mark out and organise what he or she perceives. After only a few notes from a well-known musical introduction to a commercial, the consumer may say inwardly, 'Oh ... This is an advert for XYZ. I know what this is going to be about'. It is important for the manager in charge of launching a new product to understand the rules that have already been established by consumers to structure their environment. Generally speaking, a marketer wants to position a brand within a galaxy of reference products, while at the same time making sure it stands out. Three major categorisation mechanisms have been identified.[38] Sometimes the consumer goes by level, for example price ranges ('It's expensive' or 'It's not expensive'), sometimes by association ('It's expensive, therefore, it is good quality'[39]), and sometimes by comparisons (to do with logos, colours, packaging). In this way the consumer builds up a repertoire of experiences which allow him or her to incorporate and even anticipate the new purchases he or she is going to make.[40] Within many product categories, the consumer often chooses a **typical product** or reference product, to be used as a yardstick. A product is all the more typical because it has the characteristics common to the family to which it belongs.[41] For example, in southern Europe, many consumers recognise the type of yoghurt they buy on the basis of the material used for the container. Yoghurts sold in glass jars are 'decoded' as whole milk yoghurts and immediately differentiated from other yoghurts (standard, flavoured, fruit, etc.) sold in plastic containers. Naturally, these 'codes' evolve over time. PCs were first called micro-computers to differentiate them from the traditional larger mainframe units. Now PCs are further classified into desktop machines, laptops, notebooks, and so on.

Furthermore, interpretation makes extensive use of the **symbolism** associated with certain shapes, words, objects and colours. For example, in some countries red is said to connote strength and excitement, while pastel shades imply femininity and gentleness. White is regarded as pure and virginal, while black seems mysterious, even malicious; this perhaps explains why white pearls are usually considered suitable for young women, while black pearls are felt to be appropriate for more mature and experienced women (for example, Liz Taylor has used the black pearl theme for one of her perfumes). An understanding of the symbols associated with colours, shapes, words and objects is obviously very important in advertising. When producing an advert, companies often carry out visual tests to check that the effects produced are actually the ones desired.

Consider the two adverts for the two competing anti-ageing skin-care products shown in Figures 2.11 and 2.12. Because the text is not in English, it may be even easier for non-French readers to discern the underlying symbolism. The first one (Orlane) aims to communicate the main function of the product: to fight against time. There are lots of visual elements which help it to be perceived as a product which 'reverses time': the colour coding, the implicit upward movement of the product, the clocks in the background, and the name 'Anagenese' (from the Greek word for origin), which suggests rejuvenescence. The second advertisement (Clarins) is clearly based on a scientific and educational approach. The product is dissected as though it were the topic of a scientific lesson and, on the right-hand side of the advertisement, a beautician dressed in a clinical white blouse gives elaborate prescriptive instructions of a quasi-medical nature. To understand better how symbols can be used in adverts, marketers are increasingly turning their attention to **semiology** (also called **semiotics**), a discipline entirely dedicated to the study of signs and their meanings.[42] According to semioticians, signs can be related to objects through icons, indexes and symbols.[43] An icon is a sign which is similar to the object itself. For example, the icon of a printer in the Windows 98 toolbar is used to order the PC to send a message to the printer. An index is linked to the object through an association based on some shared property. For example, the Club Med logo is a trident (Neptune's weapon) as a reminder of its sea-based leisure activities. Finally, a symbol is associated with an object through simple conventional use. For example, in most European countries, speed limits and other restrictions on traffic are indicated by street signs which are generally circular. In marketing, semiotics has been extensively used not only in advertising but also for industrial design purposes. For example, semiotic principles have been used in the design of new hypermarkets.[44]

Figure 2.11 Symbolism in advertising

Figure 2.12   Symbolism in advertising (cont.)

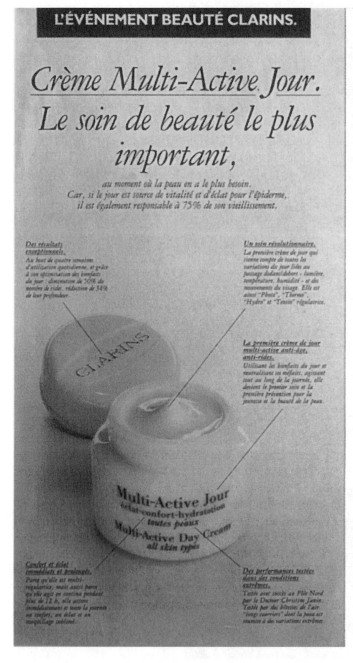

Brand image and positioning: the structure of perceptions

The principles of Gestalt psychology make an important contribution to our understanding of the perception process. They underline the necessity of being able to refer to underlying dimensions or **attributes** (proximity, similarity, contrast, etc.) in order to analyse perceptions. Such an idea provides the foundation for **brand image** research, one of the most fruitful domains of investigation in contemporary marketing.

An image is made up of all the percepts (that is, the outcomes of the perceptual process, often themselves called perceptions) that a consumer holds in relation to a product, company, person or idea. Structurally, an image can be understood as a constellation of associations between the stimulus and a given number of attributes. Therefore, a consumer statement like 'Klorane shampoo gives you beautiful looking hair but is a bit expensive to use' shows that the Klorane image is structured in relation to two dimensions: the cost of using the product and the type of results obtained. Because such judgements can only be comparative (of what value is information about the effectiveness of a product when it cannot be compared with competition?), analysing a brand image can only be effective if one understands the relevant **perceptual universe**.

Figure 2.13 An example of the universe of perceptions for given products

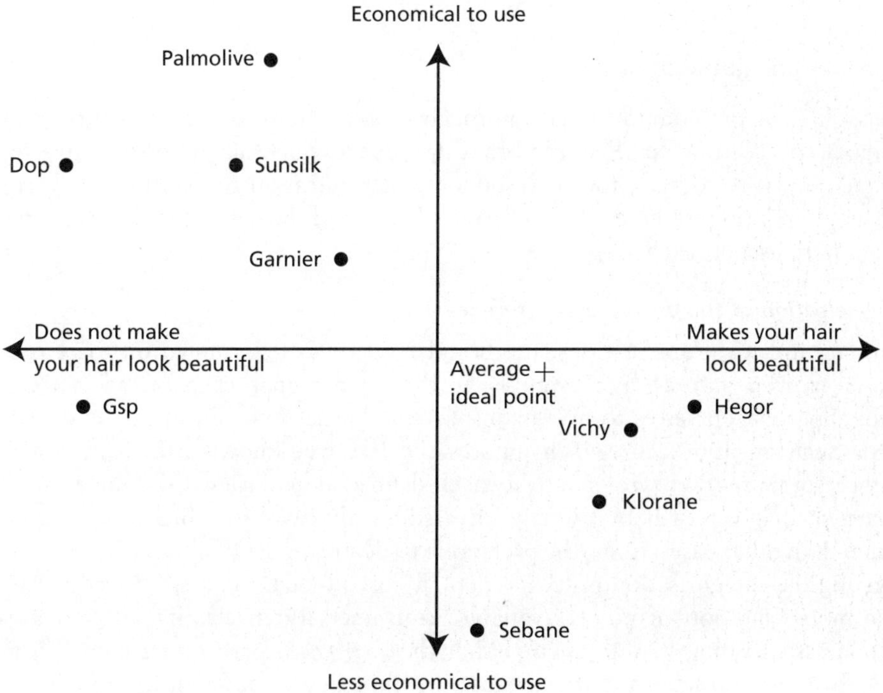

Source: B. Pras and J. Tarondeau, *Comportement de l'acheteur* (Sirey, 1981), p. 66

Perceptual universes such as the one represented in Figure 2.13 provide the basis on which **positioning** decisions are made. Positioning refers to the deliberate attempt made by a company to design its offering so that it occupies a meaningful and distinct position in consumers' minds.[45] While the positioning of a brand corresponds to a managerial decision, the brand image describes a perceptual outcome. Ideally, of course, the two should perfectly match but this is seldom the case and that's why it is necessary first to understand perceptual maps in order to prepare positioning decisions. A perceptual map reveals not only the various brand images (for example, Palmolive is perceived positively as being economical but rated as average only on performance) but also which products are close to each other and therefore in direct competition, at least in the minds of consumers. In the perceptual map depicted in Figure 2.13, Vichy and Hegor for example are perceived as being very close to each other, but Dop and Vichy are far apart.

It must be noted that the images which consumers hold in their mind are not restricted to word associations but can also include visual or other sensory elements. As we see in Chapter 3, visual properties (logos for example) can greatly facilitate memorisation.[46]

The structure of perceptions as they appear in a perceptual map suggests that there are two major measurement approaches in developing such maps: (a) the map is worked out piece by piece (the **compositional approach**) or (b) an attempt is made to capture the whole structure first, which is then broken down and interpreted (the **decompositional approach**). Let us examine these two methods in turn.

The compositional approach

According to the compositional approach, a perceptual map is built up in four stages. You need (a) to select the brands/products which make up the universe of reference; (b) to identify the corresponding attributes; (c) to position the various images in relation to these attributes; and (d) to build the map itself. Different techniques are used at each stage.

The selection of the universe of reference

In many practical applications, the brand universe is determined on the basis of actual market shares.[47] For example, in the car hire market in Europe we could probably limit ourselves to five 'main players': Hertz, Avis, Europcar, Budget and Sixt. Such an approach, which ignores the less well-known brands, assumes a rather stable market with relatively well-defined boundaries. Of course, market share calculations will be directly affected by the way in which the market is defined. In other cases, it may be preferable to define the set of alternatives by investigating the categorisation processes actually used by consumers.[48] Faced with the enormous selection of goods available, consumers often classify and categorise products according to the function that they see them performing (ends), rather than by their characteristics (the means).[49] Although very different from each other, all the products manufactured by Sony may thus appear related because they are all seen as 'entertainment goods'. Based on these classifications, consumers establish **consideration sets,** which are limited to the number of brands they feel familiar enough with to consider them in a given purchase situation. Usually, the size of these sets is quite limited but may vary depending upon the country; for instance, if the average number of cars considered in a purchase is about eight in the USA, it falls to two in Norway.[50]

The identification of attributes

A marketing manager always has some knowledge about the dimensions that customers use in perceiving his or her products. However, it is rare for attributes called up in this way to provide a structured and exhaustive picture. To enrich managers' experience and intuition, many methods are available, as detailed below:

- **Surveys**   This is the most widely used approach to tackling the problem, achieved by actually asking consumers to explain the criteria they use. The main drawbacks are that interviewees may omit things and/or rationalise their answers. For example, it seems easier for consumers to admit that they are influenced by the quality of a product than by media advertising.

- **Projective tests** (such as sentence completion tests, word associations, pictures to interpret, etc.)   The projective approach is interesting because it reveals attributes or criteria that are not immediately salient or obvious. In a study undertaken for a cigarette company, a sample of smokers and non-smokers were asked to describe the personality of Mrs Dupont and Mrs Durand from the following dialogue:

  Mrs Dupont: 'I smoke as often as I like and I see nothing wrong with that.'
  Mrs Durand: 'I don't smoke at all and I think that it is better that way.'

  The attributes interviewees suggested (modern, authoritarian, vulgar, cool) were far more numerous and vivid than those that would have been obtained from direct questioning alone.[51]

- **Kelly's repertory grid analysis**   Kelly suggested a different method for discovering people's perceptual 'repertoires'. His idea is to form triads of objects and then ask respondents systematically to compare any two objects within the triad. In so doing, Kelly claims that the interviewee reveals the underlying structure of his or her perceptions. For example, when carrying out a study on business hotels one could ask interviewees systematically to compare Hilton with Sheraton and Hyatt. Researchers would not suggest any specific criteria but would limit themselves to questions such as: 'Which two brands among those three are most similar? Which two are most dissimilar? In which ways do they differ, etc.' This method is not without limitations. The initial set of items has a heavy bearing on the results, and respondents sometimes have a tendency to go for the easiest answers.[52]

- **Observation**   Finally, direct observation of consumer behaviour is a method that has the advantage of reducing the biases introduced by questioning techniques.[53] In Bourdieu's sociological analysis of 'social distinction' and good taste, the research process included an observation sheet to be filled in by the interviewer. The idea was to record observations not only about the interviewee's housing (type of building, number of rooms, interior decoration, style of furniture) and clothing (type of clothes – working overalls, suit, casual sportswear – style and colour), but also about hair style (long or short hair, well groomed or not) and language used (well spoken, use of jargon, with or without an accent, with or without grammatical errors).[54] However, to be really useful, direct observation must be carefully monitored and sometimes supplemented by mechanical devices. In the case of measuring exposure to advertisements, for example, some researchers have used instruments such as an ocular camera, which allows them to follow the movement of the subject's eyes or to measure pupil dilation (increased dilation indicates that the person is paying attention).[55] A study carried out in 1992 by the European Association for the Promotion of Hygiene endeavoured to find out the number of people who wash their hands before leaving the toilets, the amount of time spent washing and whether they used soap or not. The people undertaking the survey (in public toilet facilities) were dressed as plumbers and hid themselves behind the main door so as 'not to influence the subjects' behaviour'. The results were surprising: one in three people does not wash their hands and the average duration of handwashing is 9.3 seconds!

The selection of attributes

At the end of the previous stage, the researcher has a number of attributes available which express the different points of view considered when the products are called to mind. The attributes are either continuous (and therefore can be dealt with as dimensions, as in the case of price) or discontinuous (consumers can simply check whether the attributes are present or absent). Abstract attributes (for example the quality of a television set) often belong to the first group, while concrete attributes (a high-definition screen) belong to the second.[56] Studies have demonstrated that the less products are immediately comparable to each other (that is to say they are not considered as true alternatives), the more consumers will have to rely on abstract attributes.[57] In fact, consumers seem to prefer to use abstract attributes even when concrete attributes are available. Concrete attributes tend to be more technical and of less relevance to consumers, especially in low-involvement situations.[58]

In general, the attributes obtained from preliminary research are too numerous to all be put on a chart. Therefore, it is a good idea to sort them out, eliminating those which are redundant or less important. The removal of **redundant** attributes can be done either by just analysing their nature (but it is then difficult to avoid arbitrariness or subjectivity in the final selection) or by using statistical data-reduction methods such as factor or correspondence analysis.[59] For example, a study of the criteria used by film-goers when choosing which film to see, as the result of a principal component analysis, recognised three underlying dimensions: (a) the

'professional' quality of the film (value of the scenario and excellence of the production); (b) its 'entertainment' value (relaxing, fun); and (c) its 'intellectual' value
(impact, originality of its underlying message).[60]

Measuring attribute **importance** can be done through direct questioning (importance ranking or rating scales) or through statistical methods.[61] In order to assess
attribute importance, one may also try to relate objective physical product characteristics to abstract perceptual dimensions. For example, in a study done on a
mobile health-care unit, it was found that a simple linear model could explain
rather well how specific 'objective' features, such as opening hours, nature and
number of personnel employed and so on, influence perceptual dimensions such as
quality and convenience.[62] In the same way it has been discovered that the manner
in which a piece of music is perceived (in particular how 'new' or difficult it is
judged) is a direct result of a limited number of psychophysical sensations (quick or
slow tempo, regular or irregular rhythm, same pitch or a higher or lower pitch, and
whether the various musical phrases are linked or separate).[63]

Once the attributes have been identified and sorted, the various brands or
products are systematically evaluated for their performance on each attribute,
usually using a set of scales such as the bipolar semantic differential scale shown
in Figure 2.14.[64] In this figure, it appears that the images of four well-known
companies (Michelin, Danone, L'Oréal, and French Railways) are the same in
certain areas (for example, the international nature of the first three companies)
but are very different in others (perceived working atmosphere, competitiveness
of salaries, etc.).

The building of the map

Finally, building the perceptual map is done either manually (especially when there
are few relatively independent attributes) or by using mapping techniques such as
the ones now readily available in many statistical packages.[65]

Figure 2.14   Images of four companies measured with the semantic differential

Large	Small
Well managed	Poorly managed
Competitive salaries	Salaries not competitive
Interesting product	Product not interesting
Dynamic	Not dynamic
Pleasant working atmosphere	Unpleasant working atmosphere
Good promotion prospects	Lack of opportunity for advancement
Offers further training	Limited training available
Innovative	Not particularly innovative
Socially responsible	Lack of social responsibility

Source: unpublished study by B. Dubois and R. Laufer (1976)

The decompositional approach

The decompositional approach rests on the principle of proximity formulated by Gestalt psychology. We start by studying the spatial proximity relationships between different brands in a given product universe, for example by asking consumers which brands seem to be the most and least similar (for example, 'Between British Airways, KLM, SAS, Lufthansa, which two airlines are the most similar? Which two are the least similar?').[66] Then, a bit like reconstructing the map of Europe from the number of kilometres between cities, we can deduce the structure of the underlying perceptions – that is, the number of attributes used and their nature – through a technique known as **multidimensional scaling.**[67] In fact, the compositional and decompositional approaches are more complementary methods than alternatives to each other.[68] In practice, it is often useful to use both approaches together in order to increase the amount of control one has, at each stage, in the analysis of brand images and people's perceptions of them.

In summary, consumers' perceptions of products and brands play a key role in buying behaviour. As we see in Chapter 4, perceptions and images provide the foundations for attitudes and preferences. The social sciences in general and the psychology of perception in particular have helped us to understand how the perception process works, and how images are formed and maintained over time. For marketing managers but also for every individual or organisation involved in communications and other exchange relationships (public authorities, consumer associations, artists, product designers, etc.) these results are highly significant.

Notes

[1] U. Neisser, *Cognitive Psychology* (Appleton-Century-Crofts, 1967) and W. N. Dember, *The Psychology of Perception* (Holt, Rinehart & Winston, 1961).

[2] C. Derbaix and F. Van den Abeele, 'Consumer Inferences and Consumer Preferences: The Status of Cognitions and Consciousness in Consumer Behaviour Theory', *International Journal of Research in Marketing*, 1985, pp. 157–74.

[3] W. Heron, 'Cognitive and Psychological Effects of Perceptual Isolation' in P. Salomon *et al.* (eds), *Sensory Deprivation* (Harvard University Press, 1961).

[4] R. H. Day, *Human Perception* (Wiley, 1969).

[5] M. W. Levine and J. M. Shefner, *Fundamentals of Sensation and Perception* (Reading, 1981); E. C. Carterette and M. P. Friedman, *Handbook of Perception*, Vol. 8: *Perceptual Coding* (Academic Press, 1978); and R. Held, H. W. Leibowitz and H. L. Teuber (eds), *Handbook of Sensory Physiology*, Vol. 8: *Perception* (Springer, 1978).

[6] V. Packard, *The Hidden Persuaders* (McKay, 1957).

[7] H. Fiss *et al.*, 'Effects of Subliminal Stimulation on Imagery and Discrimination', *Perceptual and Motor Skills*, 1963, 17, pp. 31–4; see also S. J. Segal, *The Function and Nature of Imagery* (Academic Press, 1972).

[8] See T. E. Moore, 'Subliminal Advertising: What You See Is What You Get', *Journal of Marketing*, 1982, p. 46; for an analysis of this question in more depth, see D. Dixon, *Subliminal Perception: The Nature of the Controversy* (McGraw-Hill, 1971). Also see M. Rogers and K. Smith, 'Public Perceptions of Subliminal Advertising', *Journal of Advertising Research*, March–April 1993, pp. 10–29.

⁹ J. N. Kapferer, 'Une Rumeur de la Publicité: la Publicité Subliminale', *Revue Française de Marketing*, December 1986.

¹⁰ R. I. Allison and K. P. Uhl, 'Influence of Beer Identification on Taste Perception', *Journal of Marketing Research*, August 1964, pp. 36–9. For an earlier study done on cigarettes, see R. Littman and H. M. Manning, 'A Methodological Study of Cigarette Brand Discrimination', *Journal of Applied Psychology*, 1954, 38, pp. 185–90.

¹¹ C. Bouvier, J. C. Levèque and Y. Moine, 'La connaissance des prix par les consommateurs', 1978 (HEC study, undertaken under the direction of the author). See also K. Monroe, 'Buyers' Subjective Perceptions of Price', *Journal of Marketing Research*, February 1973, 170–80.

¹² A. Gabor and C. W. J. Granger, 'Price Sensitivity of the Consumer', *Journal of Advertising Research*, December 1964, pp. 40–4; also see P. R. Dickinson and A. G. Sawyer, 'The Price Knowledge and Search of Supermarket Shoppers', *Journal of Marketing*, July 1990, pp. 42–53.

¹³ For advertising studies related to attention, see G. Brown, 'Tracking Studies and Sales Effects: A UK Perspective', *Journal of Advertising Research*, 1985, 25, pp. 52–64. On attention processes, see R. Celsi and J. C. Olson, 'The Role of Involvement in Attention and Comprehension Processes', *Journal of Consumer Research*, September 1988, pp. 210–24.

¹⁴ S. H. Britt *et al.*, 'How Many Advertising Exposures per Day?' *Journal of Advertising Research*, 1972, pp. 3–9.

¹⁵ D. L. Moore, D. Hausknecht and K. Thamodaran, 'Time Compression, Response Opportunity, and Persuasion', *Journal of Consumer Research*, June 1986, pp. 85–99. See also J. MacLachlan and M. Siegel, 'Reducing the Costs of Television Commercials by Use of Time Compression', *Journal of Marketing Research*, February 1980, pp. 52–7.

¹⁶ R. Barton, *Advertising Media* (McGraw-Hill, 1964), p. 109.

¹⁷ L. Ulin, 'Does Large Size Influence Advertising Effectiveness?' *Media/Scope*, July 1962, p. 14.

¹⁸ L. Percy, 'Ways in which the People, Words and Pictures in Advertising Influence Its Effectiveness' (Financial Institutions Marketing Association, July 1984).

¹⁹ For more on self-referential advertising and other related approaches, see S. Brown, *Postmodern Marketing* (Routledge, 1995).

²⁰ See P. H. Webbs, 'Consumer Initial Processing in a Difficult Media Environment', *Journal of Consumer Research*, December 1979, pp. 225–36.

²¹ For other examples, see S. Moriarty, *Creative Advertising: Theory and Practice* (Prentice Hall, 1986); and A. Turnbull and R. Baird, *The Graphics of Communication: Typography, Layout, Design* (Holt, Rinehart & Winston, 1975).

²² D. E. Berlyne, 'Attention to Change', *British Journal of Psychology*, 1951, pp. 269–78, and 'The Influence of Complexity and Novelty in Visual Figures on Orienting Responses', *Journal of Experimental Psychology*, 1958, pp. 289–96.

²³ D. R. Davies and R. Parasuraman, *The Psychology of Vigilance* (Academic Press, 1982).

²⁴ See R. Haley, 'Benefit Segmentation: A Decision-oriented Research Tool', *Journal of Marketing*, 1968, vol. 32, pp. 30–5. For recent research on this topic, see S. Ratneshwar, L. Warlop, D. G. Mick and G. Seeger, 'Benefit Salience and Consumers' Selective Attention to Product Features', *International Journal of Research in Marketing*, July 1997, pp. 245–60. See also S. Ratneshwar, D. G. Mick and G. Reitinger, 'Selective Attention in Consumer Information Processing', *Advances in Consumer Research*, 1990, pp. 547–53.

²⁵ J. S. Bruner and D. D. Goodman, 'Value and Need as Organising Factors in Perception', *Journal of Abnormal and Social Psychology*, 1947, pp. 33–4. See also J. S. Bruner, 'On Perceptual Readiness', *Psychological Review*, 1957, vol. 64, pp. 306–7.

²⁶ J. Shiteville, 'Psychic Defence against High Fear Appeals: A Key Marketing Variable', *Journal of Marketing*, April 1970, pp. 39–45.

²⁷ Concerning perceived risk and its use in the media, see D. Cox, *Risk Taking and Information Handling in Consumer Behaviour* (HBS Division of Research, 1967).

²⁸ On the consequences of involvement in the subject with regard to paying attention to advertising, see J. M. Agostini, 'Communication Publicitaire et Implication du Consommateur:

Conséquences Pratiques pour la Conception des Messages et le Choix des Médias' (Irep, 1978).

29 J. Engel, 'Are Automobile Purchasers Dissonant Consumers?' *Journal of Marketing*, April 1968, pp. 55–8.

30 See W. McGuire, 'The Current Status of Cognitive Consistency Theories' in J. B. Cohen (ed.), *Behavioural Science Foundations of Consumer Behaviour* (Free Press, 1972), pp. 253–74.

31 H. E. Spence and J. F. Engel, 'The Impact of Brand Preference on the Perception of Brand Names: A Laboratory Analysis' in P. R. McDonald (ed.), *Marketing Involvement in Society and the Economy* (AMA, 1970), pp. 267–77.

32 F. Heider, *The Psychology of Interpersonal Relations* (John Wiley, 1958).

33 B. Zeigarnik, 'Uber das Behalten von erledigten und unerledigten Handlungen', *Psychologische Forschungen*, 9, pp. 1–85.

34 J. H. Heimbach and J. Jacoby, 'The Zeigarnik Effect in Advertising' in M. Venkatesan, *ACR Proceedings* (ACR, 1972), pp. 746–58.

35 J. S. Bruner and A. L. Minturn, 'Perceptual Identification and Perceptual Organization', *Journal of Genetic Psychology*, 1955, pp. 21–8.

36 Even though they liked the product. See L. A. Perrachio and J. Meyers-Levy, 'How Ambiguous Cropped Objects in Ad Photos Can Affect Product Evaluations', *Journal of Consumer Research*, June 1994, pp. 190–204.

37 G. Miller, E. Galanter and D. Pribram, *The Structure of Behaviour* (Holt, Rinehart & Winston, 1960).

38 For an extensive treatment of categorisation principles, see J. S. Bruner, J. J. Goodnow and G. A. Austin, *A Study of Thinking* (Wiley, 1956).

39 About the price–quality relationship, see D. Gardener, 'Is There a Generalised Price–Quality Relationship?' *Journal of Marketing Research*, May 1971, pp. 241–3; also see M. Zollinger, 'Le Concept de Prix de Référence dans le Comportement du Consommateur', *Recherche et Applications en Marketing*, 1993, no. 2, pp. 61–78.

40 A. Rethans and J. Taylor, 'A Script Theoretic Analysis of Consumer Decision-Making' in B. Walker (ed.), *Proceedings of the American Marketing Association Educators' Conference*, 1982, pp. 71–4.

41 See B. Loken and J. Ward, 'Alternative Approach to Understanding the Determinants of Typicality', *Journal of Consumer Research*, September 1990, pp. 111–26; see also M. Sujan and C. Deklava, 'Product Categorization and Inference Making: Some Implications for Comparative Advertising', *Journal of Consumer Research*, December 1983, pp. 372–8.

42 D. Mick, 'Consumer Research and Semiotics: Exploring the Morphology of Signs, Symbols, and Significance', *Journal of Consumer Research*, September 1986, pp. 196–213. See also the special double issue of the *International Journal of Research in Marketing* (1988), ed. by C. Pinson, and *Marketing and Semiotics, New Directions in the Study of Signs for Sale,* J. Umiker-Sebeok, ed. (Mouton de Gruyer, 1987).

43 W. Nöth, *Handbook of Semiotics* (Sage, 1994).

44 J. M. Floch, 'The Contribution of Structural Semiotics to the Design of a Hypermarket', *International Journal of Research in Marketing*, 1988, pp. 233–52.

45 A. Ries and J. Trout, *Positioning: The Battle For Your Mind* (Warner, 1982).

46 G Bower, 'Imagery as a Relational Organizer in Associative Learning', *Journal of Applied Psychology*, 1977, pp. 493–8.

47 For an approach that also takes into account the 'affinity' between two brands, see B. Dubois and P. Duquesne, 'Polarization Maps: A New Approach to Identifying and Assessing Competitive Position: The Case of Luxury Brands', *Marketing and Research Today*, May 1993, pp. 115–23.

48 See V. Stefflre, 'Market Structure Studies: New Products for Old Markets and New Markets (Foreign) for Old Products', in F. M. Bass, C. W. King, and E. A. Pessemier (eds) *Application of the Sciences in Marketing* (Wiley, 1969), pp. 251–68.

49 See J. Gutman, 'A Means–End Chain Model Based on Consumer Categorization Process',

Journal of Marketing, Spring 1982, pp. 60–72. See also Hendry's model presented in D. H. Butler and B. E. Butler, *Hendro-Dynamics: Fundamental Laws of Consumer Dynamics* (The Hendry Corporation, 1970–1971).

[50] J. Hauser and B. Wernerfelt, 'An Evaluation Cost Model of Consideration Sets', *Journal of Consumer Research*, 1990, 16, pp. 393–408.

[51] E. Deutsch, 'L'Usage des Techniques dites Projectives dans les Etudes Psychosociologiques', *Metra*, 1962, pp. 71–82.

[52] G. A. Kelly, *The Psychology of Personal Constructs* (Norton, 1955).

[53] W. D. Wells and L. A. Lo Sciuto, 'Direct Observation of Purchasing Behaviour', *Journal of Marketing Research*, August 1966, pp. 227–33.

[54] P. Bourdieu, *La Distinction: Critique Sociale du Jugement* (Ed. de Minuit, 1979), pp. 605–6.

[55] E. J. Russo and L. D. Rosen, 'An Eye Fixation Analysis of Multialternative Choices', *Memory and Cognition*, May 1975, pp. 267–76, and B. C. Goldwater, 'Psychological Significance of Pupillary Movements', *Psychological Bulletin*, 1972, pp. 340–55. For examples of use see A. Millet and D. Tsiantar, 'Psyching Out Customers', *Business Week*, 27 February 1989, pp. 46–7.

[56] M. Johnson and C. Fornell, 'The Nature and Methodological Implications of the Cognitive Representation of Products', *Journal of Consumer Research*, September 1987, pp. 214–28.

[57] M. Johnson, 'Consumer Choice Strategies for Comparing Non-Comparable Alternatives', *Journal of Consumer Research*, December 1984, pp. 741–53, and M. Johnson, 'Comparability and Hierarchical Processing in Multialternative Choice', *Journal of Consumer Research*, December 1988, pp. 303–14.

[58] K. Corfman, 'Comparability and Comparison Levels Used in Choices Among Consumer Products', *Journal of Marketing Research*, August 1991, pp. 368–74. See also W. Hutchinson and J. Alba, 'Ignoring Irrelevant Information: Situational Determinants of Consumer Learning', *Journal of Consumer Research*, December 1991, pp. 325–45.

[59] For a comparison of methods used see J. Hauser and F. Koppelman, 'Alternative Perceptual Mapping Techniques: Relative Accuracy and Usefulness', *Journal of Market Research*, November 1979, pp. 495–506.

[60] J.-M. Choffray and B. Pras, 'Les Déterminants Perceptuels du Résultat Commercial des Films dans la Région Paris-périphérie', (Cahier de Recherche Ceressec, 1979).

[61] Statistical methods include, for example, using regression weights in a regression analysis where the dependent variable is an overall evaluation of the product and where the independent variables correspond to perceived performance of the product on specific attributes.

[62] S. Neslin, 'Linking Product Features to Perceptions: Self-Stated versus Statistically Revealed Importance Weights', *Journal of Marketing Research*, February 1981, pp. 80–6.

[63] M. Holbrook, 'Integrating Compositional and Decompositional Analyses to Represent the Intervening Role of Perceptions in Evaluative Judgement', *Journal of Marketing Research*, February 1981, pp. 13–28. For another example, see F. Boecker and H. Schweikl, 'Better Preference Prediction with Individualized Sets of Relevant Attributes', *International Journal of Research in Marketing*, 1988, pp. 15–24.

[64] The semantic differential method was developed by C. E. Osgood, C. J. Suci and R. H. Tannenbaum in *The Measurement of Meaning* (University of Illinois Press, 1957).

[65] Examples of statistical packages include SPSS and SAS. The interested reader will find an excellent step-by-step introduction to multidimensional scaling in F. Young and D. F. Harris, 'Multidimensional scaling', in *SPSS Professional Statistics*, release 8.0, 1997.

[66] On the concept of similarity, see F. Attneave, 'Dimensions of Similarity', *American Journal of Psychology*, 1967, pp. 133–44, and A. Tversky, 'Features of Similarity', *Psychological Review*, 1977, 84, pp. 321–7.

[67] For a recent review of multidimensional scaling techniques, see D. J. Carroll and P. Green, 'Psychometric Methods in Marketing: Part II, Multidimensional Scaling', *Journal of Marketing Research*, 1997, 34, pp. 193–205. For a European perspective, see B. Dubois and Y. Evrard, 'A

Few Problems Associated with Multidimensional Scaling of Proximity and Preference Data', ESOMAR Conference Proceedings 1975, pp. 463–84.

[68] For a comparison of the different approaches, see D. Gupta, 'Some Practical Guidelines for Selecting an Appropriate Perceptual Mapping Technique', EMAC-ESOMAR, Congress Proceedings, October 1984, pp. 107–35.

3

Learning, experience and memory

Learning objectives

After reading this chapter, you will understand that:

1 consumers buy many products and services simply out of habit, because they have learned to do so;

2 behavioural learning theories offer various explanations of the many ways in which we develop habits;

3 classical conditioning maintains that most of our learning operates through associations between stimuli and responses. Advertising and product design make extensive use of classical conditioning;

4 instrumental conditioning highlights the role of rewards and punishment in shaping our behaviour. The principles of instrumental conditioning are at the very foundation of many customer loyalty programmes;

5 human beings adapt what they have learned to cope with new stimuli, relying upon processes such as generalisation and discrimination;

6 cognitive learning emphasises the role of conscious thought processes in the development of experience. Many consumer educational strategies are based on cognitive learning mechanisms;

7 memory is a complex structure which operates at many levels (sensory, short-term, long-term) according to a variety of rules such as the semantic and the episodic principles.

Key words

habit	reinforcement	storage
learning	relationship marketing	script
behaviourism	shaping	retrieval
response	extinction	forgetting
stimulus	cognitive learning	nostalgia
classical conditioning	experience	recall
generalisation	memory	recognition
discrimination	typicality	signalling
instrumental	mental rehearsal	
conditioning	elaboration	

It is not absolutely necessary for a consumer to have a good image of a brand or a good impression of a product before they will make a purchase. Most products we consume are not important enough for us to think about them in a deep way. We buy them out of **habit**. Even for durable goods such as cars, the best indicator for the make to be purchased remains the make we currently own. This may be interpreted as reflecting a certain level of attachment to the brand but may also simply be habit.

For low-involvement products, the results are even clearer. Even a cursory analysis of consumer panel results leaves no place for ambiguity. For many product categories, the same consumers tend to buy the same items over and over again. At the base of this behaviour lies one of the fundamental mechanisms underlying human activity: **learning**.[1]

By learning we usually understand 'an enduring change in the mechanisms of behaviour that results from experience with environmental events'.[2] Learning is actually a continuous process of behavioural adjustment by the individual to the environment.[3] In the marketplace, consumers continuously learn by being exposed to commercial stimuli such as advertising and non-commercial ones such as discussions with friends.[4] Learning can take many forms: it can be direct, as when a young girl memorises a letter of the alphabet which she later recognises to the admiration of her teacher, or indirect, as when we learn vicariously (that is 'by proxy'), observing the way in which somebody carries out a task or reacts to a situation in which we could find ourselves one day. It may be premeditated (as when we decide to go to a driving school) or fortuitous (due to an unexpected event such as an accident or illness). As with perception, it is a process which many theories have attempted to elucidate.

Behaviourism

Behaviourist theories rely on the hypothesis that learning is a **response** of the organism to a **stimulus**, that is any objectively describable situation or event arising from elements external to the individual. The notion of a 'black box' is often used to describe the behaviourist model as it does not seek to explain internal psychological processes which link the stimuli and the response but limits itself to observing (and measuring) the nature and strength of their association. Two main theories have been developed to explain the stimulus–response mechanism: **classical conditioning** (also known as respondent conditioning) and **instrumental conditioning** (also known as operant conditioning).

Classical conditioning

Almost everyone has heard of the experiment conducted by Russian psychologist Pavlov, who, by ringing a bell at the same time as feeding a dog, gradually succeeded in inducing the animal to salivate when the bell was rung in the absence of any food. In this kind of experiment, we designate the bell ringing (initially) as a **neutral stimulus**, the food as an **unconditioned stimulus** (because it is enough by itself to provoke salivation), and the salivation as a **conditioned response**. After several trials, the sound becomes a **conditioned stimulus**, capable alone of provoking the conditioned response. Conditioning is thus a process of association between two stimuli which enables one of them to acquire, after repetition, the capacity to elicit a response which the other can provoke on its own.[5] Figure 3.1 summarises the functioning of this mechanism when it is reduced to its simplest form.

Five precautions must be taken before we can safely conclude the existence of a successful conditioning process:

1 the conditioned stimulus must be precisely defined;
2 the unconditioned stimulus must also be clearly defined (in general it is selected on the basis of its strength);
3 the two stimuli must be associated in a systematic manner;
4 the conditioned response must be measured after each association; and finally
5 the existence of the conditioned response must be verified when the unconditioned stimulus is no longer present.[6]

Ideally, the following conditions must also be present to ascertain a causal link:

1 the non-conditioned stimulus has to be present before the conditioned stimulus (this is often referred to as forward conditioning, in contrast to backward conditioning, which is more difficult to interpret);
2 strong associations have to be observed on a repeated number of occasions (certain conditioning processes take time to produce an effect);[7]
3 the two stimuli have to be coherent with each other (in terms of content, format, strength or style);

Figure 3.1 The classical conditioning model

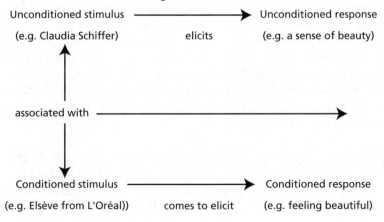

Unconditioned stimulus ⟶ Unconditioned response
(e.g. Claudia Schiffer) elicits (e.g. a sense of beauty)

associated with ⟶

Conditioned stimulus ⟶ Conditioned response
(e.g. Elsève from L'Oréal)) comes to elicit (e.g. feeling beautiful)

4 the conditioned stimulus must not be well known by the subject at the beginning (to avoid any interference with previous connotations) and;

5 the non-conditioned stimulus has, if possible, to be physically or symbolically clearly delineated (in order to reduce any ambiguity in interpretation).[8]

Classical conditioning, which has often been considered as a 'dumb' form of learning[9] and heavily criticised for that,[10] is very commonly used in advertising. For example, a company like L'Oréal associates an attractive person, say Claudia Schiffer, with one of its brands of shampoo (Elsève) in the hope that after a number of repetitions the good feelings associated with the person will be transferred to the brand, increasing the possibility that it will be chosen from a supermarket shelf. For very well-known brands, such as Coca-Cola or Avon cosmetics, we do not even need to see the brand name: a visual stimulus (the bottle) or a sound (the door bell) can be sufficient.[11]

In principle, all sorts of stimuli can be associated with a product. For example, a study has shown that it is enough to associate pleasant music with a pen for it to be chosen over another identical pen which is associated with less pleasant music.[12] Another study showed that when exposed to attractive water scenes that were systematically associated with a new brand of toothpaste people exhibited, when compared with a corresponding random group, significantly more positive attitudes towards the associated brand.[13] Even a credit card has been shown to be enough of a stimulus to facilitate spending.[14] In certain categories, products are so undifferentiated that it would be difficult indeed for a brand to offer distinct advantages. In such a case, associating an emotion with the brand through conditioning may be enough to produce a favourable response; this type of approach is often used for basic food items and cleaning products.

Of course, the strength of association depends on how often the two conditioned and unconditioned stimuli are paired. If they cease to appear together, the conditioning mechanism declines and eventually disappears. Catherine Deneuve jewellery, for example, had to be taken off the market relatively shortly after its introduction as the international movie star was seen to be wearing it less and less. Such a principle underlies the common advertising practice of frequently repeating the same message, in order to maintain the force of the association. Krugman estimates that three appearances are an absolute minimum – the first to capture attention, the second to convince and the third to secure memorisation.[15] Others go as far as recommending at least thirty repetitions.[16] At the same time, there clearly exists a limit beyond which repetition of an advertisement causes it to lose its effectiveness, not because of failure but due to an overdose of conditioning – just like a pupil who gets bored when a topic already covered in class is repeated by another teacher.

Generally speaking, classical conditioning – which assumes that the presentation order of the non-conditioned and conditioned stimuli is fully controlled – is easier to use on TV and radio than in the press or on posters, where the sequence in which the two stimuli are read is more difficult to control by the advertiser. By the same token, it is somewhat risky to associate a very famous piece of music with a product, since such a hit can usually be heard in many circumstances where the product is not present. One can, however, limit this phenomenon by using past hits rather than more current ones (or commission one's own music, as Coca-Cola does).[17]

Generalisation and discrimination

We call **generalisation** the mechanism by which a stimulus similar to a reference (conditioned) stimulus tends to provoke a response initially associated with the reference stimulus. In marketing, the generalisation principle is at the very heart of strategies emphasising sub-brands or brand extensions (for example, Mars Ice Cream).[18] Caterpillar is best known as a manufacturer of earth-moving equipment, but its reputation for durability and resilience has enabled the brand to extend into certain types of clothing and footwear – and even stationery. The generalisation principle can unfortunately also be used by counterfeiters, who, by using certain product attributes or well-known brands' symbols (Lacoste's crocodile or Rolex watch designs), hope to create confusion among consumers – to their advantage.[19] The consequences of product confusion can be dramatic: in the USA, nearly eighty people had to have medical treatment for poisoning because they drank lemon washing-up liquid thinking that it was a specific brand of lemon juice due to almost identical packaging.[20]

The mechanism of **discrimination**, on the other hand, appears when a stimulus resembling the reference stimulus does not provoke the same response. The proliferation of items in many product categories progressively forces consumers to discriminate more and more precisely between the many products offered. In the market for cameras, for example, professionals and keen amateur photographers identify the key characteristics of the products much more quickly than other camera users; the same applies for many food products such as fine wines and cheeses. Within the same product category, consumers thus practice generalisation or discrimination depending upon their degree of involvement. As they are not all involved in the same products, every market has its adherents and its indifferents and can usefully be segmented accordingly.

In general, well-established brands want to distance their customers from alternative choices or imitations and must rely on people's aptitude for discrimination: 'The choice of professionals', 'Persil washes whiter', and so on. Conversely, smaller or budget-price brands have lots to gain by being assimilated by the leader. The principles of generalisation and discrimination are, therefore, omnipresent in managerial decisions made on commercial positioning (as discussed in Chapter 2).

Instrumental conditioning

Instrumental conditioning, also known as operant conditioning, occurs when the individual memorises behaviour which has had positive results and tends to forget behaviour leading to negative consequences. Positive results (called **reinforcement**) can take the form of either rewards or absence of punishment, while negative reinforcement is the exact opposite. These concepts were developed by Skinner,[21] who observed the behaviour of pigeons and discovered that they were more readily attracted to stimuli (coloured drawers) which contained food. Today, instrumental conditioning is widely used for training purposes. It is, for example, the basis on which circus animals are trained to do tricks. In contrast to responses obtained by classical conditioning, which are involuntary and simple, instrumental responses can be quite articulated. Operant conditioning also implies the sequence:

$$\text{Behaviour} >>> \text{reward} >>> \text{learning}$$

which contrasts with the simultaneous nature of classical conditioning. By offering frequent presents to their most loyal clients or by creating (over time) good relations by personalised mailings, many companies practise instrumental conditioning. [22]

In many sectors, it is estimated that the cost of keeping an existing customer is a lot less than the cost of getting a new one. From this has arisen a new kind of marketing known as **relationship marketing**, which aims to induce customer loyalty. Programmes such as KLM Flying Dutchman perfectly illustrate this approach. Members accumulate points for each flight taken, which allow them to have future flights free. They regularly receive personal correspondence which not only updates them on the latest company information (new routes, latest timetables, etc.) but also offers them a whole range of services at preferential rates (car hire, hotels, exhibitions, concert tickets, and so on). Other schemes such as the American Express Membership Rewards Scheme and the Tesco Clubcard use the same principle.[23]

We can also consider free trial programmes or free samples as a form of instrumental conditioning. When a new car is launched, why are people invited to come and try it? Because the manufacturer hopes that the pleasure arising from driving it (positive reinforcement) will contribute to overcoming the resistance to purchase. By reversing the usual purchase followed by consumption sequence, the gratification is immediate; by making the consumption act free of charge, the importance of inhibiting factors is also minimised (no need to spend money). The driver receives a reward for which a minimum of effort has been expended. Of course, it is hoped that such a brand stimulus will be remembered at the appropriate moment – when deciding to buy a new car. In the 1993 campaign for the Volvo 850, the Swedish company thus systematically placed the emphasis on the great pleasure felt during the test drive.

The giving of free samples, very common for consumer products, rests on the same idea. All models developed to predict the adoption rate of a new product place great emphasis on the trial phase,[24] and many studies have shown that those who receive a sample are much more likely to buy the product than those who do not. Also, the rate of repurchase is higher for this group.[25]

Of course, instrumental conditioning also works in a repressive sense. In this case the sequence becomes:

undesirable behaviour >>> punishment >>> learning

or even:

absence of undesirable behaviour >>> absence of punishment >>> learning.

These principles, which are omnipresent in children's education, also lend themselves to commercial applications. Television advertising is thus classed as either positive or negative, depending on whether the products advertised lead to well-being or enable unhappiness to be avoided. The consequences of not buying can be dramatised; for example, to encourage the Belgians to check the mechanical state of their vehicles more regularly, a recent campaign showed examples of a problem occurring with a car that had not been checked over (exhaust pipe falling off, worn shock absorbers causing an accident, etc.).

The frequency and amplitude of reinforcement mechanisms (that is, reward or punishment) and their impact on **shaping** behaviour have been the subject of many studies, given the importance of promotional tactics in the commercial field.[26] All other things being equal, it would seem that:

- When rewards are offered at regular intervals (as in the case of annual sales), the response takes time to get established but is strong later on. We can thus expect better and better public reaction year after year.

- When the rewards are unpredictable (as in the case of a lottery or slot machines), the response is obtained in a very regular manner. Sales personnel who do not know when a manager – sometimes disguised as a 'ghost shopper' – will be on the shop floor tend to harmonise the level of service provided to customers, which is not the case when the times of such visits are known in advance.

- When the rewards are all the same size (amplitude), as when presents are given based on points obtained (cumulative system), the targeted behaviour to be encouraged is regular and repetitive but can disappear quite quickly if the reward is not motivating enough. In many companies, sales staff thus have a tendency to consider bonuses as a right rather than a reward over time. Behaviourists talk about response **extinction**.

- When the amplitude of the reward is variable (games and competitions), once gained, the response fades only progressively since the individual can always hope to obtain a substantial reward each time the desired behaviour is manifest – thus provoking reinforcement.

Cognitive learning

In contrast to behaviourism, cognitive learning theory highlights the internal mental processes of an individual. Learning is thus assimilated into the resolution of a problem based on the information available in the environment. Learning is no longer automatic but becomes a deliberate and creative process which rests on the development of expectations and the evaluation of results.[27] This is the mode of learning that the educational system gradually favours as the child matures. In the case of consumers, cognitive learning is frequently in operation for the purchase of expensive goods or for those being bought for the first time.[28]

Even among behaviourists, it is often admitted that the traditional Pavlovian conditioning model does not explain fully what is happening.[29] Conditioning is not this rather degrading automatic behaviour which consists of developing reflexes in an essentially passive individual. The heart of the mechanism does not lie in obtaining a response, which can depend on situational factors, but in creating a relatively solid and lasting association. Learning becomes a mental process of acquiring new, more refined knowledge from the outside world;[30] and the term 'learning' may appear too narrow to describe what takes the form of a full 'experience'.

For the neo-Pavlovians, the response resulting from conditioning is not just limited to behaviour. It can be completely cognitive and, for example, take the form of the creation of an attitude or an evaluative judgement.[31] Also, the neo-Pavlovians are not satisfied with continuity or frequency of appearance being enough to guarantee conditioning but place emphasis on the need for a deeper relationship. In their experiments they contrast the results obtained by two groups – randomly chosen – to which the two stimuli (conditioned and non-conditioned) are presented with equal frequency. For one group, the order of presentation is determined randomly; for the second, it is systematic. The neo-Pavlovians are thus led to reinterpret many previous results presented as proof of the acquisition of a reflex. Returning to the example of Claudia Schiffer and shampoo, they do not interpret the transfer of good feeling as automatic but as a rich and complex process, bringing into play many symbolic associations linked to haircare and the pleasure attached to good looks – a process which goes much further than the simple presentation of two stimuli.

From a consumer research standpoint, it is difficult to take up a position in favour of either of these approaches. On one hand, it seems that certain things are learned by consumers in quite an automatic way (for example, young children remembering brands, and particularly advertising slogans[32]). It is equally clear that there are mental processes of categorisation which allow us to classify and judge brands and products (and even people) which we do not know about. All that we think we need is a significant cue to trigger a response. For example, the use of thick glossy paper in an estate agent's brochure could be enough for customers to categorise it as top class; the reaction may not be the same if ordinary paper were used. A product's origin, particularly if it comes from the Third World, may also be enough for many people to doubt its quality.[33]

On the other hand, however, learning is much more than an accumulation of personal experience. Another powerful mechanism known as **vicarious learning** also rests on cognitive mechanisms. As indicated previously, vicarious learning consists of observing the behaviour of someone in a particular situation and basing an interpretation on the 'rewards' and 'punishments' subsequently observed. In fact, vicarious learning is partly explained by **social comparison theory**, according to which individuals compare themselves in order to develop their own attitudes and judgements.[34] In reality, the process is complex to the extent that, in many cases, the people observed are not chosen by accident but are selected as models of behaviour (positive or negative) in terms of the specific situation in which those people are found.[35] For example, young girls often develop their ideas about what it is like to be a woman by carefully observing their mothers in traditional feminine roles. Cognitive learning mechanisms based on vicarious processes are often used in commercial practice, particularly in salesforce training. Cognitive learning provides the theoretical foundation for the so-called 'demonstrative approach' to selling, which consists in explaining the different aspects associated with the purchase or the usage of a product with the help of a fictitious or real person.[36]

Whatever its specific mode, learning finally rests on two sequential steps: recognising the repetitive nature of a given environmental situation and remembering what was done in the past in similar circumstances. To understand the latter, we now move on to explain how memory works.

Memory

The process of memorising consists of acquiring and recording information in such a way that it can be retrieved later. Even though we are far from a complete understanding of the memorising process, several theories on the functioning of memory have been developed, often by analogy with the way a computer works. In both cases, information is taken in, processed and stored in a form which makes organisation and access relatively easy – randomly or sequentially.

Analysing the way in which information is stored enables us to understand the way it is represented in the memory. In general, new information which is related to that already held has more chance of being memorised. For example, brand names such as Rich Tea or After Eight are more easily remembered than abstract names, given the products to which they are attached.[37] The same applies to names which have a strong visual aspect (Jaguar cars, Guinness stout). When a piece of information is held in memory, it can be reduced to its sensory components such as a colour or a smell. When it reappears, such a trace is enough to make the whole stimulus with which it was associated reappear. For example, the sight of a luxury brand logo (let us say the Lacoste alligator) can summon up a whole series of memories linked to gifts, some of which may be very old.[38] In the same manner, many people have a preferred colour or number which they keep throughout their lives, because of the many memories which it evokes.

Elements held in memory can take many forms. Certain are completely abstract, for example the formula for calculating the volume of a sphere, while others can be concrete, generally linked to memories of a personal nature. In representing them, certain advertisements may try to recreate these memories, particularly when they relate to happy moments spent as a family or a couple. To make such moments broadly applicable, they are often presented in particularly symbolic places or circumstances (a sunset over a tropical island, a child's first smile, and so on).

Sensory memory is used for immediately recognising external stimuli. It enables us to almost instantaneously recognise the letter A or the shape of a cylinder. These impressions are very short-lived and disappear in a few seconds;[39] an example is the pleasant smell of freshly baked bread which an early morning walker notices coming from the open vent of a bakery. Even though the sensation could be brief, it could be enough to grab the attention and go beyond the frontiers of short-term memory.

Short-term memory serves as a 'holding structure' for temporary stocks of information. As in a computer, it has a limited capacity and is mainly used as workspace. It controls the treatment of current information; hence, short-term memory contains that which you are currently thinking. The main elements are grouped in configurations which enable them to be more easily remembered; for international telephone numbers, for example, the two or three numbers that are the country code are often set apart mentally.

Finally, **long-term memory** corresponds to the 'warehouse' of our knowledge. We refer to it when we speak of our intellectual capacity or our knowledge of cooking or mechanics. It comprises not only stored information (episodic memory) but also the rules which determine its manipulation (semantic memory). Long-term memory is organised according to two principles, almost like a library: the semantic principle and the temporal (also called episodic) principle. First, the **semantic principle**, which can be *ad hoc* or taxonomic (based on classifications), enables an individual to recognise a category of drinks such as beers, and also to distinguish several sub-categories (lager, stout, bitter, low-alcohol, and so on) and finally brands (Heineken, Boddingtons, Guinness, etc.).[40] This classification is based upon the perception of whether the objects evaluated possess the key attributes of the categories: for example, the alcohol content for a beer, the colour for a bitter, etc. The taxonomic structures are thus based on a prototype which, for the majority of people, summarises the relevant characteristics. The prototype serves as a standard for knowing whether or not the product belongs to the category and if it is **typical**.[41] The opportunist mode is at the origin of *ad hoc* structures linked to a specific buying situation and based upon a precise objective such as: 'the things to eat if I want to lose weight'. Following this principle, weight watchers will reject chocolate and cake in favour of water or celery, which is the champion of all dieters as eating celery burns up more calories than it provides. In contrast to taxonomic classification, *ad hoc* classification is not made based upon the nature of the objects but as a function of an ideal to attain (zero calories in this example.).[42] Second, the **temporal principle** keeps a record of the order in which events occurred. It is this principle which enables an individual to tell a story or recall their past. It is an interesting area for study in market research, for example when it concerns finding out whether the decision to buy a brand was taken before or after entering a shop. The temporal principle also enables the individual to anticipate the future and, to a certain degree, to plan it.

While it is attention which assures the transition between sensory and short-term memory, the relationship between the short- and long-term memories is controlled by two processes known as mental rehearsal and elaboration (or coding). **Mental rehearsal** implies a search for significance linked to a stimulus and the establishing of a relationship with information already held in memory.[43] An exercise in geometric calculation, for example the area of a rectangle, activates this mechanism. We must first recognise, with the help of the short-term memory, the regular form of the quadrilateral and the basic parameters – the length and width. We then get, from our long-term memory, the formula for calculating the area. Certain commercial communication, particularly that which is presented as sentences to complete or operations to carry out, rests on this principle. This is the essence of uncompleted slogans such as: 'It takes two hands ... (to handle a Burger King Whopper)'. Those who use this approach expect a better memorisation of the message based upon the mental rehearsal.

Rehearsal consists of recycling information in the memory, a little like when we repeat the licence plate number of our new car so that we do not forget it; **elaboration** (or coding), on the other hand, is a form of cognitive processing which we carry out on the information itself in order to keep it in mind. Thus, in England, people remember the colours of the rainbow by recalling the phrase 'Richard Of York Gave Battle In Vain'. We use such processes when we choose door access codes, or lottery numbers based upon birthdays or dates already memorised. In general, the more elaboration is used, the better the learning will be. This is due to the number of cognitive chains, which, a little like a network of motorway connections, increases the number of access routes.[44] Advertisers capitalise on coding processes by using word play ('You can't fit quicker than a Kwik-Fit fitter'). They can also incorporate into the message well-known elements which facilitate its interpretation.[45]

Not all experts always agree on the idea of a memory consisting of compartments and some think that, depending on the nature of the stimulus, it is one or other part of the memory which is activated.[46] The larger the processing effort the greater the chance that the information will be placed in the long-term memory. This is probably the reason why it often contains memories from our schooldays or those linked to personal events which have greatly affected us (the day our children were born, for example).

The principles governing information **storage** have also been the subject of many controversies. A number of researchers support the idea that units of information are interlinked, like the threads of a spider's web, with nodes and segments of variable length. Certain elements are at the centre of the structure and thus contribute to its definition, while others are at the periphery and may, therefore, be more easily detached. New information is said to find its position based on its relation with the existing structures.[47]

Others are more inclined towards a hierarchical system where the information is first processed at its most basic level and then at more and more abstract levels which 'consume' greater amounts of cognitive energy. When the level of processing does not result in any productive outcome, cognitive activity rapidly shifts towards

Figure 3.2 Mental associations

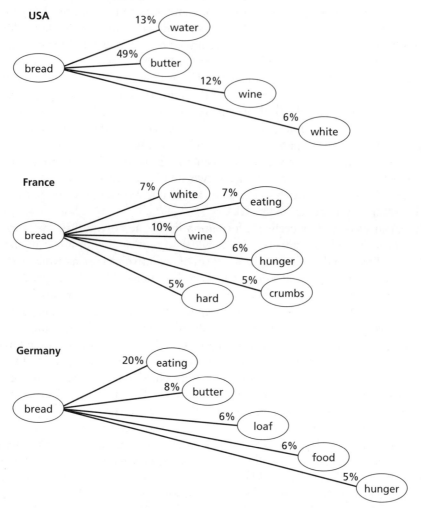

Source: W. Kroeber-Riel, 'Computer Aided Globalization of Advertising by Expert Systems', *European Advances in Consumer Research*, 1993, Vol. 1, pp. 110–17

other elements. Figure 3.2 represents such an associative structure resulting from a study recently carried out on young people's perceptions relating to bread.[48] A sample of a hundred American, German and French students were asked to indicate what they associated with the word 'bread'. The structure represented in Figure 3.2 is the 'average' one, but each individual network of associations can be analysed in the same way. We can see that the concept of bread is very tightly linked with notions such as butter and eating, but there are strong cultural variations. Such graphs reproduce corresponding structures in memory which organise and classify the knowledge and associations linked to a particular notion.

It would thus appear that memory functions along a network of connections, a bit like a railway system. One node is activated and, based upon the set of points which it commands, a whole series of associations follows: this is the experience which many people have when they try to rebuild the steps which have led them from the initial thought to the last idea when they let their mind wander freely. In general, this process travels across different levels of abstraction and alternates between specific memories and less defined ideas. From the perspective of commercial implications, it may be useful to group an individual's memories relating to a particular product into several levels according to:

- the brand and its attributes;
- advertising (message and media);
- the product category (understanding, use);
- evaluative judgements.[49]

A structure of meanings can thus be built up. Meaningful concepts (for example, Gucci and luxury) are linked to each other by propositions (or beliefs). The propositions serve to drive more complex images (for example, 'Gucci makes high-quality handbags for elegant women'). These propositions are then integrated into scenarios which become yet more complex as experience builds up. Many studies have shown that new items of information are much more easily integrated into the memory if they are compatible with existing structures.[50] The ability to go from one level of abstraction to another greatly improves the flexibility and efficiency of the system. It is for this reason that young children only gradually learn to use their intellectual potential.[51]

One kind of scheme which has direct implications for marketing is the **script**, by which we mean a series of behaviours which make up the expectations of an individual. For example, a traveller who visits a hotel or takes a flight has in their head a 'script'; they are expecting someone to show them to their room (or their seat). Consumers often rely on their script to evaluate the service provided and this explains why new automatic services (at the bank or for reserving seats on a train) encounter resistance among certain consumers.[52]

Finally, the ability to retrieve information varies widely from one situation to another. Obviously, at a point in time, a person uses only a very small portion of the amount of information available in their memory. How does information **retrieval** work? First of all, it should be recognised that the ability to retrieve information from memory is greatly affected by age. In general, older people experience a gradual decay in their ability to remember, though certain childhood memories remain present. Other factors are linked to the context in which the information was originally released and stored. The more it was continuous and following a logical progression, the more the information remains accessible. Retrieval also works better when the circumstances in which the information is retrieved from memory resemble the circumstances when it was recorded. For example, certain studies have shown that a student who usually drinks a cup of coffee while studying has a good chance of drinking one just before the exam.[53]

Finally, information retrieval also depends on certain characteristics linked to the stimuli themselves. For example, we have a greater chance of remembering a message the larger its degree of proximity and familiarity.[54] Furthermore, a stimulus which is clearly detached from its environment increases its chance of being easily remembered. Companies can use this phenomenon by accentuating the novelty of a product. This is known as the Von Restorff effect.[55] Also, certain works have shown that we memorise visual elements more easily than verbal ones.[56] This of course has important implications for designing advertising messages.[57]

Conversely, there are many factors which facilitate **forgetting**. Forgetting is an extremely common phenomenon which poses many problems for communicators. A study carried out among 13 000 adults has shown that more than half of them could not remember any written, verbal or television advertising from the previous 30 days.[58] Of course, all memory researchers have long known that memories fade away as time passes.[59] Mathematical curves have even been established to display the speed of forgetting. Another major factor is interference created by new incoming information which 'disturbs' that which is already stored in memory. For example, the associations arising from conditioning diminish if other responses are engendered by identical or similar stimuli. In adding liaisons between existing nodes, new information – particularly if it is inconsistent – decreases the strength of old links.[60] In marketing, this phenomenon helps to understand why brand information deteriorates when the number of messages relating to other brands in the same product category increases. A state of overloading results which is often harmful to brands that are already established.[61]

Finally, when a stimulus is capable of recreating a personal event, even after many years, there often follows a bitter-sweet sentiment known as **nostalgia**. Even if the memories so unearthed are happy ones, a certain sadness comes with them due to their existence in a time which is long gone and often idealised.[62] Past decades become 'the good old days' after the passage of time.

Positive emotions, formed by warm feelings arising from nostalgia, have led many companies to promote it in their commercial messages. Nostalgia provides justification for 'retro' trends and the temptation to recreate the styles and fashions of yesterday. In the field of music, for example, the 1960s have given birth to a series of associations such as style accessories, clothes and hairstyles. There also exists a market for 1950s furniture, such as Formica tables or the large sofas characteristic of the period. Consumer products have even been recreated through a special series or a promotional campaign, an old product, an outdated style or an old logo. Sometimes, an advertisement may show some or all of an old television or radio commercial, which enables companies not only to facilitate the recall of special moments but also to demonstrate their long experience and the authenticity of their know-how. This also applies to durable goods. The success of the film *Rain Man* (which featured a Buick Roadmaster) was such that General Motors reintroduced the model, originally produced between 1936 and 1958.[63] Similarly, Volkswagen has decided to relaunch its famous 'Beetle'. Restaurants and discotheques have also tried to re-establish past times for specific themed evenings or for an old-time atmosphere in general; by using period decoration and furnishings and dressing staff in appropriate costume they hark back to bygone days.

Nostalgia is also at the heart of the market for souvenirs. Today there exist numerous museums, castles, theme parks and so on which have created shops selling all kinds of objects (postcards, T-shirts, keyrings, etc.) to tourists, encouraging them to keep something material after their visit as a memento. Even hotels and restaurants compete in this market by selling bathroom accessories, ashtrays or even silverware.

Given the budgets invested in advertising, companies are of course extremely interested to know what remains in people's minds. As we have already seen, not very much. According to certain studies, less than 7 per cent of television viewers can remember the product advertised in the last commercial break they watched. It would also seem that the proportion diminishes with the endless proliferation of new media.[64]

In order to understand the impact of messages on memory, companies use two main measures: **recall** and **recognition**.[65] In a test of recall, people are simply asked if they can remember advertising recently seen or heard in the media. In the procedure known as day-after recall, viewers are questioned about what they saw the day before. Scores are calculated which are compared with norms established for each product category. In a test of recognition, on the other hand, an advertisement is shown (a page of a magazine for example) to the people being surveyed and they are asked if they remember seeing it. Even if the absolute levels are different, the two methods tend to provide comparable results when they are used in similar conditions.[66] In general, however, recognition tests provide more reliable results because they are less affected by time.[67] Of course, they display higher scores because the information made available during the test is more abundant. The two measures in fact provide different indicators. The results linked to recall seem more significant as the consumer answers questions without any assistance and must rely exclusively on memory. In contrast, recognition is more revealing because faced with a large number of supermarket facings or a large catalogue, the potential buyer has to identify a name or a product. Of course, there are limits to this process because an already well-known stimulus has sometimes less chance of attracting attention, given that we notice it less.[68]

In most European countries, advertising research companies supplement recall and recognition scores with additional information concerning the degree to which a message sent out is recreated and appreciated. A 'proven' score is thus calculated as well as an 'approval' score, which expresses the level of appreciation of the consumer for the advertisement just remembered. The scores obtained are compared with norms established by category of message and also by the level of advertising pressure.

Of course, measures of memorisation only correspond imperfectly to the contents of the memory and several kinds of bias have been identified. For example, certain individuals tend to reply 'yes' irrespective of the question asked. Others see no reason not to keep the enquirer happy and try to guess what is expected of them. Also, some people have a tendency to omit details which may embarrass them, or to generalise by levelling out their perceptions, while still others keep only very imprecise traces in their minds after a time.[69]

Naturally, all these factors contaminate the results, and memory test scores must, therefore, be interpreted with caution. Certain methods can be used to detect biases. For example, asking questions about events which never happened enables the tendency to invent the past to be controlled. Also, the theory of memory **signalling** states that each element of information has a certain 'weight' in the long-term memory; this weight increases with each exposure, starting with the first. Real stimuli as well as distracting elements thus all start with a particular value which changes little by little over time. By comparing results obtained with experimental groups which have been subjected to different treatments, we can to a certain degree ascertain causal attributions.[70]

Finally, it must be pointed out that the memorisation of an advertising message is only one of the elements which facilitates the formation of a favourable predisposition towards purchase. Emotional or evaluative reactions probably count as much as having kept a specific memory of an exposure. Many campaigns, for example that of Benetton, place more emphasis on creating an emotional shock than articulating reasons for purchase. It is not certain that remembering better facilitates the emergence of a preference. If memorisation seems a necessary condition, it is far from being sufficient and other factors contribute to the formation of an attitude. These factors affecting attitudes are examined in Chapter 4.

Notes

[1] R. A. Baron, *Psychology: The Essential Science* (Allyn & Bacon, 1989).

[2] M. Domjan and B. Burkhard, *The Principles of Learning and Behavior* (Brooks, 1986).

[3] K. L. Holyoak, K. Koh and R. E. Nisvett, 'A Theory of Conditioning: Inductive Learning Within Rule-Based Default Hierachies', *Psychological Review*, 1989, 96, pp. 315–40.

[4] S. Hoch and J. Deighton, 'Managing What Consumers Learn', *Journal of Marketing*, April 1989, pp. 1–20.

[5] R. E. Petty and J. T. Cacioppo, *Attitudes and Persuasion: Classic and Contemporary Approaches* (Brown, 1981).

[6] See T. Shimp, 'Neopavlovian Conditioning and its Implications for Consumer Theory and Research', in T. Robertson and H. H. Kassarjian (eds), *Handbook of Consumer Behavior* (Prentice Hall, 1991), Ch. 5, pp. 162–88. Also see G. Foxall, 'Radical Behaviorism and Consumer Research: Theoretical Promise and Empirical Problems', *International Journal of Research in Marketing*, 1987, 2, pp. 111–30, and by the same author, *Consumer Psychology in Behavioral Perspective* (Routledge, 1990).

[7] See T. A. Shimp, E. W. Stuart and R. W. Engle, 'A Program of Classical Conditioning Experiments Testing Variations in the Conditioned Stimulus and Context', *Journal of Consumer Research*, June 1991, pp. 1–12.

[8] F. McSweeney and C. Bierley, 'Recent Developments in Classical Conditioning', *Journal of Consumer Research*, June 1986, pp. 71–84.

[9] P. Davies, G. L. Davies and S. Bennett, 'An Effective Paradigm for Conditioning Visual Perception in Human Subjects', *Perception*, 1982, pp. 183–210.

[10] R. Rescorla, 'Pavlovian Conditioning: It's Not What You Think It Is', *American Psychologist*, March 1988, pp. 151–60.

[11] C. T. Allen and T. A. Madden, 'A Closer Look at Classical Conditioning', *Journal of Consumer Research*, December 1985, pp. 301–15.

[12] G. Gorn, 'The Effects of Music in Advertising on Choice Behavior: A Classical Conditioning Approach', *Journal of Marketing*, Winter 1982, pp. 94–101. For replications of this seminal study, see Allen and Madden *op. cit.*, and J. J. Kellaris and A. D. Cox, 'The Effects of Background Music in Advertising: A Reassessment', *Journal of Consumer Research*, June 1989, pp. 11–118.

[13] T. A. Shimp, E. W. Stuart and R. W. Engle, 'A Program of Classical Conditioning Experiments Testing Variations in the Conditioned Stimulus and Context', *Journal of Consumer Research*, June 1991, pp. 1–12.

[14] R. A. Feinberg, 'Credit Cards as Spending Facilitating Stimuli: A Conditioning Interpretation', *Journal of Consumer Research*, December 1986, pp. 348–56. This study has, however, been criticised on methodological grounds and is often not considered as a true conditioning study. See Shimp, *op. cit.*

[15] H. Krugman, 'Low Recall and High Recognition of Advertising', *Journal of Advertising Research*, 1986, pp. 79–86.

[16] W. Kroeber-Riel, 'Emotional Product Differentiation by Classical Conditioning', *Advances in Consumer Research* (ACR, 1984), pp. 538–43.

[17] C. Bierley, F. McSweeney and R. Vannieuwkerk, 'Classical Conditioning of Preferences for Stimuli', *Journal of Consumer Research*, December 1985, pp. 316–23.

[18] D. Aaker and K. L. Keller, 'Consumer Evaluations of Brand Extensions', *Journal of Marketing*, January 1990, pp. 27–41; and L. Sunde and R. J. Brodie, 'Consumer Evaluations of Brand Extensions: Further Empirical Results', *International Journal of Research in Marketing*, 1992, pp. 47–54.

[19] G. Miaoulis and N. D'Amato, 'Consumer Confusion: Trademark Infringement', *Journal of Marketing*, Spring 1978, pp. 48–55. Also see J. N. Kapferer, 'Stealing Brand Equity', *Marketing and Research Today*, May 1995, pp. 96–103; and from the same author, 'Brand Confusion: Empirical Study of a Legal Concept', *Psychology and Marketing*, September 1995, pp. 551–568.

[20] 'The Lemon Juice that Wasn't', *Newsweek*, 2 August 1982, p. 53.

[21] B. F. Skinner, *Science and Human Behavior* (Macmillan, 1953).

[22] For an application of the principles of instrumental conditioning in marketing, see G. Foxall, 'The Role of Radical Behaviorism in the Explanation of Consumer Choice' in *Advances in Consumer Research* (ACR, 1986) pp. 187–91; J. P. Peter and W. Nord, 'A Clarification and Extension of Operant Conditioning Principles in Marketing', *Journal of Marketing*, Summer 1982, pp. 102–7; W. Nord and J. P. Peter, 'A Behavior Modification Perspective in Marketing', *Journal of Marketing*, Spring 1980, pp. 36–47; and M. Rothschild and W. C. Gaidis, 'Behavioral Learning Theory: Its Relevance to Marketing and Promotions', *Journal of Marketing*, Spring 1981, pp. 70–8.

[23] For other examples see B. Biergel and C. Trosclair, 'Instrumental Learning: Its Application to Customer Satisfaction', *Journal of Consumer Marketing*, Autumn 1985, pp. 23–8, and J. R. Carey *et al.*, 'A Test of Positive Reinforcement of Customers', *Journal of Marketing*, October 1976, pp. 98–100.

[24] For an overall presentation, see G. Lilien *et al.*, *Marketing Models* (Prentice Hall, 1992), Ch. 19.

[25] Insights, *NPD Research*, June 1979–1982.

[26] For a review, see T. Shimp, *op. cit.*

[27] R. J. Meyer, 'The Learning of Multiattribute Judgement Policies', *Journal of Consumer Research*, September 1987, pp. 155–73.

[28] P. Wright and P. Rip, 'Product Class Advertising Effects on First Time Buyers' Decision Strategies', *Journal of Consumer Research*, September 1980, pp. 151–75.

[29] T. Shimp *et al.*, 'A Program of Classical Conditioning Experiments Testing Variations in

the Conditioned Stimulus and Context', *Journal of Consumer Research*, June 1991, pp. 1–12.

30 See J. Alba and J. W. Hutchinson, 'Dimensions of Consumer Expertise', *Journal of Consumer Research*, March 1987, pp. 411–54, and S. Hoch and J. Deighton, 'Managing What Consumers Learn', *Journal of Marketing*, April 1989, pp. 1–20.

31 It can also be attentional. See C. Janiszewski and L. Warlop, 'The Influence of Classical Conditioning Procedures on Subsequent Attention to the Conditioned Brand', *Journal of Consumer Research*, September 1993, pp. 171–89.

32 D. Roedder-John and J. Whitney Jr, 'The Development of Consumer Knowledge in Children: A Cognitive Structure Approach', *Journal of Consumer Research*, March 1986, pp. 406–17.

33 For an analysis of the perception of product origins, see J. Liefeld and M. Wall, 'The Effects of Intrinsic Country of Origin, and Price Cues on Product Evaluation and Choice', *European Advances in Consumer Research*, Vol. 1 (ACR, 1993), pp. 191–8; also see G. Albaum *et al.*, 'Exploring Country of Origin Perceptions by Multidimensional Scaling', *European Advances in Consumer Research*, Vol. 1 (ACR, 1993), pp. 183–90.

34 L. Festinger, 'A Theory of Social Comparison Processes', *Human Relations*, 1954, 7, pp. 117–40.

35 G. R. Goethals, and J. M. Darley, 'Social Comparison Theory: An Attributional Approach', in J. M. Suls and R. L. Miller (eds), *Social Comparison Processes: Theoretical and Empirical Perspectives* (Hemsiphere, 1977).

36 See A. Bandura, *Principles of Behavior Modification*, (Holt, Rinehart & Winston, 1968), and by the same author, 'The Self System in Reciprocal Determinism', *American Psychologist*, April 1978, pp. 344–58.

37 See M. Friestad and E. Thorson, 'Remembering Ads: The Effects of Encoding Strategies, Retrieval Cues, and Emotional Response', *Journal of Consumer Psychology*, 1993, 1, pp. 1–23.

38 K. Robertson, 'Recall and Recognition Effects of Brand Name Imagery', *Psychology and Marketing*, 4, Spring 1987, pp. 3–15.

39 G. Sperling, 'The Information Available in Brief Visual Presentations', *Psychological Monographs*, 1960, p. 74, p. 11.

40 For more on the semantic principles, see the work of Lawrence Barsalou, for example in L. W. Barsalou, 'Ideals, Central Tendency, and Frequency of Instantiation as Determinants of Graded Structure', *Journal of Experimental Psychology: Learning, Memory, and Cognition*, October 1985, pp. 629–54. See also S. Ratneshwar and A. D. Slocker, 'The Application of Prototypes and Categorization Theory in Marketing: Some Problems and Alternative Perspectives', *Advances in Consumer Research*, 1988, pp. 280–5.

41 On the notion of typicality, see B. Loken and J. Ward, 'Alternative Approaches to Understanding the Determinants of Typicality', *Journal of Consumer Research*, September 1990, pp. 111–26; M. Ashcraft, 'Property Norms for Typical and Atypical Items from 17 Categories: A Description and Discussion', *Memory and Cognition*, 1978, pp. 227–32; and P. Nedungadi and J. W. Hutchinson, 'The Prototypicality of Brands', *Advances in Consumer Research* (ACR, 1985), pp. 498–503.

42 L. Barsalou, 'Ad Hoc Categories', *Memory and Cognition*, 1983, pp. 211–32.

43 E. Rosch and B. B. Lloyd, *Cognition and Categorization* (Erlbaum, 1988).

44 T. Childers and M. Houston, 'Conditions for a Picture Superiority Effect on Consumer Memory', *Journal of Consumer Research*, September 1984, pp. 643–54.

45 M. P. Gardner *et al.*, 'Low Involvement Strategies for Processing Advertisements', *Journal of Advertising Research*, 1985, pp. 4–12.

46 See C. A. Cole and M. J. Houston, 'Encoding and Media Effects on Consumer Learning Deficiencies in the Elderly', *Journal of Marketing Research*, February 1987, 24, pp. 55–64.

47 W. A. Henry, 'The Effect of Information-Processing Ability on Processing Accuracy', *Journal of Consumer Research*, June 1980, pp. 42–8.

[48] W. Kroeber-Riel, 'Computer Aided Globalisation of Advertising by Expert Systems', *European Advances in Consumer Research*, 1993, Vol. 1, pp. 110–17.

[49] K. Lane Keller, 'Memory Factors in Advertising: The Effects of Advertising Retrieval Cues on Brand Evaluations', *Journal of Consumer Research*, December 1987, pp. 29–33. Also see G. Biehal and D. Chakravarti, 'Consumers' Use of Memory and External Information in Choice: Macro and Micro Perspectives', *Journal of Consumer Research*, March 1986, 12, pp. 382–405.

[50] S. T. Fiske and S. E. Taylor, *Social Cognition* (Addison Wesley, 1984).

[51] D. Roedder John and J. C. Whitney Jr, 'The Development of Consumer Knowledge in Children: A Cognitive Structure Approach', *Journal of Consumer Research*, March 1986, pp. 406–17.

[52] M. R. Solomon *et al.*, 'A Role Theory Perspective on Dyadic Interactions: The Service Encounter', *Journal of Marketing*, Winter 1985, pp. 99–111.

[53] Baron, *op. cit.*

[54] E. J. Johnson and J. E. Russ, 'Product Familiarity and Learning New Information', *Journal of Consumer Research*, June 1984, pp. 542–50.

[55] J. G. Lynch and T. K. Srull, 'Memory and Attentional Factors in Consumer Choice: Concepts and Research Methods', *Journal of Consumer Research*, June 1982, pp. 18–37.

[56] T. Childers and M. J. Houston, *op. cit.*

[57] T. Childers, S. Heckler and M. Houston, 'Memory for the Visual and Verbal Components of Hint Advertisements', *Psychology and Marketing*, Autumn 1986, pp. 147–50.

[58] R. Burke and T. K. Srull, 'Competitive Interference and Consumer Memory Advertising', *Journal of Consumer Research*, June 1988, pp. 55–68.

[59] G. Jenkins and K. M. Dallenbach, 'Oblivescence during Sleep and Waking', *American Journal of Psychology*, October 1924, pp. 605–12.

[60] J. W. Alba and A. Chattopadhyay, 'Salience Effects in Brand Recall', *Journal of Marketing Research*, November 1986, pp. 363–9.

[61] J. Meyers-Levy, 'The Influence of a Brand Name's Association Set Size and Word Frequency on Brand Memory', *Journal of Consumer Research*, September 1989, pp. 197–208.

[62] H. Baumgartner, M. Sujan and J. R. Bettman, 'Autobiographical Memories, Affect and Consumer Information Processing', *Journal of Consumer Research*, January 1992, pp. 53–82. See also M. Sujan, J. R. Bettman and H. Baumgartner, 'Influencing Consumer Judgments Using Autobiographical Memories: A Self-Referencing Perspective', *Journal of Marketing Research*, November 1993, pp. 422–36.

[63] R. Serafin, 'Roadmaster Re-Enters Buick Fleet', *Advertising Age*, 10 September 1990, p. 28.

[64] 'Terminal Television', *American Demographics*, January 1987, p. 15.

[65] C. A. Cole, 'Forced-Choice Recognition Tests: A Critical Review', *Journal of Advertising*, 1985, pp. 52–8.

[66] A. Finn, 'Print Ad Recognition Readership Scores: An Information Processing Perspective', *Journal of Marketing Research*, May 1988, pp. 168–77.

[67] R. Bagozzi and J. A. Silk, 'Recall, Recognition and the Measurement of Memory for Print Advertisements', *Marketing Science*, 1983, pp. 95–134.

[68] M. A. de Turck and M. Goldhaber, 'Effectiveness of Product Warning Labels: Effects of Consumers' Information Processing Objectives', *Journal of Advertising Research*, March 1989, pp. 111–25.

[69] W. A. Cook, 'Telescoping and Memory's Other Tricks', *Journal of Advertising Research*, February–March 1987, pp. 5–8.

[70] See S. N. Singh and G. A. Churchill Jr, 'Response-Bias-Free Recognition Tests to Measure Advertising Research, *Journal of Advertising Research*, June–July 1987, pp. 23–6. A. Tastichian *et al.*, 'Signal Detection Analysis and Advertising Recognition: An Introduction to Measurement and Interpretation Issues', *Journal of Marketing*, November 1988, pp. 397–405.

4

Attitudes and preferences

Learning objectives

After reading this chapter, you should understand:

1 the two related concepts of attitude and preference as well as the reasons why they play a central role in consumer behaviour analysis;

2 the interrelationships between the cognitive, affective and conative elements of an attitude;

3 how a number of multi-attribute models have been used to measure and predict attitudes and behaviour;

4 why preferences are not always a good predictor of behaviour;

5 how the process of communication works;

6 how attitudes change over time, often under the influence of persuasive communications;

7 which elements increase the effectiveness of a communication strategy.

Key words

attitude	value–expectancy models	persuasion
preference	conjunctive model	self-perception theory
cognitive component	disjunctive model	uses and gratifications
image	lexicographic model	theory
affective component	communication	theory of social
conative component	source	judgement
consistency	message	psychological reactance
emotions	media	elaboration likelihood
moods	audience	model
multi-attribute models	feedback	sleeper effect

A mong the various factors advanced to explain purchasing behaviour, attitudes and preferences indisputably occupy a central position. Studies dedicated to them, in both the social sciences and commercial research, are numerous. A brief look back at the three previous chapters will help explain why.

In Chapter 1 – dedicated to motivation, involvement and personality – the role of individual needs and interests in the emergence of a pattern of behaviour was emphasised. At the same time it has been pointed out that an approach based on the identification of an individual's internal motives could not possibly account for all the reasons for a purchase. If most consumers get deeply involved before acquiring a product that they consider essential (a flat, a second home, a family holiday), the purchase of a less important item (a packet of chewing gum bought at the supermarket checkout, a pack of cigarettes, a newspaper) seldom obliges them to resolve an acute conflict of contradictory motives. In such a case, the elements characterising the purchasing environment (presentation of products on shelves, displays, special offers) may also account for consumers' choices. The mechanisms mediating perception and habits, as detailed in Chapters 2 and 3, obviously also play a significant role. When stocking up on sugar, salt or tea, many shoppers are most likely to place either the first product to hand or the one they normally buy in their trolley; in the first case, perceptual factors will predominate, while learning will account for the second.

However, in a majority of cases, the purchasing act is a combined result of internal psychological processes and exposure to external stimuli. The complementary explanatory power provided by notions such as motivation, perception and previous experience suggests that they may be integrated within the framework of more 'global' concepts such as attitudes and preferences.

The question of attitude has formed the basis of so many discussions that psychologists such as Allport, Thomas and Znaniecki have made it the focal point of their work.[1] Normally an attitude describes how the body is positioned or inclined, or, in a figurative sense, a manifestation of one's frame of mind or intentions. Thus, for example, one may speak of a deferential or a disrespectful attitude. In consumer research, the term is not used any differently; following the psychologists' approach,[2] one defines the **attitude** to a product or a brand as an enduring inclination or tendency to respond towards the said product or brand in a specific way.[3] The concept of **preference** expresses the same idea when two or more objects are concerned. Thus a consumer will prefer, say, Lux to Imperial Leather if his or her attitude to the first brand is more favourable than to the second.

Although many theories and measurement methods regarding attitudes and preferences have been developed, a majority of researchers consider today that an attitude is structured around three components: cognitive, affective and conative.[4] The **cognitive component** includes the knowledge, beliefs and associations held regarding the object. So the attitude of a consumer in relation to UNICEF, for example, will be based upon what he or she already knows or believes about UNICEF: it is a non-profit association, it is international, it is dedicated to the improvement of children's well-being, etc. As already explained in Chapter 2, the constellation of these impressions is referred to as the consumer's **image** of UNICEF. The **affective component** corresponds to the evaluation of the image profile. It incorporates the positive or negative feelings experienced as well as the emotions involved: is UNICEF useful or useless, professional or disorganised in its operations, honest or dishonest in its management of funds, etc.? Finally, the **conative component** is linked to behavioural intentions: do people want to give money to UNICEF, attend a conference, buy some greetings cards? In commercial research, a detailed knowledge of purchasing intentions towards a product or service takes on considerable importance in view of its implications for sales forecasting. The same goes for 'political marketing', and a proliferation of opinion polls on voting intentions is regularly observed prior to election times.

Setting out the components of an attitude helps one to understand how it integrates motivation, perception and consumer experience. The cognitive dimension relies directly on perceptions 'blended' with memory, and while evaluation operates according to criteria expressing needs and motivations, intentions correspond to the resulting propensity to act: 'I am going to buy UNICEF Christmas cards because I feel it is a valuable organisation, given what I know'. In their definition, Krech and Crutchfield summarise an attitude as follows: 'the lasting organisation of the motivational, emotional, perceptive and cognitive processes with regard to a particular aspect of the individual's world'.[5]

Beliefs, emotions and actions

The cognitive component of attitude has already been extensively discussed in Chapter 2. We will not return to it here except to mention results obtained on the relationships connecting the various perceptions of an object. On the whole, the findings converge and point to a marked **consistency** of global images.[6] When we think of a product or a brand, we tend to regard it as a structured, ordered entity, and often as something more homogeneous than it really is. For example, research done on attitudes towards gold jewellery items reveals that they are strongly influenced by the great value attached to gold itself, which bears strong symbolic and emotive connotations. It follows that consumers systematically overestimate the price of individual pieces of jewellery, for example estimating at £500 a gold bracelet priced at £300. Such a discrepancy presents both a commercial obstacle and an opportunity – an obstacle because it distances a group of potential customers who think, perhaps wrongly, that they cannot afford such jewellery, and an opportunity because when a customer comes to make the purchase, an astute jeweller can take advantage of a situation where the products on offer appear to be 'less expensive than I thought'.

The different perceived attributes of an object are thus linked to one another by a subtle network of inferences. All car manufacturers know that a large number of drivers assess the solidity of a car that they are not familiar with on the basis of the sound of the door closing. Similarly, the movement of the brake pedal is often used as an 'indicator' of braking power. Some years ago a study showed that consumers had rejected a new silent mixer because they judged it to be less powerful than the noisy appliances which they were used to.[7] Consumers' insistence on coherent images explains such phenomena. In many purchasing situations we cannot evaluate all the characteristics of a product. Therefore we choose indicators which, once identified, lead us to form broadly based judgements. In other words, we operate by selective sampling.

Different aspects of a product may carry connotations which have a distant relation to reality. When ice-blue is used in the packaging of frozen fish dishes, for example, the objective is to convey the idea of freshness; similarly, orange or red labels are often used to suggest the strength of an instant coffee.

As we have already seen in the jewellery example, inferential processes also underlie the price–quality relationship.[8] In general consumers associate, rightly or wrongly, higher prices with higher quality. The Joy perfume from Jean Patou would perhaps be held in lower esteem if it were not positioned as 'the most expensive perfume in the world! However, the strength of the perceived price–quality relationship varies according to the nature of the product and the type of consumer. Overall, it is more pronounced in three situations:

1 when the consumer has very little information on the product, in which case the price serves as a departure point for evaluation;

2 when the consumer considers him or herself incapable of making a judgement, although at the same time acknowledging that there are differences in quality between the products offered;[9] or

3 when the quality is difficult to estimate before purchase, as in the case of many services.[10]

Conversely, when the differences are visible (carpets, rugs) or the consumers are experienced (everyday food products), the price is less often used as an indication of quality.[11]

In the tri-component theory of attitude structure, the **affective component** is usually presented after the cognitive component, which would tend to indicate that feeling always follows knowledge. In fact, many attitudes develop in this way: we like so-and-so because we know him to be intelligent; we dislike someone else because her beliefs are opposed to ours. However, such a process is not automatic and the affective evaluation of an object or an individual can take place *before* the acquisition of information concerning him or her. In this case, knowledge appears to justify rather than determine choice: here we consider so-and-so intelligent *because* we like him (and not the reverse). More recently, several researchers have developed a hypothesis according to which affect and cognition are unrelated systems which may be activated independently from each other.[12] Feelings could then emerge without prior cognitions. Experiments have even demonstrated the existence of a mere 'exposure effect': both humans and animals miss an object which

111

they have grown to love simply because it was a familiar part of their environment. The mere fact that they saw it regularly was enough to create an attachment, irrespective of any other reason which might justify this sentiment.[13] Moreland and Zajonc, for example, have shown that when subjects are exposed to Chinese ideograms, which have no particular significance to them, they will express a preference for those which they have already seen, *even if they do not recognise them*.[14] Zajonc also refers to another experiment where a group of consumers were asked to test headphones:[15] some had to simulate a jogging movement and so nodded their heads; others were asked to imagine a bicycle ride and so moved their heads from side to side. Although the music played through the headphones was the same, those who nodded their heads found the experience more enjoyable and judged the headphones more favourably. According to Zajonc, the simple action of nodding the head – a sign of agreement – was enough to induce a favourable attitude.[16]

Generally speaking, it seems that **emotions**, sentiments and feelings exert a strong influence on the purchase and consumption of goods and services.[17] In the case of jewellery, for example, consumers often remember 'heart-stopping' purchases where, passing by a jewellery shop, they felt an 'irresistible' need to go in and buy themselves a 'special treat'. Estate agents are well aware that couples will not always buy a house because it corresponds exactly to their (long) list of requirements, but because they experience 'love at first sight' when viewing it for the first time. Similarly, in the United States, the rejection of new, improved Coke and the demand for a return to old-style Coke is not best explained by taste preferences but by an emotional attachment to the values symbolised by the old-style 'classic' Coke.[18]

By showing a black woman breastfeeding a white child, Benetton is not merely addressing our intellect, but something more fundamental: it is not trying to elicit a favourable comparison of the brand (I prefer Benetton pullovers because …) but to provoke an 'associative punch' induced by a strong, easy to remember image. The same principle underlies all companies' attempts to associate their brands with universal values such as beauty, love or friendship; by using puppies Andrex, for example, immediately conveys tenderness.

Attempts at understanding the role of emotions in the formation of attitudes are often faced with difficult methodological problems: how can one measure a feeling or mood with precision? There are physiological processes associated with strong emotions (changes in sweating, for example), but the available types of apparatus to measure them, such as the skin galvanometer, are hardly practical to use on consumers.[19] Furthermore, experimental procedures which seek to induce either a good or bad feeling in the consumer (for example, congratulating them or criticising their lack of expertise in a game of skill) can be misleading: factors other than emotions (self-confidence, for example) may come into play at the same time. To assess emotional states, it therefore seems preferable to rely on 'natural' situations.[20] However, new marketing research tools are constantly being developed. For example, two American researchers a number of years ago proposed the 'warmth monitor', an instrument which, like the encephalograph, draws the curve of emotions experienced by a consumer (directly transcribed by him or her by a pen revolving on a drum) as they watch advertisements.[21] It is also possible to ask consumers to describe their emotional state with the help of instruments such as the PAD (pleasure–arousal–dominance) scale developed by psychologists; but, of course, self-reported emotions may not correspond exactly to the ones experienced in real situations.[22]

In fact, it is because they give us reasons to choose that emotions play such an important role in purchasing. By associating images, music or strong symbols, emotional advertising seeks to make us *like* the brand so that we end up buying it. As time passes, it becomes our 'favourite' brand and the affective padding which we wrap it up in protects it against eventual switching. The process fuels itself because, except in the case of a disappointing result, the good performance associated with the brand reassures us of the soundness of our choice and makes us like it all the more.

In a related area, research carried out on **moods** has also generated interesting conclusions.[23] For example, it has been shown that a consumer who is in a good mood:

1 follows instructions (the waiter's recommendation, the shopkeeper's advice) more readily;
2 takes on shopping-related tasks more willingly (for example, packing their own shopping bags or seeing to the installation of an electrical appliance themselves);
3 is more favourable to appeals to generosity (giving to charities and national causes for example); and finally
4 being in a good mood facilitates the purchasing act itself if it is immediate (telephone ordering or on-line shopping in the case of a direct marketing operation) and has a clearly identifiable positive effect (for example, the purchase of fittings to make the home more comfortable).

For companies, there are many ways to put consumers in a good mood. In the shop, decor and atmosphere can be improved (by music and elegant design, for example), access can be made easier (by store guides and clear instructions), and staff can be trained to handle different customer moods (a discipline known as 'mood management' in the USA). For example, many department stores have discovered that Christmas sales go up when Christmas carols are played in-store.[24] As for advertising, some studies have shown that it is better received if it is inserted into programmes which engender a good mood (sitcoms, comedy shows) or feature characters who themselves generate good humour (for example, Mr Bean in Europe). One might even wonder if it might not be appropriate to vary the cost of TV slots depending on whether they appear before or after the endless catalogue of catastrophes which currently characterise the daily news.[25]

The **conative component**, finally, corresponds to various behavioural drives associated with a specific attitude. Somebody who has a very positive attitude towards a particular political party will often want to become a member of it, to participate in its demonstrations and subscribe to its magazines. In marketing, it is primarily the **purchasing intention** which is deemed important, given the possibilities which it opens up as regards sales forecasts (and therefore production rationalisation, reduction of stock and better financial management).

Normally, a consumer will tend to buy the products or brands his or her attitudes are most favourable towards, and there is a logical link between the brand's preference score and its share in the purchases.[26] However, as we see below, the ability to predict behaviour from attitudinal data is far from perfect. Numerous commercial studies on product and brand attitude seek to identify consumers' purchasing intentions. For example, in tests carried out on new products, it is usual to ask:

'Which of the following phrases best describes how you feel about the product?'
- I would definitely buy it   1
- I would probably buy it   2
- I don't know whether I would buy it or not   3
- I would probably not buy it   4
- I would definitely not buy it   5

Answers given to such questions help to estimate the acceptance level that the new product or brand will receive. Marketing research companies that regularly conduct this sort of study, such as the Burke Institute in Europe, have generated norms which they use to evaluate with more or less accuracy (+ or − 20 per cent according to Burke) the probability of success of a new product.[27] For example, a food product with a score of less than 50 per cent in the 'definitely' category is usually not considered worth launching. In international studies, results are often adjusted to take into account cultural differences in expressing intentions.[28] It is rare for Japanese consumers, for example, to use the two extreme response categories (1 and 5) as this would be inappropriate in view of their tradition of moderation. In Japan, more weight would therefore be given to the 'probably' response than in an American survey, where opinions are expressed more openly.

Today, investigating purchasing intentions allows economists to anticipate consumer trends; for example, in France it is from the surveys carried out three times per year in 7500 households that INSEE, the National Statistics Institute, draws up its economic forecasts for a variety of sectors. However, it is not necessarily true that actual behaviour will correspond to reported intentions. According to INSEE, only 16 per cent of households that intended to buy a dishwasher had realised their intention a year later.[29] Percentages observed for other durable goods (washing machines 23, refrigerators 17, freezers 15 and televisions 27) are in the same range. The score is somewhat higher for cars (45 per cent) but still remains under the threshold of 50 per cent. Even more sophisticated indicators of purchasing desire such as 'consumer sentiment', an index of American origin which integrates different methods of determining buyers' intentions (through questions like 'Do you expect your situation to improve, deteriorate or remain the same in the next few years?'), fail to obtain better results.[30]

Many factors can intervene to undo the connections between intention and purchase.[31] In Europe, there are many drivers who prefer Ferrari to all other makes of car, but only a few hundred cars are sold every year. In other cases, products may not be available when they are within financial reach. Social environment may also restrict purchasing trends; children, whose parents sometimes object to their desire for treats and games, know this only too well. Knowing how a 'significant other' will feel about a purchase may be more important in determining behaviour than the decision maker's own preferences.[32] The role played by the immediate social environment is discussed at length in Chapter 5. Finally, an individual may modify, change or abandon his or her decision on consideration of the risks it might involve.[33] For example, a woman might decide not to go through with cosmetic surgery because of the risks associated with surgical procedures; in other cases, the perceived risks might be primarily financial (stocks and shares) or social (*avant-garde* fashion or furniture).

Generally speaking, it seems that purchasing intentions are most strictly adhered to when:

1 the time lag between intention and final decision is short;
2 the nature of the decision makes it less dependent on external influences or events;[34] and
3 it involves durable goods, in which consumers usually invest more financially and emotionally (household fittings, holidays, etc.).[35]

The structure of attitudes

The breaking down of an attitude into cognitive, affective and conative components makes both its nature and its structure easily understandable. It has long been observed that both consumer attitudes and preferences are primarily structured on the basis of criteria used by consumers to categorise the endless supply of items on offer, as well as the various images of rival options. It is therefore important to understand the links which unite the former to the latter in the formation of preferences. Studies carried out on this subject have given rise to the concept of **multi-attribute models**.[36] This is illustrated by the following example.

Mrs Miller has decided to buy a dishwasher with twelve settings and has limited her choice to four brands: Bauknecht, Whirlpool, Miele and Zanussi. She has decided to take four criteria into account: price attractiveness, design, level of water and electricity consumption, and quality of after-sales service. The impressions she has of the four brands on each of these criteria are shown in Table 4.1. All scores appear in the form of marks out of 10 (10 corresponds to maximum satisfaction). So Mrs Miller judges the Bauknecht to be high (7/10) on the price and design scales, average in after-sales service but rather inadequate from the point of view of water and electricity consumption. The other brands are compared according to the same system. Mrs Miller has also expressed the relative importance she

Table 4.1 The purchase of a dishwasher

Brand	Price attractiveness	Design	Consumption	After-sales service
Bauknecht	7	7	3	5
Whirlpool	5	8	4	5
Miele	2	9	7	5
Zanussi	7	2	3	6
Importance	9	2	3	6
Minimum	5	7	3	5

attaches to each attribute as well as the minimum level required using the same numerical system. What, then, can one conclude from the information in Table 4.1, and, most importantly, how might one predict Mrs Miller's preferred brand? This will depend on the hypothesis used. If we assume that Mrs Miller is working by a process of compensation – that is, she accepts that a low score on one attribute can be 'compensated for' by a better score on another – she will choose the brand whose total score is the highest; here it is Miele with 28 points, well ahead of Whirlpool and Bauknecht (22 points). However, such a system assumes that all attributes carry the same weight, something which we know to be incorrect. If one were to incorporate the importance scores as weights, Mrs Miller's results would alter: now Bauknecht with 109 points would be in the lead, followed by Zanussi (104) and Miele (103).

These two models (or hypotheses) are known as linear additive models or **value–expectancy** models. Used extensively in commercial research because of their simplicity and their diagnostic power, they were first developed in social psychology, notably under the influence of researchers such as Rosenberg and Fishbein.[37]

Following Katz's theory,[38] which claims that the individual forms his or her propensity towards a certain object according to the functions (for example self-enhancement or some other value-expressive function[39]) he or she expects it to fulfil, Rosenberg has developed a simple model explaining the formation of attitudes. Rosenberg's model, expressed symbolically, is:

$$A_o = \sum_{i=1}^{n} I_i V_i$$

where:

A_o = attitudes towards object o

$\sum$ = sum of

I_i = 'perceived instrumentality', that is, the perceived capacity of the object to procure a value expressing a desirable result

V_i = importance of this value for the individual

n = number of 'values' or desirable qualities.

In a commercial context, this model indicates that a consumer will buy an Electrolux vacuum cleaner rather than a Miele if he or she thinks that the most important requirement in view of their purchasing values (efficient cleaning, safe use, improved self-image) will be better fulfilled (that is, made instrumental) with Electrolux rather than Miele. *Value* is here the desired result – that is, impeccable cleaning – while *instrumentality* corresponds to the consumer's expectations with regard to the vacuum cleaner's cleaning capacity. If the Electrolux cleans better than the Miele, it will benefit from a partial preference on the part of the consumer. The final judgement will be made once all the purchasing criteria (values) have been taken into account. A product will obtain higher scores if it corresponds to the consumer's expectations in terms of the criteria expressing his or her values. Hence the generic term of this class of models: value–expectancy models. In fact, Rosenberg's functionalist approach is very similar to the Lancaster model (discussed in Chapter 2), which holds that products are bought more for the benefits they bring than for their intrinsic characteristics. In practice, this model has allowed the prediction of consumer choice in many domains such as modes of transport, restaurants or even choice of dishes on a restaurant menu.[40]

In his early writings, Fishbein adopts the same theory, but with a slightly different approach. He maintains that attitudes towards objects can be explained by knowledge of the object's attributes and by the value attached to each attribute (its more or less desirable nature).[41] Symbolically, Fishbein's formula is the same as Rosenberg's:

$$A_o = \sum_{i=1}^{n} B_i V_i$$

with the following key:

B_i = strength of the perceived relationship between attribute i and object o (that is, the probability that the object possesses the attribute)
A_i = value of attribute i

For example, if I like sports cars and I think the new Alfa Romeo is a particularly sporty model, my attraction to this model will grow. Note that two conditions must be fulfilled: the performance of the product according to given criteria and the attraction of these criteria for the consumer.

The value–expectancy model has had a considerable influence on commercial research by providing a simple and yet operational method of diagnosing the image problems met by products, brands and even corporations.[42] For example, the aim of a study carried out for the Centre National d'Études Spatiales (the French equivalent of NASA) was to discover the attitudes of the French towards space and national space politics.[43] The approach chosen was the following: the average French citizen's attitude towards space research would be favourable to the extent it would be perceived as a contribution to the problems he or she considered important. Questions were therefore put to a representative cross-section of the

Table 4.2 Expectations regarding space activities

Domain	% People feeling that a given domain is very important	% People feeling that a given domain will benefit a lot from space research
Medicine	88.2	11.9
Pollution control	81.7	9.6
New sources of energy	80.4	15.0
Agriculture	65.4	7.7
Petrol research	61.7	8.3
Mines	58.4	6.8
Telecommunications	50.6	16.0
Metallurgy	47.2	5.0
Aid to developing countries	36.6	3.8
Meteorology	46.0	19.7
Navigation	45.5	10.7
Atomic research	38.4	12.0
Computers	31.0	10.7
Military defence	29.5	12.8
Astronomy	27.0	23.9
Television	21.2	13.3
Photography	14.1	7.6

population about which areas they believed to be most important and what contribution space research might make. The results are shown in Table 4.2. According to these results, it appears that space and space research are not of major importance to the French. Other areas interest them more, a conclusion which confirms opinions expressed during the qualitative part of the study:

'I wouldn't give priority to spending money on space research when there are people dying of hunger and people who are ill. I'd give priority to medical research.' (Office worker, 30)

'I think the most important research is on biology and health ... they're the most important things as far as I'm concerned ... space research definitely comes second.' (Student, 22)

How can these findings be explained? By combining the results of the two parts of Table 4.2 (which is exactly what the value–expectancy model does), the matrix reproduced in Figure 4.1 is obtained. All becomes clear. Attitudes towards space are not very favourable because:

1 the areas in which space research is making progress are, with the exception of new energy sources, of little interest to the public;

2 the contribution of space to important subject areas (medicine and agriculture, for example) is not perceived as significant.

Such information was used by the CNES to shape its public relations policy and, most importantly, the nature of the information it makes available to the public during the bi-annual Le Bourget international aeronautics show. More generally,

Figure 4.1   A value–expectancy matrix

Perceived importance of domain

		Strong	Weak
Perceived impact of space research	Strong	New sources of energy	Telecommunications, TV, navigation, meteorology, atomic research, defence, astronomy
	Weak	Medicine, petrol, agriculture, pollution, mines	Aid to development, computers, photography, metallurgy

there are five ways in which a company can improve its image:

1 by strengthening its favourable perceived relationship with a desirable attribute;
2 by reinforcing the perceived importance of an attribute on which it is favourably positioned;
3 by improving its position on a top-priority attribute;
4 by influencing negatively competitive perceptions; or
5 by adding a new attribute on which it could develop a sustainable competitive advantage.

Although it seems logical – and has been used to explain the choice of products as diverse as toothpaste, lipstick, toilet paper, concentrated orange juice and bras,[44] – the value–expectancy model has a number of limitations. First, it assumes a thorough knowledge of the choice criteria (attributes) used by consumers. In the dishwasher example, the factors taken into account were the price attractiveness, the design of the appliance, its consumption level and the perception of after-sales service. Other criteria, for example the length of guarantee or the dishwasher dimensions, which may also have played a part in the choice, were ignored. Consumers are not always conscious of their choice criteria or may not want to reveal them, for example if they think they might be damaging or shameful – some surveys have revealed that it is the interviews in *Playboy* which are considered the most interesting features of the magazine!

Furthermore, the value–expectancy model assumes that the consumer attaches value to any improvement of every attribute considered. For example, preference

119

for a product is expected to grow as its price decreases. It does not necessarily work like this all the time: a lower price will sometimes be interpreted as an indicator of poorer quality, a stock that must be disposed of or an out-of-date item. Similarly, certain drivers may prefer a small car to a large one, especially where they antici- pate parking or manoeuvrability difficulties. Finally, the value–expectancy model makes it necessary to assess the relative importance of these factors. As we have seen in Chapter 2, such information is difficult to obtain. To overcome some of these problems, the incorporation of 'an ideal position' on every attribute (to be defined by the consumers themselves) has been proposed, as has the measurement of preferences in terms of deviation from this ideal. The value–expectancy model then appears as follows:

$$A_O = \sum_{i=1}^{n} \mid I_i - A_i \mid B_i$$

where A_O, A_i and B_i are defined as above, and I_i represents the ideal position of attribute i, for example the ideal size (for a garment) or temperature (for a drink like tea taken either hot or iced but rarely lukewarm)

Obviously, not all consumers will state the same ideal position and it is, in fact, very useful for a company to segment its customers according to their ideal expecta- tions.[45] The toothpaste market thus comprises many brands, each one aimed at a particular benefit: protection against gum disease (Mentadent), the fight against decay (Colgate), fresh breath (Aquafresh), etc.

The ideal-profile model assumes that consumers have a precise idea of what they would like to have, which is only true for products they know relatively well and in which they are involved. However, the information it contains is more detailed, and therefore the model is often found to be a better indicator of preferences.[46] It proved superior to the original Fishbein model in predicting students' preferences for business schools, for example.[47]

Is it true to say, then, that value–expectancy models, especially when enriched with the ideal profile, always predict consumer preferences? Of course not. In reality it largely depends on the assumptions made, based on underlying psychological prin- ciples. The models examined so far all assume a **compensatory** choice process where, just as school exam results depend on a number of coefficients giving weight to the various disciplines, a brand's weakness in one area can be compensated for by strength in another. Do consumers always judge brands or products like this?

In certain cases, for example with hi-fi systems or electrical goods, it seems that **thresholds** which must not be exceeded are used. These thresholds, for example budgetary limits, do not have compensatory safeguards; a product which does not pass the threshold will not be able to redeem itself by its other qualities. In our example, Mrs Miller has already indicated her thresholds for each of the selected attributes (5/10 for price, 7/10 for attractiveness, etc.; see Table 4.1). By applying them – that is, by eliminating all the brands which fail to reach them – she would limit her choice; she would no longer prefer Miele (too expensive) or Zanussi (not attractive enough) but would opt for Bauknecht or Whirlpool. It is worth noting that the 'threshold' model, also known as the **conjunctive** model, does not necessarily designate an outright winner but simply isolates the brands which fulfil all the requirements. A complete rank ordering requires the formulation of additional hypotheses. The conjunctive model seems appropriate in situations where consumers hesitate between several brands which are all deemed acceptable, after rejecting others which are not. Studies carried out on choice of video recorders, washing machines and lawnmowers tend to support the threshold model.[48]

The conjunctive model is also used implicitly in the comparative tests carried out in Consumers' Association magazines. Usually, the recommended purchase is one which fulfils all the requirements. It is important to note that the model does not take the performance of the brand beyond the required threshold into consideration, and that it is non-compensatory. It may be that a consumer will reject all brands held up for consideration because of a threshold relating to higher demands. In this case the model predicts that the consumer will not make any purchase (or at least postpone it), as no brand has yet proved satisfactory.

Another model, related to the conjunctive model but less widely used, is the **disjunctive** model. It assumes that the consumer chooses products because of their superiority in one *or* other of different criteria. This is perhaps the method that a coach would use to choose his football team: to be one of the members, you need to be either an excellent attacker *or* an excellent defender (but not necessarily both, as is required in the conjunctive model). This model is not compensatory either as it eliminates, with no second chances, all the players who are neither one nor the other. In the commercial world, the disjunctive model can explain buyers' hesitations when it comes to choosing holidays (the seaside or the mountains?) or property (a flat in the centre of town or a house in the suburbs?).

Like the conjunctive model, the disjunctive model does not, in general, lead to a conclusive classification. This is not the case for the **lexicographic** model, the final model to be discussed here. The lexicographic model takes its name from the structured manner, comparable to the ordering of a dictionary, in which it places products in a hierarchy. According to this model, the product which obtains the highest score on the most important attribute wins the competition. If all scores are equal, the second most important attribute is considered – and so on until a complete classification is obtained. In Mrs Miller' case, the following would constitute her preference order: (a) Bauknecht (due to its superiority over Zanussi with regard to consumption); (b) Zanussi; (c) Whirlpool and (d) Miele. The lexicographic model is particularly appropriate when one attribute dominates all the others in the eyes of the consumer. Because many discount shops (Argos for jewellery, Food Giant for groceries, or PC World for electrical goods) estimate that the price (or the percentage of discount) is the only aspect that really captures consumers' attention, they direct their advertising almost exclusively to this issue.

Given the number of alternative models available, it would be natural to ask which is the most effective: the value–expectancy, conjunctive, disjunctive or lexicographic model? This question, far from being confined to marketing researchers' interests, has many concrete implications, notably in the field of communication.[49] In advertising, for example, two questions often recur in the development of a campaign: how many themes to include and how strongly should the themes be emphasised? Some claim that it is better to emphasise a single theme, especially if the brand has a clear advantage there. This is the essence of USP (unique selling proposition) theory. Others reckon that by playing on several themes one 'reaps more reward'. The debate surrounding the force of the arguments to be presented is no less controversial. Some maintain that you must drive the point home as forcibly as possible (for example, through heavy message repetition in the media), while others say that by presenting both the product's advantages and limitations more credibility is gained.

The nature of the choice model assumed to be used by the audience determines the appropriate mode of communication. For a 'lexicographic' consumer, only the most important attribute counts and any deficit in the brand performance on this attribute is enough to make a difference. A USP approach administered with as much strength as possible (within of course the confines of the law and the reality of the product) is therefore justified: here the technological superiority of the product or its price might be the element most fêted. A 'compensatory' consumer on the other hand is better suited to a more balanced advertising campaign which presents a variety of arguments; estate agents' commercial arguments (discussing location, aspect, area, price, etc.) are based upon this method. Faced with a 'conjunctive' audience there is no need to go beyond the required thresholds, especially when many criteria are considered. An advertisement which shows the product attaining the expected levels is, in theory, sufficient; exaggerated claims are not necessary and could result in a loss of credibility. To summarise, the number of arguments to be presented in an advert as well as their strength depends upon assumptions made about information-processing modes used by the audience.

More generally, understanding the choice models used by consumers helps brand managers to decide about the best positioning strategy for their brands. If, for example, it has been established that consumers are operating in a compensatory manner, it becomes possible either to reinforce emphasis on an important dimension (improvement strategy), to highlight an advantage which is already strong (differentiation strategy), or even to add a new attribute (as in mature products).

Studies which empirically compare the performance of different multi-attribute models abound.[50] In general, they focus on the predictive power attached to each type of model in one or more product categories. On the basis of the results obtained, one has to admit that a single superior model does not exist that would work whatever the circumstances; each model is more or less appropriate depending upon the situation encountered. The fewer the number of options under consideration, the more effective is the value–expectancy model. Conversely, non-compensatory models perform better when the number of products or brands available is very high and the consumer wishes to use a preliminary screening process before turning his or her attention to the most interesting ones. Sometimes, more than one model will be needed to explain the final choice made by a consumer. Lindon, in an empirical analysis of the electoral process, concludes that, for a general election, the combination of conjunctive and value–expectancy models is the most effective for predicting votes.[51] First, voters eliminate the candidates who do not suit them (small or unknown political parties, candidates judged as extreme, etc.). Among the few remaining names, they make a compensatory comparison according to the problems which worry them – unemployment, pollution, health, etc. – and the perceived capacity of the candidate to bring a solution to these problems.

Even though their predictive power is far from perfect, the analysis of attitudes and preferences is very useful for a good understanding of purchasing behaviour. Unlike social psychologists, who work on 'big' societal issues (such as racism, violence, political ideologies) which are unlikely to change much in a short period of time, marketers are confronted with a constantly changing environment where brand positions are never established for long and where innovative products perpetually threaten the current market structure. This perhaps explains why, beyond their efforts to understand the nature and structure of brand attitudes and preferences, managers are even more interested in modifying them to their advantage – a topic which we consider in the second part of this chapter.

Attitude change and persuasion

Tracking surveys made on the attitudes towards an issue such as advertising show that these attitudes change over time with, especially among young people, alternating periods of fascination and scepticism.[52] How does an attitude evolve over time and how can one modify it? To answer this double-headed question, one first has to understand the persuasion process, a process to which many studies have been devoted, particularly in advertising research.[53]

In order to understand better how persuasion works, it will be useful to recall the principles of the **process of communication**. Every communication has a source, a message, a channel or medium, and an audience (see Figure 4.2). The **source** is the origin of the message; it determines its content and its format. In a commercial environment, the source is usually a company keen to promote its products. To communicate successfully, it is necessary to **encode** the **message**, that is, to choose its structure and symbolism at the same time as taking into account its intended objectives. Meanwhile, the **media** are selected from the reading and listening habits of the audience. Choosing the media is as important as selecting the message since the impact of what is said depends upon where it is said. The **audience** then **decodes** and interprets this message according to its own sphere of experience, and 'noise' is often likely to interfere with the reception of the communication. Finally, the receivers are likely to give some **feedback** containing their reaction to the message: Have they paid attention to it? Have they understood it? Are they following what it says? Do they want to buy the advertised product? Naturally, the source will be

Figure 4.2 The process of communication

Source ——► Encoding ——► Message/Media ——► Decoding ——► Audience

Feedback

very interested in the audience's feedback, which is the basis for measuring the communication's effectiveness. Each year, many companies invest a proportion of their annual advertising budget to monitor its impact, either in terms of sales or, more commonly, in terms of recognition and perception.

One could, therefore, define **persuasion** as a communication aimed at influencing the attitudes of an audience. There are two alternative strategies for persuading people: the **adaptation** strategy, which moulds its message to pre-existing attitudes; and the **disruption** strategy, which attempts to modify the audience's point of view. Generally speaking, it is a lot easier to adapt to a pre-existing attitude than to modify it. The first strategy assumes nothing more than a good knowledge of the attitudes prevalent in the target market; it is then sufficient to insert a new element into this collection of predispositions to reinforce their cohesion and consistency. Many people consider Formula 1 to be a macho sport, for example. Therefore, it is appropriate to associate a brand of cigarettes like Marlboro with it by sponsoring a racing team. Similarly, targeting young people in advertisements for chewing gum or soft drinks is in line with this approach. In contrast, trying to make hats or gloves appeal to the young may prove more difficult given their generally negative attitudes towards such products.

In many different markets (detergents, cooking oil, newspapers and magazines), it turns out to be much easier, and more profitable, to keep existing customers than to convert new ones. Loyalty cards, points to redeem for gifts, special prices and offers to old clients are effective ways for a company to keep its clients interested and satisfied. As we have already seen in Chapter 2, Leon Festinger's theory of cognitive dissonance reinforces this idea by suggesting that a consumer who has just made an important decision needs positive information about it in order to be reassured that he or she has made the right choice.[54] Guarantees and post-purchase customer satisfaction surveys have this objective in mind, but promotion schemes, users' clubs and supporters' groups take it one step further by making satisfied customers into active sellers of the product; trying to convince someone of something is usually the best way to believing in it oneself! This view is also supported by Bem's **self-perception theory**, which holds that people attempt to explain their behaviour by justifying it afterwards. They achieve this in the same way a scientist would reach a conclusion: by observing the environment and his own actions and interpreting the associations which are thus brought into view – 'since I always buy this brand of beer, it must be good'.[55]

Modifying an attitude is more difficult. While the traditional communication model implicitly assumes that the audience primarily consists of passive receivers who simply need to be convinced, more recent communication research reveals that in many cases, receivers are active, goal-driven and – as suggested by **uses and grat-ifications theory** – decide whether or not to accept a message depending upon what's in it for them.[56] Today, under the influence of factors such as the wide diffusion of remote-control devices and the Internet, many forms of communication are interactive and this makes it more difficult for marketers to get their messages across.[57] However, results obtained from studies conducted on persuasion reveal some interesting points. For example, beliefs which are at the heart of our system of values evolve less rapidly than more vulnerable, peripheral attitudes.[58] The **theory of social judgement**, formulated by Sherif and his students, explores this phenomenon in depth.[59] According to Sherif, every individual has an acceptance zone (I agree), a rejection zone (I disagree), and an indifference zone (I don't care) with respect to any given subject. Existing beliefs, therefore, provide an anchor point for evaluating every additional perception. A new message judged to be very close to the acquired positions is rapidly assimilated, to the point of being distorted at times in the interest of an even stronger convergence. On the other hand, if the new message does not match with existing feelings, it will be perceived as being even further away and therefore rejected.[60] This is why political leaders easily enthuse about people whose ideas are similar to their own and mock their opponents' positions. In general, the more an individual is involved in a issue, the more his or her tolerance zone is reduced. In extreme circumstances, for example when he or she declares, 'This is what I believe and there is nothing you can say which will make me change my mind', the tolerance zone is nil.

Assessing acceptance and rejection zones is important in commercial research because the success of a new product largely depends upon a good understanding of their relative magnitude. They are measured by surveys in which participants are presented with a series of graduated questions, from 'This brand really is the best on the market' to 'There's no way I'd buy this brand'. Obviously, acceptance and rejection zones evolve with time. A new brand must first have its existence accepted, then establish its parity, and finally its superiority.

For persuading, a progressive attack is therefore often more effective than direct combat. In many European countries, the strategy used to convince drivers to wear seatbelts was carried out in stages: first on motorways and fast roads, then on trunk roads, and lastly, in towns. A direct attack with immediate legislative power would, in all probability, have led to a wave of protestations quoting individual rights and freedom. Using the AIDS argument to reform a drug addict is bound to fail. Suggesting a maximum (and progressively smaller) daily intake is more realistic: it is the 'foot in the door' technique well known to door-to-door salesmen and all those who offer a sample, an introductory video or a trial 'with no obligation to buy'.[61] Even the reversal of a deep belief is possible if one knows how to find the appropriate opening. The American company Green Giant was well aware of this when it tackled southern European consumers, at a time when the majority of them considered sweetcorn to be a food for animals. Rather than trying to convince them to eat hot corn as an accompanying vegetable, as northern Europeans do, or attempting to sell the product on the cob (which would have reinforced the perception of an animal food), they attempted to win them over first by presenting corn as an ingredient for mixed salad. The first product launched was Mexicorn, a salad with tomatoes, peppers and corn – the corn being a legitimate ingredient because of its Mexican origin. Once the first step had been taken, the company introduced cans of sweet corn, suggesting to customers that it would be more fun for them to create the salad themselves. The company then launched white corn for cooking and, finally, corn on the cob in cans or wrapped in plastic.

Generally speaking, studies on the process of persuasion have found some further basic rules of thumb.

The cognitive component is usually easier to influence than the feeling component. It is, therefore, somewhat easier to modify somebody's attitude by appealing to their reason than to their heart; this is an approach often used by trade negotiators and all those who wish to 'take the heat out of the debate'. Similarly, advertising research shows that making use of fear or humour, two essentially emotional appeals, can prove inadequate.[62] For a long time it was thought that the impact of a communication based on **fear** was proportional to the degree of anxiety created: later studies have shown that, on the contrary, a moderate message is more effective.[63] Fear has an inhibiting effect which activates the individual's defence mechanism, allowing him or her to avoid exposure to the message, deny the argument presented, distort its content or even to consider the proposed solution as unrelated to the extent of the danger. It is estimated that around 15 per cent of advertisements today play on fear, at least to some extent.[64]

For many years, a TV advertisement was run featuring the hero of the American series *Mission Impossible*, who, straight after being given his mission, telephoned an insurance company to obtain insurance cover! Is a message based on **humour** effective? Many experts have their doubts.[65] It would appear that an appeal to humour gains attention and warmth but is detrimental to the comprehension of the message and memorisation of the brand. A humorous advertisement may easily grab the attention, but the viewer will not necessarily remember what was being advertised. Amusing communication and effective communication should not be confused. David Ogilvy, one of advertising's gurus, claims that humour is used too much in advertising: 'Clowns make people laugh', he says, 'but they don't sell anything to them'.[66] The golden rule is to integrate the humour in the content of the message. He also recommends reserving humour for well-established brands; mentioning the brand immediately so as to avoid the risk of diluting the image; and checking the compatibility of humour with the nature of the product (he warns against using it for banks, health services and property sales). The same arguments also hold for sex-related appeals.[67]

An attitude which relies on tenuous beliefs will change more rapidly than an attitude anchored in firm convictions. This is the approach constantly used in political advertising, where the majority of campaigns are aimed at neither the militant, already convinced believers, nor inflexible opponent, who are quick to produce counter-arguments, but the 'in-betweens', who are more open to considering alternative choices.

Attitudes which correspond to a high level of involvement are more resistant than others. Certain individuals identify strongly with the products and brands that they buy, whether they be cars, cigarettes or leisure pursuits. Faithful consumers are more difficult to influence, and persuasion attempts are more efficient when they are directed towards less involved people. This is often called the paradox of communication. With contraception, for example, the families who could benefit most from it are those who have the most children. However, these families are the most difficult to influence. The communicator is thus faced with a dilemma: ought he or she to focus all the resources on winning over the reluctant ones; alternatively, would it be better to reach a larger number of people, even though they are less affected by the problem? In the first case, the communicator would invest in a massive short-term persuasion strategy; in the second, an indirect method of social pressure, probably a longer-term strategy (sometimes even over a generation), would be relied upon.

Attitudes are easier to modify when they are discordant. As seen in Chapter 2, Heider's theory states that when our beliefs and attitudes are in conflict, a new balance needs to be established.[68] A person living in downtown Amsterdam, for example, might experience contradictory feelings towards the Chrysler Voyager: she might be attracted to the spacious interior but concerned about the vehicle's manoeuvrability. She would then become very much interested in any information relating to this particular aspect of the car. At the same time, there is a risk of counter-productivity if the pole of rejection is so negative (here Amsterdam's traffic congestion) that it will prevail over any other argument. Such a phenomenon raises the problem of the testimonial and celebrity endorsement approach in communication – that is, using well-known personalities to promote products.[69] Communication is balanced if, according to Heider's terms, the different elements reinforce one another: I like Mr Bean and he advises me to buy the new Volkswagen, therefore it must be a good idea. But what happens if I don't like Mr Bean? Clearly, the perceptions of each of the sides of the Me–Mr Bean–Volkswagen triangle will evolve depending upon my decision and its consequences.

Many studies on the modification of attitudes have also led to a whole list of suggestions for creating advertisements. Observers have noted that various literary forms,[70] such as the narrative and dramatic (that is, novels or plays) formats,[71] including rhetorical figures such as metaphors or resonance,[72] are used in advertising. The main practical suggestions concern the usefulness of an implicit or explicit conclusion, the relevance of either a single or plural argument, the order of presentation of arguments, and the effects of distraction, repetition and source identity. The **conclusion** of advertisements is, obviously, vital. The following discussion highlights pitfalls and positives.

It is common in advertising to distinguish between warm and cold adverts. A cold advert is unstructured and its conclusion is left open, unlike a warm advert. Traditionally, the advertising profession prefers to create warm adverts, because of the risk of misunderstanding and bad attribution of the message to the brand. In fact, it is estimated that while one in two people pays attention to the brand on a TV advert, only one in three connects it with the intended message![73] Moreover, adverts relating to secondary brands are, in cases of doubt, attributed to leading brands. However, it has also been demonstrated that a less conclusive communication is more likely to attract the consumer's attention and stimulate his or her intellect, and consequently tends to be better remembered. This last phenomenon seems to intensify over time due to an effect called **psychological reactance**, according to which a very obvious message induces a negative 'boomerang' effect.[74] In fact, everything depends on the relationship with the audience.[75] It is better not to make the conclusion explicit when the audience does not trust the source. A hostile audience will in all likelihood develop an opposite explicit conclusion leading to a direct confrontation. A more ambiguous conclusion, if it does not succeed in modifying opinions, will at least cast doubt on the nature of the final message (what did it really say?). Many applications of this principle can be found in political marketing. For example, certain leaders of the traditional right refuse to condemn the extreme right's policies on immigration too overtly in order to retain part of their electorate.

It is better to avoid explaining the conclusion when the message is simple and the audience is sophisticated. In Chapter 2, we showed that if a communication's conclusion is left open-ended, the cognitive effort which the audience makes to complete it facilitates memorisation. With a simple communication (and therefore no great risk of miscomprehension) and with an informed audience (capable of easily deciphering the hidden sense of the message), this closure effect will work well. It would, therefore, be counter-productive to frustrate the audience by explicitly announcing a conclusion which is obvious.

When the communication relates to problems of a personal nature, the audience might be opposed to a direct conclusion which they consider to be 'interfering'. A few years ago, a study of the various arguments which could be used in the public relations campaign against AIDS showed that simply saying 'sex is risky' worked better than emphasising the possibility of death from AIDS.[76] In a European country, they even used as a slogan: 'Condoms wish you happy holidays'. A normative campaign based on recommendations (do this, don't do that) would probably have been less effective because it would have interfered with a domain that a large part of the audience considers to be strictly private.

Generally speaking, it appears that a certain ambiguity in the advertisement is often more effective than a precise script. By leaving to the audience the task of forming their own conclusions and thus determining whom the product is aimed at and what the conditions of use are, advertisers succeed in enlarging their market: not all Drambuie drinkers are old ladies sipping liqueur in their living rooms, and some Peugeot 205 Junior buyers are well past their fiftieth birthday. Explicit conclusions are better adapted to products that are complex or have a very specific use.

The problem of the **method of presentation of the communication** has also given rise to many studies, notably those of Hovland and his Yale colleagues.[77] One of the problems they have been particularly interested in concerns the choice between one-sided and two-sided presentation: should an advertisement mention only the advantages of the product or its limitations as well? Intuitively speaking, better results ought to be shown with the first approach. This is exactly how propaganda (and its correlate, censorship) is engineered. However, the second method can be equally legitimate, even when it comes to advertising. In 1990, for example, a traditional household magazine conducted a very successful poster campaign with the message, 'Who says our magazine is only about little paper doilies?' and 'Who says our magazine recipes are boring?' In fact everything depends, again, on the audience's original attitude and the probability of them being exposed to counter-communications in the future.

One-sided presentation is all the more effective if the audience is already favourable to the point of view presented. Conversely, a two-sided message is more appropriate in the case of a hostile audience. This result is easily explained if one considers the possibility of counter-argumentation. A favourable audience has neither the idea nor the reason for formulating counter-arguments; on the contrary, they have every reason to be satisfied with arguments which are in line with their own convictions. On the other hand, a hostile audience might be surprised by hearing their own theories presented by their 'enemy'. So they lower their guard, endow the communicator with more credibility and, perhaps, increase their chances of being seduced! This principle has numerous commercial applications. A brandy with an unrivalled reputation and prestige has little to gain in creating a complex and elaborate argumentation as the brand name 'speaks for itself'; the reverse is true for a newcomer product which has to establish its legitimacy and credibility.

A two-sided message is more effective for an audience which is likely to be subjected to counter-propaganda. By mentioning the product's limitations, a manufacturer will outstrip his rival, a bit like vaccine protects from illness. Clearly, one should inoculate as is necessary to combat counter-propaganda only and not deprecate the product itself. A good way of practising the art of two-sided communication is to present weaknesses as strengths. Avis has long used its challenger's position as a trump card: 'We're number 2 so we try harder [than number 1 Hertz to serve you]'.

The **order of presentation of the communication** remains an unresolved issue. Some recommend immediate presentation of decisive arguments in order to reap the benefit of a shock effect. Others prefer a progressive approach which culminates in a sledgehammer argument. Here, again, the audience's attitude exerts an influence. With a captive and favourable audience the order is of little importance, whereas with a hostile audience, 'rubbing them up the wrong way' seems to be more effective.[78]

Researchers are well aware of the role counter-propaganda can play in reducing an advertisement's coherence and, therefore, effectiveness. Some experts claim that by introducing elements of **distraction** which capture the audience's attention, they are reducing such a risk;[79] for example, by accelerating the rhythm of images or by incorporating incongruous elements in order to surprise the audience. Once again, overall results are mixed.[80] Some studies report the effectiveness of such a 'distraction effect',[81] while others deny it.[82] In fact, the main risk relates to the erosion of message comprehension. In incorporating elements of distraction at all costs, one might end up with a confused message and a main argument which is diluted. Is it worth the risk?

Repetition is often considered to be a key factor in the success of a campaign. At the heart of the learning process, as studied in Chapter 3, repetition allows a progressive familiarisation with the message and therefore a better recall of its content. At the same time, it has been established that beyond a certain number of exposures, a campaign ceases to have an effect. Sometimes, excessive exposure even leads to rejection due to irritation.[83] The inevitable 'wearout' effect appears to be more pronounced for high-density messages and in situations where the audience is not greatly involved.[84] Furthermore, certain themes (humour, for example) wear out more quickly than others. Generally speaking, it appears that (a) a single exposure has almost no effect, (b) after three showings weariness begins to set in, and (c) optimal repetition is therefore situated between these two poles but obviously varies according to the nature of the communication and its audience. The challenge is to find the proper balance between the two factors of familiarity and boredom.[85]

Finally, work concerning the impact of the **nature of the source** on the effectiveness of the communication has highlighted the importance of **perceived credibility and attractiveness**. While credibility is granted on the basis of such factors as perceived expertise and trustworthiness, attractiveness is primarily influenced by physical appearance and social status (especially if similar to the receiver's). One would normally assume that persuasion is easier when the communicator's credibility has been firmly established. In fact, this is true when the audience is not very familiar with the product[86] but, again, everything depends upon the audience's original attitude. Several studies have shown that a source with weak credibility may have more impact than a source with very strong credibility when the preliminary attitude is already favourable. The source's weak credibility seems to have a stimulating effect on the audience.[87]

In general, 'beauty sells' and attractive sources have more persuasive power than less attractive ones; this is why so many companies use top models and other celebrities to promote their products.[88] In fact, this approach is more or less effective depending upon the 'fit' between the star and the product. According to the match-up hypothesis,[89] celebrity endorsement works best where receivers establish a direct link between the source and the message. Thus, Claudia Schiffer is more credible when she promotes cosmetics (L'Oréal) than cars (Citroën).

Some studies have explored the conditions in which credibility works better than attractiveness (and vice versa). The nature of the product and the nature of the audience both play a role. Experts tend to be more persuasive than celebrities when the product presents a high functional (rather than social) risk and when the audience makes autonomous decisions (with little influence from the social environment). The level of involvement is again critical. According to the elaboration like-lihood model (ELM), a highly involved audience is likely to engage in a cognitive processing of the message and will respond positively to the rational arguments provided by the expert. Conversely, when consumers do not care that much about the product being advertised, the stimuli external to the message will play an important role and an attractive celebrity may prove very effective. In the first case, the receiver is said to follow the **central route** to persuasion, while in the second, he or she adopts the **peripheral route**.[90]

Regardless of whether a highly credible or highly attractive source is used, studies have shown that source effects will decay over time – a phenomenon known as the **sleeper effect**.[91] It works rather as if, with the passage of time, the source and the message lose their connections. An alternative explanation is that memory works selectively and if the message is strongly encoded, its impact will eventually prevail over the source.[92]

Attitude change and persuasion tactics represent a vast domain of study because of the issues (and advertising money) at stake. A deep knowledge of the attributes underlying the market structure and the positions attached to the various brands available, as well as their evolution, provides answers to many business questions:[93]

- What are the attributes that the market demands and which are not satisfied by existing products?
- If I reposition my brand by trying to alter perceptions, what type of competition will I be faced with?
- Is it better to move my brand towards the ideal positioning or try to move the ideal positioning towards my brand?
- Should I improve the positioning of my product or destabilise that of my rivals, for example by using comparative advertisements?

At the same time, the reader will also have certainly noticed that many results obtained concerning persuasion strategies and tactics are often mixed and some-times contradictory. No single principal recommendation applicable to all com-munications and audiences exists. This may appear to be paradoxical. Every year, the press, radio and television unload hundreds of thousands of communications on people and yet their impact or the way they function cannot be fully appreci-ated. It must be pointed out that the modification of an attitude is a fundamentally complex phenomenon which is at the heart of the social interaction process so characteristic of human nature. There is no doubt that additional studies will con-tinue to enrich our future knowledge of the factors which accelerate or inhibit per-suasion.

Notes

[1] See G. Allport, 'Attitudes', in C. A. Murchinson (ed.), *Handbook of Social Psychology* (Clark University Press, 1935) pp. 798–844. Also see M. Fishbein, *Readings in Attitude Theory and Measurement* (J. Wiley & Sons, 1967).

[2] For a comprehensive text on the psychology of attitudes, see A. Eagly and S. Chaiken, *Psychology of Attitudes* (HBJ College & School Division, 1993).

[3] D. T. Campbell, 'Social Attitudes and Other Acquired Behavioural Dispositions', in S. Koch (ed.), *Psychology: A Study of a Science*, Vol. 6 (McGraw-Hill, 1963).

[4] D. Krech, R. Crutchfield and E. Ballachey, *Individual in Society* (McGraw-Hill, 1962).

[5] *Ibid.*, p. 139.

[6] C. Osgood and P. H. Tannenbaum, 'The Principle of Congruity in the Prediction of Attitude Change', *Psychological Review*, 1953, Vol. 62, pp. 42–55.

[7] R. Forman, *You Can Get What You Want* (Prentice Hall, 1953).

[8] See A. Rao and K. B. Monroe, 'The Effects of Price, Brand Name and Store Name on Buyers' Perceptions of Product Quality: An Integrative Review', *Journal of Marketing Research*, August 1989, pp. 351–7. Also see W. B. Dodd, K. B. Monroe and D. Grewal, 'Effects of Price, Brand and Store Information on Buyers' Product Evaluations', *Journal of Marketing Research*, August 1991, pp. 307–19.

[9] C. Obermiller and J. Wheatley, 'Beliefs in Quality Differences and Brand Choice', in E. C. Hirschmann and M. C. Holbrook (eds), *Advances in Consumer Research* (ACR, 1985), pp. 75–8.

[10] K. B. Monroe, 'The Influence of Price Differences and Brand Familiarity in Brand Preferences', *Journal of Consumer Research*, June 1976, pp. 42–9.

[11] J. J. Wheatley, J. S. Y. Chiu and A. Goldman, 'Physical Quality, Price and Perceptions of Product Quality: Indications for Retailers', *Journal of Retailing*, Summer 1981, pp. 100–16.

[12] See P. Anand, M. Holbrook and D. Stephens, 'The Formation of Affective Judgments: The Cognitive–Affective Model Versus the Independence Hypothesis', *Journal of Consumer Research*, December 1988, pp. 386–91.

[13] R. Zajonc, 'The Attitudinal Effects of Mere Exposure', *Journal of Personality and Social Psychology*, 1968 supplement, pp. 1–17. See also R. Zajonc, 'Feeling and Thinking: Preferences Need No Inferences', *American Psychologist*, 1980, 2, pp. 151–75. For a discussion of mere exposure effects in a consumer research context, see C. Janiszewski, 'Pre-attentive Mere-Exposure Effects', *Journal of Consumer Research*, December 1993, pp. 376–92. See also M. Vanhuele, 'Why Familiar Stimuli are Better Liked. A Study on the Cognitive Dynamics Linking Recognition and the Mere Exposure Effect', *Advances in Consumer Research*, 1995, pp. 171–5.

[14] R. Moreland and R. Zajonc, 'Is Stimulus Recognition a Necessary Condition for the Occurrence of Exposure Effects?' *Journal of Personality and Social Psychology*, 1977, pp. 191–9.

[15] G. L. Wells and R. E. Petty, 'The Effect of Overt Head Movement on Persuasion: Compatibility and Incompatibility of Responses', *Basic and Applied Social Psychology*, 1980, 1, pp. 219–30.

[16] See R. Zajonc and H. Markus, 'Affective and Cognitive Factors in Preferences', *Journal of Consumer Research*, September 1982, pp. 123–31. For a résumé of the debate generated by these works, see Y. Tsal, 'On the Relationship Between Cognitive and Affective Preferences: A Critique of Zajonc and Markus', *Journal of Consumer Research*, December 1985, pp. 358–64.

[17] For a review, see J. B. Cohen and C. S. Areni, 'Affect and Consumer Behavior', in T. S. Robertson and H. H. Kassarjian (eds), *Handbook of Consumer Behavior*, (Prentice Hall, 1991), pp. 188–240.

[18] Robert Enrico, *La Guerre des Colas* (Intereditions, 1986).

[19] D. Mueller, 'Psychological Techniques of Attitude Measurement', in G. Summers (ed.), *Attitude Measurement* (Chicago: Rand McNally, 1970), pp. 534–52.

[20] R. Hill and J. Ward, 'Mood Manipulation in Marketing Research: An Examination of Potential Confounding Effects', *Journal of Marketing Research*, February 1989, pp. 97–104.

[21] D. Aaker, D. M. Stayman and M. Hagerty, 'Warmth in Advertising: Measurement, Impact and Sequence Effects', *Journal of Consumer Research*, March 1986, pp. 365–81. For recent research on the Warmth Monitor, see P. Vanden Abeele and D. MacLachlan, 'Process Tracking of Emotional Responses to TV Ads: Revisiting the Warmth Monitor', *Journal of Consumer Research*, March 1994, pp. 586–600.

22 A. Mehrabian and J. Russell, *An Approach to Environmental Psychology* (MIT Press, 1974). For an alternative approach, see the scale developed by R. Plutchik in R. Plutchik, *Emotion: A Psycho-evolutionary Context* (Harper & Row, 1980). For a comparison of the two scales in a consumption context, see W. Havlena and M. Holbrook, 'The Varieties of Consumption Experience: Comparing Two Typologies of Emotion in Consumer Behavior', *Journal of Consumer Research*, December 1986, pp. 394–404.

23 M. P. Gardner, 'The Consumer's Mood: An Important Situational Variable', in T. C. Kinnear (ed.), *Advances in Consumer Research* (ACR, 1984). Also see M. P. Gardner, 'Mood States and Consumer Behavior: A Critical Review', *Journal of Consumer Research*, December 1985, pp. 281–300.

24 G. Gorn, 'The Effects of Music in Advertising on Choice Behavior: A Classical Conditioning Approach', *Journal of Marketing*, Winter 1982, pp. 94–101. Also see R. Milliman, 'The Influence of Background Music on the Behavior of Restaurant Patrons', *Journal of Consumer Research*, September 1986, pp. 286–9; and, from the same author, 'Using Background Music to Affect the Behavior of Supermarket Shoppers', *Journal of Marketing*, Summer 1982, pp. 86–91.

25 See M. E. Goldberg and G. J. Gorn, 'Happy and Sad TV Programs: How They Affect Reactions to Commercials', *Journal of Consumer Research*, December 1987, pp. 387–403.

26 For expansion of this point see K. Nakamoto, 'Alternatives to Information Processing in Consumer Research: New Perspectives on Old Controversies', *International Journal of Research in Marketing*, 1987, pp. 11–28.

27 Source: Burke Marketing Research, commercial document.

28 See J. A. Cote and P. S. Tansuhaj, 'Culture Bound Assumptions in Behavior Intention Models', *Advances in Consumer Research*, 1989, pp. 105–9.

29 R. Claude, 'La Réalisation des Intentions d'Achat', *Economie et Stratégie*, January 1981, pp. 49–83. For other works on the intention–behaviour relationship, see D. H. Granbois and J. O. Summers, 'Primary and Secondary Validity of Consumer Purchase Probabilities', *Journal of Consumer Research*, March 1975, pp. 31–8; P. W. Miniard, C. Obermiller and J. J. Page Jr, 'A Further Assessment of Measurement Influences on the Intention–Behavior Relationship', *Journal of Marketing Research*, May 1983, pp. 206–12; and B. L. Bayus and S. Gupta, 'An Empirical Analysis of Consumer Durable Replacement Intentions', *International Journal of Research in Marketing*, 1992, pp. 257–68.

30 G. Katona, 'Contribution of Psychological Data to Economic Analysis', *Journal of the American Statistical Association*, 1947, Vol. 42, pp. 449–59. See also G. Katona and E. Mueller, 'A Study of Purchase Decisions', in L. H. Clark (ed.), *Consumer Behavior: The Dynamics of Consumer Reactions* (New York University Press, 1955); and A. Macquin and G. Laurent, 'Analyse Explicative du Faible Pouvoir Prédicatif du 'Sentiment du Consommateur' (Cahier de Recherche du CESA, 1985).

31 See M. R. Warshaw and F. D. Davies, 'Disentangling Behavioral Intention and Behavioral Expectation', *Journal of Experimental Psychology*, 1985, 21, pp. 213–28. Also see R. H. Fazio and M. P. Zanna, 'On the Predictive Validity of Attitudes: The Role of Direct Experience and Confidence', *Journal of Personality*, June 1978, pp. 228–43.

32 M. Ryan and E. H. Bonfield, 'The Fishbein Extended Model and Consumer Behavior', *Journal of Consumer Research*, 1975, pp. 118–36.

33 D. Cox, *Risk Taking and Information Handling in Consumer Behavior* (Division of Research, Harvard Business School, 1967). For an international comparison, see B. Verhage *et al.*, 'Perceived Risk: A Cross Cultural Phenomenon?', *International Journal of Research in Marketing*, 1990, pp. 297–303.

34 See J. Cote, J. McCullough and M. Reilly, 'Effects of Unexpected Situations on Behavior–Intention Differences: A Garbology Analysis', *Journal of Consumer Research*, September 1985, pp. 188–94; and R. E. Smith and W. R. Swinyard, 'Attitude–Behavior Consistency: The Impact of Product Trial Versus Advertising', *Journal of Marketing Research*, August 1983, pp. 257–67.

35 For the role of attitude accessibility, see R. H. Fazio *et al.*, 'The Role of Attitude Accessibility in the Attitude-to-Behavior Process', *Journal of Consumer Research*, December 1989, pp. 280–8.

36 R. Lutz and J. R. Bettman, 'Multi-attribute Models in Marketing', in A. Woodside, J. Sheth and P. Bennet (eds), *Consumer and Industrial Buying Behavior* (North Holland, 1977), pp. 137–40.

37 M. Rosenberg, 'Cognitive Structure and Attitudinal Aspects', *Journal of Abnormal and Social Psychology*, November 1956, pp. 367–72; and M. Fishbein, 'An Investigation of the Relationships Between Beliefs about an Object and the Attitude Toward that Object', *Human Relations*, 1963, pp. 233–40.

38 D. Katz, 'The Functional Approach to the Study of Attitudes', *Public Opinion Quarterly*, Summer 1960, pp. 163–204. See also R. J. Lutz, 'Changing Brand Attitudes through Modification of Cognitive Structure', *Journal of Consumer Research*, March 1975, pp. 49–59.

39 J. S. Johar and M. J. Sirgy, 'Value-Expressive Versus Utilitarian Advertising Appeals: When and Why to Use Which Appeal', *Journal of Advertising*, September 1991, pp. 23–34.

40 F. Hansen, 'Consumer Choice Behavior: An Experimental Approach', *Journal of Marketing Research*, November 1969, pp. 436–43. For other examples of application of this model in commercial research, see S. W. Bither and S. Miller, 'A Cognitive Theory of Brand Preference', in P. R. McDonald (ed.), *Marketing Involvement in Society and the Economy* (AMA, 1969), pp. 210–16.

41 For a complete explanation of the model, see M. Fishbein and I. Ajzen, *Belief, Attitude, Intention and Behavior: An Introduction to Theory and Research* (Addison-Wesley, 1975); and I. Azjen and M. Fishbein, *Understanding Attitudes and Predicting Social Behavior* (Prentice Hall, 1980).

42 See, for example, M. B. Holbrook and W. J. Havlena, 'Assessing the Real-to-Generalizability of Multi-attribute Models in Tests of New Product Designs', *Journal of Marketing Research*, February 1988, pp. 26–35. See also 'Lever Brothers Uses Micromodel to Project Market Share', *Marketing News*, 27 November 1981.

43 J. N. Kapferer and B. Dubois, *Echec à la Science* (NER, 1981).

44 See F. A. Bass and W. Talarzyk, 'Attitude Model for the Study of Brand Preference', *Journal of Marketing Research*, February 1972, pp. 93–6. Also see J. N. Sheth and W. W. Talarzyk, 'Perceived Instrumentality and Value Importance as Determinants of Attitudes', *Journal of Marketing Research*, February 1972, pp. 6–9.

45 See R. I. Haley, 'Benefit Segmentation: A Decision-Orientated Research Tool', *Journal of Marketing*, July 1968, pp. 5-13; R. I. Haley, 'Benefit Segmentation 20 years later', *Journal of Customer Marketing*, 1988, pp. 5–13; and R. I. Haley, 'Beyond Benefit Segmentation', *Journal of Advertising Research*, August 1971, pp. 3–8.

46 See J. L. Ginter, 'An Experimental Investigation of Attitude Change and Choice of a New Brand', *Journal of Marketing Research*, February 1974, pp. 30–40; and D. R. Lehmann, 'Television Show Preference: Application of a Choice Model', *Journal of Marketing Research*, February 1972, pp. 44–55.

47 B. Dubois, 'A Comparison of Brand Image and Brand Preference Models and Measurement Methods', doctoral thesis, Northwestern University, 1973.

48 For examples, see B. Weitz and P. Wright, 'Retrospective Self-Insight on Factors Considered in Product Evaluations', *Journal of Consumer Research*, December 1979, pp. 280–94; and P. Wright and B. Weitz, 'Time Horizon Effects on Product Evaluation Strategies', *Journal of Marketing Research*, November 1977, pp. 429–41.

49 R. Angelmar and B. Pras, 'Advertising Strategy Implications of Consumer Evaluation Process Models', *European Journal of Marketing*, 1977. Also see Y. Yi, 'An Investigation of the Structure of Expectancy–Value Attitude and Its Implications', *International Journal of Research in Marketing*, December 1989, pp. 71–84.

50 See, for example, W. Wilkie and E. Pessemier, 'Issues in Marketing's Use of Multi-attribute Models', *Journal of Marketing Research*, November 1973, pp. 428–41; and M. B. Mazis,

O. T. Athola and R. E. Klippel, 'A Comparison of Four Multi-attribute Models in the Prediction of Consumer Attitudes', *Journal of Consumer Research*, June 1975, pp. 38–52. Also see A. d'Astous and D. Rouziès, 'Selection and Implementation of Processing Strategies in Consumer Evaluative Judgement and Choice', *International Journal of Research in Marketing*, 1987, pp. 99–110.

51 D. Lindon, *Modèle de Choix d'un Député*. (Ed. de Minuit, 1983).

52 See D. M. Boush, M. Friestad and G. Rose, 'Adolescent Skepticism Toward TV Advertising and Knowledge of Advertiser Tactics', *Journal of Consumer Research*, June 1994, pp. 165–75; R. Pieters and H. Baumgartner, 'The Attitude Toward Advertising of Advertising Practitioners, Homemakers, and Students in the Netherlands and in Belgium', *European Advances in Consumer Research*, 1993, pp. 39–45; and L. Feick and H. Gierl, 'Skepticism about Advertising: A Comparison of East and West German Consumers', *International Journal of Research in Marketing*, 1996, pp. 227–35.

53 For a comprehensive and recent treatment, see R. Cialdini, *Influence: The Psychology of Persuausion*, 1993.

54 L. Festinger, *A Theory of Cognitive Dissonance* (Harper & Row, 1957).

55 D. Bem, 'Self-Perception Theory', L. Berkowitz (ed.) *Advances in Experimental Social Psychology* (Academic Press, 1968), pp. 319–23. See also from the same author, 'Attitudes as Self-Descriptions: Another Look at the Attitude–Behavior Link', in A. Greenwald, T. Brock and T. Ostrom (eds), *Psychological Foundations of Attitudes* (Academic Press, 1968).

56 See S. O'Donohoe, 'Advertising Uses and Gratifications', *European Journal of Marketing*, 1994, 8/9, pp. 52–75.

57 D. L. Hoffman and T. P. Novak, 'Marketing in Hypermedia Computer-Mediated Environments: Conceptual Foundations', *Journal of Marketing*, July 1996, pp. 50–68.

58 See R. E. Petty and J. T. Cacioppo, *Attitudes and Persuasion* (W. C. Brown, 1981).

59 C. W. Sherif, M. Sherif and R. E. Nebergall, *Attitude and Attitude Change* (New Haven: Yale University Press, 1961).

60 See J. Meyers-Levy and B. Sternthal, 'A Two-Factor Explanation of Assimilation and Contrast Effects', *Journal of Marketing Research*, August 1993, pp. 359–68.

61 J. L. Freedman and S. C. Fraser, 'Compliance Without Pressure: The Foot in the Door Technique', *Journal of Personality and Social Psychology*, August 1966, pp. 195–202. See also A. M. Tybout, B. Sternthal and B. J. Calder, 'Information Availability as a Determinant of Multiple-Request Effectiveness', *Journal of Marketing Research*, August 1988, pp. 280–90; and D. H. Furse, D. W. Stewart and D. L. Rados, 'Effects of Foot-in-the-Door, Cash Incentives on Survey Response', *Journal of Marketing Research*, November 1981, pp. 473–8.

62 A. Chattopadhyay and K. Basu, 'Humor in Advertising: The Moderating Role of Prior Brand Evaluation', *Journal of Marketing Research*, November 1990, pp. 466–76.

63 I. L. Janis and L. Feshbach, 'Effects of Fear-Arousing Communications', *Journal of Abnormal and Social Psychology*, 1953, pp. 78–92. For a complete discussion of the issue, see M. Ray and W. Wilkie, 'Fear: The Potential of an Appeal Neglected by Marketing', *Journal of Marketing*, 1970, pp. 59–62. See also J. F. Tanner, Jr, J. B. Hunt and D. R. Eppright, 'The Protection Motivation Model: A Normative Model of Fear Appeals', *Journal of Marketing*, July 1991, pp. 36–45.

64 L. S. Unger and J. M. Stearns, 'The Use of Fear and Guilt Messages in Television Advertising: Issues and Evidence,' in P. E. Murphy *et al.* (eds), *AMA Educators' Proceedings* (AMA, 1983) pp. 16–20.

65 B. Sternthal and S. Craig, 'Humor in Advertising', *Journal of Marketing*, October 1973, pp. 12–18 and 'Humor is Best Utilized with Established Products', *Marketing News*, 1 October 1982. See also J. P. Kelly and P. J. Solomon, 'Humor in Advertising', *Journal of Advertising*, Summer 1975, pp. 31–5; and T. J. Madden and M. G. Weinberger, 'The Effects of Humor on Attention in Magazine Advertising', *Journal of Advertising*, 1982, 3, pp. 8–14.

66 D. Ogilvy, *Confessions of an Advertising Man* (New York: Free Press, 1985).

[67] B.G. Yovovich, 'Sex in Advertising: The Power and the Perils', *Advertising Age*, 2 May, 1983, pp. 4–5.

[68] F. Heider, *The Psychology of Interpersonal Relations* (J. Wiley & Sons, 1958).

[69] See H. H. Friedman and L. Friedman, 'Endorser Effectiveness by Product Type', *Journal of Advertising Research*, 1979, 5, pp. 63–71.

[70] B. Stern, 'Literary Criticism and Consumer Research: Overview and Illustrative Analysis', *Journal of Consumer Research*, December 1989, pp. 322–34.

[71] J. Deighton, D. Romer and J. McQueen, 'Using Drama to Persuade', *Journal of Consumer Research*, December 1989, pp. 335–43.

[72] E. F. McQuarrie and D. G. Mick, 'On Resonance: A Critical Pluralistic Inquiry into Advertising Rhetoric', *Journal of Consumer Research*, September 1992, pp. 180–97.

[73] 'Only 38% of TV Audience links Brands with Ads', *Marketing News*, 6 January 1984, p. 10.

[74] See J. W. Brehm, *Responses to Loss of Freedom: A Theory of Psychological Reactance* (General Learning Press, 1972).

[75] F. R. Kardes, 'Spontaneous Inference Processes in Advertising: The Effects of Conclusion Omission and Involvement on Persuasion', *Journal of Consumer Research*, September 1988, pp. 225–33.

[76] R. P. Hill, 'An Exploration of the Relationship between AIDS-related Anxiety and the Evaluation of Condom Advertisements', *Journal of Advertising*, 1988, 4, pp. 35–42.

[77] See C. I. Hovland, A. A. Lumsdaine and F. D. Sheffield, *Experiments on Mass Communications* (Princeton University Press, 1948). For more recent findings, see L. L. Golden and M. I. Alpert, 'Comparative Analysis of the Relative Effectiveness of One and Two Sided Communication of Contrasting Products', *Journal of Advertising*, 1987, 16, pp. 18–25; M. A. Kamins and H. Assael, 'Two-Sided Versus One-Sided Appeals: A Cognitive Perspective on Argumentation, Source Derogation and the Effect of Disconfirming Trial on Belief Change', *Journal of Marketing Research*, February 1987, pp. 29–39; and C. Okechuku *et al.*, 'The Moderating Effect of Disclaimer Importance on the Effectiveness of Two-Sided Advertising', *European Advances in Consumer Research*, Vol. 1 (ACR, 1993), pp. 168–75.

[78] Hovland, Lumsdaine and Sheffield, *op. cit.*

[79] See R. A. Osterhouse and T. C. Brock, 'Distraction Increases Yielding to Propaganda by Inhibiting Counterarguing', *Journal of Personality and Social Psychology*, 1970, pp. 344–58.

[80] R. Petty *et al.*, 'Distraction Can Enhance or Reduce Yielding to Propaganda: Thought Disruption versus Effort Justification', *Journal of Personality and Social Psychology*, 1977.

[81] S. W. Bither, 'Effects of Distraction and Commitment on the Persuasiveness of Television Advertising', *Journal of Marketing Research*, February 1972, pp. 1–5.

[82] D. Gardner, 'The Distraction Hypothesis in Marketing', *Journal of Advertising Research*, December 1970, pp. 25–31.

[83] G. E. Belch, 'The Effects of Television Commercial Repetition on Cognitive Response and Message Acceptance', *Journal of Consumer Research*, June 1982, pp. 56–65. See also M. Burke and J. Edell, 'Ad Reactions over Time: Capturing Changes in the Real World', *Journal of Consumer Research*, June 1986, pp. 114–18.

[84] See C. S. Graig, B. Sternthal and C. Leavitt, 'Advertising Wearout: An Experimental Analysis', *Journal of Marketing Research*, November 1976, pp. 365–72.

[85] See A. Rethans, J. Swasy and L. Marks, 'Effects of Television Commercial Repetition, Receiver Knowledge, and Commercial Length: A Test of the Two-Factor Model', *Journal of Marketing Research*, February 1986, pp. 50–61.

[86] S. Ratneshwar and S. Chaiken, 'Comprehension's Role in Persuasion: The Case of Its Moderating Effect on the Persuasive Impact of Source Cues', *Journal of Consumer Research*, June 1991, pp. 52–62.

[87] R. Dholakia and B. Sternthal, 'Highly Credible Sources: Persuasive Facilitators or Persuasive Liabilities', *Journal of Consumer Research*, March 1977, pp. 223–32.

[88] See L. R. Kahle and P. Homer, 'Physical Attractiveness of the Celebrity Endorser: A Social

Adaptation Perspective', *Journal of Consumer Research*, March 1985, pp. 954–61. See also M. J. Baker and G. A. Churchill, Jr, 'The Impact of Physically Attractive Models on Advertising Evaluations', *Journal of Marketing Research*, November 1977, pp. 538–55; and C. Derbaix and L. Sjöberg,'Movie Stars in Space: A Comparison of Preference and Similarity Judgements', *International Journal of Research in Marketing*, 1994, pp. 261–74. For other perspectives on celebrity endorsement, see G. McCracken, 'Who is the Celebrity Endorser? Cultural Foundations of the Endorsement Process', *Journal of Consumer Research*, December 1989, pp. 310–21.

[89] M. Kamins, 'An Investigation into the "Match-Up" Hypothesis in Celebrity Advertising: When Beauty May Be Only Skin Deep', *Journal of Advertising*, 1990, 1, pp. 4–13. See also M. R. Solomon, R. Ashmore and L. Longo, 'The Beauty Match-Up Hypothesis: Congruence Between Types of Beauty and Product Images in Advertising', *Journal of Advertising*, December 1992, pp. 23–34.

[90] The ELM is described in detail in R. E. Petty, J. T. Cacioppo and D. Schumann, 'Central and Peripheral Routes to Advertising Effectiveness: The Moderating Role of Involvement', *Journal of Consumer Research*, September 1983, pp. 135–46. For consumer research related to the ELM, see M. J. Bitner and C. Obermiller, 'The Elaboration Likelihood Model: Limitations and Extensions in Marketing', *Advances in Consumer Research*, 1985, pp. 420–5; R. A. Higie, L. F. Feick and L. L. Price, 'The Importance of Peripheral Cues in Attitude Formation for Enduring and Task-Involved Individuals', *Advances in Consumer Research*, 1991, pp. 187–93; and J. Craig Andrews and T. Shimp, 'Effects of Involvement, Argument Strength, and Source Characteristics on Central and Peripheral Processing in Advertising', *Psychology and Marketing*, Fall 1990, pp. 195–214.

[91] See H. C. Kelman and C. I. Hovland, 'Reinstatement of the Communication in Delayed Measurement of Opinion Change', *Journal of Abnormal Psychology*, 1953, 3, pp. 327–35.

[92] See D. Hannah and B. Sternthal, 'Detecting and Explaining the Sleeper Effect', *Journal of Consumer Research*, September 1984, pp. 632–42. See also D. Mazrusky and Y. Schul, 'The Effects of Advertisement Encoding on the Failure to Discount Information: Implications for the Sleeper Effect', *Journal of Consumer Research*, June 1988, pp. 24–36.

[93] See H. Boyd, M. Ray and E. Strong, 'An Attitudinal Framework for Advertising Strategy', *Journal of Marketing*, April 1972, pp. 27–33.

5

Groups and opinion leaders

Learning objectives

After reading this chapter, you will understand:

1 the nature and diversity of groups which have an influence on purchase and consumption behaviour;

2 the conditions under which group influence may or not prevail;

3 the mechanisms underlying interpersonal influence;

4 what it takes to be an opinion leader and the assessment of opinion leadership;

5 the various simulation and stimulation strategies used by companies to capitalise upon interpersonal influence;

6 the mechanisms underlying the diffusion of an innovation.

Key words

social environment	membership and	word-of-mouth
primary and secondary	reference groups	communication
groups	identification function	opinion leadership
nuclear family	normative function	key informant method
socio-groups and	two-step flow of	sociometry
psycho-groups	communications	self-designating method
formal and informal	opinion leaders and	empathy
groups	followers	influenceability

Motivations, perceptions and attitudes are a logical point of departure for understanding consumers but are not enough. They are a logical point of departure because buying decisions are always ultimately individual in nature. They are not sufficient, however, because although they enable us to understand preferences and intentions, they do not necessarily help predict subsequent behaviour.[1] As seen in the previous chapter, most studies exploring the link between intentions and actions have concluded that intentions have a rather weak, if any, predictive value.[2] Two main factors are put forward to account for the discrepancies: the situ-

ation and the social environment. The situation often rel:
cumstances, which can lead to a last-minute change in
example, a customer at a sales outlet discovers that her p
stock and decides to buy another. Situational variables are
The other factor, the **social environment**, is the subject of th

A number of studies testify to the significant influence of the
that is the influence of other people, on purchase decisions. Con
market survey done on small household electrical appliances. In
question: 'What was the most important source of information in bu,
uct?' friends, neighbours and acquaintances were mentioned in 50 per cent of
as against only 8 per cent for advertising and 1 per cent for the salesperson.[3] In a
study carried out by the Pernod-Ricard company, 'discussions with friends' was
identified as a very important information source for aperitifs (with a 26% score),
just after labels attached to products (28%) and well ahead of advertising (15.2%),
promotions (15.1%) or the advice of a salesperson (12.5%). Even if, in such
studies, social influence may be somewhat overestimated due to the fact that few
people openly admit that they have been influenced by advertising or promotions,
its impact in terms of percentages remains impressive and has been observed for a
number of other products: 29 for food;[4] 42 for the choice of a garage;[5] 53 for a
hotel;[6] 58 for doctors;[7] and up to 82 for a book.[8] A study done in the USA revealed
that the diffusion pattern of air-conditioning units observed in blocks of flats was
linked to interpersonal relationships between the inhabitants:[9] the networks of
friends could almost be recreated by looking at the dates on the invoices! Today, a
number of sociologists consider that social influence on consumption has never
been stronger, due to the reduction of inequality in expenditure levels. Given the
pervasive nature of interpersonal influence, it is essential to understand the nature
of social groups as well as their various modes of operation.

A typology of groups

The concept of a group, as currently defined in social science, differs somewhat
from that used in everyday language. In daily life, we consider any gathering of several people as a group; for a social scientist, such a gathering must also have a
common objective. The passengers on an aircraft do not constitute a group in themselves. They become one if an event occurs (such as an accident or a delay) which
triggers a collective consciousness. Even under this restricted definition, the multi-
plicity and diversity of human groups remains extraordinary. Social affiliation and
interaction represent perhaps the most distinctive human traits, with the group con-
stituting the basic building block of any known society. Human beings are social
animals and their preferences are inevitably influenced by group memberships.
Given such a proliferation of groups, a system of classification is needed. It has
become customary to distinguish different types of group according to their (a) size,
(b) purpose, (c) structure and (d) status.

the point of view of size, social scientists make a distinction between **pri-** **mary groups** and **secondary groups.**[10] By virtue of its limited size, a primary group is characterised by the possibility of a direct and almost permanent contact between its members. The **nuclear family**, composed of parents and their children, is probably the best-known example. In a secondary group, on the other hand, one can easily detect the existence of sub-groups as well as of specific interaction processes made necessary by the broader membership. This is, for example, the case with a professional association or a group of sports fans. The distinction between primary and secondary groups is important for marketing purposes. Communication directed towards primary groups is made more difficult due to the very large number of such groups and the therefore atomistic nature of the audience. On the other hand, after having obtained access to one member, the communication is almost immediate and straightforward. In many cases it is enough to show a child an advertisement in order for the rest of the family to become aware of it! For secondary groups, the problem is just the opposite: their targeting is made easier given their smaller number as well as larger size, but the message can circulate very poorly or not at all if the most appropriate internal channels have not been identified first. In this chapter we will discuss primary groups, while secondary groups, especially social classes and cultural communities, comprise the topics of Chapters 6 and 7 respectively.

According to the group purpose, social scientists establish a distinction between **socio-groups** and **psycho-groups.**[11] In a socio-group, contact between members is only a means to achieve an objective. For example, computing user groups only get together to exchange experiences of using a computer or software. On the other hand, in a psycho-group, contact between members is an end in itself. A few fellow students who decide to spend an evening together, without knowing exactly what they are going to do, would fall into this category. Of course, few 'pure' socio-groups or psycho-groups exist, and most groups are to some degree both at once, though not necessarily in equal proportions. Here again, the distinction has some relevance for understanding buying behaviour and consumption. For a socio-group, a company will try to position its products in a functional manner: for example, a new support service promoted among a user group. In a psycho-group, however, it is the capacity of the product to express interpersonal relations which will be valued. In Europe, for example, a leading brewery has decided to position beer consumption as a collective emotional experience with its slogan: 'Create those great moments'.

According to their structure, it has become customary to separate **formal** and **informal** groups.[12] The formal group is characterised by the existence of rules and rituals determining how the group functions (sometimes even preceding their existence, such as for company legal structures: public limited company, joint venture, and so on). In the informal group, the norms are communally established and not always easy to detect by an external observer: in a class, for example, the designated leader is not necessarily the one who would have been elected by their comrades. Virtual communities such as those rapidly burgeoning on the Internet usually function as informal groups.[13]

Finally, considering status has resulted in the notions of **memb** reference groups.[14] Membership groups comprise all groups of ual is a part, whether voluntarily or not – going as far as gender, tat. Conversely, reference groups, which have been defined imaginary group conceived of having significant relevance u evaluations, aspirations or behaviour',[15] are usually based on a ation (or repulsion). The 'jet set society' thus represents an ideal and an anti-model for others. Certain reference groups are distant (for example, movie stars), while others are closer (relatives, friends).[16] Depending upon the social environment, the role of a product, and therefore its purchase and consumption patterns, can be more or less loaded with symbolic meanings. In buying a T-shirt with the emblem of an American university on it, a British school child is using an image which he or she judges valuable (reference group). However, the desired effect will only be obtained in full if his or her friends (membership group) hold similar values.

Research done on groups has generated innumerable studies and forms an essential part of the psycho-sociological domain. Two questions seem to have obsessed researchers: what is a group for, and how does it work? The answers provided by social psychologists are rich in implications for the understanding of buying and consumption phenomena.

The double function of a group

Two functions are most commonly put forward to justify the existence of groups: the identification function and the normative function.[17] We will examine each of these in turn.

The identification function

Paradoxical as it may seem, human beings affirm their identity via their social affiliation. There are many different groups to which we belong which, considered together, enable us to know who we are and to what we aspire. If you are not convinced about this, try to compile your *curriculum vitae* or even consider how you would introduce yourself to a stranger. In such exercises, the number of references, explicit or implicit, made to social groups is impressive. How could we identify ourselves without making reference to the family, our social surroundings, our professional environment, our school record, or even our leisure activities, which are often spent with other people? In fact, throughout our lives, we spend a lot of time comparing ourselves with people like us or close to us in order to evaluate ourselves, and most of our seemingly 'individual' tastes and preferences for such things as music or sports emerge from such continuous social benchmarking.[18] Normally, we tend to use people of equivalent standing when performing such social comparisons, and we tend to accept the information they give us as more trustworthy relevant. For example, a study revealed that women prefer the judgements of similar others' when choosing cosmetics.[19]

Given the pervasive nature of comparative influence processes, the **identification function** of a group opens up some interesting perspectives to understand the purchase and consumption of numerous goods and services. Almost every product or brand can enable us to express membership of a group. Figure 5.1 sums up the results obtained from twenty studies dedicated to this theme. Four situations emerge depending upon whether social influence affects the product category (generic impact) or the choice of a particular brand (specific impact). Two factors seem to account for the observed differences: the private or public nature of product consumption and its perceived necessity.[20]

Thus, necessities consumed in the home (light bulbs, mattresses, soap) are not particularly susceptible to group influence given their limited potential for social exchange. Conversely, 'outside' products corresponding to more discretionary spending (golf clubs, cigarettes, cars) offer excellent opportunities for interpersonal interaction. The group then simultaneously influences the acquisition of the product and the choice of the brand; all the other products occupy an intermediate position. Note that the consumption environment is more important than the product itself. Thus we do not buy the same alcoholic drinks to entertain friends as for our own personal consumption.[21] To capitalise upon social influence, a company therefore has two possibilities: either (a) 'externalise' the product (in the United States, T-shirts were first confined to the role of underclothes); or (b) bring it out of its daily and humdrum status, perhaps via the choice of original concepts (for example, pasta or rice positioned as ethnic or exotic food).

Figure 5.1   Group influence on product and brand

Influence on the product

		Weak	Strong
Influence on the brand	Strong	Suits, clothes, furniture, magazines, colour TV, wrist watches	Cars, cigarettes, beer, medicines, hi-fi equipment, sports equipment (skis, tennis rackets)
	Weak	Blankets, soap, detergents, cooking utensils, refrigerators, radios, mattresses, electric light bulbs	Air-conditioning equipment, Instant coffee, black-and-white TV, video discs, electric knives, electronic games

Source: Adapted from F. Bourne, 'Group Influence in Marketing and Public Relations', in R. Likert and S. P. Hayes (eds), *Some Applications of Behavioural Research* (UNESCO, 1957). See also W. O. Bearden and M. J. Etzel, 'Reference Group Influence on Product and Brand Purchase Decisions', *Journal of Consumer Research*, September 1982, pp. 183–94; and T. L. Childers and A. R. Rao, 'The Influence of Familial and Peer-based Reference Groups on Consumer Decisions', *Journal of Consumer Research*, September 1992, 198–211.

More generally speaking, it has been shown that group influence and, by extension, personal contact channels are stronger:

1 when the product is expensive, or perceived as such (luxury goods);

2 when the purchase is considered to be risky (financially, physically or socially);

3 when it is new or little diffused;

4 when it is intangible (services) or complex (for example, hi-fi equipment); and

5 when the consumption takes place in a public setting, watched by others.[22]

Conversely, the impact declines when the consumer feels relatively well informed or even an 'expert' in the product category, or when concerns to please the group are smaller, for example because of a lesser attraction (or credibility) of the group.

It should be noted that group influence is not always positive. Sometimes, people may wish to avoid being affiliated with their reference groups. For example, Richard Branson, president of Virgin, wears jeans and open shirts in sharp contrast to other multinational company leaders. Psychologists have coined the word 'reactance' to describe such behaviour.[23]

The normative function

The **normative function** of a group is perhaps even more revealing. Some years ago at European business school, an unusual study was carried out. A group of students proposed three brands of mineral water to thirty of their comrades in a 'blind test', that is to say with products from which all brand identification had been removed (anonymous bottles, product identification using single letters). The three products were, in fact, the same but the subjects involved in the test did not know this. These subjects were grouped into fours and were invited, after the tasting, to reveal their preferences. The group of four was artificial: it was composed of only one 'real' subject and three 'stooges' acting on the instructions of the experimenters and presented as 'experts'. In the control condition the subject was always invited to speak first whereas in the experiment he or she was always asked to speak last, after the three experts had given their opinion (they always chose the second product – brand B – either spontaneously or after some hesitation). The results are presented in Table 5.1. They speak for themselves. When the subjects spoke first, there was no reason for them to prefer one product over another and, the brands being all the same, their preferences were distributed more or less at random (control situation). In the opposite case (experimental situation 1), they had to face up to a 'norm' created by three people who had just unanimously expressed a strong preference for one brand (brand B in this case); it was then difficult for them not to prefer the same brand and their behaviour was adjusted to conform with that of the group. On the other hand, when the stooges were hesitant (experimental situation 2), the norm was 'destroyed' and the subjects could again express their own choice.

This experiment replicated, in a consumer research context, a famous study conducted many years ago by an American psychologist, Asch, who showed that when

Table 5.1 An experiment of conformity to group norms

	Results Brand A	Brand B	Brand C
Control situation			
30 subjects speaking first	9	10	11
	(30%)	(33%)	(36%)
Experimental situation 1			
30 subjects speaking last after three definitive 'experts'	6	16	8
(expressing a strong preference for Brand B)	(20%)	(53%)	(27%)
Experimental situation 2			
30 subjects speaking last after three hesitant 'experts'	10	11	9
(but still preferring B)	(33%)	(37%)	(30%)

confronted with a group norm, individual subjects could go as far as admitting a result totally contradictory to their own perceptions (in his study, recognising that a straight line was longer than another, obviously equal one, simply because all the stooges had dictated this choice).[24] Such an experiment has been repeated with similar results with other products such as men's suits,[25] and can even be observed in daily life, for example during a show of hands at a trade union meeting. In many social situations, there is a strong pressure to conform to group norms. There are many reasons for people to conform to group norms, including cultural pressures, fear of deviance and self-interest.[26]

Other social science research results testify to the impact of group influence on individual choice. It has been shown for example that, in a group situation, subjects often have a tendency to adopt more extreme attitudes that they would do alone, as if the presence of other people removes inhibiting factors.[27] On special occasions such as Mardi Gras or New Year's Eve, it may almost appear as if individual identities are submerged within a group, a phenomenon sometimes called **de-individuation**. It has also been shown that group members are inclined to accept riskier decisions, probably because of a perceived diffusion of responsibility. On other occasions, subjects become less involved than they would normally be, delegating some unpleasant or financially unattractive tasks to others. In the USA, for example, it has been shown that when dining at a restaurant, people tip less (per person) when they are in group than when they are alone.[28] As a result, a growing number of restaurant owners automatically add 10 or 15 per cent to the bill for groups of six people or more. On the other hand, other studies have established that shoppers tend to buy more when they shop with friends,[29] and certain retailers try to encourage such 'friendship' shopping.

The pressure to conform to group norms is at the heart of the way society works (imagine the societal chaos if norms like driving on a particular side of the road or paying income taxes ceased to be observed). In rewarding conformist behaviour and 'punishing' non-conformists, groups enable a society to survive by assuring the transmission of values, norms and rituals from the oldest to the youngest. As soon as group pressure is reduced, individuals recover some freedom of choice. For example, a recent study revealed that during weekends, 20 per cent of men choose not to shave.[30] Given their pervasive nature, it is not surprising that the impact of groups concerns all aspects of life in society – including, of course, buying and consumption.

A number of strategies and tactics exist for a distributor as well as a manufacturer to capitalise on the phenomenon of conformity to peer pressure. In retailing, it may take the form of a peddler and their cronies who, at the right moment, make some purchases in order to prime the pump. For manufacturers, it may be the case of an advertising message such as the one presented in Figure 5.2, which invites people losing their hair to contact their doctor immediately.

Social interaction and interpersonal influence

Given the two key functions identified above,[31] how does a group operate? There are few topics in social psychology which have generated more interest among researchers than this one. Generally speaking, three modes of group influence have been distinguished, depending upon whether the primary purpose of the interpersonal contact is (a) information ('I will ask someone who knows, in order to make a better choice'); (b) a concern to conform with others ('I'll take the advice of my parents so that I'm sure they'll approve'); or (c) a concern for self-expression ('I will take the advice of someone I admire and with whom I want to be associated').[32] From the extensive body of research carried out on the first of them – that is, **informational influence** – an early hypothesis has emerged, still at the heart of current debate and practice: the **two-step flow of communication**. In all social systems, resources, power and prestige are unequally divided. Certain people enjoy a privileged position within their group: these are called **opinion leaders**. Others submit to their influence, they are **followers**. The influence of opinion leaders on the behaviour of followers has been demonstrated on many occasions. The political studies conducted by Lazarsfeld and Gaudet[33] have shown how leaders, more exposed to the media, diffuse information around them, thus influencing the opinion of their entourage. Studies have shown similar results in the field of health[34] and rural sociology,[35] among many others.[36]

In marketing, the existence of opinion leaders opens up many interesting perspectives for a company. For example, a pharmaceutical laboratory may use more innovative doctors to promote new drugs by inviting them to seminars and lunches, and organizing various other 'events' for them;[37] similarly, a pop record company has demonstrated that, by distributing records to opinion leaders, an effective salesforce becomes available – and is much more credible as it is not subjected to commercial pressures.[38] It would seem that for more and more products and services, word-of-mouth communication is now more effective than advertising, especially for changing people's attitudes (rather than creating new ones), as it is systematically backed up by social pressure to conform to recommendations. In order to

Figure 5.2   A normative strategy

Today you and your doctor can do
something about your hair loss.

A new prescription only pharmaceutical
product is now available from pharmacies
in Scandinavia.

Call your doctor!

exploit this phenomenon, however, it is necessary to be able to identify and manage opinion leaders.

For a long time, sociologists believed in the existence of generalised (also called 'polymorphic') opinion leaders[39] who, by reason of their knowledge, personality or social position, have authority in a wide variety of domains.[40] Consumer researchers even attempted to characterise them: younger, socially active and often of a privileged socio-economic status, opinion leaders are exposed to a lot of information and have very favourable attitudes towards innovations – but only on condition that such innovations are not so revolutionary as to call into question their status.[41] In this sense, opinion leaders differentiate themselves from 'innovators', who are often defined as 'those who tend to adopt an innovation more rapidly than others'[42] and who are identified from either the moment of adoption, or the number of new products owned.[43] It should be noted that, in contrast with opinion leaders, innovators take their decisions independently of any interpersonal exchange.[44] They also have a tendency to process information more quickly and in a less elaborated manner than do opinion leaders.[45]

Similarly, researchers believed that opinion leaders were placed on top of the social pyramid and that their influence could only be downwards, according to the so-called 'trickle-down' effect: once the 'trend setters' had expressed themselves, it was believed, the crowd would follow.[46] Social scientists now recognise that reality is much more complex and that influence patterns are horizontal as much as vertical.[47] As a result, opinion leaders are primarily local and operate in a limited sphere of influence (monomorphic rather than polymorphic leaders).[48] In other words, because a person is very knowledgeable about cooking it is not the case that she will necessarily be consulted on DIY matters. Besides, a 'similarity effect' has been demonstrated: we are more easily influenced by someone that we feel close to.[49] For example, insurance salespeople are more successful with clients that resemble them psychologically or even physically. At times, word-of-mouth influence can be even more powerful than one's own perceptions. In the case of furniture, a study showed that consumers' opinions about whether their friends would like it was a better predictor of what they bought than their own product evaluations.[50] Social reality thus drives a complex network of influences. This obviously leads to difficulties in identifying and measuring opinion leadership.

Measuring opinion leadership

Unfortunately, there is no universally applicable method for identifying opinion leadership. For more restricted groups, researchers often use direct methods. Among these, the **key informant** technique, borrowed from ethnography, a social science discipline traditionally concerned with 'primitive' cultures, consists of asking someone who is well informed about the predominant networks of communication in the group under investigation.[51] The accuracy of the information supplied depends of course on the quality of the informant and the method is difficult to use for large groups, but with certain well-defined populations (a group of children, a company, a holiday club, etc.), it gives valuable results.

Another method, arising this time from social psychology, is **sociometry** and in particular the sociogramme, developed by Moreno.[52] Establishing a sociogramme consists of asking all group members (or a representative sample) to indicate who they consider as a leader (or 'to whom they would go for advice' if a less direct approach is preferred). The replies obtained result most often in a 'star' network in which the leaders can easily be located by their central position (that is, they are mentioned in the largest proportion). Here also, the method is interesting but most applicable to small-sized groups. For example, it has been used in a college environment in order to measure the relative perceived credibility of students in terms of music and records, as part of an experiment aimed at analysing the diffusion of pop music among teenagers.[53] Sociometry is particularly useful for understanding referral behaviour.[54]

Finally, the most direct method consists of asking people to evaluate themselves in terms of opinion leadership.[55] This **self-designating method** works via questions such as: 'When it comes to buying a new . . ., do many people ask your advice?' This method is far from perfect as it can lead to biased responses, especially in countries where leadership is socially valued, but it is by far the most practical and consequently the most frequently used in commercial studies.[56] Alternatively one could try to measure the '**influenceability**' of a consumer, that is their propensity to be a follower. Such a characteristic is often linked to other personality traits such as self-confidence or self-esteem.[57] Table 5.2 presents a scale, expressed in two dimensions (tendency to conform to others' judgements and tendency to accept them more certainly than one's own), which has been tested and used in fields as diverse as the choice of jeans in a shop, a colour TV or a car.[58]

Table 5.2 A scale of measurement of sensitivity to interpersonal influence

1 I often consult other people in order to help me choose the best product possible.
2 If I want to be like someone, I often buy the same brands as they do.
3 It is important that others like the brands and the products that I buy.
4 To reassure myself that I have made a good choice, I often watch what others buy and use.
5 I rarely buy the latest fashion if I'm not sure my friends will approve of it.
6 I often identify myself with others when buying brands and products that they buy.
7 If I have little experience of a product, I often ask my friends about it.
8 When I buy products, I generally buy brands which others approve of.
9 I like to know which products and brands make a good impression on others.
10 I often inform myself via friends and family regarding a product that I want to buy.
11 For a product that other people will see me using, I often buy the brand that they are expecting me to buy.
12 I feel closer to people if I buy the same products and brands as they do.

Source: Adapted from W. O. Bearden, R. G. Netemeyer and J. E. Teel, 'Measurement of Consumer Susceptibility to Interpersonal Influence', *Journal of Consumer Research*, March 1989, pp. 473–81. Also see from the same authors, 'Further Validation of the Consumer Susceptibility to Influence Scale', *Advances in Consumer Research* (ACR, 1990), pp. 770–6.

Finally, one may measure opinion leadership indirectly, that's to say using the traits which characterise an opinion leader for a given product category. The following characteristics have thus been used:

1 frequency and amount of purchase (opinion leaders are often the largest buyers of the product category);

2 brand loyalty or company affinity (as measured, for example, by possession of a fidelity card); or

3 behaviour relating to exposure to specialised media (opinion leaders are often the largest consumers of reviews and magazines within their sphere of interest). For example, a study of financial opinion leaders found that they were more likely to read books and watch TV programmes devoted to financial issues.

Sometimes, consumer researchers can also use indicators of leadership in other domains (electoral mandate, responsibility in an association, etc.).

What makes an opinion leader?

Even if it is difficult to provide a complete profile, certain key characteristics of opinion leaders have been identified. Kelman has suggested three qualities, much sought after in the identification and management of today's leaders.[59] The first is **perceived expertise**. In order to be a leader, an individual needs first to be recognised as an authority within his or her sphere of influence. This authority confers upon a leader the credibility which is needed to support his or her statements. Who best to cover the Tour de France? An ex-participant. Who can speak authoritatively about AIDS? A medical professor doing research in this area. Conversely, a school student normally has little influence over a schoolteacher. Similarly, a non-consumer is rapidly excluded from a focus group debate over the purchasing criteria for the corresponding product. It is worth pointing out that perceived expertise is more important here than real expertise. From the moment the supposed expert is considered as such by his public, it is of little consequence whether or not he or she is actually a specialist in this field. All the members of staff in a pharmacy do not necessarily have a pharmaceutical qualification, but they all wear a white coat in order to win the confidence of the customer. In one interesting study, two American researchers varied the level of perceived expertise of record shop staff. Salespeople had to sell a record-cleaning kit, and they sold three times more when they spoke with authority than when they admitted they didn't know much about it.[60]

Perceived expertise is a necessary but not sufficient condition for opinion leadership. For example, numerous university researchers, while honoured by their university, turn out to be totally incapable of exciting the interest of their audience. **Empathy** is also required, that is the capacity to put oneself 'in the shoes' of one's audience to the extent that they identify with the speaker, thinking 'It's amazing how he understands our problems and how he seems so close to us!' Certain celebrities, such as Cilla Black and Jay Leno, seem to enjoy a high level of empathy with their public. In adopting a straightforward manner or using direct language, they appear less distant, greatly increasing their ability to influence. Less admired than authorities, they seem perhaps more real.

Finally, opinion leaders must be seen to be **disinterested**. Leaders are much better accepted if their actions are perceived to be in the general interest, rather than being partisan. This makes all the difference between humanitarian and commercial communications. In calling on a celebrity to convince people to send donations, UNICEF knows that no member of the audience will question the good faith and independence of the endorser, which significantly reinforces the credibility of the message. Conversely, it is usually very difficult for a salesperson to appear neutral and objective in a face-to-face contact with a potential customer. It is worth noting that, as for expertise, the perception of impartiality or disinterest counts more than disinterest itself.

Expertise, empathy and disinterest are qualities which we rarely encounter to a large degree in the same individual; therefore, it is no surprise that only a small number of leaders are universally recognised as such. It is possible, however, that certain people can succeed in providing the right mix between the three ingredients. Good examples include Mother Teresa, Nelson Mandela and John F. Kennedy; but such opinion leaders are few and are obviously difficult to control.

Yet, certain companies succeed in putting in place a strategy for managing opinion leaders. These are often the companies which do not have free access to the media either because of their limited resources (small business, non-profit associations) or because of regulation (for example, tobacco, alcoholic drinks). For example, a medium-sized European company (CSL), which makes and sells solar energy products, has identified two different categories of leader: the 'leader-user', which it tries to access via trade fairs and exhibitions, and the 'leader-influencer'. This last group comprises both professionals and pressure or influence groups. The first are not all managed in the same way. If they are installers or heating engineers, they are offered expenses-paid sales conferences aimed at establishing good relations between them and CSL. For design offices and architects, CSL prepares press packs and maintains regular contact with professional bodies and unions. CSL has also identified numerous pressure and influence groups: ecologists, to whom it supplies documentation and support for literature destined for the specialist press; DIY associations; consumer organisations (preparation of technical documentation such as comparative tests); and journalists and political personalities. Overall, the CSL programme has proven to be very effective.

Similarly Pernod-Ricard (the French group) has for a long time undertaken actions aimed at opinion leaders via its 'propaganda' department. Three kinds of operation are in place. First, propaganda at the place of consumption uses the traditional salesforce and consists of identifying 'key café owners', who indicate their regular customers. Targeted offers are then proposed by the sales rep at the time aperitifs are served and the café owner receives a gift. Second, propaganda at leisure and entertainment spots is carried out by reps specially trained in public relations.

From information supplied by the key café owners, Pernod-Ricard identifies the leaders in certain selected sports such as fishing or rugby. Parties are held at weekends in popular places. The support of the company is not limited to the organisation of the parties; it also includes team sponsoring, free sports equipment, training support, the giving of cups and trophies, and targeted offers during competitions. Finally, propaganda at the place of work is implemented with the help of a 'commando force' specialising in direct contact. Typical sectors are chosen (butchers' shops, garages, repair shops) and contacts are established with the owners or workshop supervisors, always in consultation with the key café owners. Aperitifs or presents are offered at the place of work (after hours). The idea is to pick out the key consumers, who in turn will pass on their opinions.

Many car manufacturers also employ PR consultants, who prepare product launches by sending information to 'car fans' identified from appropriate databases and by organising 'road tests' for selected journalists, who are taken to fancy places where they are wined and dined. In the domain of cosmetics, a company like L'Oréal has identified four opinion leader categories:

1 journalists, regularly contacted by public relations staff;

2 'specialists' such as popular hairdressers or pharmacists;

3 professionals (for example, dermatologists); and

4 leader-users.[61]

It should be noted that public relations campaigns do not always succeed. In particular, they cannot compensate for a major deficiency in the product or an inadequate price positioning.

More generally, companies wanting to take advantage of the phenomena of opinion leadership and interpersonal influence can adopt two main strategies: **simulation** and **stimulation**.

Simulation and stimulation

A strategy of **simulation** consists of 'doing as if' a process of social diffusion was supporting the product or the brand. A number of approaches are available: one possibility, for example, is to simulate product use by a person considered to be a leader. This is the essence of the testimonial and celebrity endorsement approaches: Nigel Mansell, former world motor racing champion, advises you to drive a certain make of car; Gary Lineker eats Walker's Crisps; Elizabeth Hurley models for Estée Lauder; and so on. The budgets required vary according to the fame of the star and the company's financial resources. Pepsi-Cola spent hundreds of millions of dollars on Michael Jackson before the contract was terminated.

In order to be effective, this approach must rely on a leader who is both attractive and credible.[62] As already discussed in Chapter 3, the importance of credibility varies according to the nature of the audience. For an uninvolved viewer, the credibility of the source has little relevance. In the case of deeper involvement, on the other hand, a highly credible source reinforces the impact of the message and reduces the number and strength of counter-arguments.[63] Additionally, it would appear that a highly credible source increases the level of yielding.[64] However, managing a celebrity is sometimes a delicate exercise. Most companies who used the services of 'Magic' Johnson (for example, Nestlé, Pepsi-Cola, Nintendo) re-examined their position when he announced on television that he was HIV-posi-tive.[65] To avoid such problems, companies may prefer to 'create' their own 'celebrities', whose lives then become easier to manage – the Mario character cre-ated by the Nintendo company to promote its video games is one such 'celebrity'. In 1994, Nintendo even moved on to create Wario, the 'negative double' of Mario, who ranks number four in children's all-time favourite heroes. Finally, studies have shown that multiple product endorsements by the same celebrity tend to reduce their overall impact,[66] unless the products are highly related to each other and pre-sented within a relevant context.[67]

A second approach consists of developing the idea that 'others' are buying the product. This method has been used successfully by Electrolux for its household appliances. The aim is to reveal to the consumer their status as follower and, in making them feel a little guilty, to 'bring them back into the club' by making them participate in some positive word of mouth. It is also the approach of a bookstore chain in Europe, which emphasises this in its slogan: 'Each year, 300 000 readers recommend us to their friends. It is our best advertisement'. In recent years, a number of company, product and brand 'clubs' have been created as a way of maintaining permanent contact with customers. For example, the Nintendo hotline receives about 300 000 calls daily. Banks have also created 'affinity cards', which can be tied to almost any type of membership group.[68] In the USA, it is estimated that over 2700 different affinity cards are now available and that they are carried by over 26 million people.

A third approach consists of granting the status of a leader to a potential customer in the hope of triggering a feeling of pride which will lead to a purchase. Business peri-odicals regularly target management students towards the end of their studies with messages like this: 'In a few months, you will be taking on some important responsi-bilities. Your job will require a perfect understanding of the world around you and how it is changing. To prepare you …' (a subscription offer follows). Similarly, par-ticular retailing groups have chosen to develop an image for their salespeople as experts – specialists in a product category – but relatively 'neutral' and 'independent' with regard to the different brands on sale in the shop. Virgin Megastore staff, for example, are trained to be able to provide their assistance in the choice of music or equipment but without necessarily recommending particular brands. By publishing the results of comparative tests (limited, it's true, to products and brands on sale in the store), by organising events and exhibitions, Virgin seeks to appear as an opinion leader – and a reference in the world of music and leisure equipment.

A different strategy consists of **stimulating** personal influence. The idea is now to trigger the process of social interaction rather than just give the illusion of it. Several mechanisms can be used for this. The first one consists of using existing opinion leaders. The launch of Rubik's Cube in France was helped by sending 1600 specimens to the press and show business personalities. Similarly, when Ford re-launched its Thunderbird model in the USA, invitations to try it were sent to 400 000 managers and professionals. More than 15 000 people took advantage of the offer; though only 10 per cent said they were interested in buying one, 84 per cent indicated that they would recommend the car to their friends.[69] In the same manner, most pharmaceutical laboratories try to maintain good relations with national and international specialists, to whom they confide their tests and studies carried out on compounds that they have just brought out.

A slightly different method consists of supplying local opinion leaders with the product in the hope that their network of influence will promote it. This strategy has been used in southern Europe by companies selling swimming pools in resi-dential areas. They install the swimming pool extremely cheaply (sometimes even free) in a house where the owner is well known locally. Word of mouth is supposed to do the rest. A few years ago, an interesting experiment took place to demonstrate the power of opinion leadership phenomena. A new pop record was produced and sent to university students identified (through sociometric methods) as local opin-ion leaders in terms of music and records. For control purposes, the record was also randomly mailed to students at other universities. It rapidly became a hit in those universities where opinion leaders were used but did not succeed at all elsewhere.[70]

A more common approach is to help people to talk about their recent purchase. This technique builds on the phenomenon of cognitive dissonance discussed in Chapter 2. Buyers often seek to justify a purchase they have just made (especially if the decision took a long time and was difficult to make) and the most natural way to do it is to talk to others about it. The buyer thus becomes an excellent salesper-son, being so much more credible because they have no commercial interest. Referral and sponsorship programmes such as those used by American Express and the airline companies work on this principle. Sometimes complete commercial structures are put in place. A classic example is Tupperware, a company selling plastic containers sold exclusively (and almost without advertising) via a network of 12 500 housewives acting as 'Tupperware hostesses'. Each hostess organises, at regular intervals, a gathering of 'friends', getting together a dozen acquaintances who are shown the company's products.[71] Tupperware's results are impressive: 700 000 meetings are held each year, and seven million people are thus contacted. Two and a half million people buy at least one product, which corresponds to an impressive conversion rate of more than a third! Avon is a similar case: it contacts around a million women each year via 70 000 'Avon ladies', chosen from its best clients and managed by 360 'regional advisors'.

A final approach stimulating interpersonal influence consists of getting people to talk about a product by creating a 'stunt' around it. It is expected that subsequent word of mouth will promote sales. This approach is exemplified by 'teasing'-style advertising campaigns. The principle is always the same: the first message is quite enigmatic, capturing one's attention. Waiting until the level of 'suspense' has risen, the solution is then provided in a second message. The risk, of course, is that the second message does not meet the expectations created by the first. The results can however be spectacular: some years ago, IBM placed the first 'musical advert' in a magazine insert, a microprocessor being used to play a tune when the page was opened. The edition of the European magazine in which this was inserted was sold out almost as soon as it was published. Several companies such as Peter Kim and Event International specialise in the management of such events and suggest all kinds of things designed to arouse interest in a new product.

In summary, the management of influence processes turns out to be a rather powerful tool in developing exchange relationships with consumers. Less visible than advertising, it is also usually cheaper to implement. Very flexible in nature, it builds upon mechanisms of interpersonal interaction which are at the heart of the way human society works. Because of this, it can be extremely effective.

Notes

1 This limitation has led Fishbein and his associates to enrich the attitudinal model described in the previous chapter and develop their 'Theory of Reasoned Action', which takes into account two additional factors: social norms and the individual motivation to comply with them. See I. Ajzen and M. Fishbein, *Understanding Attitudes and Predicting Social Behaviour* (Prentice Hall, 1980). For consumer research done on the theory of reasoned action, see M. J. Ryan and E. H. Bonfield, 'The Fishbein Extended Model and Consumer Behavior', *Journal of Consumer Research*, 1975, 2, pp. 118–36; and B. H. Sheppard, J. Hartwick and P. R. Warshaw, 'The Theory of Reasoned Action: A Meta-Analysis of Past Research with Recommendations for Modifications and Future Research', *Journal of Consumer Research*, December 1988, pp. 325–43.

2 On this point see A. Wicker, 'Attitudes versus Actions: The Relationship of Verbal and Overt Behavioural Responses to Attitude Objects', *The Journal of Social Issues*, 1969, pp. 41–78; S. J. Gross and C. M. Niman, 'Attitude–Behaviour Consistency: A Review', *Public Opinion Quarterly*, Autumn 1975, pp. 358–68; I. Ajzen and M. Fishbein, 'Attitude–Behaviour Relations: A Theoretical Analysis and Review of Empirical Research', *Psychological Bulletin*, September 1977, pp. 888–918; and M. U. Kalwani and A. J. Silk, 'On the Reliability and Predictive Validity of Purchase Intention Measures', *Marketing Science*, Summer 1982, pp. 243–86.

3 J. Ardnt, 'Roles of Product Related Conversations in the Diffusion of a New Product', *Journal of Marketing Research*, August 1967, pp. 291–5.

4 T. S. Robertson, *Innovative Behavior and Communications* (Holt, Rinehart, & Winston, 1971)

5 J. L. Moulins, 'Etude des Phénomènes de Leadership dans le Domaine des Services Auto-mobiles', Aix-en-Provence, 1978, unpublished document.

6 Study carried out in 1989 by the British Market Bureau, on a sample of one thousand adults.

7 S. P. Feldman, 'Some Dyadic Relationships Associated with Consumer Choice', in R. M. Haas (ed.), *Proceedings of the American Marketing Association* (AMA, 1966), pp. 758–75.

8 B. Audard *et al.*, 'L'Influence Interpersonnelle'. FNAC/ISA study, December 1990, conducted under the author's supervision.

9 W. H. Whyte Jr, 'The Web of Word of Mouth', *Fortune*, November 1954, pp. 140–3.

10 See P. Hare, E. F. Borgatta and R. Bales (eds), *Small Groups* (New York: Knopf, 1955).

11 D. Krech, R. Crutchfield and E. Ballachey, *Individual in Society* (New York: McGraw-Hill, 1962), p. 383.

12 See for example F. J. Roethlisberger and W. J. Dickson, *Management and the Worker* (Cambridge, Mass.: Harvard University Press, 1939).

[13] J. Hagel III and A. G. Armstrong, *Net Gain: Expanding Markets Through Virtual Communities'* (Cambridge, Mass.: Harvard Business School Press, 1997).

[14] H. Hyman, 'The Psychology of Status', *Archives of Psychology*, 1942, 269, pp. 94–102. See also from the same author, 'Reflections on Reference Groups', *Public Opinion Quarterly*, 1960, 24, pp. 383–96.

[15] R. Burnkrant and A. Cousineau, 'Informational and Normative Social Influence in Buyer Behavior', *Journal of Consumer Research*, December 1975, pp. 206–15.

[16] A. B. Cocanougher and G. D. Bruce, 'Socially Distant Reference Groups and Consumer Aspirations', *Journal of Marketing Research*, August 1971, pp. 79–81.

[17] Some authors prefer to distinguish between the normative and informational functions of a group. The latter refers to using the behaviour and opinions of other group members as a source of information for one's own decisions. Although the informational function has been well documented (for a review, see Cialdini's *Influence: The Psychology of Persuasion*, 1993), we believe the identification function is a broader concept, as it does not necessarily assume informational influence through observation.

[18] Leon Festinger, 'A Theory of Social Comparison Processes', *Human Relations*, 4 May 1994, pp. 117–40.

[19] G. P. Moschis, 'Social Comparison and Informal Group Influence', *Journal of Marketing Research*, August 1976, pp. 237–44.

[20] See W. Bearden and M. J. Etzel, 'Reference Group Influence on Product and Brand Purchase Decisions', *Journal of Consumer Research*, September 1982, pp. 183–94; also see T. L. Childers and A.R. Rao, 'The Influence of Familial and Peer-Based Reference Groups on Consumer Decisions', *Journal of Consumer Research*, September 1992, pp. 198–211.

[21] P. Miniard and J. B. Cohen, 'Modeling Personal and Normative Influences on Behavior', *Journal of Consumer Research*, September 1983, pp. 169–80.

[22] J. D. Ford and E. A. Ellis, 'A Re-examination of Group Influence on Member Brand Preference', *Journal of Marketing Research*, February 1980, pp. 125–32.

[23] J. W. Brehm, *A Theory of Psychological Reactance*, (Academic Press, 1960).

[24] S. E. Asch, ' Effects of Group Pressure on Modification and Distortion of Judgements', in H. Guetzkow (ed.), *Groups, Leadership, and Men* (Carnegie Press, 1951).

[25] M. Venkatesan, 'Experimental Study of Consumer Behaviour Conformity and Independence', *Journal of Marketing Research*, November 1966, pp. 384–7. For another application in the fashion industry, see L. L. Davis and F. G. Miller, 'Conformity and Judgements of Fashionability', *Home Economics Research Journal*, June 1983, pp. 37–42.

[26] J. W. Thibault and H. H. Kelley, *The Social Psychology of Groups* (New York: John Wiley, 1959).

[27] V. Rao and J. Steckel, 'A Polarization Model for Describing Group Preferences', *Journal of Consumer Research*, June 1991, pp. 108–18.

[28] S. Freeman, M. Walker, R. Borden and B. Latané, 'Diffusion of Responsibility and Restaurant Tipping: Cheaper by the Bunch', *Personality and Social Psychology Bulletin*, 1978, pp. 584–7.

[29] D. Granbois, 'Improving the Study of Customer In-Store Behavior', *Journal of Marketing*, October 1968, pp. 28–32.

[30] S. Brown, 'It really is a man's world', *Marketing News*, 1994, July 28, p. 1.

[31] For additional reading, see Harold H. Kelley, 'Two Functions of Reference Groups', in H. Proshansky and B. Siedenberg (eds), *Basic Studies in Social Psychology* (New York: Holt, Rinehart & Winston, 1965), pp. 210–14.

[32] M. Deutsch and H. Gerard, 'A Study of Normative and Informational Social Influences Upon Individual Judgement', *Journal of Abnormal and Social Psychology*, 1955, vol. 51, pp. 624–36. For a detailed description of each mode of influence, see C. Whan Park and V. Parker Lessig, 'Students and Housewives: Differences in Susceptibility to Reference Group Influence', *Journal of Consumer Research*, September 1977, p. 102.

[33] P. F. Lazarsfeld, B. Berelson and H. Gaudet, *The People's Choice* (Columbia University Press, 1948); see also E. Katz and P. F. Lazarsfeld, *Personal Influence* (Free Press, 1955).

[34] J. R. Coleman, 'Social Process in Physicians' Adoption of a New Drug', *Journal of Chronic Diseases*, 1959, pp. 1–19. See also J. Coleman, E. Katz and H. Menzel, 'The Diffusion of an Innovation Among Physicians', *Sociometry*, December 1957, pp. 253–70.

[35] B. Ryan and N. C. Gross, 'The Diffusion of Hybrid Seed Corn in Two Iowa Communities', *Rural Sociology*, March 1943, pp. 15–24.

[36] E. M. Rogers; *The Diffusion of Innovations* (Free Press, 1983).

[37] See M. Rawlins, 'Doctors and Drug Makers', *The Lancet*, 1984, 15 October, pp. 20–1.

[38] See M. L. Richins, 'Word of Mouth Communication as Negative Information', *Advances in Consumer Research* (ACR, 1984), pp. 697–702.

[39] R. Merton, *Social Theory and Social Structure* (Free Press, 1957).

[40] See R. Marcus and R. Bauer, 'Yes, There Are Generalized Opinion Leaders', *Public Opinion Quarterly*, Winter 1964, pp. 628–32; and E. J. Gross, 'Support for a Generalized Marketing Leadership Theory', *Journal of Advertising Research*, November 1969, pp. 49–52.

[41] J. H. Myers and T. S. Robertson, 'Dimension of Opinion Leadership', *Journal of Marketing Research*, February 1972, pp. 41–6. See also T. S. Robertson and J. H. Myers, 'Personality Correlates of Opinion Leadership and Innovative Buying Behavior', *Journal of Marketing Research*, May 1969, p. 168.

[42] E. Rogers and F. Shoemaker, *Communication of Innovations* (Free Press, 1971).

[43] See J. N. Kapferer and G. Laurent, 'Peut-on identifier les Innovateurs?' *Revue Française du Marketing*, 1980, 83, pp. 21–39; G. Roehrich, 'Les Consommateurs Innovateurs: Un essai d'identification', doctoral thesis, cited in G. Roehrich, 'Nouveauté perçue d'une innovation', *Recherche et Applications en Marketing*, 1987, 1, pp. 1–15; C. Kohn and J. Jacoby, 'Operationally Defining the Consumer Innovator', *Proceedings of the American Psychological Association Conference* (APA, 1973); and R. Goldsmith and L. Reinecke, 'Identifying Innovators in Consumer Product Markets', *International Journal of Research in Marketing*, 1992, 12, pp. 42–55.

[44] D. F. Midgley and G. R. Dowling, 'Innovativeness: The Concept and its Measurement', *Journal of Consumer Research*, March 1978, pp. 229–42. For an empirical scale measuring the tendency to innovate, see R. E. Goldsmith and C. Hofacker, 'Measuring Consumer Innovativeness', *Journal of the Academy of Marketing Science*, 1991, 19, (3), pp. 209–21. Such a scale has been validated both in Europe and in Canada.

[45] G. R. Dowling and D. F. Midgley, 'The Decision Processes of Innovative Communicators and Other Adopters', *Marketing Letters*, 1993, 4, pp. 297–308. See also G. R. Foxall and S. Bhate, 'Cognitive Style and Personal Involvement as Explicators of Innovative Purchasing of Health Food Brands', *European Journal of Marketing*, 1993, 27, pp. 5–16; R. J. Fisher and L. L. Price, 'An Investigation into the Social Context of Early Adoption Behavior', *Journal of Consumer Research*, December 1992, pp. 477–86; and S. L. Holak, D. R. Lehmann and F. Sultan, 'The Role of Expectations in the Adoption of Innovative Consumer Durables: Some preliminary Evidence', *Journal of Retailing*, Fall 1987, pp. 243–59.

[46] C. W. King, 'Fashion Adoption: A Rebuttal to the Trickle Down Theory', in J. U. McNeal (ed.), *Dimensions of Consumer Behaviour* (Appleton-Century-Crofts, 1969).

[47] See D. F. Midgley and G. Wills, *Fashion Marketing Lateral Marketing Thoughts* (Bradford: MCB Prem, 1979).

[48] See A. Silk, 'Overlap Amongst Self-Designated Opinion Leaders: A Study of Selected Dental Products and Services', *Journal of Marketing Research*, August 1966, pp. 255–9; C. W. King and J. O. Summers, 'Overlap of Opinion Leadership Across Consumer Product Categories', *Journal of Marketing Research*, February 1970, pp. 43–50; and D. Montgomery and A. J. Silk, 'Clusters of Consumer Interest and Opinion Leaders' Spheres of Influence', *Journal of Marketing Research*, August 1971, pp. 317–21.

[49] See P. Busch and D. J. Wilson, 'An Experimental Analysis of a Salesman's Expert and Referent Bases of Social Power in the Buyer–Seller Dyad', *Journal of Marketing Research*, February 1976, pp. 3–11.

[50] See J. H. Myers and T. S. Roberston, *op. cit.*

[51] P. A. Adler and P. Adler, 'Membership Roles in Field Research', *Qualitative Research Methods*, Vol. 6 (Sage, 1987).

[52] J. L. Moreno, *Foundations of Sociometry* (Paris: PUF, 1954).

[53] J. R. Mancuso, 'Why Not Create Opinion Leaders for New Product Introductions?' *Journal of Marketing*, July 1969, pp. 20–5.

[54] P. Reingen and J. B. Kernan, 'Analysis of Referral Networks in Marketing: Methods and Illustration', *Journal of Marketing Research*, November 1986, pp. 370–8.

[55] E. Rogers and D. G. Cartano, 'Methods of Measuring Opinion Leadership', *Public Opinion Quarterly*, Autumn 1962, pp. 435–41. See also J. Jacoby, 'Opinion Leadership and Innovativeness: Overlap and Validity', *Proceedings of the 3rd Annual Conference of the Association for Consumer Research*, M. Venkatesan (ed.), 1972, pp. 632–49.

[56] See T. Childers, 'Assessing the Psychometric Properties of an Opinion Leadership Scale', *Journal of Marketing Research*, May 1986, pp. 184–8.

[57] See W. McGuire, 'Personality and Susceptibility to Social Influence', in E. F. Borgatta and W. W. Lambert (eds), *The Handbook of Personality Theory and Research* (Rand McNally, 1968), pp. 1130–87; J. E. Stafford and B. A. Cocanougher, 'Reference Group Theory' in *Selected Aspects of Consumer Behavior* (Superintendent of Documents, US Government Printing Office, 1977), pp. 361–80; and C. W. Park and P. V. Lessig, 'Students and Housewives: Differences in Susceptibility to Reference Group Influence', *Journal of Consumer Research*, September 1977, pp. 102–10.

[58] W. O. Bearden, R. G. Netemeyer and J. E. Teel, 'Measurement of Consumer Susceptibility to Interpersonal Influence', *Journal of Consumer Research*, March 1989, pp. 473–81. Also see the same authors: 'Further Validation of the Consumer Susceptibility to Influence Scale', *Advances in Consumer Research* (ACR, 1990), pp. 770–6.

[59] H. C. Kelman, 'Processes of Opinion Change', *Public Opinion Quarterly*, Spring 1961, pp. 57–78.

[60] A. C. Woodside and J. W. Davenport, 'The Effect of Salesman Similarity and Expertise on Consumer Purchasing Behaviour', *Journal of Marketing Research*, May 1974, pp. 198–202.

[61] P. Aubron *et al.*, *La Gestion des Leaders d'Opinion. Étude réalisée sur le Marché des Cosmétiques*. HEC study 1990 carried out under the author's supervision.

[62] See M. J. Baker and G. A. Churchill Jr, 'The Impact of Physically Attractive Models on Advertising Evaluations', *Journal of Marketing Research*, November 1977, pp. 538–55; and L. R. Kahle and P. M. Homer, 'Physical Attractiveness of the Celebrity Endorser: A Social Adaptation Perspective', *Journal of Consumer Research*, March 1995, pp. 954–61.

[63] B. Sternthal, R. Dohlakia and C. Leavitt, 'The Persuasive Effect of Source Credibility: Test of Cognitive Response', *Journal of Consumer Research*, March 1978, pp. 252–60; also see R. Dohlakia and B. Sternthal, 'Highly Credible Sources: Persuasive Facilitators and Persuasive Liabilities', *Journal of Consumer Research*, March 1977, pp. 223–37.

[64] B. Sternthal, 'Persuasion and the Mass Communication Process', doctoral thesis, Ohio State University, 1972.

[65] 'Advertisers Forced to Rethink "Magic" as their Spokesman', *Marketing News*, 9 December 1991, p. 1.

[66] C. Tripp *et al.*, 'The Effects of Multiple Products Endorsements by Celebrities on Consumers' Attitudes and Intentions', *Journal of Consumer Research*, March 1994, pp. 535–47.

[67] T. B. Heath *et al.*, 'Spokesperson Fame and Vividness Effects in the Context of Issue-relevant Thinking: The Moderating Role of Competitive Setting', *Journal of Consumer Research*, March 1994, pp. 520–34.

[68] J. Graham, 'Affinity Card Clutter: Number of Tie-ins Raises Doubts About Continued Use', Special Report: Financial Services Marketing, *Advertising Age*, 14 November 1988.

[69] M. Cox, 'Ford Pushing Thunderbird with VIP Pan', *Wall Street Journal*, 17 October 1983, p. 37.

[70] J. R. Mancuso, *op. cit.*

[71] L. Strazewski, 'Tupperware Locks in New Strategy', *Advertising Age*, 8 February 1988, p. 30.

6

Social classes and lifestyles

Learning objectives

After studying this chapter, you should understand:

1 the meaning attached to the concept of social class;
2 the various ways in which social class standing is measured and categorised;
3 how social class affiliation affects consumer behaviour;
4 how social class classification can be used by marketing managers for segmenting their targets, positioning their products and managing the marketing mix;
5 the meaning attached to the lifestyle concept;
6 the differences between social class and lifestyle;
7 how lifestyles are measured and used in marketing;
8 the limits attached to lifestyle systems.

Key words

social stratification	class consciousness	social structure
social class	socio-professional	lifestyle
social mobility	categories	psychographics
status symbols	social status	centres of interest

For a special edition dedicated to the twenty-first century, a European news magazine carried out a poll asking youngsters which career they would like to follow, from a choice of six in three categories.[1] The results, presented in Table 6.1, are revealing. Such lists express, through judgements made about relative **occupational prestige**, a hierarchical system characteristic of living in society.[2]

In all known human groups, and some animal societies (as studies have shown the existence of a 'pecking order' for birds[3]), there exists a process by which power, authority and prestige are unequally divided among the various members making up the group. This mechanism, known as **social stratification**, determines their

Table 6.1

List 1 *'Prestigious' jobs*		List 2 *'Intermediate' jobs*		List 3 *'Doing' jobs*	
1 Journalist	28%	1 Computer programmer	51%	1 Secretary	54%
2 Engineer	27%	2 Teacher	22%	2 Salesperson	29%
3 Doctor	19%	3 Nurse	17%	3 Postman	8%
4 Professor	11%	4 Sales representative	5%	4 Lorry driver	7%
5 Company manager	10%	5 Supervisor	3%	5 Factory worker	2%
6 Banker	5%	6 Farmer	2%	6 Doorkeeper	0%

access to resources and leads to a separation of society into levels (or strata) corresponding to rungs on a social ladder.[4] In societies with closed structures, we call these groups 'castes'; in more modern and flexible societies, they are called social classes.

What is a social class?

Given that social class is the central concept of sociology, it is not surprising that there are many definitions of it.[5] Rather than examining and comparing them one by one, we will take one of the better-known definitions and try to identify its essential aspects. According to Krech, Crutchfield and Ballachey, social class is 'a division of society made up of persons possessing certain common social characteristics which are taken to qualify them for intimate, equal-status relations with one another, and which restrict their interaction with members of other social classes'.[6] From this definition, five elements emerge. Social classes are (a) large aggregates, (b) stratified, (c) evolving, (d) multidimensional but (e) relatively homogeneous:

- **Large aggregates** Social classes are secondary groups, that is groups in which communication between members is neither direct nor interactive. It follows that – in contrast to smaller social groups such as households, neighbours, colleagues, groups of friends, where interpersonal influence is a key factor – the impact of social class affiliation is more symbolic by nature. Today, people can buy and use a variety of products and services that express to which social class they belong.

- **Stratified** As opposed to age groups or lifestyles, which are juxtaposed mosaics of human attributes, social classes always include the idea of superior or inferior status. This characteristic is important for understanding consumption patterns for many publicly consumed products. Consider clothing. To a large extent, the way people dress tends to express their social position. Sociologists have thus coined the expression 'blue collar workers' to refer to manual workers.

- **Evolving** In contrast to castes, social classes are neither rigid nor closed. The very existence of an open social stratification system encourages members of the inferior class to climb up the social ladder. The phenomenon of upward (or downward) mobility explains a good number of purchasing decisions. In buying a top-of-the-range attaché case, an employee recently promoted to office supervisor is trying to materialise the progression; he or she also wants to make sure everyone notices the difference.

- **Multidimensional** Social class does not equate to occupation, income or level of education. A lorry driver, even if earning about the same as a schoolteacher, does not belong to the same group. They do not consider themselves as 'equals', may not feel at ease in each other's company and will probably spend their money very differently. On the other hand, all these factors – among others[7] – help to define social class identity. By its very nature, social class is a multifaceted concept.

- **Relatively homogeneous** Holding the same position on the social chessboard, sharing the same core values, the members of a given social class tend to behave in a similar manner. In particular, they tend to use their money in similar ways. It is this last characteristic which is of particular interest to marketing managers.[8] This homogeneous behaviour, for example the tendency to dress in the same way, to have the same leisure activities and share the same interests, enables marketers to define social class groupings. Equally important, the specific products bought by the social classes are often intended to convey to the other groups where they stand socially. Products and services thus become **status symbols**. We imagine a factory worker dressed in overalls rather than in a three-piece suit. For marketers, a means of differentiating their products, mode of communication and distribution systems becomes available. In a number of sectors, the airline industry for example, companies may adopt a two-tiered marketing strategy with separate offering for upmarket (that is, 'first class') and downscale (that is, 'economy') consumers.

Beyond their common core, the numerous definitions of social class diverge greatly. It has become customary to oppose the 'objective' approaches, which rely upon external, observable indicators, to 'subjective' approaches, in which a key element is 'class consciousness'. Beyond theoretical differences, such a distinction directly affects the problem of **measurement**.

How do we measure social class?

Numerous methods for measuring social class have been suggested. We first analyse those based on the subjective orientation and then those relying on the objective approach.

For European sociologists such as Lukacs[9] or Halbwachs,[10] who make class consciousness a key aspect of the concept of social class, a method based on direct questioning is well founded. Two procedures have been used: self-classification and the method based on reputation. According to the **self-classification** method,[11] the individual is asked to indicate on a list, either directly or by comparison with others, to which social class they think they belong.[12] Alternatively, researchers can invite them to give themselves a 'score' (from 1 to 10) on the social ladder, or even place themselves in a pyramid or on a step.[13] In the method based on **reputation**, researchers ask a well-informed person to indicate the social class affiliation of people belonging to their community, relying on their own perception or by referring to activities considered superior or inferior.[14] These two methods have their limits. In Europe, where egalitarianism tends to be valued, the method of self-classification often results in an enlargement of the middle class; most people pick intermediate categories when asked to indicate their social standing. The reputation method, on the other hand, is slow, costly and – critically – depends upon the qualifications and objectivity of the researcher. It can only be applied to limited groups. For these reasons, subjective methods are little used in marketing except for verification purposes.

The first 'objective' approach to social class was put forward by Karl Marx, who, even though he used several criteria to define a class (including class consciousness), made the relationship to the means of production a key indicator. He clearly distinguished the 'haves', who control resources, and the 'have-nots', who depend on their labour to survive. On this basis, he identified and analysed three classes: (a) workers; (b) capitalists; (c) and landowners.[15] In later works, he even went as far as seven[16] or eight class groupings.[17]

The difficulties involved in classifying the numerous intermediate categories, coupled with the evolution of economic structures, have rendered this approach a little out of date and no longer usable.[18] Marketing specialists currently prefer approaches based on socio-economic criteria, notably those developed in American sociology under the influence of Max Weber.[19] We can regroup these approaches around two poles according to whether they rely on a unique criterion or on a series of indicators.[20] Single-criterion methods are the oldest. Three variables have been traditionally used for identifying social class: income, socio-professional category, and educational level. Only the first two are taken into account in classification systems routinely used in commercial research.

The ABCD classification

Marketing research bureaux, especially those maintaining consumer panels, have highlighted **income** as a privileged indicator of social class. Secodip, a member of the Europanel network (together with other European research companies such as GfK and Taylor Nelson), has thus defined the four-group ABCD structure, in which group boundaries correspond to monthly revenues adjusted for household size. The ABCD classes are respectively defined as upper, upper middle, lower middle and lower (or modest).

This system, extensively used in marketing analyses, has the advantage of simplicity but is not without limitations. First, the cut-offs are relatively arbitrary; second, they have to be reviewed each year to adjust for inflation; third, and more importantly, the ABCD system reduces the notion of social class to that of an income level (which is not even known with precision). National statistical institutes, for their part, make little use in their analyses of the idea of social class, tending to prefer that of 'social category'. Most of them have developed a classification based on **socio-professional categories**.

Often used in marketing research and projects requiring an understanding of the sociological background of respondents, socio-professional categories are a complex concept with a long history. In fact, the divisions established successively by analysts tend to reflect the stages society itself has gone through over time. Consider the case of France.[21] In 1851, when the national census (usually conducted every ten years) first asked a question on occupation, four categories were used: 'managers, employees, workers and domestic staff'. The underlying logic subsequently evolved to cover first the split between those economically active and inactive, then the hierarchical position (that is, employers versus employees) and the sector/profession interface. This finally resulted in the 1950s in the notion of socio-professional categories, used during the following thirty years. For the 1982 census, and in order to take account of the 'transformation of the professions and their relative positions (in which) income and qualification play a major part', INSEE, the French national statistics institute, again modified the classification system and proposed a new list of 'professions and socio-professional categories'.[22] The newly adopted socio-professional categories integrate three variables: (a) the employee's status – self-employed/salaried; (b) the type of occupation; and (c) for salaried workers, the employer's status – private or public. On the basis of the many socio-professional divisions resulting from such distinctions, INSEE has put in place four classification groups (also labelled ABCD), thus mirroring, at least implicitly, scales based on occupational prestige[23] (see Figure 6.1).

Figure 6.1   The ABCD classification according to profession

A:	Company heads Liberal professions Senior managers
B:	Middle managers Small business owners Craftspeople
C:	Factory workers Clerical staff
D:	Economically under-privileged active (agricultural workers, manual labourers) Economically under-privileged inactive (unemployed, retired workers)

Table 6.2 Income and socio-professional categories (vertical presentation)

	% Pop.	A	B	C	D
Farmers	3	1	1	3	11
Small business owners	6	6	6	5	6
Senior managers	8	29	10	3	0
Intermediary professions	13	22	18	11	3
Employees	11	6	13	13	8
Workers	22	5	19	27	29
Retired	37	31	33	38	43

Source: Secodip

Table 6.3 Income and socio-professional categories (horizontal presentation)

	%	Farmers	Small business owners	Senior managers	Intermediary professions	Employees	Workers	Retired
A	15	2	15	53	24	8	4	13
B	30	13	34	35	40	35	26	27
C	40	34	35	12	33	47	50	42
D	15	51	16	0	3	10	20	18

Source: Secodip

To a large extent, such a system suffers from the same limitations as the preceding classification.[24] A certain confusion also seems to exist in commercial research due to the fact that the two structures, although they have the same letters, only partially overlap, as is shown in the case of France in Tables 6.2 and 6.3. Table 6.2 reveals that if category A (defined on the basis of income) mostly comprises senior managers, it also consists of a high proportion of middle managers and economically inactive people. Conversely, Table 6.3 shows that a large proportion of senior managers belong to category B, while retired people seem to be almost unclassifiable. The limits of single-criterion approaches probably explain the success of multidimensional indicators such as socio-economic indices.

Socio-economic indices

Although he has also elaborated a method based on reputation, known as 'evaluative participation', American sociologist Lloyd Warner is generally credited with the first viable system for measuring social class empirically.[25] The ISC (index of status characteristics) which he developed combines profession (coefficient 4), source of income (3), type of habitation (2) and area of residence (1). Using the ISC, Warner cut American society into six major classes (see Figure 6.2), often used in marketing studies as we see shortly.

A. Hollingshead, also an American sociologist, developed another index called

Figure 6.2 Social classes according to Warner (and their British equivalents)

In the USA	In the UK
	A
1 Upper-Upper	(*according to RSC*)
Aristocracy – around 1.4% of the American population	(Upper Middle Class)
2 Lower-Upper	B
Nouveaux-riches – 1.6%	(Middle Class)
3 Upper-Middle	C_1
10.8%	(Lower Middle Class)
4 Lower-Middle	C_2
Mostly white collar – 28.1%	(Skilled Working Class)
5 Upper-Lower	D
Blue collar – 32.6%	(Working Class)
6 Lower-Lower	E
Homeless, jobless and marginals – 25.2%	(Lower Class)

the ISP (index of social position), which in the simplified version relies on only two factors: profession and education, measured on a scale of 1 to 7 according to the scoring system displayed in Figure 6.3.[26]

Richard Coleman, a third American sociologist, has more recently proposed a social class measurement system known as CSI (computerised status index), which takes into account: (1) and (2) the educational level of each of two spouses (that of a single person is doubled); (3) the profession of the head of the family (allotted a coefficient 2); (4) the total income of the family; and (5) the reputation of the area in which they live. From this system, he has identified four classes: superior, average, worker and inferior.[27]

In Europe, a comparable method has been proposed by ESOMAR (the European Society for Marketing Research). The ESOMAR system suggests an allocation of points according to the scoring grid presented in Table 6.4.[28] Such a system, which measures social class according to a score varying from 35 to 75 points, is increasingly used in pan-European studies. It has been rearranged further into seven categories according the scheme presented in Table 6.5. ESOMAR has also proposed an index of status (see Figure 6.4) based on the possession of durable goods (colour TV, second car, video-recorder, etc.),[29] an approach also used in France by the ISL Institute.[30] In the UK, Acorn developed a similar system based upon trading area (see Figure 6.5).

The preceding discussion makes it clear that there is no universally accepted method for measuring social class. Some studies have found that raw indicators such as education or income sometimes perform better than composite indices,[31] while indices have been criticised for being outdated and overly focused on traditional family structures.[32] As already mentioned, the way social class is measured at a particular moment depends upon prevailing views about the structure of society at that time.

Figure 6.3 Social classes according to Hollingshead

Profession scale	Diploma scale
1 Senior managers, liberal professions	1 Specialised university diploma
2 Medium-sized company managers	2 University diploma
3 Civil servants, small business managers	3 Two years at university
4 Employees, technicians	4 Bachelor's degree
5 Skilled workers	5 Secondary schooling
6 Semi-skilled workers	6 Primary schooling
7 Unskilled workers	7 No diploma at all

The scores are then weighted (coefficient 7 for the profession and 4 for education) and added up to arrive at the ISP score, which provides the basis for class attribution, according to the following scale:

Social class	ISP score
I	11–17
II	18–27
III	28–43
IV	44–60
V	61–77

Table 6.4 The European measurement system for social class

Education	University or equivalent	Further education 19+	Educated until 17 to 19	None or until 16–
Occupation				
E1 Gen. Managers/6+	75	69	64	64
E2 Professionals/self.	74	66	66	66
E3 Professionals/empl.	72	72	59	59
E4 Gen. Managers/5−	73	65	60	60
E5 Middle Mgnt/6+	71	66	63	62/60*
E6 Middle Mgnt/5−	70	62	61	60/58*
E7 Business/6+	64	64	64	61
E8 Other Office Workers	65	59	57/55*	50/48*
E9 Business/5−	65	65	56	50/48*
E10 Students	67	58	52	42
E11 N.-Off. Workers/N.-Man	68	53	51	39/35*
E12 Farmers/20 H.*	57	57	57	40
E13 Farmers/19/H.-	56	56	56	41/36*
E14 Housewives	67	58	52	42
E15 N.-Office Worker man.	47	47	43/41*	38/37*

* with/without apprenticeship/professional training

Source: ESOMAR Working Group

Table 6.5 The seven European social classes

Education level (age at the end of studies)	Professions						
	E1/4	E2/6	E3/5/9	E7/8	E11	E14	E12
21+						D	
17–20	A		B		C		
15–16	C			E1			
14					E2		
13		D	E2			E3	

Figure 6.4   Economic status in Europe (average score by country)

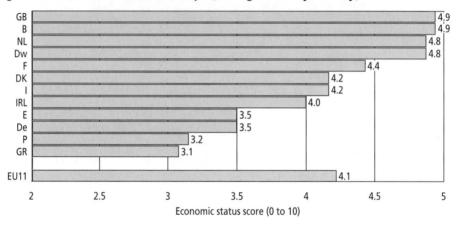

Average socio-economic status scores based on ownership of 10 durables
(Dw = West Germany. De = East Germany)

Source: Eurobarometer 34, EC/INRA Europe, October 1990

European social maps

The ESOMAR classification has enabled the identification of the European social structure in a relatively coherent manner across all the member countries. By way of illustration, Figure 6.6 shows the average results obtained for eleven EU countries and for the two extremes – Denmark and Portugal. It is worth pointing out that these results, based on very large samples (more than 10 000 people), arise from an identical definition of the divisions between social categories in all countries concerned. This is extremely useful for pan-European market studies. Of course, given the different level of industrialisation achieved by each country, the numbers of individuals in each category vary widely. If one prefers to use social groups of comparable size in different countries (for example in order to compare

Figure 6.5   Acorn profiles in Great Britain

CACI's ACORN classification profiles customers in a trading area or on a database into six Categories, 17 Groups and 54 Types (plus one unclassified), so that marketers can understand more about their likely consumer characteristics. The table below shows the ACORN profile of CACI's 1996 population projections for Great Britain.

ACORN categories	ACORN groups		ACORN types	Number	Percent of total
A THRIVING	1 Wealthy achievers, Suburban areas	1.1	Wealthy suburbs, large detached houses	1,456,317	2.5
		1.2	Villages with wealthy commuters	1,808,297	3.2
		1.3	Mature affluent home-owning areas	1,535,783	2.7
		1.4	Affluent suburbs, older families	2,110,439	3.7
		1.5	Mature, well-off suburbs	1,707,149	3.0
	2 Affluent greys, rural communities	2.6	Agricultural villages, home-based workers	917,402	1.6
		2.7	Holiday retreats, older people, home-based workers	396,699	0.7
	3 Prosperous pensioners, retirement areas	3.8	Home-owning areas, well-off older residents	799,894	1.4
		3.9	Private flats, elderly people	539,332	0.9
B EXPANDING	4 Affluent executives, family areas	4.10	Affluent working families with mortgages	1,218,440	2.1
		4.11	Affluent working couples with mortgages, new homes	728,231	1.3
		4.12	Transient workforces, living at their place of work	200,275	0.4
	5 Well-off workers, family areas	5.13	Home-owning family areas	1,478,659	2.5
		5.14	Home-owning family areas, older children	1,716.884	3.0
		5.15	Families with mortgages, younger children	1,273,309	2.2
C RISING	6 Affluent urbanites, town and city areas	6.16	Well-off town and city areas	525,710	1.1
		6.17	Flats and mortgages, singles and young working couples	426,313	0.7
		6.18	Furnished flats and bedsits, younger single people	253,214	0.4
	7 Prosperous professionals, metropolitan areas	7.19	Apartments, young professional singles and couples	649,844	1.1
		7.20	Gentrified multi-ethnic areas	554,248	1.0
	8 Better-off executives, inner city areas	8.21	Prosperous enclaves, highly qualified executives	425,761	0.7
		8.22	Academic centres, students and young professionals	372,521	0.7
		8.23	Affluent city centre areas, tenements and flats	254,919	0.4
		8.24	Partially gentrified multi-ethnic areas	405,370	0.7
		8.25	Converted flats and bedsits, single people	497,232	0.9
D SETTLING	9 Comfortable middle agers, mature home owning areas	9.26	Mature established home-owning areas	1,379,911	3.3
		9.27	Rural areas, mixed occupations	1,971,732	3.5
		9.28	Established home-owning areas	2,287,361	4.0

▶

ACORN categories	ACORN groups		ACORN types	Number	Percent of total
		9.29	Home-owning areas, council tenants, retired people	1,511,276	2.5
	10 Skilled workers, home owning areas	10.30	Established home-owning areas, skilled workers	2,573,232	4.5
		10.31	Home owners in older properties, younger workers	1,739,087	3.0
		10.32	Home-owning areas with skilled workers	1,765,548	3.1
E ASPIRING	11 New home owners, mature communities	11.33	Council areas, some new home owners	2,167,029	3.8
		11.34	Mature home-owning areas, skilled workers	1,754,556	3.1
	12 White collar workers, better-off multi-ethnic areas	12.36	Home-owning multi-ethnic areas, young families	640,400	1.1
		12.37	Multi-occupied town centres, mixed occupations	1,035,085	1.8
		12.38	Multi-ethnic areas, white collar workers	511,082	1.1
	13 Older people, less prosperous areas	13.39	Home owners, small council flats, single pensioners	1,084,613	1.9
		13.40	Council areas, older people, health problems	970,162	1.7
	14 Council estate residents, better-off homes	14.41	Better-off council areas, new home owners	1,371,484	2.4
		14.42	Council areas, young families, some new home owners	1,709,433	3.0
		14.43	Council areas, young families, many lone parents	895.361	1.6
		14.44	Multi-occupied terraces, multi-ethnic areas	485,456	0.8
		14.45	Low-rise council housing, less well-off families	1,013,944	1.8
		14.46	Council areas, residents with health problems	1,098,931	1.9
F STRIVING	15 Council estate residents, high unemployment	15.47	Estates with high unemployment	542,154	1.1
		15.48	Council flats, elderly people, health problems	383,176	0.7
	16 Council estate Residents, greatest hardship	16.50	Council areas, high unemployment, lone parents	1,055,036	1.8
		16.51	Council flats, greatest hardship, many lone parents	518,991	0.9
	17 People in multi-ethnic, low-income areas	17.52	Multi-ethnic, large families, overcrowding	363,689	0.6
		17.53	Multi-ethnic, severe unemployment, lone parents	565,629	1.0
		17.54	Multi-ethnic, high unemployment, overcrowding	299,507	0.5
	Unclassified			290,834	8.5
	TOTAL			57,139.635	100.0

Source: OPCS and GRO(S)

Figure 6.6   Social structure in Europe

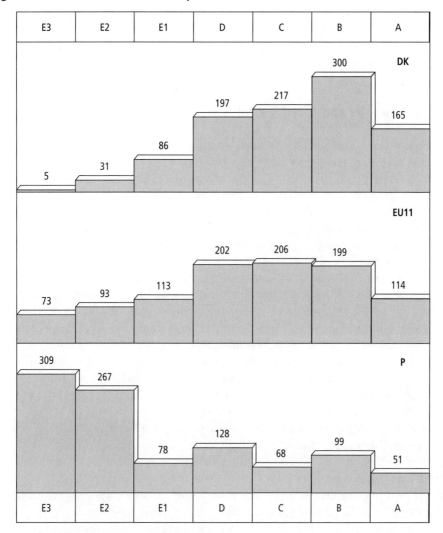

Key: DK: Denmark. Read: 16.5% of Danish populations belong to A class
     EU11: Average results for 11 EU countries
     P: Portugal

Source: Y. Marbeau, *op. cit.*

the 10 per cent most wealthy consumers in each country) then it is better to rearrange the dividing lines between the social classes. In Western Europe, it has been estimated that households with access to more than 100 000 Euros per year represent less than 5 per cent of the population but account for more than one-quarter of total EU discretionary income.[33]

Social structure and market analysis

The representations of social structure, notably those which lend themselves easily to social mapping, frequently serve as a basis for market analysis – particularly in commercial research. For example, a study of leisure activities based on an approach developed by French sociologist Bourdieu[34] resulted in the perceptual map represented in Figure 6.7. However, this kind of map, commonly used when assessing product positioning, must be interpreted with care given the risk of bias introduced by the geographical metaphor. Thus the proximity of the *Nouvel Observateur* and school teachers clearly does not imply that all the readers of the news magazine *Le Nouvel Observateur* are school teachers, or that all school teachers read the *Le Nouvel Observateur*; it simply indicates that the 'centre of gravity' for *Nouvel Observateur* readership is situated as positioned on the map. Naturally, a detailed analysis of readership data prevents incorrect interpretation.

Beyond simple observation and in contrast to basic socio-demographic variables, social class, because it relies on a body of propositions forming a theory, enables the formulation of specific hypotheses related to buying behaviour and consumption. For example, Bourdieu holds that, even for the same amount of total resources (which Bourdieu calls global capital), 'the distribution of economic capital (as measured through income and possessions) differs sharply from that of cultural capital (as measured through education and diploma)' among social classes.[35] He then observes that purchase and consumption behaviour reflects such differences: corporate managers more often own their homes, are more likely to have a boat and holiday regularly in hotels, while university professors or public sector managers (who enjoy a similar income level) read more books, visit museums or go to concerts more regularly, and are more likely to own an FM radio. Furthermore, observations made about social mobility help analysts to refine their understanding of human behaviour. An American study carried out among 1000 people living in large cities examined the proportion of members of a range of social classes living within one mile of their parents. The results range from 55 per cent for the lower classes to 12 per cent for the upper classes.[36] This proximity phenomenon even goes as far as affecting the relationship between spouses; it has been observed that when two couples go out together in a car, men belonging to the working classes tend to sit together in the front while their wives are in the back, whereas among the upper-middle classes there is more chance of seeing the couples sitting together in the front and back.[37]

Theories relating to social class mobility also help in anticipating behaviours.

Figure 6.7   Social class and leisure

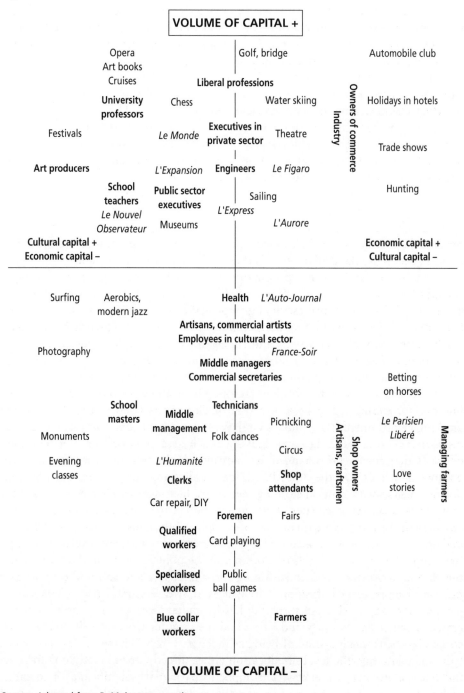

Source: Adapted from B. Moingeon, *op. cit.*

Thus, the 'social trajectory' concept introduced by Bourdieu enables him to interpret the behaviour of 'the middle manager of ascetic virtues and cultural willingness which shows itself in many ways – by taking evening classes, by registering with libraries, by being a collector – expressing quite clearly the aspiration to rise to the next level, the objective of those occupying the inferior position'.[38]

Many studies have shown the link between social class and buying behaviour. Most of the time, European research has relied on one of three common indicators of social class: income, educational level and profession. The studies relating to income having been presented in Chapter 1; only the works covering education or profession are illustrated in this chapter. American research, on the other hand, has mainly used multidimensional indicators. Results will be presented by relating them successively to each major marketing variable.

The product

Beyond their utilitarian value, objects possess a 'social significance' according to French sociologist Baudrillard.[39] It is thus understandable that the level of ownership and/or consumption of a product or brand varies according to social class.[40] A study carried out among 7000 households revealed that, even at similar income levels, the various socio-professional groups make very different choices regarding the number of items of clothing bought and the quality of these clothes (see Figure 6.8). Compared with technicians and supervisors, salespeople value quality more than volume. The impact of fashion is also visible. In fact, the use to which clothes are put and the concern to conform to social norms (or conversely to differentiate oneself from them) are the two key factors which underpin buying patterns. For farmers, for example, the basic function of clothing is to meet the needs of the working environment: they thus buy relatively few simple and durable clothes for themselves; in contrast, they will make a much greater effort for their children, whose requirements are changed by meeting children from other social backgrounds at school. On the other hand, the middle-range professions such as first-line managers spend a lot on clothing relative to their income. Moreover, what they buy depends on whether they work in the public or private sectors. In private companies, men buy large quantities of straight cloth trousers, long-sleeved shirts and above all ties. Their concern to assimilate into management levels encourages them to invest in typical kinds of clothing. In the public sector, on the other hand, the clothing norms are less constraining for similar levels of job and men tend to dress in a more relaxed fashion – long-sleeved sweaters, polo necks and leather jackets. Even so, this lack of formality has its limits. Jeans of all kinds are not tolerated, women prefer skirts and shirts and men tighter trousers.[41] In many ways, social class is as much a state of being as much as it is of having.[42]

In a similar way, the level of education either directly or indirectly (via income) influences a number of markets. The impact is particularly significant for so-called 'cultural' goods. Table 6.6 reveals great variation in the levels of possession of books, cameras, videos, etc., and how often 'cultural' activities are undertaken

Figure 6.8   Quality and number of clothing purchases according to social class

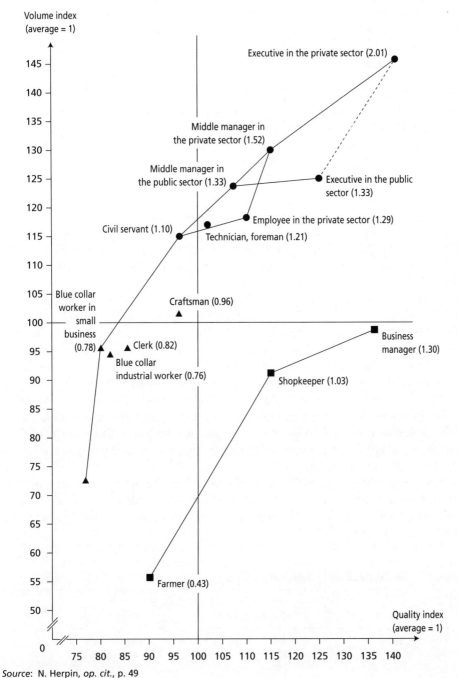

Source: N. Herpin, op. cit., p. 49

Table 6.6 Level of education and cultural goods (percentage)

						Own:		Have gone during the last 12 months to:	
	At least one book	A camera	Hi-fi equip.	An audio recorder	At least one record		Theatre	Concert	Museum
Education:	%	%	%	%	%		%	%	%
No diploma	61.3	35.6	6.5	15.2	54.1		2.9	1.2	14
Primary	72.2	45.4	9.3	18.3	57.1		3.8	3.7	20.9
Secondary	90.5	45.7	19.3	36.7	81.2		10.1	7.5	33.9
University	97.1	44.4	24.9	50.3	85.4		28.2	20.4	55.6

Source: Adapted from *Cultural Practices of the French* (French government publications)

(theatre, concerts, museum visits) according to the level of education.[43] The educational level is an important segmentation criterion in this case. Studies of social class have also revealed a strong link with household equipment buying patterns. It has been shown, for example, that the lower classes spend more willingly on the kitchen than the living room, in contrast to the middle classes.[44] Purchases of furniture are particularly affected due to their high visibility.[45]

Social class also influences consumption practices. Marketers are very interested in learning how the various social classes use their products and services since this may affect the positioning strategies they adopt. For example, for a similar level of card ownership, the upper classes use their credit cards more often due to their convenience (no need to carry money or a cheque book), while the lower social levels most often use credit cards for credit purposes (that is, to delay payment).[46] The relation is linear, as is shown in Table 6.7. Such differences in turn lead to differences in the way of acquiring and using credit. Hence, the upper and middle classes more willingly approach banks for a loan, while the lower classes turn to their friends or specialist credit companies.[47] In addition, the lower classes use their cards mostly for day-to-day purchases, while the upper classes do not hesitate to use one for luxury goods purchases.[48] Generally speaking, the working classes tend to prefer products and services which correspond to immediate needs and tend to avoid those which appear less familiar (such as, for example, vacation trips to out-of-the-way places).[49]

Table 6.7 Social class and credit card usage

Social Class	Credit card usage	
	Convenience %	Credit %
I Upper class	48	52
II Upper middle class	38	62
III Lower middle class	29	71
IV Lower class	24	76

Source: Mathews and Slocum, *op. cit.*

In many areas it is the concern for social visibility which explains social class differences in consumption behaviour. As a result, in comparison with income, social class is a better predictor of purchase of products with a strong symbolic content. The upper classes are much more sensitive to fashion, for example when they choose clothes,[50] household equipment,[51] sporting goods,[52] food products[53] or even a telephone handset.[54] Conversely, social class seems to play a less important role for less visible products such as washing machines and dishwashers. For luxury goods, which are both expensive and symbolic, social class and income considered together are better predictors than each variable considered alone.[55]

Price

Beyond the obvious indirect effects of social class through income,[56] the attitudes and behaviours relating to price are also directly influenced by social class affiliation. Generally speaking, lower-class consumers are less well informed about price[57] and more inclined to buy products on promotion.[58] Conversely, the better-off classes are less likely to use price as an indicator of quality, considering themselves better at judging the intrinsic value of the products they are buying.[59]

However, Coleman considers that members of a social class are not necessarily homogeneous in their attitudes towards price. Analysing car purchases, he showed that in each class one could determine the existence of 'over-privileged' and 'under-privileged' categories. For example, in the upper middle class, young professors have an income lower than the average for the class even though their level of education and their cultural aspirations are similar. Conversely, a skilled worker of fifty years of age enjoys a greater income than the average for the class and is in a position to keep some discretionary money, which, for example, could be used to buy a comfortable car. Coleman thus observed that the 'over-privileged' in each class had a tendency to buy large cars, while the 'under-privileged' bought compact cars.[60]

Distribution

Despite the broad frequentation of hypermarkets and supermarkets for fast-moving consumer goods, there remains (especially for specialty products), a well-documented link between social class and the type of sales outlet visited. In the textile sector for example, a study of 1000 American consumers, categorised according to Warner's method, resulted in the findings presented in Table 6.8.[61] These percentages show quite a diversity in sales outlets visited: as may be expected, department stores are frequented by a wealthier clientele and the opposite is true for discount stores. Mail order occupies a mid-range position. The purchasing frequency also varies according to social class, as is the time set aside for shopping (less time is spent shopping as we move up the social scale). On the other hand, the authors of the study concluded that sources of information used (brochures, advertising, press, etc.) and the influence of word of mouth were not greatly differentiated. However,

Table 6.8 Social class and preferred shop

Preferred shop	Lower Lower %	Upper Lower %	Lower Middle %	Upper Middle %	Lower Upper %	Upper Upper %
Department store	51	60	77	83	88	91
Discount store	14	11	6	2	–	–
Variety store	2	6	6	5	–	–
Mail order	9	14	5	2	3	–
Corner shop	11	2	1	1	3	–
Others	11	5	4	7	–	–

Source: Rich and Jain, op. cit.

a later English study covering food and household electrical goods purchases contradicted these latter results.[62]

A French study, again in the textile sector, showed that for purchases of shoes, accessories and cloth, managerial levels visited specialist shops, while workers and craftspeople tended to go to larger stores and farmers to market stalls.[63] Other works have shown that the lower classes in general prefer corner shops and avoid large commercial centres.[64] The middle classes visit discount stores for low-risk products or those dominated by major brands; however, they do visit specialist shops for products which involve a higher degree of personal taste (furniture, cloth, jewels, etc.).[65]

All these findings, supported by more recent studies,[66] enable store managers to identify their customer base and as a result alter their assortment ranges and sales techniques. Generally, it is estimated that if location accounts for 30 to 40 per cent of the customer base, social class accounts for 15 to 20 per cent.[67]

Promotion

Finally, it has long been established that social class influences how advertising messages are received and the media used.[68] According to studies by Social Research Inc., consumers in the less well-off classes are more receptive to advertising which is visual, lively and proposes practical everyday solutions, whereas the upper classes respond better to symbolic representation.[69] Even slogans often have to be differentiated to the extent that the linguistic codes are not the same.[70] The upper classes may talk of hedonism when the lower classes speak about pleasure. In the UK, the tone of Harrod's advertising cannot be the same as that of MFI.

Many studies of media audience, even if they use the notion of socio-professional category rather than that of class, reveal that the media viewed are socially determined. Even within a specific category, for example television, programme audiences are not the same. Other studies show that the middle and upper classes read magazines and newspapers more often, watch less television and when they do watch it, look at films and news more than soap operas, drama series, game shows or sitcoms.[71] Also, managers and the intermediate professions (who usually represent less than 10 per cent of the population) represent one-fifth of the cinema audience in Europe. In contrast, those sometimes classified as 'inactive' (retired, pupils, etc.) (about one-third of the total) represent less than one-fifth of cinema goers. Such elements are clearly useful to those involved in advertising management, as much for defining targets as for the design and planning of campaigns.[72]

From social class to lifestyle

Socio-demographic variables and social class provide only a relatively aggregated and descriptive analysis of consumers. To get into more depth, it is of course possible to turn to individual motivation studies and focus group interviews, but problems arise linked to small sample sizes and the difficulties of interpretation of what people have said (that is, handling the verbatim reports). Under these conditions, it is tempting to want to bring together the advantages of large-scale studies with a more refined understanding of consumers' attitudes and behaviour. It is precisely from this perspective that the notion of **lifestyle** arose and was promoted from 1970 onwards. Few concepts have, in such a short time, developed such notoriety and level of use in commercial studies. The object of the second part of this chapter is to present and discuss lifestyle research. The first section covers the notion of lifestyle itself; the second presents the different approaches, developed in both Europe and the United States, as well as the corresponding measures. The final section reviews the various fields of application of lifestyle – its limits and its evolution.

What is lifestyle?

While the origin of the concept is attributed either to the sociologist Max Weber,[73] who used it to characterise the social status of a group, or to the psychologist Adler, who used it to 'describe the rules developed by an individual to achieve life's goals',[74] we had to wait until the beginning of the 1960s for the notion of lifestyle to be applied to purchasing and consumption phenomena.[75] Lazer, one of the first consumer researchers to get interested in this area, gave lifestyle the following definition:

> lifestyle refers to the distinctive or characteristic mode of living, in its aggregate and broadest sense, of a whole society or segment thereof. It is concerned with those unique ingredients or qualities which describe the style of life of some culture or group, distinguish it from others. It embodies the patterns that develop and emerge from the dynamics of living in a society. Lifestyle, therefore, is the result of such forces as culture, values, resources, symbols, license, and sanction. From a marketing perspective, the aggregate of consumer purchases, and the manner in which they are consumed, reflect a society's lifestyle.[76]

Even though a number of other definitions have been proposed,[77] based on Lazer's statement we can identify three major approaches, respectively centred on (a) values; (b) the types of product bought and consumed; and (c) attitudes, interests and opinions.

The value-based approach

This approach, the most culturally oriented, has mainly developed in Europe and particularly in France under the influence of two research institutes: Cofremca and CCA (Centre de Communication Avancé). In the United States, even though they are numerous and diverse,[78] the works on values have not been well integrated into the lifestyle research tradition, with the double exception of the Yankelovitch Monitor and the VALS system (value and life styles segmentation) developed by A. Mitchell of the Stanford Research Institute (SRI).

The Yankelovitch Monitor takes the form of an annual survey based on a scale of thirty-one key values revealing major trends at the heart of the evolution of American culture.[79] Based upon these trends, a certain number of population segments such as the 'trend setters', the 'disoriented', etc. have been identified. The monitor is used by many companies both to research new product opportunities and to renew advertising themes.

A. Mitchell and his team at SRI originally divided American society into three lifestyle segments articulated around three corresponding values: needs constraint, external orientation and orientation towards the self. The first group is further divided into survivors (4%) and sustainers (7%), the second into belongers (35%), emulators (10%) and achievers (22%), and the last one into 'I am me' (5%), experientials (7%), societally conscious (8%) and integrateds (2%). To each lifestyle group corresponds a particular mode of purchasing.[80] The VALS classification was developed from the works of Riesman and Maslow (see Chapter 1), for whom the strongest motivations are first linked to fundamental needs (survivors and sustainers), before growing towards others (belongers, emulators), crystallising on the self (achievers, 'I am me', experientials), and finally culminating in serenity and equilibrium (societally conscious and integrateds).

A comparison between the USA and Europe based on the VALS system has been made; it is reproduced in Figure 6.9. The VALS system, even if it has been the object of certain criticisms,[81] has been used by over 200 companies both to segment their markets and to target new product launches. Marketing managers are little interested in the first two VALS segments because of their weak purchasing power but follow the others closely. Table 6.9 presents the results of an American study of jewellery buyers. These figures reveal that the 'I am me' are common purchasers of jewellery, but the average value of their purchases remains low. The 'achievers' on the other hand represent a major part of the market considering average purchasing price. Finally, the 'belongers' buy little but, given their number, cannot be ignored. To each group correspond distinct products and differentiated approaches (advertising and sales outlets). For example, the 'I am me' are most interested in

Table 6.9 Lifestyle and jewellery purchase

Lifestyle group	Acquisition rate (%)	Average price (US$)	% of total in value
Survivors	9.8	209	1.3
Sustainers	12.0	289	1.1
Belongers	6.8	429	23.0
Emulators	10.6	498	7.0
Achievers	12.8	905	55.0
I Am Me	40.5	197	1.2
Experientials	13.8	516	3.6
Societally conscious	9.6	473	7.7
Integrateds	NS	NS	NS
Average	9.9	580	100.00

costume jewellery sold as fashion accessories in gift shops; the Achievers prefer gold jewellery sold in traditional shops.

The VALS typology was revised in 1989 and the US population is now divided into eight groups determined not only by psychological characteristics but also by access to 'resources' such as income, education, energy levels and eagerness to buy. In VALS 2, groups are structured vertically according to the number of resources they have access to and horizontally in terms of their basic psychological orientation (see Figure 6.10). The eight groups are defined as follows: actualizers are successful consumers with access to many resources. Fulfilleds are satisfied, reflective and comfortable; they are sensitive to functional value. Achievers are more career-oriented and prefer predictability over risk. Experiencers, on the other hand, are impulsive and enjoy self-discovery. The next three groups, which have access to fewer resources, include believers, who have strong principles and like strong brands; strivers, who are very much concerned about social approval; and makers, who focus their efforts on self-sufficiency. Strugglers, finally, are primarily concerned with their own survival – very much like the survivors and sustainers of the previous classification.

In France, approaches centred around values have dominated lifestyle research. As mentioned before, they have mainly been developed and implemented by two organisations: Cofremca and CCA. Cofremca, inspired by the work of Yankelovitch, has created a way of following sociocultural trends (3SC) upon which are based lifestyle groups. Cofremca questionnaires comprise more than two hundred questions grouped into five parts (values, specific themes, media exposure, product consumption and socio-demographic characteristics[82]). Sociocultural types are thus defined by identifying the individuals obtaining the 25 per cent highest scores on each of the topics. Some of them are quite close to the VALS studies (for example, those based on the egocentric–sociocentric dimension).

At a European level the RISC (Research Institute for Social Change) has come up

Figure 6.9   The VALS system in Europe and the USA

Comparison of European and USA lifestyle types	Survivor	Sustainer	Belonger	Emulator	Achiever	I am me	Experiential	Societally conscious	Integrated
United States	Old; intensely poor; fearful; depressed; despairing; far removed from the cultural mainstream; misfits.	Living on the edge of poverty angry and resentful; streetwise; involved in the underground economy	Ageing; traditional and conventional; contented; intensely patriotic; sentimental; deeply stable.	Youthful and ambitious; macho; show-off; trying to break into the system, to make it big.	Middle-aged and prosperous; able leaders; self-assured; materialistic; builders of the 'American dream'.	Transition state; exhibitionistic and narcissistic; young; impulsive; dramatic; experimental; active; inventive.	Youthful; seek direct experience; person centred; artistic; intensely oriented toward inner growth.	Mission-oriented; leaders of single-issue groups; mature; successful; some live lives of voluntary simplicity.	Psychologically mature; large field of vision; tolerant and understanding; sense of fittingness.
France	Negligible number, but attributes as in USA, some older. Belongers and Sustainers share characteristics.	Old peasant women and retireds; poor; little education; fearful; live by habit; unable to cope with change.	Ageing; need family and community; concerned about financial security, appearance, surroundings, health; able to cope with change, but avoid it.	Youthful, but older and quieter than in the USA; better educated; entertain at home rather than outside; consider ideologies to be dangerous; concerned about health.	Two groups: older, more mature are similar to USA, younger are more intuitive; both groups less materialistic than USA achievers; both concerned about ecology, environment, etc.	Older (20–30); well educated; contemplative; little concern for financial security, social success or materialism; enjoy their work.	Young; predominantly male; highly educated; not fulfilled by work, but by leisure: enjoy the present; hedonistic.	Too few to be statistically significant, although more people have stronger societally conscious tendencies than in the USA.	Same as in USA.
Italy	Similar to USA survivors; live in northern urban slums.	Ageing; uneducated; uprooted from agrarian society; dependent; concerned with health and appearance; escapist.	Ageing; poorly educated; strongly authoritarian; self-sacrificing for family or church; fearful of change; fatalistic; save rather than spend; reject industrial society and its problems.	Youthful; mostly male; highly educated; reject family ties; highly materialistic; insensitive to nature; read more than average.	Middle-aged; predominantly female; links to family and religion; indifferent to self-fulfilment from work; want success and prestige, but otherwise escapist.	Highly educated; middle- to upper-class; 25–35 age; reject both traditional and consumer/industrial societies; political extremists; live now; bored; take light drugs.	Too few to be statistically significant, although some I am me's exhibit experiential characteristics.	Well educated; generally fairly young; led by protagonists of 1968 protests; satisfied; want more education, socially committed	Same as in USA.
Sweden	Two categories: an older	Wealthier than others; fearful of children's	As in the USA, but more suspicious of	Slightly older than others;	As interested in status as in money; save	Older than in the USA; entrepreneurial; experience and	Hedonists; risk takers; crave experience and	Want simpler, more basic ways of life; active in communities;	Same as in USA.

	group similar to USA; a very young group of unemployed school dropouts who are alienated, apathetic.	economic future; concerned with own economic security and pensions; afraid of big government and big business.	government and big business.	concerned with prestige; want beautiful homes; prefer quieter lifestyles.	more than USA achievers; buy valuables for their children to inherit; this group is the most middle-class of all.	self-expressive; concerned about self-improvement; reject drugs and alcohol; seek rich inner and emotional life, warm relationships.	excitement; enjoy dangerous pursuits.	questioning and critical; concerned about physical environment and impersonality of large organizations.	Same as in USA.
United Kingdom	Two groups similar to those in Sweden: older group is very similar to that in the USA. The younger, unemployed, are more aggressive than those in Sweden – form cliques.	Working-class values; concerned about economic security; family-centred; afraid of government and big business; mainly complaining; the youngest group is 35 years and over.	Two groups: one as in the USA, with the other traditional but more active, more concerned about education, creativity, emotions.	Older than others; mostly female; more interested in social status than job status; sacrifice comfort and practicality for fashion.	Too few to be statistically significant; status geared to social position; wealthy become more inner-directed; older people are unwilling to change.	Too few to be statistically significant; exhibit self-expressive characteristics, but are more societally conscious.	Highly educated; want excitement and adventure; risk takers; creative and self-expressive; want meaningful work; want to demonstrate abilities.	Family-oriented, young; well educated; creative; want personal growth and meaningful, satisfying work; question authority and technology.	
West Germany	Survivors in a psychological sense, not economic or demographic; fearful, envious and alienated; concerned about social position, physical appearance; antibusiness; many are women.	Sustainers in a psychological sense only; negative feelings toward all aspects of life; resigned and apathetic; high level of hypochondria.	As in the USA, although wealthier and better educated; more concerned about prestige and social standing.	Fairly young; well educated; mostly male; conscious about job status and social standing; concerned about physical safety.	As in the USA, although more are politically active and more concerned about the environment.	Older than in the USA; find work meaningful and self-fulfilling; want to have an impact on society; have a high level of anxiety; emotional vacuum, looking for ideologies.	Too few to be statistically significant.	Too few to be statistically significant.	Same as in USA.

Source: Arnold Mitchell, 'Nine American Lifestyles: Values and Societal Change', *The Futurist*, 18 (August 1984), 4–13

Figure 6.10　The VALS 2 system

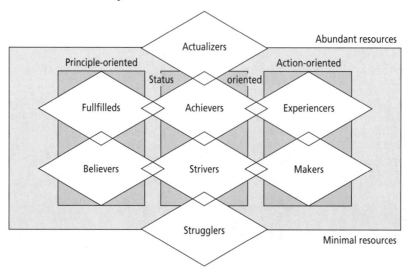

Source: SRI International, Menlo Park, California

with a typology in six categories based upon twenty-four trends measured among 30 000 Europeans:

1 Traditionalists (18%), attached to their history and their country's culture;

2 Home lovers (14%), rooted to their immediate environment;

3 Rationalists (23%), who end to analyse the world around them, even if they are uncertain about it;

4 Epicureans (17%), sensitive to their emotions and pleasure;

5 Fighters (15%), trying to carve out their own destiny; and

6 Trend setters (13%), keen to innovate and promote novelty.

CCA has developed and communicated a representation of lifestyles which has been extensively used in France.[83] Globally speaking, the approach is quite similar to that of Cofremca. Thirteen sociocultural trends are first identified, based on focus group discussions, and from this base are defined a number of 'sociostyles' or groups of individuals of similar behaviour, among them the 'Displaced', the 'Rigorists', the 'Egocentrists', the 'Activists' and the 'Materialists'. B. Cathelat describes them as follows:

> The displaced are typical of those that were formerly known as the young elite. They are intellectuals benefiting from a higher level of education. We find them amongst managers comfortably installed in commercial life. However, even though they are privileged, they are not found amongst the leaders of today ... The displaced have decided to invest little in work and a great deal in their private life. They are excited by new technologies and have a taste for adventure and risky enterprises. Available, they are within a society which

does not offer them a great deal: they only see controlling managers whilst waiting for the invaders.

At the other end of the spectrum are the rigorists (20% of the population). Instead of hiding in the future, they wrap themselves in the values of the past. The hard core of these rigorists tends to be found in industry amongst the craftsmen, small businessmen, the middle class. Their micro-economic liberalism transforms into macro-economic protectionism. They accept technological modernism, but they are extremely conservative on moral issues.

The egocentrists are a third family of lifestyles. They represent 23 per cent of the French, but 40 per cent of the young. They live in the suburbs of large towns. Mostly workers, clerical staff, or small business employees, they represent the impoverished classes, those who have felt the full force of recession. There are three times as many unemployed amongst them as the other groups. They are equally thirsty for consumption as financially frustrated.

The activists like to talk. First a broad picture of the state of the world we live in today is painted. If you ask him about himself, the activist does not reveal many details about his deeper personality. He prefers to talk about work, highlighting his responsibilities, the time he spends there, or how much he earns. If he introduces you to his family, it is to show off his wife, very involved in the parents' association at school, or to tell you about his childrens' school results ... and before you become too indiscreet, he asks you to meet up, to join him at his aerobics class or on the tennis court. The activist has a very busy schedule, but he loves that ...

Finally, materialists give priority to sound organisation and quality of life. What they call rigour or austerity is a restriction on the abundant society. In recession times, the desire to consume material goods takes a back seat. To still be able to consume something against the odds, is for them a statement of survival.[84]

Figure 6.11   Six European lifestyle mentalities

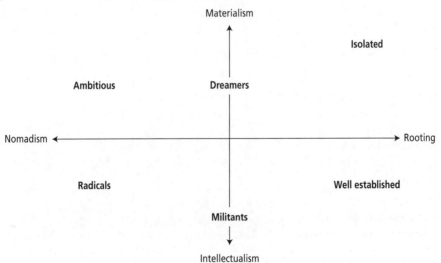

Source: Les Euro-socio-styles (CCA International and Europanel)

The CCA system has recently been extended to Europe, and the resulting map is shown in Figure 6.11. For a number of years, the European Commission has also conducted a survey called CTS (Continuous Tracking Survey), designed to 'investigate the importance of a number of values among Europeans and provide insight into the extent to which these values are shared throughout the European Union'.[85] Figures 6.12 to 6.15 show the results obtained for four values: involvement in creating a better society, traditionalism, materialism and self-development. It appears that:

1 despite all the concerns about individualism in our society, Europeans are still very concerned about creating a better society. Country results show that societal values are strong in all member states;

2 for quite a substantial proportion of Europeans, the image of a better society is 'the world as it used to be', with 68 per cent agreeing that they want a world in which people live by traditional values;

3 financial success is also a value many Europeans adhere to, with two in four saying that making a lot of money is important. Such a feeling, however, is more prevalent in Portugal and Spain than in northern Europe;

4 finally, one's own development is also highly valued – but even more so in Portugal, Spain and Greece than in the UK, France and Sweden.

Figure 6.12 The importance of being involved in creating a better society

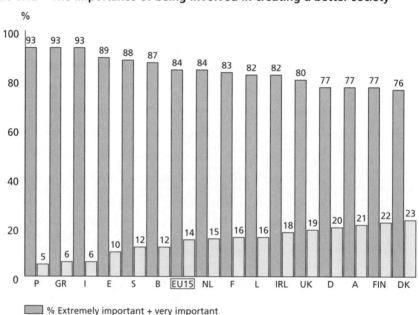

Figure 6.13 'I want a world where people live by traditional values'

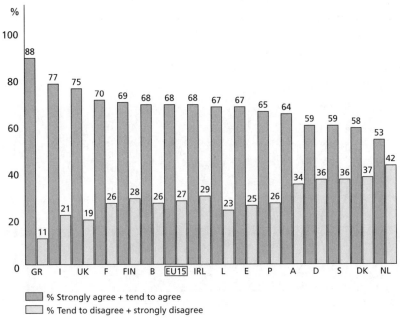

Figure 6.14 The importance of making a lot of money

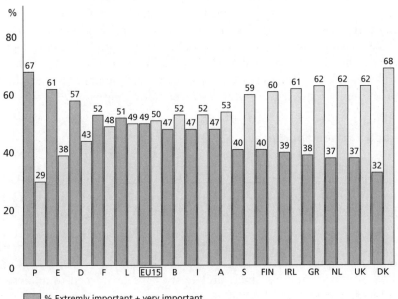

Figure 6.15   The importance of putting more time and effort into your personal development

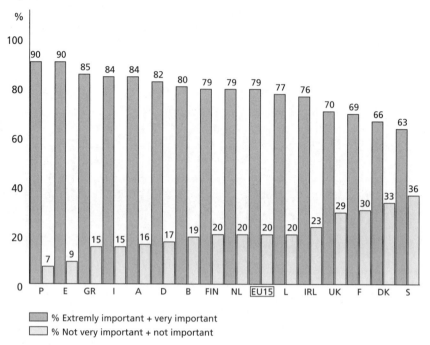

% Extremly important + very important
% Not very important + not important

It should be noted that, as is the case in Figure 6.15, materialism (which may be defined as 'the importance people attach to their worldly possessions) is often used in lifestyle representations.[86] This is not really surprising since, as mentioned before, the consumption of goods and products is not only affected by but is also an essential ingredient of one's lifestyle, especially through their symbolic dimensions.[87] This explains why, as will be discussed now, a number of researchers have attempted to infer lifestyle from product consumption patterns.

The product-based approach

As just mentioned, this approach is based on the hypothesis that the products and services bought or consumed by an individual or a household reflect their lifestyle.[88] In comparison with values, it is both more concrete and more contextual. In practical terms, the product-based approach consists of analysing consumption and purchase trends (often from survey information, consumer panels or scanner data) and identifying significant groups, thus enabling the definition of types or styles of purchaser.[89]

In the USA, for example, Alpert and Gatty have proceeded to analyse eighty products and services bought by 5000 consumers and have proposed a typology of sixteen fundamental profiles: the 'big drinker', the 'car fanatic', the 'traveller', etc. With each profile is associated a particular purchasing and consumption style. Hence the 'car fanatic' buys many more car accessories than the average, consumes more cleaning products and reads a greater number of car magazines. It therefore follows that marketers can, to some extent, associate the positioning of their brands in a given domain (for instance, beer) with these typical consumer profiles.[90]

In Europe, a similar approach has been used to understand the market for liqueurs,[91] and that of consumption of everyday products.[92] The pragmatic orientation of this approach is both its main strength and its principal weakness. The fact that it links directly to product groups makes it very operational, particularly for purposes of market segmentation or consumer typologies. The profiles thus created are, on the other hand, limited to a single domain or product category. The product-based approach has, however, been instrumental in highlighting product complementarity, either functional or symbolic.[93] For example, the yuppies of the late 1980s were often portrayed as possessing a BMW, a pair of Nike shoes, a Rolex watch and a squash racket.

Activities, interests and opinions

The value-based approach remains very general and may appear quite distant from the immediate preoccupation of understanding purchasing and consumption patterns. It can seem too abstract to a marketing manager. The product-based approach is, in contrast, more concrete but not easily generalised: it often poorly relates to other descriptive demand variables such as socio-demographics. The approach by activities, interests and opinions (AIO), also known as **psychographics**, suggests a middle path. It attempts to understand consumers based on what they do and what they think in a vast range of situations in society.

Essentially developed in the USA, it is not without links to the study of **centres of interest**, which appeared in Europe at the beginning of the 1970s.[94] The central idea of this approach was to study those areas in which a person declares an interest (politics, television, cooking, etc.) then to proceed to group people on the basis of the relationships between these areas and other variables of interest to the researcher (for example, product consumption level or media exposure). In France, Agostini and Boss have established a connection between ninety-one areas of interest, thirty socio-economic variables and how often twenty-five magazines are read.[95] Certain areas of interest could help explain magazine readership but, overall, the results remained quite limited – probably because the notion of a centre of interest is not enough, considered alone, to define a lifestyle. Completed by other attitudinal or behavioural variables, it can prove to be interesting, as the AIO approach shows.

Even though many variations in the AIO approach have emerged, most studies have taken the form of a rather a-theoretical (that is, with few research hypotheses) empirical perspective based on information touching upon a wide variety of daily life subjects. Among the various frameworks which have been proposed by aca-

Figure 6.16   Activities, interests and opinions

Activities	Interests	Opinions
Work	Family	Themselves
Hobbies	Home	Social issues
Social events	Job	Politics
Vacation	Community	Business
Entertainment	Recreation	Economics
Club membership	Fashion	Education
Community	Food	Products
Shopping	Media	Future
Sports	Achievements	Culture

Source: W. D. Wells and D. Tigert, *op. cit.*

demics and marketing research companies, the one presented in Figure 6.16, arising from the work of Wells, Tigert, Hustad and Pessemier,[96] is probably the most widely used in the USA as well as in Europe. The idea of this approach is to take account of lifestyle via a range of indicators covering:

- **activities**, especially those concerning leisure pursuits, daily life and work. For marketing purposes, a particular emphasis is naturally given to purchasing behaviour;
- **interests**, especially those related to the family, the home and the surrounding social community; and
- **opinions**, revealing the systems of beliefs and values of the person interviewed.

From a practical standpoint, and even if different methodological approaches are available,[97] the most common procedure consists of creating questionnaires containing a large number of items relating to these areas. The next step is to analyse and structure the large amount of data thus gathered to produce the different categorisations, often called psychographic profiles.

The AIO approach has been used for both domestic and international comparisons.[98] For example, a multi-country psychographic segmentation project carried out by the Ogilvy and Mather advertising agency resulted in ten profiles, including such segments as 'basic needs', 'look-at-me', 'visible achievement', 'socially aware' and 'fairer deal'. Few Australians were classified in the 'visible achievement' cluster, contrary to the USA, Canada and Japan. A disproportionate percentage of British respondents fell into the 'fairer deal' cluster, while Germans were strongly represented in the 'look-at-me' segment.[99]

Lifestyle and consumption

The applications of lifestyle in the field of consumption are quite numerous and concern both strategic analyses, such as market segmentation or positioning, and more tactical commercial decisions, particularly in the area of advertising and distribution. The success of lifestyle studies may be explained by the fact that marketing researchers are always looking for novel approaches and new insights which will allow them better to understand their customers.

In the USA, as in Europe, lifestyle studies have been used in order to segment many markets such as, among many others, takeaway food,[100] food products,[101] credit cards,[102] domestic energy consumption,[103] air traffic,[104] television watching,[105] ready-cooked meals[106] and holidays.[107] For example, in this last category, the following groups were recently identified in Europe:

1 the 'stay-at-home' (33%);

2 the 'small family holidaymakers' (24%), who spend their holidays with their families;

3 the 'convivial escapists' (15%), hungry for low-budget adventure;

4 the 'blue white residents' (5%), keen on tanning by the seaside;

5 the 'green residents' (8%), who primarily want a change of atmosphere and to rediscover nature; and

6 the 'budget groups' (15%), who like to be looked after and provided with entertainment.

In order to improve understanding of media consumption, McCann Erickson, London, identified the four following lifestyles: avant-guardians (interested in change), pontificators (traditionalists, very British), chameleons (follow the crowd) and sleepwalkers (contented underachievers). Similarly, D'Arcy, Masius, Benton and Bowles classified Russian consumers into five groups: 'kuptsi' (merchants), 'Cossacks', 'students', 'business executives' and 'Russian souls'. Cossacks are described as ambitious, independent and status seeking, while Russian souls are passive, fearful of choices and hopeful. While Cossacks would drive a BMW, smoke Dunhill cigarettes and drink brandy, Russian souls would drive a Lada, smoke Marlboros and drink vodka.

Many companies, including Carrefour, Shell and Danone, have used lifestyles to segment their market. In France, the Crédit Agricole bank has, similarly, identified five basic lifestyle target groups, for which specific products and methods of distribution have been developed.[108]

Lifestyle has also been used to research new product concepts or reposition existing products. Hence, following a study which identified three major client groups – the enthusiasts, the amateurs and the 'nouveaux riches' – an interior decoration company developed new products for each group: DIY kits for the first, pre-assembled decoration kits for the second and complete design services for the last. Examples of repositioning helped by lifestyle are equally numerous. When the Ford Pinto was launched in the United States, its initial positioning was that of a 'trouble-free, compact and romantic' car. A study carried out among potential buyers revealed a much more prosaic lifestyle; they were most interested in the practicalities when choosing a car, the 'only function of which was to transport'.

They rejected the idea that 'the kind of car one owns gives an image of oneself to others'. Following this, the Pinto was successfully repositioned as a highly functional and economic means of transport.[109]

As far as commercial tactics are concerned, it is in the area of advertising where lifestyle has perhaps achieved its major results. In the field of advertising, both the elaboration of the messages and the choice of media have benefited from lifestyle studies. According to some, lifestyle provides a particularly rich and vivid description of the intended target audience which allows advertising people to be more efficient, balancing both preconceptions and prejudgement.[110] A lifestyle study has, for example, resulted in a complete modification of a campaign aimed at promoting a particular kind of hand soap. Originally the theme was a mechanic with greasy hands working in a garage under difficult conditions. The study revealed that the typical user was a woman, very proud of her home and family. These women led quite a traditional life and attached a lot of importance to moral values and cleanliness. The campaign was repositioned around the family and the soap presented as a solution to children's dirty hands.[111]

Information on lifestyle has also helped to analyse, evaluate and select media. For example, Michaels found that the adoption of traditional values was often linked to the reading of certain magazines – religious and agriculture journals, ecology and geographical magazines, etc.[112] These results, confirmed by other studies, are not surprising as the exposure to media is often a descriptor used in identifying lifestyles.

Finally, in the area of distribution, some researchers have highlighted the contribution of lifestyle studies to the development of new distribution channels such as hire centres.[113] Others have shown that it is possible to differentiate department store and supermarket customers according to their lifestyle.[114] For example, Leisser and Hughes have classed American shoppers into seven basic types: (a) inactive (15%), (b) active (13%), (c) service (10%), (d) traditional (14%), (e) dedicated fringe (9%), (f) price (10%) and (g) transitional shoppers (7%). This typology seems particularly robust since it was simultaneously observed in seventeen American cities.[115] In Europe, a similar study has concluded that three major variables are highly important: (a) interest in shopping (b) store loyalty and (c) purchasing styles (planned or impulsive).[116]

Limits and perspectives

Since their origin, lifestyle studies have been subject to numerous criticisms. They have been attacked for having (a) a very loose or even absent conceptual framework; (b) measuring techniques which are not perfectly reliable or kept secret; (c) unstable results; and (d) a weak predictive power. We will examine each of these points in turn.

The lack of a conceptual framework

In contrast to social class, lifestyle does not rest on a theoretical base enabling precise hypotheses to be postulated. It is partly based on a moving unit of analysis which, changing between the individual (at the data collection level) and the group (at the level of presentation of results), limits the ability of researchers to capitalise upon social science generally. This may explain why the central concepts (lifestyle, psychographics, sociocultural trends), borrowed from different disciplines, are badly defined and operationalised. Snippets are utilised from various fields – indicators taken from here and there – and their relationship with reality is often ambiguous.

In addition, the colourful language used to describe lifestyle profiles has been criticised for its magical aspects; general unease has been expressed that it is working in a loose, elastic manner. The graphical representations of CCA tend to heighten this confusion. They lead us to believe that the two axes of the graphs are (a) sufficiently exhaustive to account for all information gathered; (b) polar opposites (but does materialism actually oppose intellectualism?); and (c) of equal importance. Furthermore, the groups appear very homogeneous, being simply located by their centre of gravity.

The limited reliability and transparence of measurement methods

Lacking strong theoretical underpinnings, lifestyle measurement scales are often developed in an *ad hoc* and intuitive manner, without being subjected to classical tests of reliability and validity.[117] Researchers concerned about this discovered that the reliability of lifestyle instruments left a lot to be desired.[118] Interviewed at six-month intervals, people gave answers to the same items; only 60 to 70 per cent of these answers correlated.[119] The internal reliability coefficients reached the desirable 80 per cent level in less than one of two cases.[120] In Europe such tests have not been published as most commercial lifestyle instruments remain proprietary.

The instability of results and relationships

We have already pointed out that the CCA and Cofremca typologies are somewhat divergent, while the basic reference groups are the same.[121] How do we explain such differences? Is it simply due to the diversity of the techniques? In the case of CCA, it is difficult to accept that a new mentality – the displaced (extracted from 'cultural flows' defined as 'dynamic trends which modify the hierarchy of values *over the long run*') – was totally absent in 1977, had overcome one French person in five three years later, and this group had then lost a fifth of its number in the four years that followed.

A weak predictive power

By not providing good causal explanations, since they are based on simple statistical associations, lifestyles also have a weak predictive power.[122] Most studies investigating their ability to predict product and brand consumption have resulted in correlation coefficients between 0.2 and 0.3 when lifestyle variables are considered alone, and between 0.5 and 0.6 when they are used in combination with other descriptors.[123]

A French study using information from consumer panels has compared the predictive power of CCA and Cofremca with that of the classic socio-demographic variables.[124] The results revealed that for forty-three product categories (including food, cleaning and cosmetics), the prediction of purchases of the CCA classification was significant in only six cases and that of Cofremca in thirty-one cases (but with a proportion of explained variance never exceeding 3 per cent). In contrast, the socio-demographic variables had a significant coefficient for all products, and their predictive power could be as high as 36 per cent (for butter). Even a single socio-demographic variable, such as the profession of the household main wage earner, was a better predictor than the CCA or Cofremca classifications.

Based on this, should we reject the concept of lifestyle? Probably not. As noted by Wells, even if the reliability and the validity have not been perfectly established, lifestyle information brings an additional perspective, obtained with cost-effective methods, considering alternative ways of gaining access to the same type of data.[125] In conclusion, it thus appears that the major contribution of lifestyle studies lies in their ability to generate working hypotheses and to facilitate the emergence of creative ideas.[126] They should, however, never be the sole basis for making marketing decisions.

Notes

[1] See 'Quand j'aurais 20 ans, moi, je voudrais être ...', L'Expansion, 1992, 15 October, pp. 138–9.

[2] A. J. Reiss et al., Occupations and Social Status (Free Press, 1961).

[3] T. Schjelderup-Ebbe, 'Social Behaviour of Birds', in G. Murchinson (ed.), A Handbook of Social Psychology (Clark University Press, 1935).

[4] B. Barber, Social Stratification: A Comparative Analysis of Structure and Process (Harcourt, Brace and World, 1957). For a discussion on the existence of process, see K. Davis and W. Moore, 'Some Principles of Stratification', American Sociological Review, 1945, pp. 242–9; and M. Tumin, 'Some Principles of Stratification: A Critical Analysis', American Sociological Review, 1953, pp. 387–93.

[5] For a compilation, see T. Lasswell, Class and Stratum: An Introduction to Concepts and Research (Houghton Mifflin, 1965), Chaps 1–8.

[6] D. Krech, R. Crutchfield and E. Ballachey, Individual in Society (New York: McGraw-Hill, 1962), p. 338.

[7] For a list of 12 key variables, see B. Berelson and G. Steiner, Human Behavior (Harcourt, Brace and World, 1964), p. 54.

[8] J. Carman, The Application of Social Class to Market Segmentation (University of California Press, 1965).

[9] G. Lukacs, History and Class Consciousness (Ed. Minuit, 1980).

[10] M. Halbwachs, *Esquisse d'une Psychologie des Classes Sociales* (Ed. Rivière, 1964).

[11] R. Curtis and E. Jackson, *Inequality in American Communities* (Academic Press, 1977).

[12] T. de Boisriou *et al.*, *Mesure Subjective de la Classe Sociale*, HEC Study carried out under the author's supervision (HEC, November 1992).

[13] R. Centers, *The Psychology of Social Class* (Russell & Russell, 1961), p. 233.

[14] For an elaboration of this approach using conjoint analysis, see A. K. Jain, 'A Method for Investigating and Representing Implicit Social Class Theory', *Journal of Consumer Research*, June 1975, pp. 53–9.

[15] Karl Marx, *Das Kapital* (PUF, 1956).

[16] Karl Marx, *Les Luttes de Classe en France* (Editions Sociales, 1952).

[17] Karl Marx, *Revolution and Counter-revolution in Germany* (Editions Sociales, 1952).

[18] See, however, M. Cherkaoui and L. Lindsey, 'Problèmes de Mesure des Classes Sociales: Des Indices du Statut aux Modèles d'Analyse des Rapports de Classe', *Revue Française de Sociologie*, 1977, pp. 233–70.

[19] See H. H. Gerth and C. W. Mills, *From Max Weber: Essays in Sociology* (Oxford University Press, 1946), as well as M. Weber, *The Theory of Social and Economic Organisation*, with an introduction by Talcott Parsons (Free Press, 1947).

[20] For a comparative criticism, see L. Dominguez and A. Page, 'Stratification in Consumer Behavior Research: A Re-Examination', *Journal of the Academy of Marketing Science*, Summer 1981, pp. 250–71.

[21] A. Desrosières, 'Eléments pour l'Histoire des Nomenclatures Socio-Professionelles', in *Pour une Histoire de la Statistique, Ouvrage Collectif* (INSEE, 1977), Tome 1, pp. 155–231.

[22] B. Seys, 'De l'Ancien Code à la Nouvelle Nomenclature des Catégories Socio-Professionnelles', *Economie et Statistique*, February 1983, pp. 55–81.

[23] The best-known of these scales is certainly that of North and Hatt, which is based on a list of 30 professions with which a perceived prestige score is associated. See C. G. North and P. K. Hatt, 'Jobs and Occupations: A Popular Evaluation', *Opinion News*, September 1947, pp. 3–13. See also O. D. Duncan, 'A Socio-Economic Index for all Occupations', in Reiss, *op. cit.*

[24] For example, an English study has revealed great instability in the classifications. Questioned at ten-monthly intervals, between 35 and 40% of the respondents had changed their socio-professional category! See S. O'Brian *et al.*, 'Can We at Last Say Goodbye to Social Class?', *Journal of the Market Research Society*, July 1988, pp. 289–324.

[25] L Warner *et al. Social Class in America* (Harper & Row, 1949).

[26] A. Hollingshead and F. Redlich, *Social Class and Mental Illness* (Wiley, 1958).

[27] See R. Coleman, 'The Continuing Significance of Social Class to Marketing', *Journal of Consumer Research*, December 1983, pp. 265–80.

[28] N. Rohme and T. Veldman, 'Harmonisation of Demographics', *ESOMAR Congress Proceedings*, 1982, pp. 1–20. Also see ESOMAR Working Group, 'A Step Forward in International Research: Harmonisation of Demographics for Easier International Comparisons', *European Research*, October 1984, pp. 182–9; ESOMAR Working Group, 'Harmonising Demographics: Can We Afford Not To?' progress report, 1989; and Y. Marbeau, 'Harmonisation of Demographics in Europe 1991: The State of The Art', *Marketing and Research Today*, March 1992, pp. 33–40.

[29] J. Quatresooz and D. Vancraeynest, 'Using the ESOMAR Harmonised Demographics: External and Internal Validation of the Eurobarometer Test', *Marketing and Research Today*, 9 March 1992, pp. 42–7.

[30] J. Roussel, 'Mesure du Standing', *ISL Information*, 32, June 1987, pp. 2–5.

[31] See J. Mager and L. Kahle, 'Is the Whole More than the Sum of the Parts? Re-evaluating Social Status in Marketing', *Journal of Business Psychology*, in press.

[32] D. W. Hendon, E. L. Williams and D. E. Huffman, 'Social Class Systems Revisited', *Journal of Business Research*, November 1988, p. 259.

[33] Eurostat statistics. For access to more European statistics, one may consult

http://europa.eu.int. For a summary analysis, see P. S. H. Leeflang and W. F. van Raaij, 'The changing consumer in the European Union: A meta-analysis', *International Journal of Research in Marketing*, 1995, pp. 373–87.

[34] For a recent discussion of Bourdieu's approach in a consumer behaviour context, see D. Holt, 'Does Cultural Capital Structure American Consumption?' *Journal of Consumer Research*, June 1998, pp. 1–25. For more on Bourdieu's theory, see P. Bourdieu and L. Wacquant, *An Invitation to Reflexive Sociology* (University of Chicago Press, 1992); and C. Calhoun, E. LiPuma and M. Postone (eds), *Bourdieu: Critical Perspectives* (University of Chicago Press, 1993).

[35] See P. Bourdieu, *Distinction: A Social Critique of the Judgement of Taste* (Cambridge University Press, 1984).

[36] R. Coleman, *op. cit.*

[37] P. Fussell, *Class: A Guide Through the American Status System* (Summit Books, 1983).

[38] See P. Bourdieu, *op. cit.*

[39] J. Baudrillard, *Le système des objets* (Mediations, 1976).

[40] J. M. Munson and W. A. Spivey, 'Product and Brand User Stereotypes Among Social Classes', *Advances in Consumer Research* (ACR, 1981), pp. 696–701.

[41] N. Herpin, 'Habillement et Classe Sociale', *LSA*, October 1986, pp. 65–89.

[42] See M. R. Solomon, *Consumer Behaviour: Buying, Having, and Being*, 3rd edition (Allyn and Bacon, 1997).

[43] *Pratiques Culturelles des Français* (Dalloz, 1982).

[44] P. Bennett and H. Kassarjian, *Consumer Behavior* (Prentice Hall, 1972), p. 119.

[45] K. Prasad, 'Socioeconomic Product Risk and Patronage Reference of Retail Shoppers', *Journal of Marketing*, July 1975, pp. 42–7.

[46] H. L. Mathews and J. W. Slocum Jr, 'Social Class and Commercial Credit Usage', *Journal of Marketing*, January 1969, pp. 71–8; and J. W. Slocum Jr and H. L. Mathews, 'Social Class and Income as Indicators of Credit Behavior', *Journal of Marketing*, April 1970, pp. 69–74.

[47] P. Martineau, 'Social Class and its Very Close Relationship to the Individual's Buying Behavior', in Martin L. Bell (ed.), *Marketing: A Maturing Discipline* (American Marketing Association, 1960), p. 191.

[48] Mathews and Slocum, *op. cit.*

[49] J. F. Durgee, 'How Consumer Sub-Cultures Code Reality: A Look at Some Code Types', *Advances in Consumer Research* (1986), pp. 332–7.

[50] A. H. Roscoe Jr, A. Le Claire Jr and L. Schiffman, 'Theory and Management Applications of Demographics in Buyer Behavior', in A. Woodside, J. Sheth and P. Bennett (eds), *Consumer and Industrial Buying Behavior* (North Holland, 1977), pp. 74–5.

[51] S. Levy, 'Social Class and Consumer Behavior', in J. W. Newman (ed.), *On Knowing the Consumer* (John Wiley & Sons, 1966), pp. 146–60.

[52] D. W. Bishop and M. Ikeda, 'Status and Role Factors in the Leisure Behavior of Different Occupations', *Sociology and Social Research*, January 1970, pp. 190–208.

[53] C. Grignon and Ch. Grignon, 'Styles d'Alimentation et Goûts Populaires', *Revue Française de Sociologie*, 1980, 29(4).

[54] Roscoe, Le Claire and Schiffman, *op. cit.*

[55] B. Dubois and G. Laurent, 'Is There a Euroconsumer for Luxury Goods?' in F. van Raaij and G. J. Bamossy (eds), *European Advances in Consumer Research*, 1993, pp. 58–69.

[56] For direct comparisons between the predictive power of social class and income (with controversial results), see H. Myers, R. Stanton and A. Haug, 'Correlates of Buyer Behavior: Social Class Versus Income', *Journal of Marketing*, October 1971, pp. 8–15; and C. Schaninger, 'Social Class Versus Income Revisited: An Empirical Investigation', *Journal of Marketing Research*, May 1981, pp. 192–208.

[57] A. Gabor and S. W. J. Granger, 'Price Sensitivity of the Consumer', *Journal of Advertising Research*, December 1964, pp. 40–4, and D. Caplovitz, *The Poor Pay More* (Free Press, 1963).

58 F. E. Webster, 'The Deal Prone Consumer', *Journal of Marketing Research*, August 1964, pp. 32–5.

59 J. N. Frey and F. H. Siller, 'A Comparison of Housewife Decision Making in Two Social Classes', *Journal of Marketing Research*, August 1970, pp. 333–7.

60 R. Coleman, 'The Significance of Social Stratification in Selling', in Martin L. Bell, *op. cit*, p. 177. Also see W. Peters, 'Relative Occupational Class Income: A Significant Variable in the Marketing of Automobiles', *Journal of Marketing*, April 1970, pp. 74–7.

61 S. U. Rich and S. C. Jain, 'Social Class and Life Cycle as Predictors of Shopping Behavior', *Journal of Marketing Research*, February 1968, pp. 41–9.

62 G. Foxall, 'Social Factors in Consumer Choice', *Journal of Consumer Research*, June 1975, pp. 60–4.

63 N. Herpin, 'L'Habillement, la Classe Sociale et la Mode', *Economie et Statistique*, May 1986, pp. 35–54.

64 L. Richards, 'Consumer Practices of the Poor', in F. D. Sturdivant (ed.), *The Ghetto Marketplace* (Free Press, 1969), pp. 42–60.

65 V. K. Prasad, 'Socio-Economic Product Risk and Patronage Preferences of Retail Shoppers', *Journal of Marketing*, July 1975, pp. 42–55.

66 See S. Dawson *et al.*, 'An Empirical Update and Extension of Patronage Behavior Across the Social Class Hierarchy', *Advances in Consumer Research* (ACR, 1990).

67 J. Nevin and M. J. Houston, 'Image as Component of Attraction to Inter-Urban Shopping Areas', *Journal of Retailing*, Spring 1980, pp. 73–93.

68 L. Schatzman and A. Strauss, 'Social Classes and Modes of Communication', *American Journal of Sociology*, January 1955, pp. 329–38.

69 Levy, *op. cit.*

70 B. Bernstein, *Langages et Classes Sociales* (Edirions de Minuit, 1975).

71 D. Glick and S. J. Levy, *Living with Television* (Aldine, 1962).

72 See J. M. Munson and W. A. Spivey, 'Product and Brand-User Stereotypes Among Social Classes: Implications for Advertising Strategy', *Journal of Advertising Research*, August 1981, pp. 37–45.

73 M. Weber, 'Die Wirtschaftsethik der Weltreligionen', *Archiv fur Sozialforschung*, 1915, Vol. 41.

74 A. Adler, *The Science of Living* (Greenburg, 1929).

75 For a historical analysis of the lifestyle concept, see H. L. Ansbacher, 'Life Style: A Historical and Systematic Review', *Journal of Individual Psychology*, 1967, pp. 191–212.

76 W. Lazer, 'Life-Style Concepts and Marketing', in S. Greyser (ed.), *Toward Scientific Marketing* (American Marketing Association, 1963), pp. 103–9.

77 See L. L. Golden, 'Life-Style and Psychographics: A Critical Review and Recommendation', *Advances in Consumer Research* (ACR, 1983), p. 405.

78 See the section on values in Chapter 7.

79 D. Yankelovitch, 'What New Life Style Means to Market Planners', *Marketing Communications*, Vol. 29, June 1971.

80 A. Mitchell, *Nine American Values: Who We are and Where We are Going* (Macmillan, 1983).

81 See for example S. Yuspek, 'Syndicated Values/Life Style Segmentation Schemes: Use Them as Descriptive Tools, Not to Select Targets', *Marketing News*, 25 May 1984, pp. 1–12.

82 A. de Vulpian, 'Description et Suivi Périodique des Courants Socio-Culturels en France', *IREP*, May 1974, pp. 117–62.

83 B. Cathelat, *Styles de Vie* (Ed. d'Organisation, 1983); and B. Cathelat and M. Cathelat, *Panorama des Styles de Vie 1960–1990* (Ed. d'Organisation, 1991).

84 B. Cathelat, *op. cit.*

85 *Europinion*, November 1997, pp. 1–20.

86 M. L. Richins and S. Dawson, 'A Consumer Values Orientation for Materialism and Its Measurement: Scale Validation and Development', *Journal of Consumer Research*, December 1992, pp. 303–16.

87 M. T. Douglas and B. C. Isherwood, *The World of Goods* (Basic Books, 1979). See also M. Solomon, 'The Role of Products as Social Stimuli: A Symbolic Interactionism Perspective', *Journal of Consumer Research*, December 1983, pp. 319–29; and D. Miller, *Material Culture and Mass Consumption* (Blackwell, 1987).

88 S. Levy, 'Symbolism and Life Style', in S. Greyser (ed.), *Towards Scientific Marketing* (American Marketing Association, 1962). See also M. Solomon, 'Mapping Product Constellations: A Social Categorisation Approach to Symbolic Consumption', *Psychology and Marketing*, 5, 1988, pp. 233–58.

89 W. Wells, 'Backward Segmentation', in J. Ardn (ed.), *Insights into Consumer Behaviour* (Allyn and Bacon, 1968), pp. 85–100.

90 M. Alpert and R. Gatty, 'Product Positioning by Behavioural Life Styles', *Journal of Marketing*, April 1969, pp. 65–9.

91 J. Stoetzel, 'A Factor Analysis of Liquor Preferences of French Consumers', *Journal of Advertising Research*, May 1969, pp. 7–11.

92 L. Uusitalo, 'Identification of Consumption Style Segments on the Basis of Household Budget Allocation', *Advances in Consumer Research* (ACR, 1979), pp. 451–9.

93 S. C. Cosmas, 'Life Styles and Consumption Patterns', *Journal of Consumer Research*, March 1982, pp. 453–65.

94 J. Cehra,'The Limits of Influence', *European Research*, 1974, pp. 141–51.

95 J. M. Agostini and J. F. Boss, 'Classifying Informants in Consumer Surveys According to Their Areas of Interest', *European Research*, January 1973, pp. 20–5.

96 W. D. Wells and D. Tigert, 'Activities, Interests, and Opinions', *Journal of Advertising Research*, August 1971, pp. 27–35; E. A. Pessemier and D. Tigert, 'Personality, Activity, and Attitude Predictors of Consumer Behaviour', in J. Wright and J. Goldstucker (eds), *New Ideas for Successful Marketing* (American Marketing Association, 1966), pp. 332–47; and T. Hustad and E. A. Pessemier, 'The Development and Application of Psychographic Life Style and Associated Activity and Attitude Measures', in W. Wells (ed.), *Life Style and Psychographics* (American Marketing Association, 1974), pp. 33–70.

97 F. D. Reynolds and W. E. Darden, 'Construing Life Style and Psychographics', in W. D. Wells, *op. cit.*, pp. 71–96.

98 See S. Segnit and S. Broadbent, 'Life Style Research', *European Research*, January 1973, pp. 6–13, and March 1973, pp. 62–8. See also D. Tigert, 'Can a Separate Marketing Strategy for French Canada be Justified: Profiling English and French Markets Through Life Style Analysis', in D. M. Thompson and D. S. Leighton (eds), *Canadian Marketing: Problems and Prospects* (John Wiley, 1973), pp. 113–42.

99 'Value Segments Help Define International Market', *Marketing News* (November 21, 1988), p. 17. On Europe, see V. Latham, 'Do Euroconsumers Exist?' *Marketing*, 24 June 1993, p. 3.

100 D. Tigert *et al.*, 'The Fast Food Franchise: Psychographic and Demographic Segmentation Analysis', *Journal of Retailing*, Spring 1971, pp. 81–90.

101 T. Lunn, S. Baldwin and J. Dickens, 'Monitoring Consumer Life Styles', *Admap*, November 1972, pp. 368–72.

102 J. T. Plummer, 'Life Style Patterns and Commercial Bank Credit Card Usage', *Journal of Marketing*, April 1971, pp. 35–41.

103 R. Arellano *et al.*, 'Le Comportement du Consommateur d'Energie Domestique: Une Analyse Causale', *Actes du 4e Congrès de l'Association Française du Marketing*, Montpellier, 5–6 May 1988.

104 Behavior Science Corporation, *Developing the Family Travel Market* (Better Home and Gardens, 1972).

105 K. Villani, 'Personality/Life Style and Television Viewing Behavior', *Journal of Marketing Research*, November 1975, pp. 432–9.

106 S. Segnit and S. Broadbent, 'Clustering by Product Usage: A Case History', *ESOMAR Congress Proceedings*, September 1974, pp. 577–99.

107 W. Darden and W. D. Perreault, 'A Multivariate Analysis of Media Exposure and Vacation Behavior With Life Style Covariates', *Journal of Consumer Research*, September 1975, pp. 93–103.

108 A. Pugnet and J. C. Coutin, 'L'Application du Style de Vie à la Clientèle Bancaire: Une Approche Spécifique au Crédit Agricole', *Revue Française du Marketing*, 1982/1983, pp. 55–64.

109 W. D. Wells, 'Psychographics: A Review', *Journal of Marketing Research*, July 1985, pp. 196–213.

110 R. Ziff, 'The Role of Psychographics in the Development of Advertising Strategy and Copy', in W. D. Wells, *op. cit.*, pp. 127–66.

111 S. Douglas, 'L'Analyse du Style de Vie: Problèmes Actuels et Perspectives', *Encyclopédie du Marketing*, 1976, 4, pp. 1–32.

112 P. Michaels, 'Life Style and Magazine Exposure', in B. W. Becker and H. Becker (eds), *Marketing Education and the Real World and Dynamic Marketing in A Changing World* (American Marketing Association, 1973), pp. 324–31.

113 See C. Hodock, 'The Use of Psychographics in the Analysis of Channels of Distribution', in W. Wells, *op. cit.*, pp. 205–21.

114 E. M. May, 'Psychographics in Department Store Imagery', MSI working paper, October 1971. See also W. Bearden, J. Tell and R. Durand, 'Media Usage, Psychographics and Demographic Dimensions of Retail Shoppers', *Journal of Retailing*, 1978, pp. 65–74; and M. Crash and S. Reynolds, 'An In-depth Profile of the Department Store Shopper', *Journal of Retailing*, 1978, pp. 23–32.

115 J. A. Leisser and M. A. Hughes, 'The Generalizability of Pychographic Market Segments Across Geographical Location', *Journal of Marketing*, January 1986, pp 18–27.

116 B. Dizambourg, 'Style de Vie et Fréquentation des Points de Vente', thèse de doctorat 3e cycle en sciences de gestion. Université de Paris 1-Sorbonne.

117 Y. Wind and P. Green, 'Some Concepts of Measurement and Analytical Problems in Life Style Research', in W. D. Wells, *op. cit.*, pp. 97–126.

118 J. Lastovicka, 'On the Validation of Life Style Traits: A Review and Illustration', *Journal of Marketing Research*, February 1982, pp. 126–38.

119 A. E. Pessemier and A. V. Bruno, 'An Empirical Investigation of the Reliability and Stability of Activity and Attitude Measures', Reprint Series No. 391, Krannert Graduate School of Industrial Administration, 1971; and A. Burns and A. Harrison, 'A Test of the Reliability of Psychographics', *Journal of Marketing Research*, 1979, pp. 32–8.

120 W. Darden and F. Reynolds, 'Predicting Opinion Leadership for Men's Apparel Fashion', *Journal of Marketing Research*, August 1972, pp. 324–8.

121 See P. Valette-Florence, *Les Styles de Vie: Bilan Critique et Perspectives* (Nathan, 1994).

122 See D. Tigert and W. Wells, 'Life Style Analysis as a Basis for Media Selection', in W. D. Wells, *op. cit.*, 1971, pp. 30–47.

123 See for example C. L. Wright and J. J. Coldstucker (eds), *op. cit.*, pp. 30–47.

124 J. N. Kapferer and G. Laurent, 'Une Analyse des Relations entre les Classifications Socioculturelles et de Style de Vie et l'Achat des Produits Courants', *IREP Conference Proceedings*, pp. 205–20.

125 W. Wells, *op. cit.*, pp. 196–213. See also T. Novak and B. McEvoy, 'On Comparing Alternative Segmentation Schemes: The List of Values (LOV) and Values and Life Styles (VALS)', *Journal of Consumer Research*, June 1990, pp. 105–9.

126 For a recent book on the topic, see L. R. Kahle and L. Chiagouris (eds), *Values, Lifestyles and Psychographics* (Laurence Erlbaum Associates, 1997).

7

Culture and value systems

Learning objectives

After reading this chapter, you should understand:

1 what is meant by culture and the various ways in which this concept has been approached and studied;

2 how values and value systems are defined, monitored and used for marketing segmentation and positioning purposes;

3 how myths, norms, conventions and rituals shape and give meaning to consumer behaviour;

4 how socialisation and acculturation processes underlie cultural change;

5 the conditions under which marketing should be globalised or, on the contrary, locally adapted.

Key words

culture	ethnocentrism	global marketing
values	national character	etic and emic
norms	role	perspectives
conventions	socialisation	ethnoconsumerism
myths	acculturation	
rituals	cultural change	

German, Italian, Spanish, British or European?

When it launched its 1000 instant camera, the Polaroid Company used different advertisements for each European country. Figure 7.1 presents the campaign used in Germany, while Figure 7.2 illustrates the Italian one. Even though the camera is identical and the general structure of the advert is similar, the people represented, the slogans used, and more generally the context and tone are rather different. They are matched to the 'national character'.[1] On the other hand, when Lufthansa sends a message to its prospective business clients, it does it in exactly

Figure 7.1 Polaroid in Germany

Figure 7.2 Polaroid in Italy

the same way (except for the language) throughout the various countries of Europe: see for example the advertisements shown in England and Spain (Figures 7.3 and 7.4). Why is there such a variation in approach? How do we explain why one company decides to take into account the differences (real or imagined) between consumers of different nationality while another ignores them, relying on the existence of a homogeneous supranational group (European businessmen in this particular instance)?[2] To account for such decisions and the mechanisms supporting them, it is necessary to call upon the notion of **culture**.

The impact of culture on purchase and consumption phenomena is well documented today and most theories advanced to explain consumer behaviour integrate, in one form or another, the cultural factor.[3] Yet if we admit that culture plays a role, we do not completely understand the origin of this influence. In marketing in particular, managers as well as researchers have abused the concept of culture – most notably in international comparisons – to explain away any observed differences. For example, a study of the types of products consumed by French- and English-speaking Canadians attributed all differences not explained by income level or social class to culture.[4] Culture has progressively become a 'dustbin concept' receiving residual and unclassified data. Such a situation is particularly surprising as culture has been the subject of numerous scientific writings over many decades. Several disciplines (ethnology, anthropology, anthropological psychology, and so on) have been almost entirely devoted to this topic and have developed a considerable body of knowledge.[5] It is only recently that consumer researchers have become increasingly interested in the cultural aspects of consumption.[6]

Figure 7.3   Lufthansa in the UK

Figure 7.4   Lufthansa in Spain

The object of this chapter is to examine the cultural factor and its impact on buying behaviour and consumption. It consists of three parts: first, the concept of culture and its principal dimensions are examined; second, in a series of sections, the influence of culture on individual and social behaviour is analysed; the third part is dedicated to the marketing implications relating to these elements.[7]

How do you define culture?

The first and perhaps the major obstacle met in the study of cultural phenomena is the ambiguity which surrounds the notion of **culture**. In a seminal paper, Kroeber and Kluckhohn, two American anthropologists, collected, analysed and compared up to 164 definitions – without being able to resist adding one of their own![8] Let us take as a starting point one of the oldest 'omnibus' definitions, that given by Tylor: 'The complex whole which includes knowledge, beliefs, art, law, morals, custom, and any capability and habits acquired by man as a member of society'[9], and let us focus on its four key underlying ideas: a culture is *global*, *shared*, *transmissible* and *evolving*.

The meaning attached by social scientists to the word 'culture' is quite different to that of the layperson. Culture is not the sole prerogative of a 'cultivated' person with an advanced education and a taste for the arts and literature; it covers all characteristic elements of society. In this sense, a TV commercial or a toothbrush is as legitimate a cultural artefact as is classic poetry.[10] In its most observable form, culture first appears as a group of distinctive **behaviours** or patterns of living – that which immediately differentiates one culture from another. Perhaps it is a certain way of eating, dressing, living, speaking or expressing feelings. Essential though they are, however, notably from the point of view of their marketing implications (for products, services, modes of distribution and styles of communication), these behaviours are only the tip of the iceberg.[11] They are merely the manifestation of a variety of **norms** (that is, prescriptions controlling society) which themselves reveal a system of **values** expressing, via certain ideas (for example individual freedom, equality), the objectives of a culture and its preferred way of functioning as determined by its members. It is through our value system that we judge the behaviour of an individual as moral, immoral or even 'normal'.

Values, norms and behaviours represent a distinctive way for a society to cope with the problems posed by its environment, and in this sense a culture is necessarily collective and shared. It is not the peculiarity of a particular value – or even of the complete value system – which characterises a culture but the fact that the individuals making up a society adhere to it. In this way, a culture forges a common bond between its members. Being composed of elements that are not innate but acquired, a culture is transmissible from one generation to the next and this ensures its survival. Primarily oral in primitive societies, the process of cultural heritage transmission has acquired a great complexity in developed societies through institutions as diverse as the family, the educational system and the media.

Finally, in spite of its communal and transmissible character, a culture is not rigid. Technological innovation, the evolution of ideas and the development of means of communication make it impossible to live in a vacuum and to survive – a society has to evolve.[12] The development of the fast-food business in Europe is an excellent example of cultural change.[13]

To sum up, culture appears as the framework in which people interact and the lens through which they view the world. Articulated around a system of values, norms and behaviours, it enables a group of individuals to live as a society. Transmitted from the oldest to the youngest or to newcomers, it assures the group's survival. Under the influence of internal pressure or external events, caused notably by the contact with other cultures, it evolves in order to preserve its adaptation to the outside world.

Shaping the way of life of a society, culture is necessarily present in all aspects of consumer behaviour as well as in the objects of consumption themselves.[14] Cultural influences are therefore fundamental elements marketers need to understand and to which they must address attention.

Culture and buying behaviour

Since culture manifests itself in many forms, it is helpful to distinguish three principal domains of influence: first, the **social mould** against which interaction between marketers and consumers takes place; this is reflected in the core cultural values of a society, in its social institutions, in its conventions and rituals, and in its communication and language systems. Second, cultural influences emerge in the formation of **individual behaviour patterns**, in daily life rhythms and use of time and place, in the modes of emotional expression, and in the dominant personality types and traits of society or a social group. Finally, culture influences the **dynamics of social interaction**, the learning of social roles and behaviour and their evolution and change.

The landscape of values

As just mentioned, the core of a culture consists of a set of key values.[15] These values are at the heart of the functioning of a society and support its evolution; their identification, therefore, is essential. For example, in US middle-class culture, cleanliness is 'next to godliness' and those who smell, do not wash and are genenerally perceived as 'dirty' run the risk of being treated as social outcasts. The success of Procter and Gamble's mythical hero 'Mr Clean' is a direct reflection of the potency of the cleanliness appeal in influencing consumer behaviour.

Examining the most widespread myths in a society is a powerful (and amusing) way of identifying its core values. A **myth** is a story full of symbolic elements which express the ideals of a culture.[16] As noted by Lévi-Strauss, many mythical stories are based on an opposition, for example between good (Cinderella) and evil (Cinderella's stepmother), and as such provide models for personal conduct.[17] However, the identification of a particular value matters less than the system which links values together.[18] In the USA, for example, many efforts have been made to characterise the American value system. Thus, Kluckhohn and Strodbeck have put forward four dimensions (rapport with nature, relation to time, personal activity and relation to others) enabling the identification of cultural orientations and variations among the American people.[19] Similarly, Rokeach has discerned eighteen terminal values, that is to say values expressed as desirable goals (for example world peace, family security, freedom) and eighteen instrumental values, or preferred ways of acting and being (for example honesty, responsibility, ambition).[20] Kahle has more recently introduced and used in a variety of contexts a list called LOV, limited to nine values: the sense of belonging, the need for stimulation, enjoyment, warm relations with others, personal development, the sense of accomplishment, being respected, security, and self-respect.[21]

In Europe, Hofstede, after studying IBM employees in a large number of countries, suggested four dimensions to account for cultural variations (at least in a work-related context): (a) power distance, which refers to interpersonal relationships; (b) uncertainty avoidance; (c) masculinity/feminity; and (d) individualism/collectivism.[22] Such a framework, which is not without its critics, has been used on a number of occasions to account for cross-cultural differences in consumer research.[23]

Also in Europe, RISC has identified eight fundamental 'sociodynamic' forces:[24]

1 *personal development*, built on the belief in one's own potential;

2 *hedonism*, or the priority given to the search for pleasure in the different aspects of life;

3 *'plasticity'*, the aptitude to move and adapt to an environment in constant evolution;

4 *connectivity*, the speed of building and also of withdrawing from networks of relations with others;

5 *ethics*, the quest for authenticity and meaning;

6 *vitality*, the capacity to mobilise one's physical and mental energies;

7 *sense of belonging*, a concern to rediscover one's origins, history and identity; and

8 *inertia*, or resistance to change.

From studies measuring the degree of attachment of individuals to each of these values, RISC has developed tools such as the Euroscan indicating the major dimensions of social change. In turn, these tools have been used for positioning products and brands, for example in the luxury market.[25]

Finally, in France, Cofremca has detected thirty 'sociocultural trends' underlying the attitudes and behaviours of the French.[26] Among these: individualism and originality, hedonism, lack of respect for authority and order, and willingness to change. For its part, the Centre de Communication Avancé has drawn up a fairly similar list of thirteen sociocultural factors from the results of creative focus groups.[27] An analysis of the evolution of these trends over ten years reveals an increase of conservative values and a relative equilibrium between sensualism and materialism. We can also detect a tendency to focus attention on oneself, on family life and on the immediate environment, in other words a desire for 'cocooning'.[28] Such results could be compared with other countries a few years ago through an interesting study carried out among Europeans about the values parents would like to inculcate to their children (see Figure 7.5).

Values influence purchasing behaviour in many ways. To a large extent they determine the goals to be pursued, the level of involvement, the benefits sought and the activities carried out; they therefore explain the selection of products as well as the style of consumption. For example, a link has been established between cultural affiliation, as defined by Kluckhohn and Strodtbeck, and car ownership:[29] collectors of 'beautiful automobiles' believe more in hierarchical relationships than in conviviality. Similarly, a relationship has been observed between the values as measured by Rokeach's RVS system and the type of magazines read.[30] In the same vein, Lancôme admits to having launched its 'Magie noire' perfume based on a market positioning derived from the Cofremca studies.[31]

Social institutions

The institutions of a society, its political and economic system, its social structure

Figure 7.5 Qualities deemed important in the education of children in different European countries

	EU	FR	UK	WG	IT	NL	DK	BE	SP	IR
Honesty	73*	76	[79]	74	77	[79]	76	70	(47)	73
Tolerance	51	59	[62]	(42)	43	57	58	45	44	56
Good manners	49	(21)	[68]	42	55	59	49	47	54	65
Responsibility	46	39	24	[63]	46	55	[63]	37	[63]	(22)
Politeness	35	[51]	27	29	37	42	51	48	(20)	23
Loyalty	32	36	36	22	[43]	24	24	23	29	(19)
Self control	29	30	33	30	20	34	(12)	30	[37]	31
Independence	27	(16)	23	47	23	27	[55]	20	24	30
Obedience	25	18	[37]	16	27	23	(14)	28	30	34
Hard work	23	36	16	22	13	14	(2)	33	[42]	24
Thrift	21	32	(9)	31	19	17	15	[36]	11	15
Determination	19	18	17	[27]	17	16	11	21	13	(10)
Religious faith	17	11	14	17	22	14	(8)	17	22	[41]
Unselfishness	15	23	[40]	4	(2)	9	23	14	4	22
Patience	14	10	[16]	14	[16]	15	(9)	13	15	12
Imagination	13	12	11	14	(8)	11	11	(8)	[24]	(8)
Leadership	10	(2)	4	[32]	3	4	(2)	6	8	7

◯ = lowest score for the quality

▢ = highest score for the quality

Source: Halman *et al.*, *Traditie, secularisatie en individualisering*, Tilburg University Press, 1987, p. 342; see also Harding and Philips (1986), pp. 20, 21

and organisation, its arrangements for enforcing law and order, the place it accords to religion and the family, and the principles according to which education is organised and children are reared reflect the dominant value system of a culture. In any given society, the social institutions thus give values a formal, tangible and more easily accessible mode of expression.[32] For example, a value such as responsibility is learned both at school and in the family. Through punishments and rewards, the educational and legal systems make sure that values such as individual property and dignity are recognised and enforced.

In as far as they define the legal and social framework for living in society, institutions exert a very strong influence on purchase and consumption activities. In prescribing or censuring certain forms of behaviour, religion for example affects the fate of certain products (such as condoms) and services (such as the voluntary termination of pregnancy), as well as imposing limits on distribution networks and communication strategies. Thus in several European countries there is strong religious opposition to Sunday shopping and, as a result, store opening hours are restricted. Similarly, public bodies, in campaigning against alcohol or tobacco, affect the consumption of the corresponding products. At a broader level, laws also define what is and what is not fair commercial practice as well as what is in the best interest of merchants or consumers. As a result, many strategic alliances – such as the one negotiated between British Airways and American Airlines, for example – run into difficulties with European Commissioners who feel they may result in too many restrictive practices. Similarly, the duty-free industry constantly had to engage in lobbying activities to protect its very existence in Europe.

Conventions and rituals

Conventions and rituals, such as eating habits or rites of passage from one phase of life to another (for example from childhood to adulthood), also contribute to defining the way society exists and works. To be convinced, one has only to consider the huge variety of ways of celebrating or marking life events such as birth, puberty, marriage and death across the world.[33] While conventions usually correspond to simple rules to follow in daily life, rituals may take the form of very elaborate scripts governing the 'proper way' to behave in very specific circumstances. As indicated above, rituals are often associated with transitional moments – periods with before and after stages or involving a metamorphosis (from private to public life for example). But both conventions and rituals reflect the dominant value system in a given society. For example, a study has shown that the convention of tipping differs widely across varying cultural contexts. While in total contradiction to hospitality values in countries such as Polynesia, tipping is common practice in societies where it was seen as reinforcing status and social distance – one of the key values investigated by Hofstede.[34] Obviously, people tend to consider the prevailing conventions in their own culture as the 'right' ones: an attitude known as **ethnocentrism**. Rituals, which may be defined as a precise sequence of symbolic behaviours to be repeated periodically,[35] affect certain aspects of daily life such as grooming or gift giving[36] but are particularly visible during the celebration of ceremonies such as birthdays, graduations, weddings and funerals.[37] In many countries in Europe there are, for example, very specific rituals attached to the celebration of Christmas, as is the case with Thanksgiving and Halloween in the USA.[38] It is important to understand not only the functional but also the symbolic dimensions of such types of behaviour, as part of a complete consumption system.[39] Hence, depending upon the specific context, drinking coffee may mean many different things: giving oneself a moment of relaxation after a significant effort, building up energy to start the whole day, sharing a moment with a friend, or even, for a school pupil perhaps, helping to mark the passage into adulthood. But strong variations may exist in the various cultures. For example, as a proportion of income, Christmas gifts represent a much more important expenditure in Mexico than in Europe.[40]

Such rituals have a fundamental relevance in understanding the purchase context of many products (jewels, small household goods, sweets, toys, etc.) as well as its evolution over time. Today, the 'solitaire' diamond ring traditionally offered as an engagement present is facing a difficult marketing problem as five 'cultural shocks' have negatively affected it:

1 a decline of the marriage rate;

2 a reduction in the number of marriages preceded by an engagement ceremony;

3 the decline in popularity of rings as engagement presents;

4 a fall in the number of rings containing diamonds compared with the total number of rings offered as engagement presents; and

5 an increasing tendency in favour of giving existing family rings rather than buying a new one.

The communication and language system

Beyond institutions and rituals, all cultures also develop a specific system of communication and language.[41] In the armed forces, the terms 'slotted' and 'scran' are readily understood, and all pupils know what 'prep' is. Teenagers, businesspeople and tramps – even bars and nightclubs – have their own jargon and speech patterns in the same way that English or Japanese consumers do.

The language and means of communication of a culture serve to ensure bonding between its members and to reinforce their feelings of belonging to a community. Someone who hesitates over the meaning or use of words or signs is immediately identified as a stranger or uninitiated. In most European countries, we can divide up the population according to the kind of words that are used in dialects or slang. In a commercial context, any effort to inform or persuade thus requires a knowledge and understanding of the system of communication and language of the audience being addressed. Complete control however, is often difficult to achieve. In Japanese, there exist three different ways of expressing the same concept (for example eating) depending on whether one wants to be abrupt (*taberu*), polite (*agaru*) or deferential (*itadaku*).[42] It is thus not surprising that many blunders have been made in the choice of names and slogans: General Motors had to change the name of its Nova model in Puerto Rico because it realised that in Spanish 'No va' means 'it doesn't work'; the slogan 'Come alive with Pepsi' was translated into German as 'Reincarnate with Pepsi' and 'Pepsi brings your ancestors back to life' in Chinese;[43] and the Rexona deodorant brand could not be launched in Portugal under that name because of obscene connotations.

Living the culture: the impact on the individual

An individual lives their culture day to day, through ordinary gestures and the way in which they express their feelings and emotions. At a more subtle level, culture also influences one's perception and interpretation of the environment as well as general personality traits.

Gestures and day-to-day expressions

Gestures used in daily life, and the use of time and space, vary fundamentally from one society to another.[44] For example, a handshake is regularly used in certain cultures as a daily greeting, whereas in others it is used only to symbolise an important agreement. In the USA, men shake hands only when they meet for the first time. In southern Spain, the habit of taking an afternoon siesta break and a late evening meal provides a means of coping with high midday temperatures, and shopping activities usually take place in the early evening. Attitudes towards time also vary even within mainland Europe. In northern Europe, time is often considered a scarce resource and therefore carefully apportioned for separate activities: people tend to be punctual and activities scheduled; clocks are found everywhere and watches are kept in working order; many housewives make out shopping lists and plan what they will buy for the week in order to economise on the time spent shopping. In southern Europe, time does not have the same material significance: people frequently don't respect schedules, with the philosophy that what is not done today can de done tomorrow. The conventions relating to the space to maintain between two people during a conversation are also quite different. In Anglo-Saxon countries, it is considered correct to keep a certain distance and to limit physical contact to a minimum; in Latin countries, on the other hand, such behaviour could be interpreted as a sign of coldness or lack of sensitivity. Such rules have an important impact on the organisation of buyer and seller relations, including the requisite time for the negotiation of a sale, the desire for personal contact at the point of sale, and the spatial arrangements of selling activities. While in some cultures the jostling crowded atmosphere of open-air markets or bazaars is preferred, others are attracted by the cold impersonal efficiency of a supermarket or the remote luxuriousness of high-class department stores.

By the same token, ways of expressing sentiments such as anger, anxiety or humour are far from being identical everywhere, and concepts such as beauty, politeness and respect depend very much on cultural context.[45] Ideas about what is beautiful or pleasing to the eye thus vary: the delicate, often understated lines of oriental design contrast with the more expressive, sometimes exaggerated styles typical of Western culture. In Japan, for example, Mattel has had to reduce the size of its Barbie dolls' eyes, which had frightened young Japanese girls.

Humorous advertising messages, in particular those using national stereotypes, are rarely transferable without adaptation. In certain regions of the world it is seen as wrong to enter into the details of a commercial negotiation immediately, though such behaviour is considered natural in North America. Such aspects of course affect interpersonal relations linked to the act of purchase. In a famous book, the anthropologist Edward Hall tells the story of the failure of a commercial transaction worth millions of dollars between an American and a Mexican due to lack of understanding of the respective behaviours; while the American was not able to hold back from discussing the details of the sale, the Mexican first wanted to understand the personality of the manager with whom he was negotiating such an important business deal.[46] He wanted the American to visit his town and meet his family, things which the American considered to be a waste of time.

Perceptual patterns and ways of thinking

Beyond behavioural differences which are immediately observable, culture exerts an influence over an individual's cognitive systems.[47] The familiarity with certain reference objects plays an important role in the perceptive process in so far as it affects the way an ambiguous stimulus is interpreted. Thus a drawing of a triangle on top of a square is interpreted as a house by Western children, while it represents a temple for Orientals. Also, symbolic associations with objects or colours can vary widely. Carlsberg had to add a third elephant to its logo in Africa, as two elephants seen together were considered a bad omen.[48] In Africa, Nestlé is called the 'brand with the birds', a concept easier to understand and remember in countries where the rate of illiteracy is still relatively high. Superstitions about numbers, ladders, black cats and so on also differ from country to country. While in many European countries, '13' is unlucky, in Italy, '17' is the fated number and cannot be issued for hotel rooms or racing cars.

In broader terms, culture determines the boundaries between the sacred and the profane.[49] While profane consumption involves ordinary products and activities, sacred consumption is set apart as requiring special attention. While the words may suggest a link with religion, all types of entity including places, events, people and even ideas, may be consumed in a sacred or profane manner. Before it became the site where Diana Princess of Wales died, for example, the Parisian underpass where her car crashed was just an ordinary road tunnel, like many others in Paris. The fatal pillar is now almost permanently adorned with fresh flowers. In Europe, many people consider their home a special place (a sanctuary) where they can isolate themselves from the harassing outside world. As a result, they make special efforts to personalise it, for example by displaying a muliplicity of family portraits.[50] An international hotel chain recently discovered that one of the first things that many businesspeople who travel frequently do when they enter their hotel room is to rearrange it so as to make it 'look like home'. Similarly, 'sacred' events such as the soccer World Cup or 'historic' rock concerts create a huge market for memorabilia. Conversely, religious symbols such as crosses tend to lose their sacred character when they become costume jewellery items.

Culture and personality

Finally, though it remains somewhat controversial, it would appear that a society's culture exhibits itself in some of the personality traits of its members; indeed, culture is often said to cause the emergence of a 'basic personality' or 'national character'.[51] Following this line of argument, Russians are said to be characterised by 'a tendency for social interaction, great sensitivity, an absence of an elaborate system of defence, and obstinacy'.[52] Similarly, Japanese managers are often considered to be more long-term oriented than their American colleagues, even if they are more tense and seem less happy in their jobs.[53] It has also been shown that American Jews are more favourably disposed toward innovation.[54] Finally, a Franco-German comparative study carried out using the LOV list has shown that social values (in particular relations with others) were more important in France than in Germany.[55]

Though it is somewhat risky to associate one kind of personality with a particular culture, the identification of characteristic traits can help the understanding of buying behaviour and, notably, of attitudes towards products, brands, and advertising messages and media. For example, it has been shown that members of a given culture tend to prefer advertising consistent with their national character.[56] This perhaps explains the success of the Marlboro cowboy in the United States (while in Hong Kong, the image evoked only that of a cowherd and it was necessary to use a white horse to give it prestige) or the campaign promoting energy conservation by the French government ('In France, we don't have any oil, but we have ideas').

Similarly, studies have shown the existence of a 'patriotic bias': in industrialised countries, consumers have a tendency to prefer products and brands from their own country (the opposite is true for developing countries).[57] The acceptance of foreign products is in fact linked to such personal characteristics as gender,[58] age (negative correlation)[59] and educational level (positive correlation). Additionally, many consumers seem to evaluate the quality as well as the price of a foreign product based on its country of origin.[60]

Culture and social interactions

Beyond its influence on social institutions and its impact on individual behaviour, culture also affects interpersonal relations. This intermediate level of analysis is examined successively via the distribution and learning of 'social roles', the social-isation process and the mechanism of social change.

Cultural casting: the distribution of roles

In a given society, every individual is a member of various groups in which they occupy a particular place (see Chapter 5). The same individual may, simultaneously, be head of a family, company manager and administrator of a sports club. To each of these positions is associated a number of specific behaviours and expectations which express the way society feels the **role** should be carried out.[61] Such roles inevitably influence the nature of products deemed adapted to a given situation. For example, a study on household attitudes towards instant coffee has shown that in certain environments, the main obstacle to consumption was its per-ceived incompatibility with the traditional image of a 'good housewife'– an image according to which the coffee was properly prepared for the family and for guests. Use of soluble coffee was associated with laziness and over-familiarity on the part of the householder and the product was judged as somewhat demeaning.[62]

Role perceptions also affect market positioning and, therefore, the way products are promoted. A mistake made by an American company when promoting dish-washers in Switzerland consisted of highlighting the labour-saving dimension. This argument, which had been proved to work in the USA, was considered by the Swiss housewife to contradict the importance she attached to the task – a value judge-ment which prevented her accepting that the job could be done by a machine. As a result, the company had to change the positioning of the product by emphasising the hygienic nature of the washing process.[63]

Socialisation and acculturation

The behavioural norms which are attached to different social roles and the values which underpin them are handed down from one generation to the next via the process of 'socialisation'.[64] According to this process, an individual learns pro-gressively and through multiple networks (family, school, and so on) what is acceptable and what is deviant in a wide variety of social interaction situations.

This learning mechanism also exists in the case of an individual who is trans-planted from one culture to another, and the learning process is then called accul-turation. Both socialisation and acculturation mechanisms enable the emergence of stable behaviours common across most members of a given society. A number of studies have shown how children learn to behave as consumers and choose a pur-chasing strategy by observing their parents or friends.[65] A French study revealed, for example, that buying and usage habits of cosmetics resulted from a reciprocal influence between mothers and daughters.[66] Similarly, it has been shown that Hispanic-Americans have a consumption style deriving from their cultural affilia-tion[67] and, in the case of Mexican immmigrants, this is notably different from white American culture.[68] Bilingual Canadians, to take another example, are situated an equal distance between Canadian francophones and anglophones on a scale of values and specific behaviours.[69]

Cultural change

Whether under the influence of internal or external factors, a culture must evolve. A society changes either because of innovative actions by its members or through the assimilation of elements borrowed from other cultures.

In every culture, there are individuals or organisations who are more dynamic than others and wish to advance the value system and the prevalent state of technological and economic development.[70] Such individuals or organisations either develop new ideas themselves or play a crucial role in their diffusion into the social system. In particular, they play a key role in the rhythm of diffusion of new products and the resulting pattern of buying behaviours and consumption habits. It is thus important to identify them and analyse their role. In many countries, high-income, achievement-motivated, better-educated members of society have often been identified as more likely to be innovators and to play a pioneering role in the spread of new products and services.[71] In industrial contexts, several studies have been devoted to similar 'lead' customers.[72]

Finally, a culture may also evolve as a result of contact with other environments. In the modern era the development of new means of communication, and particularly the Internet, is weakening traditional cultural barriers and gives birth to new supranational groups with specific and homogeneous behaviour patterns.[73] This explains, for example, the emergence of an international ecologist or consumerist subculture.[74] Sometimes, the mechanism of 'cultural exportation' meets a certain resistance on the part of the culture being 'invaded'. In Europe, all products 'made in the USA' do not spread at the same speed: peanut butter and popcorn have not met with the same success as chewing gum and soft drinks.[75] A great deal depends on the perceived compatibility with the predominant value system in the receiving culture.[76]

Marketing implications

A manager can take into account the cultural factor in many ways, both when making strategic decisions and in the implementation of tactical operations. At the strategic level, an understanding of cultural influences can suggest opportunities for segmenting strategies and for transferring or expanding operations into other cultural settings. At the tactical level, cultural factors often impose significant constraints on how strategies will be carried out, especially in reference to product, price, distribution and communication policy decisions.

Differentiated or global marketing?

A detailed understanding of cultural practices, conventions, taboos, rituals and folklore can considerably facilitate the identification of motivational and social forces operating in different cultural settings and situations; it can, therefore, provide a sound basis for segmenting markets. In the USA, for example, the importance of black and Hispanic ethnic groups has justified the implementation of specific strategies, expressed at the level of each element of the marketing mix. Thus, complete product ranges (shampoo, beauty products, food products, and so on) have been developed, and there are specialised advertising agencies and media for the promotion of these products.[77] Conversely, the universal nature of certain societal phenomena – such as conflict between generations or sex role orientation – means that cultural sub-groups can adopt similar modes of response, even if they are living in different national contexts.[78] Teenagers thus show numerous similar characteristics across the world. The markets for motor bikes, pop CDs and trainers, along with grooming products, take a homogeneous form with multiple national sub-segments.[79]

The two preceding remarks, discussing segmentation and potential homogeneity, show how the assimilation of the concept of culture into that of country is dangerous. The decision to ignore certain national markets sometimes rests on a presumed incompatibility between the product or service that is being sold and the typical cultural profile of the country's consumer.[80] However, because in the past a product has been judged incompatible with a given society does not mean that it cannot, ultimately, be sold successfully. Thus in France, after a very slow start, the market for breakfast cereals has taken off: 2300 tonnes in 1978 but fifteen times that figure twenty years later. In such cases, management can play an active role as an 'agent' stimulating the process of cultural change. In the past, this development has often occurred in the context of the international product life-cycle.[81] Product or strategy ideas – such as PCs or the Internet – developed in the high-income, technologically intensive culture of the USA find outlets in other countries as high-income segments of their populations, with similar desires for easy access to information, grow in sufficient numbers to provide an adequate market base.

Overall, it is both the relative importance of intra-country cultural differences (as opposed to inter-country differences) and the manager's own willingness to innovate and adapt which determine strategic choices. Three main approaches are possible.[82] The first consists of using a uniform, standardised strategy; in this case, the target market and the product positioning are the same all over the world and this is called 'global marketing'. According to Levitt, one of the principal defenders of this approach:

> The differences due to culture, tastes, or national norms are vestiges of the past. The current power of technology is driving the world into a convergent community. Thus only the truly global companies are assured long term success by concentrating on what everyone needs rather than the details about what they think they want.[83]

Coca-Cola, Kodak, Honda, Bic and Gillette are prime practitioners of global marketing, thus benefiting from substantial economies of scale in production as well as marketing. Coca-Cola has calculated that it saves $8 million every year by using the same advertising themes everywhere.[84] Similarly, Gillette managers explain that 'whether they live in London, Caracas, or New York, lawyers or accountants tend to have the same attitudes towards shaving'.[85] A global marketing strategy also suits the small company which does not have the means to adapt its products to each market; such companies can target only a well-defined segment in each country. Firms in the luxury sector follow this approach: Hermès and Patek Philippe sell the same products across the world. Another argument in favour of globalisation is competition: a 'sprinkler approach' takes the speed of the competition as against a 'waterfall approach', which leaves it the time to adapt country by country. To a large extent, global marketing is based on an **etic** perspective, which emphasises similarities across cultures. An etic approach is analytical and assumes an external and objective search for general cultural categories.[86]

At the other extreme, a second approach consists of developing a strategy specifically adapted to the local environment and cultural system. 'The Nescafé that one buys in Switzerland does not have the same taste as that drunk in France, just the other side of the border', Nestlé explains. Unilever and Kraft have adopted the same local approach. It seems particularly appropriate because in the area of food and drink, consumers develop expectations which are very different between one country and another, and eating and drinking habits are very difficult to change because of their central position in the cultural system. Giving up all the advantages of standardisation, this strategy considers each cultural sub-group as a specific market. To a large extent, such an approach is based on an **emic** perspective, which assumes each culture is unique and should be analysed from an insider's viewpoint, an approach also known as **ethnoconsumerism**.[87]

Finally, a third strategy is an intermediate one; it consists of offering essentially the same product or service but modifying certain aspects of the marketing policy in response to local considerations. Such a strategy is particularly suited to the situation where the same product satisfies a different need in each market, or even links into the cultural system of each country in a different way. Even McDonald's, often considered to be a champion of global marketing, has to adapt its formula and points of sale. While in the USA McDonald's customers essentially consist of families, in Europe and in Japan they are mostly teenagers, and the concept as well as the location of the restaurant has to take this into account. Also, the drinks are served according to local customs: guarana in Brazil, exotic drinks in Thailand and beer in France.[88] Sometimes, the way in which a product is promoted enables it to be adapted to a particular market. Thus, an English company successfully launched a mint-flavoured chocolate, apparently alien to French food habits, by positioning it as an exclusive, sophisticated product to be eaten after dinner, as in the best British social circles – thus capitalising upon the high value attached by the French to British upper-class traditions.[89] Such a strategy may, therefore, be appropriate if a product which appears to contravene relevant cultural habits can be connected with other favourable elements within the value system.

Marketing mix decisions

Cultural factors are important not only for strategic purposes but also because of their impact on the implementation of the various elements of a company's marketing mix – namely its product, price, distribution and communication policy.

The product

In certain categories such as food, the products commonly consumed are far from being the same everywhere. In a Spanish supermarket, for example, the shelves dedicated to olive oil are far more important than in the UK. This product occupies second place after milk in terms of overall consumption in Spain. Other products, such as 'ensaimadas' (pastries made from milk bread), are completely unknown in the UK. Beyond the product itself, its positioning, its appearance and the way it is packaged are largely influenced by culture.

A product is not only a physical entity dedicated to a given function, it is also an object which is intertwined with the fabric and customs of life, and to which are attached many symbolic associations. Let us consider a bicycle. Sold as a means of transport accessible to almost everyone in many developing countries, it is the sporting and environmentally friendly aspects which are promoted in Western countries. Even though the product is basically the same, its meaning for consumers demands completely different market positioning in the two situations. Similarly, the BMW car make is not positioned in the same way across Europe: in Germany and Austria prestige is placed to the fore, in Italy it is the road holding, and in Switzerland the impression of discretion conveyed by the make is emphasised.[90]

Preferences in terms of aesthetics and style are also predominantly culturally determined. Sommers and Kernan have shown that for a given standard of living, Canadian consumers prefer simpler, less eye-catching products than the nearby Americans.[91]

The choice of packaging (material, shape, colour) cannot ignore symbolic meanings prevalent in the cultural environment. A manufacturer of frozen products exporting to Mexico was surprised to see a level of sales which could not be attributed to either the product or the price. It was discovered that, completely by accident, the packaging was the attraction: it was green, white and red – the colours of the national flag.[92]

The price

Even though pricing decisions are largely made on the basis of economic considerations such as production or distribution costs, or in response to competitors' strategies, cultural factors also play a role in their definition. Cultural factors influence in particular the **political and legal framework** within which pricing decisions are made, as well as the **perceptions and attitudes** of both consumers and intermediaries.

The value system of a culture supplies the foundation of legislation relating to price, especially in relation to perceptions of trade activities. In certain countries, price competition is considered to be a fundamentally healthy aspect of the economic environment, whereas in others it is seen as threatening to the social order. Thus, the practice of price fixing, predominant in planned economies, is perceived in the United States as a grave offence threatening the effective functioning of a free trade economy.

Cultural norms relating to money and material possessions also influence consumers' attitudes towards price and credit terms, and determine the psychological context surrounding the purchase. For example, the strength with which the notion of quality is linked to that of price varies from one culture to another,[93] as does price as a purchasing criterion. Compared with non-Hispanics, Mexican-Americans visit nearby shops more often, where the prices are more familiar to them.[94] Additionally, the reluctance of certain consumers to use credit, often of a religious or moral origin, can reduce its effectiveness as a promotional weapon for the sale of durable goods such as household appliances.[95]

The possibility of using price as a marketing tool is also closely linked to the customs and habits prevailing in a given culture. In India, distributors are somewhat reluctant to enter into price wars, which are felt to be incompatible with retaining their dignity.[96] In such a context, it is difficult for a company to adopt a price-cutting strategy. Conversely, while in the West the price indicated on a product is in general what it sells for, it acts only as a basis for negotiation in a number of oriental cultures.[97] The price at which the transaction is finally made can differ considerably from the initial figure, according to the relative skill and power position of the parties involved.

Distribution

The cultural system of a society exerts an influence as much over the nature of **distribution outlets** as over **consumer reactions to point-of-sale service**. It is essential to understand such influences due to the extent that they define the context in which distribution decisions are made and affect strategic managerial choices (such as the selection of distribution channels or the partition of functions between the different channels) as well as tactical decisions (services offered at point of sale, sales approach).

Key characteristics of a distribution system such as the number, the diversity, the cost and the promotional value of the various channels are, in any given culture, related to the values and the social organisation which predominate. In Japan, for example, the importance attached to individual enterprise explains the number and complexity of Japanese distribution networks.[98] Also, several studies have shown the impact of social institutions such as the family unit on the structure of distribution systems.[99] In Mediterranean countries, for example, the predominance of traditional retailing structures is often attributed to the exclusive recruitment of employees from within the owner's family.

The characteristics of the distribution system define the options managers have regarding the building of sales networks and the division of production, inventory, transport and credit functions between the various intermediaries. The habits and customs of a culture often have a direct influence in this area. In Nigeria, for example, the Tupperware company had to modify its sales approach of home meetings because such an approach was considered incompatible with the cultural habits of the country.[100] Also, Hoover discovered that the door-to-door sales technique it used to operate was impractical in countries where custom forbids a wife to open the door to strangers when her husband is not there. Decisions concerning which services to offer at the point of sale, and how to offer them, are also strongly influenced by the cultural context. In Belgium, Inno superstores had to stop selling clothes on a self-service basis as many local consumers place a great deal of importance on the help and advice of a salesperson. The layout and decoration also have to be adapted to the sociocultural environment. Jewellers in London's Regent's Street cannot lay out their window displays in the same manner as the clock sellers in the area.

Finally, sales techniques have to be adjusted to people's expectations. The aggressive, hard sell approach common in the United States is judged inappropriate in India and Japan, where it is better not to move too quickly or to impose oneself too strongly.[101] Such factors affect the salesperson's approach, and also the recruitment, training, motivation and reward systems for the salesforce.

Communication

Given that culture is at the heart of social interaction, it is not surprising that its impact on communication processes is easily identifiable. On one hand it affects the nature of the **targets** selected, and on the other the **messages** and **media** used.

The distribution of social roles exerts a direct influence over the choice of communication targets. The increasing role children play in purchasing decisions is observed in a number of countries; in response, Kellogg's directly targets them by showing cornflakes advertisements during peak viewing times for children (for example, during Disney programmes). Many experts now believe that, as the world's borders shrink, more and more pan-European targets will be identified; currently, the affluent and the young are already being exposed to pan-European marketing.[102]

The choice of theme, most notably the use of humour or fear, is also dictated by the importance of sticking to prevailing values and using culturally specific modes of expression. For example, Mexican consumers, in comparison with their neighbours, perceive much less risk in the purchase of most products due to a cultural tradition which tends to be fatalistic.[103] It therefore follows that an advertising campaign stressing the reliability attached to a prestigious brand will be less effective there than elsewhere. In Europe, on the other hand, Sony-CBS could use the same campaign showing two young people surfing on the crest of a wave in fifteen countries, exploiting the fact that young people use similar modes of expression.[104] In contrast, a Camay campaign which showed a man entering the bathroom while his wife was bathing was badly received in Japan. Seen as amusing in France, it was felt to be indecent by the Japanese.

The development of the overall message – including the copy platform, the structure, the relationship between text and illustration, and the layout – clearly depends upon the communication system and language of the target audience. An advertisement for a brandy targeted at the Bantu market showed a couple at a table with a bottle which, due to its positioning, appeared to many viewers to be placed on the head of the lady. The woman was thus seen in her traditional role of servant, not at all compatible with the modern image of the advert.[105] As a matter of fact, there exist few universal rules governing the production of advertising. For every example of a successful global campaign (Coca-Cola, Marlboro, De Beers), there are numerous ones which are adapted to particular situations. For example, Apple Computers has developed specific messages for each country.[106] Even companies marketing luxury goods, which are aimed predominantly at a global market, sometimes have to fine-tune their message. The image of a dark woman dressed in black used for the perfume Shalimar (Guerlain) in Europe could not be transferred to the United States as French perfumes had acquired a light image in comparison with those made in the USA; a delicate blonde woman, dressed in white, was used instead.

The amount of advertising spending, and its allocation between various media, is also subject to the influence of consumer lifestyles and habits. In Africa, radio is a powerful medium, particularly for publicity of an informative nature.[107] Nowadays, TV programmes shown on satellite channels (such as Sky, MTV and Eurosport in Europe) have altered the international advertising landscape, even though they still represent only 3 per cent of European TV audiences.[108]

Finally, decisions relating to other promotional means are also tightly linked to hypotheses made relating to the habits and customs of the targeted audiences. In Japan, the success of savings stamps and promotional contests has been noted, this kind of commercial tactic being consistent with the interest of many Japanese consumers in games. Here again, an in-depth analysis of the characteristic values, norms and behaviours of a culture is an essential initial step when thinking about which sales promotion tactics are most suitable.

Conclusion: almost virgin territory

As we have seen in the different sections of this chapter, the current body of knowledge about culture already enables many valuable conclusions to be drawn. We must not, however, assume that this represents the full contribution that a concept as rich and diversified as culture could potentially make. The studies currently available have only scratched the surface of a largely unexplored area. First, the impact of culture on purchasing and consumption remains relatively unknown compared with other cultural phenomena such as kinship or systems of religious belief. Second, most company research on the subject has, up to this point, taken the form of international comparisons of behaviour or attitudes, while it is accepted that the concept of culture cannot be reduced to that of a country. We should recognise that equating cultures with countries represents a rather limited perspective. Differences within countries – such as regional (Scottish vs English; Flanders vs Wallonia), ethnic (black vs white in the USA or France), or religious ones – can be larger than those between countries.

A research effort is therefore necessary. Regarding the work carried out on values, most international research has thus far taken the form of polls. In taking account of the rich symbolic significance attached to cultural issues, the survey is not the only or even the best approach. Rather than asking questions, it would perhaps be better, as recommended by anthropologists,[109] to 'live' for some time among consumers in order better to understand them. This 'participant observer' method is beginning to be used to analyse commercial phenomena.[110] For example, an in-depth analysis, led over four days by a team of three researchers, on the workings of a flea market provided some interesting results. Beyond the economic dimension (exchange of new and used goods), it was found that the flea market represents an adult form of treasure hunting, a surviving anachronism of ancient markets which brings the same feelings of excitement and adventure, and the joy – potential or actual – of discovering a rare pearl.[111]

Future studies should facilitate the structuring and cumulative progression of knowledge, given a better articulation of the theoretical bases and methodological implications. Furthermore, such research needs to be carried out, certainly in Europe, on another basis than one limited solely by national boundaries. Future studies could, for example, go about identifying the sub-cultures existing within one country, or focus on the similarities present between sub-cultures common to different countries. Even if this research requires significant effort, the potential that it holds merits it being undertaken. It represents the basis of the strategic and tactical interest which managers must have in order to take account of cultural phenomena.

Notes

[1] See T. Clark, 'International Marketing and National Character: A Review and Proposal for an Integrative Theory', *Journal of Marketing*, October 1990, pp. 66–79.

[2] See V. Latham, 'Do Euroconsumers Exist?' *Marketing*, 1993, June 24, p. 3; see also P. S. H. Leeflang and W. F. van Raaij, 'The Changing Consumer in the European Union: A Meta-analyis', *International Journal of Research in Marketing*, 1995, pp. 373–87.

[3] See, for example, J. Engel, R. Blackwell and P. Miniard, *Consumer Behavior*, 7th edition (Harcourt, Brace and World, 1993) and M. Solomon, *Consumer Behavior: Buying, Having, Being*, 3rd edition (Prentice Hall, 1997). For European texts, see M. Evans *et al.*, *Applied Consumer Behaviour* (Addison-Wesley, 1996), and R. East, *Consumer Behaviour: Advances and Applications in Marketing* (Prentice Hall, 1997). See also the various models of buying behaviour which have been presented in the literature and are discussed in the concluding chapter of this book: J. Howard and J. Sheth, *The Theory of Buyer Behavior* (Wiley, 1969) and F. Nicosia, *Consumer Decision Processes* (Prentice Hall, 1966).

[4] C. Schaninger *et al.*, 'French–British Canadian Subcultural Consumption Differences', *Journal of Marketing*, Spring 1985, pp. 82–92.

[5] R. Benedict, *Patterns of Culture* (Houghton Mifflin, 1934); A. L. Kroeber, *Anthropology* (Harcourt, Brace and World, 1948); F. L. K. Hsu, *Psychological Anthropology*, (Dorsey Press,

1961); C. Levi-Strauss, *Anthropologie Culturelle* (PUF, 1961); L. Schneider and C. Boujean, *The Idea of Culture in the Social Sciences* (Cambridge University Press, 1973).

6 See G. McCracken, *Culture and Consumption: New Approaches to the Symbolic Character of Consumer Goods and Activities* (Indiana University Press, 1988) and J. F. Sherry (ed.), *Contemporary Marketing and Consumer Behavior: An Anthropological Sourcebook* (Sage Publications, 1995).

7 This chapter borrows its structure from S. Douglas and B. Dubois, 'Culture and Consumer Behavior: Time for a Fresh Look?' 1977, Marketing Science Institute Report No. 77–106.

8 A. L. Kroeber and C. Kluckhohn, 'Culture: A Critical Review of Concepts and Definitions', *Anthropological Papers*, Peabody Museum No. 4 (1952).

9 E. Tylor, *Primitive Culture* (Murray, 1913).

10 See R. A. Peterson, *The Production of Culture* (Sage Contemporary Social Science Issues, 1976).

11 R. Linton, *The Cultural Determinants of Personality* (Dunod, 1963).

12 H. G. Barnett, *Innovation: The Basis of Cultural Change* (McGraw-Hill, 1953).

13 For other examples of (and concern for) the 'Americanisation' of the world, see G. Ger and R. Belk, 'I'd Like to Buy the World a Coke: Consumptionscapes of the Less Affluent World', *Journal of Consumer Policy*, 1996, pp. 271–304.

14 G. McCracken, 'Culture and Consumption: A Theoretical Account on the Structure and Movement of the Cultural Meaning of Consumer Goods', *Journal of Consumer Research*, June 1986, pp. 71–84.

15 M. Rokeach, *The Nature of Human Values* (Free Press, 1973). F. Kluckhohn and F. Strodtbeck, *Variations in Value Orientations* (Row Peterson, 1961). Also see L. Kahle, *Social Values and Social Change* (Praeger, 1983). For a comparison, see S. Beatty *et al.*, 'Alternative Measurement Approaches to Consumer Values: the List of Values and the Rokeach Value Survey', *Psychology and Marketing*, 1985, Vol. 3, pp. 181–200.

16 J. Campbell, *Myths, Dreams and Religion* (Dutton, 1970).

17 C. Lévi-Strauss, 'The Principle of Reciprocity', in L. A. Coser and B. Rosenberg (eds), *Sociological Theory* (Macmillan, 1965).

18 W. Kamakura and T. Novak, 'Value-System Segmentation: Exploring the Meaning of LOV', *Journal of Consumer Research*, December 1992, pp. 119–32.

19 F. Kluckhohn and F. Strodtbeck, *op. cit.*; also see D. Yankelovitch, 'What Lifestyle Means to Marketers', *Marketing Communications*, 1971, 6, pp. 38–45; and G. Hofstede, *Culture's Consequences: International Differences in Work Related Values* (Sage, 1980)

20 M. Rokeach, *op. cit.* Several researchers have suggested reducing Rokeach's list. See J. Veroff, E. Dowman and A. Kulka, *The Inner American* (Basic Books, 1981). For a different classification, see S. Schwartz and W. Bilsky, 'Toward a Universal Psychological Structure of Human Values', *Journal of Personality and Social Psychology*, 1987, pp. 550–62 and 'Toward a Theory of the Universal Content and Structure of Values: Extensions and Cross-Cultural Replications', *Journal of Personality and Social Psychology*, 1990, pp. 878–91.

21 L. Kahle, *Social Values and Social Change: Adaptation to Life in America* (Praeger, 1983).

22 G. Hofstede, *Culture's Consequences* (Sage, 1990).

23 See L. M. Milner, D. Fodness and M. L. W. Speece, 'Hofstede's Research on Cross-Cultural Work-Related Values: Implications for Consumer Behaviour', *European Advances in Consumer Research*, 1993, pp. 70–6.

24 'Mapping the Forces of Change', *RISC Observer*, April 1993.

25 B. Dubois and P. Duquesne, 'The Market for Luxury Goods: Income vs Culture', *European Journal of Marketing*, 1993, 1, pp. 35–44.

26 Alain de Vulpian, 'Les Courants Socio-Culturels en France', summary of *Journées de l'IREP*, 27 March 1974, pp. 117–62.

27 C. Matricon, M. Burke and B. Cathelat, 'L'importance de l'environnement socio-culturel', *IREP*, May 1974, pp. 40–94.

[28] F. Popcorn, *The Popcorn Report* (Harper Business, 1992).

[29] W. Henry, 'Cultural Values Do Correlate with Consumer Behaviour', *Journal of Marketing Research*, May 1976, pp. 116–17.

[30] Y. Evrard and E. Tissier Desbordes, 'Les Systèmes de Valeur et les Lectures dans la Famille', *Actes du séminaire international de Recherche en Marketing d'Aix-en-Provence*, May 1985. For other examples, see P. Valette-Florence and A. Jolibert, 'Un Essai Empirique de Clarification des Approches de Style de Vie', *Actes du colloque de l'Association Française de Marketing*, 1985, pp. 133–57.

[31] Personal communication with the author.

[32] M. Herskovitz, *Economic Anthropology* (Knopf, 1952).

[33] M Gluckman, *The Rites of Passage: Essays on the Ritual of Social Relations* (Manchester University Press, 1962). For an analysis of buying behaviour for toiletry products, see D. Rook, 'The Ritual Dimension of Consumer Behaviour', *Journal of Consumer Research*, December 1985, pp. 251–64.

[34] M. Lynn, G. Zinkhan and J. Harris, 'Consumer Tipping: A Cross-country Study', *Journal of Consumer Research*, December 1993, pp. 478–85.

[35] D. Rook, 'The Ritual Dimension of Consumer Behavior', *Journal of Consumer Research*, December 1985, pp. 251–64; and M. A. Stansfield Tetreault and R. E. Kleine III, 'Ritual, Ritualized Behavior, and Habit: Refinements and Extensions of the Consumption Ritual Construct', *Advances in Consumer Research*, 1990, pp. 31–8.

[36] J. Sherry, 'Gift Giving in Anthropological Perspective', *Journal of Consumer Research*, September 1983, pp. 157–68.

[37] On funeral rituals, see L. D. Compeau and C. Nicholson, 'Funerals: Emotional Rituals or Ritualistic Emotions', *Advances in Consumer Research*, 1994, p. 692.

[38] R. W. Belk, 'Halloween: An Evolving American Consumption Ritual', *Advances in Consumer Research*, 1990, pp. 508–17; and M. Wallendorf and E. Arnould, 'We Gather Together: The Consumption Rituals of Thanksgiving Day', *Journal of Consumer Research*, June 1991, pp. 13–31.

[39] S. Levy, 'Symbols for Sale', *Harvard Business Review*, 1959, Vol. 37, pp. 117–124 and 'Interpreting Consumer Mythology: A Structural Approach to Consumer Behavior', *Journal of Marketing*, Summer 1981, pp. 49–61.

[40] A. Jolibert and C. Fernandez-Moreno, 'A Comparison of French and Mexican Gift Giving Practices', *Advances in Consumer Research*, Vol. X, 1983, pp. 191–6.

[41] D. Hynes (ed.), *Language in Culture and Society* (Harper & Row, 1964).

[42] H. Shadara, 'Honorific Expressions of Personal Attitudes in Spoken Japanese' (Center for Japanese Studies – University of Michigan Press, 1962).

[43] D. Ricks, *Big Business Blunders: Mistakes in Multinational Marketing* (Irwin, 1983).

[44] W. Labano, 'The Cultural Basis of Emotions and Gestures', *Journal of Personality*, 16, pp. 49–68.

[45] M. J. Eysenck, 'National Differences in Sense of Humour', *Character and Personality*, 1944, 13, pp. 37–44.

[46] E. T. Hall, *The Silent Language of Business* (New York, 1971).

[47] H. Tajfel, 'Social and Cultural Factors in Perception', in G. Lindsey and E. Aronson (eds), *Handbook of Social Psychology* (Addison-Wesley, 1969); H. Triandis, 'Cultural Influence on Cognitive Processes', in I. Berkowitz (ed.), *Advances in Experimental Psychology*, Vol. 1 (Academic Press, 1964).

[48] J. D. McCornell, 'The Economics of Behavioral Factors in the Multinational Corporation', in F. C. Allvine (ed.), *Combined Proceedings of the American Marketing Association*, 1971, p. 260.

[49] R. W. Belk, M. Wallendorf and J. Sherry, 'The Sacred and the Profane in Consumer Behavior: Theodicy on the Odyssey', *Journal of Consumer Research*, 1989, pp. 1–38.

[50] G. McCracken, 'Homeyness: "A Cultural Account of One Constellation of Goods and

Meanings"', in E. C. Hirschman (ed.), *Interpretive Consumer Research* (Association for Consumer Research, 1989), pp. 168–84.

51 See T. Clark, 'International Marketing and National Character: A Review and Proposal for an Integrative Theory', *Journal of Marketing*, October 1990, pp. 66–79. Also see V. Barnow, 'Studies in National Character', in *Culture and Personality* (Dorsey Press, 1973); W. Kassarjian, 'Systematic Approaches to the Study of Interdependence of Culture and Personality', in J. B. Cohen (ed.), *Behavioral Science Foundations of Consumer Behaviour* (Free Press, 1969); A. Inkeles and D. I. Levinson, 'National Character: The Study of Modal Personality and the Sociocultural System', in G. Lindzey and E. Aronson (eds), *op. cit.*

52 A. Inkeles, E. Haufmann and H. Reier, 'Modal Personality and Adjustment to the Soviet Socio-Political System', *Human Relations*, Vol. II (1958), pp. 3–22.

53 R. Lynn, *National Differences in Anxiety and Extroversion: Progress in Experimental Research* (Wiley, 1982).

54 E. Hirschmann, 'American Jewish Ethnicity: Its Relationship to Some Selected Aspects of Consumer Behaviour', *Journal of Marketing*, Summer 1981, Vol. 6, pp. 5–20.

55 P. Valette-Florence *et al.*, 'Une Comparaison Franco-Allemande de l'Adhesion aux Valeurs Personnelles', *Recherche et Applications en Marketing*, 1991, Vol. 6, pp. 5–20.

56 H. Kassarjian, 'Social Character and Differential Preference for Communications', *Journal of Marketing Research*, November 1971, pp. 409–18.

57 M. Han C., 'Country Image Halo or Summary Construct?' *Journal of Marketing Research*, May 1990, pp. 222–7.

58 R. Schooler, 'Bias Phenomena Attendant to the Marketing of Foreign Goods in the US', *Journal of International Business Studies*, 1971, pp. 71–80; W. T. Anderson and W. H. Cunningham, 'Gauging Foreign Product Promotion', *Journal of Advertising Research*, February 1972, pp. 29–34. .

59 W. K. Li and K. Monroe, 'The Role of Country of Origin Information on Buyers' Product Evaluationss', *AMA Proceedings* (American Marketing Association, 1982), pp. 247–80.

60 W. J. Bilkey and E. Nes, 'Country-of-origin Effects on Products Evaluation', *Journal of International Business Studies*, 1982, 13, pp. 89–99; D. Maheswaran, 'Country of Origin as a Stereotype: Effects of Consumer Expertise and Attribute Strength on Product Evaluations', *Journal of Consumer Research*, September 1994, pp. 354–65.

61 T. Sarbin and V. Allen, 'Role Theory', in G. Lindzey and E. Aronson (eds), *op. cit.*

62 M. Haire, 'Projective Techniques in Marketing Research', *Journal of Marketing*, 1950, pp. 649–52.

63 R. Buzzell, 'Can You Standardize Multinational Marketing?' *Harvard Business Review*, November–December 1968, pp. 102–13.

64 D. Goslin, *Handbook of Socialization Theory and Research* (Rand McNally, 1969); and S. Ward, 'Consumer Socialization', *Journal of Consumer Research*, September 1974, pp. 1–14.

65 B. C. Miller, 'Intergenerational Patterns of Consumer Behaviour', in M. J. Schlinger (ed.), *Advances in Consumer Research*, Vol. 2 (ACR, 1975); J. Arndt, 'A Research Note on Intergenerational Overlap of Selected Consumer Variables', *Markeds Kommunikasjon*, Vol. 3 (1971); S. Ward and D. Wackman, 'Effects of Television Advertising on Consumer Socialization' (Marketing Science Institute, 1973).

66 E. Tissier-Desbordes, 'Interaction Familiale et Comportement d'Achat des Mères et des Filles', *Actes du 10e séminaire International de Recherche d'Aix,* 1983.

67 M. Wallendorf and M. Reilly, 'Ethnic Migration, Assimilation, and Consumption', *Journal of Consumer Research*, December 1983, pp. 292–303; for other results, see R. Deshpandé *et al.*, 'The Intensity of Ethnic Affiliation: A Study of the Sociology of Hispanic Consumption', *Journal of Consumer Research*, September 1986, pp. 214–19; M. Laroche *et al.*, 'Acculturation of Italians towards French and English Cultures and Its Impact on Lifestyles'; and K. Gronhaug *et al.*, 'Barriers and Incentives in Consumer Acculturation', *European Advances in Consumer Research*, Vol. 1 (ACR, 1993), pp. 269–86.

[68] L. Peñaloza, 'Atravesando Fronteras/Border Crossings: A Critical Ethnographic Exploration of the Consumer Acculturation of Mexican Immigrants', *Journal of Consumer Research*, June 1994, pp. 32–53.

[69] C. Schaninger, L. Bourgeois and W. C. Russ, 'French–English Canadian Subcultural Consumption Differences', *Journal of Marketing*, 1985, pp. 82–7.

[70] E. Rogers, *Diffusion of Innovations* (Free Press, 1983). For an international comparison, see R. T. Green and E. Langeard, 'A Cross-national Comparison of Consumer Habits and Innovator Characteristics', *Journal of Marketing*, July 1975, pp. 34–41.

[71] T. Robertson, *Innovative Behavior and Communication* (Dryden Press, 1971).

[72] E. von Hippel, 'Learning from Lead Users', in R. D. Buzzell (ed.), *Marketing in an Electronic Age* (Harvard Business School Press, 1985) pp. 308–17.

[73] E. Hagen, *On the Theory of Social Change* (Dorsey Press, 1962).

[74] See, for example, R. Anderson and J. Engledow, 'A Factor Analytic Comparison of US and German Information Seekers', *Journal of Consumer Research*, March 1977, pp. 185–96.

[75] M. Sommers and J. Kerman, 'Why Products Flourish Here, Fizzle There', *Columbia Journal of World Business*, Vol. 2 (March–April 1967), pp. 89–97; D. E. Robinson, 'US Life Style Invades Europe', *Harvard Business Review*, September–October 1968.

[76] B. Dubois, 'A Cultural Approach to the Study of Diffusion and Adoption of Innovations', in M. Venkatesan (ed.), *Proceedings of the Third Annual Conference of the Association for Consumer Research*, November 1972.

[77] R. Bauer and S. M. Cunningham, *Studies in the Negro Market* (MSI, 1970); D. Sexton, 'Black Buyer Behavior', *Journal of Marketing*, October 1972, pp. 36–9, D. Yankelovitch, *Spanish USA* (Skilly and White, 1981); and J. Sondheim *et al.*, 'Hispanic Marketing: The Invisible Giant', *Advertising Age*, April 1979, pp. 5–20.

[78] E. Zah, 'The European Marketplace: Social Change and the Consumer's Choice', in J. Hess and P. Cateora (eds), *International Marketing* (Irwin, 1973); for some applications in the luxury sector, see B. Dubois and G. Laurent, 'Is There a Euroconsumer for Luxury Goods', *European Advances in Consumer Research*, Vol. 1, 1993, pp. 58–69 and B. Dubois and P. Duquesne, 'The Market for Luxury Goods – Income versus Culture', *European Journal of Marketing*, 1993, No. 1, pp. 35–44.

[79] J. C. Usunier, *Intercultural Marketing*, 2nd edition (Prentice Hall, 1995).

[80] Y. Wind and S. Douglas, 'Segmenting International Markets', *European Journal of Marketing*, Spring 1972, 1.

[81] L. T. Wells (ed.), *The Product Life-Cycle and International* Trade (Harvard Business School, 1972).

[82] R. D. Buzzell, *op. cit.*, pp. 102–3; and W. Keegan, 'Multinational Product Planning: Strategic Alternatives', *Journal of Marketing*, January 1969, pp. 38–62.

[83] T. Levitt, 'Only One Market: The Universe', *Harvard Business Review*, January 1983, pp. 6–17. For a response, see J. J. Boddewyn, 'Standardization in International Marketing: Is Ted Levitt in Fact Right?' *Business Horizons*, November–December 1986, pp. 69–75.

[84] 'The Ad Biz Glooms onto Global', *Fortune*, November 1984, pp. 61–4.

[85] 'The Razor Edge', *Brandweek*, 24 April 1995.

[86] See G. McCracken, 'Account of the Structure and Movement of the Cultural Meaning of Consumer Goods', *Journal of Consumer Research*, June 1986, pp. 71–84; and K. Applbaum and I. Jordt, 'Notes Toward an Application of McCracken's "Cultural Categories" for Cross-Cultural Research', *Journal of Consumer Research*, December 1996, pp. 204–18.

[87] A. Venkatesh, 'Ethnoconsumerism: A Proposal for a New Paradigm to Study Cultural and Cross Cultural Consumer Behavior', in J. A. Costa and G. Bamossy (eds), *Marketing in a Multicultural World: Ethnicity, Nationalism, and Cultural Identity* (Sage, 1995), pp. 26–67.

[88] 'Mc World? McDonald's Can Make a Big Mac Anywhere, but Duplicating its Culture Abroad Won't Be Easy', *Business Week*, 13 October 1986, pp. 60–6.

[89] P. M. Kraushar, 'The Cost Effectiveness of Market Research with Particular Application to the

Search for New Product Ideas in Fast Moving Consumer Goods', *ESOMAR Congress Proceedings*, 1974.

[90] M. Silverstein, *The European Challenge in Consumer Goods* (Boston Consulting Group, May 1993).

[91] M. Sommers and J. Kernan, *op. cit.*

[92] G. Miracle, 'International Advertising Principles and Strategies', *MSU Business Topics*, Autumn 1968, pp. 36–7.

[93] R. Buzzell, *op cit.*

[94] J. Slagert *et al.*, 'Characteristics of Mexican American Consumers', *Journal of Consumer Research*, June 1985, pp. 104–9.

[95] H. Boyd and J. Percy, 'Marketing to the British Consumer', *Business Horizons*, Spring 1963.

[96] D. Carson, *International Marketing* (Wiley, 1967).

[97] R. Bartels (ed.), *Comparative Marketing: Wholesaling in Fifteen Countries* (Irwin 1963), p. 145.

[98] G. Figas and L. P. David, 'Wholesaling in Japan' in R. Bartels, *op. cit.*

[99] R. Bartels, *op. cit.*

[100] J. Goldstucker, 'The Influence of Culture on Channels of Distribution', in R. L. King (ed.), *Marketing and the New Science of Planning* (AMA, 1968).

[101] D. Carson, *op. cit.*

[102] K. Cote, 'The New Shape of Europe', *Advertising Age*, 9 November 1988, p. 98.

[103] R. Hoover et al., 'A Cross National Study of Perceived Risk', *Journal of Marketing*, July 1978, pp. 102–8.

[104] J. C. Usunier, *op. cit.*

[105] S. Douglas and B. Dubois, 'Looking at the Cultural Environment for International Marketing Opportunities', in B. Enis and K. Cox (eds), *Marketing Classics: A Selection of Influential Articles*, 7th edition (Allyn and Bacon, 1991), pp. 542–62.

[106] Y. Wind and S. Douglas, 'Le Mythe de la Globalisation', *Recherche et Applications en Marketing*, October 1986, pp. 5–26.

[107] J. Théault, 'Démarche Marketing dans les PVD', *Moci*, November 1984, p. 23.

[108] See J. C. Usunier, *op. cit.*

[109] See G. McCracken, 'Culture and Consumer Behaviour: An Anthropological Perspective', *Journal of the Market Research Society*, Vol. 32(1), pp. 3–10.

[110] J. Sherry Jr, 'Anthropology of Marketing and Consumption: Retrospect and Prospect', in J. Sherry Jr (ed.), *Contemporary Marketing and Consumer Behavior: An Anthropological Sourcebook* (Sage, 1995), pp. 435–45.

[111] R. Belk *et al.*, 'A Naturalistic Enquiry into Buyer and Seller Behaviour at a Swap Market', *Journal of Consumer Research*, March 1988, pp. 449–70.

Part 2

Purchase and consumption dynamics

In the first part of this book we considered a number of perspectives which help us to understand a purchasing decision. However, a purchase is rarely based on a single decision taken at a specific time and in a particular place. In buying a car, the Martins had to solve various problems and were faced with many choices: make of vehicle, model, sales outlet, payment terms, etc. Also, many people played a part in the decisions: Mr Martin, his wife, their son, their friends, colleagues, the mechanic, the salesperson, and so on. To take into consideration all these aspects of a purchase, we now need to abandon the snapshot view adopted up to this point and open up a longer-term, cinematic perspective describing the various stages of a purchase decision. This is the objective of the second part of this book. Not all purchases resemble each other. We can classify purchase situations on the basis of two criteria: the level of consumers' involvement in the corresponding product category, and their capacity to perceive differences between the various products and brands available on the market. It is self-evident that consumers are much more involved in certain products (for example dresses, perfumes) than others (batteries, toilet paper), depending upon the extent to which the purchase decision is central to their self-concept.

When a consumer is involved and finds strong differences between brand or product alternatives, one can talk about an **extended problem-solving** context as the purchase act comprises a series of steps and moments spread over time. We thus have to analyse not a decision but a **process**. This is the theme of Chapter 8.

It is also usually true that several people will take part in a complex purchase. We can thus no longer speak of a consumer as if they were a single unique individual; rather the consumer is a **decision-making unit**. Chapter 9 covers this topic.

Finally, when the level of involvement is low and brands are not strongly differentiated, the purchase has every chance of becoming a habit, dominated by **routine decision-making** procedures. The key factors now become the contextual elements characterising the purchase and consumption **situation**. This is the subject of Chapter 10.

8

The purchasing process

Learning objectives

After reading this chapter, you will understand how:

1 the various steps of the consumer decision-making process have been conceptualised and structured;

2 consumers recognise the emergence of a problem;

3 they retrieve and process internal as well as external information;

4 they formulate decisions;

5 they experience post-purchase feelings such as satisfaction or dissatisfaction.

Key words

purchasing process	information processing	store loyalty
arousal	psychology of	brand loyalty
need recognition	simplification	impulse buying
standard of comparison	psychology of	post-purchase
diffusion	complication	phenomena
information search	economics of	satisfaction
internal search	information	dissatisfaction
external search	comparative advertising	reflex
perceived risk	categorisation	
protocols	prototype	
information display	heuristics	
boards	atmosphere	

The idea of a **purchasing process** refers to a sequence of successive stages until the final decision. The implicit assumption is that a purchase decision always corresponds to a response to a consumer problem.[1] There exist many conceptualisations of this process, but a number of studies and observations of complex purchases have suggested the existence of a four-step structure:

1 the arousal phase, which triggers the idea to purchase;

2 the information search and processing stage;

3 the formulation and implementation of the choice;

4 the evaluation of the post-purchase consequences.

Arousal and problem recognition

Sylvia Jones is visiting London Zoo with her French penfriend. It is hot. The two girls head towards the drinks stand and order refreshments. Meanwhile, Sylvia's mother is preparing dinner. She has decided to bake them an apple pie, but on opening the cupboard discovers that she has hardly any flour left. Quickly, she takes off her apron and runs to the corner shop for more. Her husband, coming home from work, goes past the news-stand at the tube station. He buys his usual evening paper but noticing a new musical magazine decides to buy it also. That evening, while the Joneses are watching TV, their favourite programme is interrupted because the set breaks down. This isn't the first time that the Joneses have had doubts about the health of their old set. The previous day they had visited their friends' house to watch an opera on their TV – the latest Sony with large screen and stereo sound. Returning home, the Joneses had exchanged opinions about the high quality of their friends' new TV. In opening their mail, Sylvia's parents find a bank statement indicating that a larger than expected bonus has been paid in. The Joneses are now decided. They are going to buy a new TV.

How does a decision to buy come about? What triggers the idea to acquire a product or service? The preceding examples all reveal an initial phase of **problem recognition**. A problem or need arises whenever consumers perceive a gap – big enough to trigger a reaction – between reality, as they see it, and another state judged as more desirable. In our first example, reality is the thirst created by the hot weather – happiness is a cold Coke. In the final example, the problem arises from a badly functioning TV set, exacerbated by the friends' brand new state-of-the-art model. Since the recognition of a problem is almost always at the origin of a purchase, it is necessary to explain how the initial gap is detected. Here, the mechanisms vary.

In the case of Sylvia and her friend, the process is essentially an internal one, in which physiological mechanisms play a key role. The combination of weather conditions and the exercise cause thirst to develop. Thirst, hunger, fatigue, ageing or a malfunctioning bodily organ are at the origin of the buying process for many products and services, particularly in the areas of food and medicines. The example of the apple pie is also quite simple. The mere observation that something has run out explains a large number of food repurchases. The difference between this situation and the previously described physiological process is based mainly on the necessity of an explicit assessment stage. On preparing the pie, Sylvia's mother discovers that flour stocks are too low for what she wants to do. Without this 'discovery', the packet could have lasted perhaps another week or month. Hunger and thirst on the other hand, can stand little delay.

The music magazine illustrates a phenomenon known as **variety seeking**.[2] For certain product categories, for example seasonings or biscuits, it is often observed that consumers become bored by constantly using the same things. In addition, the considerable variety of the offering arouses their curiosity. There follows multiple purchasing behaviour according to which several product or brand alternatives are bought by the same consumer either simultaneously or sequentially. The latter situation corresponds to brand or product **switching**: rich tea biscuits today, perhaps digestives or shortbread tomorrow. In this case, the consumer chooses brands without a real evaluation but more as a result of their feelings at the time and their willingness to change – not necessarily linked to prior dissatisfaction. Companies playing in such markets must take advantage of (or protect themselves against) variety-seeking behaviour. The leading brands will offer a product assortment large enough to keep their customers loyal. Challengers will try to get into the market via promotions, special offers and other incentives.

The case of the TV set is more complex and several mechanisms are being brought into play. A feeling of discontent appears with the set while it is being used by Sylvia's family. Additionally, their friends' Sony contributes to raising the level of expectations by altering the **standard of comparison**. A problem is recognised not only because of a deterioration of the **actual state** ('the TV set does not work') but also because the **ideal state** has been moved upward, thus creating an opportunity ('it would be nice to have a large-screen and stereo TV set like our friends'). In many cases, needs arise for reasons which are either physical (for example linked with the ageing process) or psychological (as in the case of fashion). Fashion designers, manufacturers of appliances and producers of entertainment and educational goods have all become masters in the art of renewing their products as part of a strategy of planned obsolescence – the consumer is always discovering that the 'latest model' is rooted in the past!

In our example, we can also observe that the discontent is reinforced by two contextual factors: the dinner with friends and the extra bonus payment. As discussed in Chapter 5, the behaviour of an individual is often affected by their desire to identify with reference groups. A change brought via the social environment thus can lead to modifications of behaviour. In the case of new products, the **diffusion** phenomenon directly results from this mimicking effect.[3] For many innovations, we actually observe an introductory phase, which is often quite slow and confined to pioneers, hungry for novelty and innovation. Then, under the influence of word-of-mouth recommendation, many additional consumers decide to follow suit, leading to an acceleration of the diffusion process. Beyond a certain level, mere social pressure, as measured by the number of people having already acquired the product and expressing positive feedback, can be enough to trigger a purchase among the sceptical. Such a process, reflecting the evolution of the product throughout its life-cycle, explains the success of many household appliances (electric carving knives, coffee machines, etc.) which, even if they do not correspond to a strong need, make up a part of the modern household.

Finally, problem recognition can emerge from a modification in the situation of the buyer (as in the case of the bonus in our example). The birth of a child, schooling, the transition into adult life, marriage – these are all events generating new needs for food, clothing, appliances or even homes. If Mrs Jones decides to go back to work once Sylvia has reached university age, then she will be faced with a whole series of new requirements: transportation, a new wardrobe, etc. A job move, an inheritance, a promotion or an accident may all contribute to trigger needs. A salesperson who accepts a job abroad has to move house, perhaps buy a new car and adapt to a new cultural environment. It is worth noticing that in this case purchase decisions feed off one another. The purchase of a house leads to the need for furniture, which in turn requires accessories. Certain studies have explored the links existing between specific activities: 50 per cent of hunters are also fishermen, but the reverse is true only in 20 per cent of cases.

Relatively little research has been conducted on thresholds above which a difference between the ideal and the actual is enough to activate a decision process.[4] It would appear, however, that such thresholds strongly vary from one individual to the next. The smallest stain on a carpet could trigger the search for the most suitable cleaning product in a very house-proud homemaker, while another person may not even notice it.

The problem recognition phase is over when a consumer admits the reality of the need and the necessity of a corresponding purchase. Depending on the case, priorities previously established can be modified (the holiday is shortened because a new car is needed) or the shopping list is simply lengthened.[5] Of course, the economic context can also have a strong impact on the way consumers define their needs. Given the relatively high level of unemployment in Europe, many studies have been conducted on the purchasing behaviour of the unemployed.[6] Generally speaking, people who have lost their job tend to feel alienated in a consumer society, as the gap between what they would like to have and what they can afford increases. However, a number of them manage to preserve their self-esteem by re-emphasising the value of a simple, less materialistic life. In the USA, however, a paradox has been observed in difficult economic times: both discounted goods and luxury items sell well. On the one hand, the affluent worry less about high interest rates and stockpile luxury items; on the other, modest consumers engage in comparative shopping.[7] The degree of optimism or pessimism about the future can also affect need recognition. For example, in Europe, the percentage of people who believe that 'my children will be less prosperous than I am when they grow up' varies from a low of 25 per cent (in the Netherlands) to a high of 65 per cent (in Italy).[8] Obviously, when people are pessimistic, they tend to redefine their priorities. Whatever the initial circumstances, a consumer alerted by a problem will look for a solution. Most often, he or she will engage in information search and processing activities.

Information search and processing

Consumers are typically in one of two situations when exposed to commercial information. Most often, they are in a state of passive reception. In this case, and as explained in Chapter 2, messages often reach them in a form strongly altered by perceptual filters. Obviously, the amount of information received by a consumer depends upon many factors, including occupation and lifestyle; a news reporter thus receives much more information than a farmer. In the second situation, however, especially when they are personally involved in the decision-making process, consumers are much more active in the search for information relating to their problem.[9] The initiative has now shifted from the company broadcasting the message to the consumer.

Given the pivotal role played by a good understanding of the information search process – particularly its value in advertising – it is not surprising that many studies have tried to identify the nature and quality of information **sources,** as well as the quantity, sequence and impact of information used by consumers when reaching their purchasing decisions. For example, several studies have shown that recommendations from friends and proximity to home or to place of work were the two most important pieces of information in the selection of a bank.[10] More generally, it has been discovered that the degree of information search undertaken depended upon the consumer's prior **expertise:** it was greatest for those with an average, intermediate level of knowledge.[11] The reason is easy to understand: not all information used during a purchase is gathered at the moment of the decision; in many cases the consumer uses information already held in memory (**internal** instead of **external search**). In Chapter 3 we studied how the memorisation process works and so do not return to it here; suffice it to say that internal search is particularly used by experts and people who already have acquired some experience with the product category.[12] Thus, while connoisseurs can rely upon their own memory, people with very limited knowledge do not feel capable of absorbing a lot of unfamiliar information and do not know where to start.[13] Similarly, while experts engage in selective search, novices look for more general and 'pre-packaged' information.[14]

Another factor influencing the amount and type of information search is the level of **risk** perceived in the purchase of a product and the resulting consumer uncertainty about its acquisition.[15] Up to five types of risk have been identified:[16]

- financial risk (the risk of losing money or spending it inappropriately);
- functional risk (the risk that the product will not work properly or less well than alternative ways of performing the same task);
- physical risk (the risk of being hurt or physically diminished);
- social risk (the risk of feeling embarrassed in front of other people); and
- psychological risk (the risk of losing self-esteem or self-confidence because of a bad decision).

A Scandinavian study found that buyers perceiving a high level of risk in a purchase have a strong tendency to rely on friends' advice and recommendations.[17] However, the type of risk perceived in a given purchase largely depends upon the product and the person.

To explore these issues, difficult methodological problems have to be overcome: how do we get access to information search and processing strategies? The post-purchase investigation is not particularly appropriate here. Its retrospective nature introduces a memory (do consumers remember all the sources of information consulted during a purchase?) and rationalisation bias (do they wish to communicate them all?). Two approaches have been used which enable a more in-depth analysis: **protocols** and **information display boards**. Simply put, the protocol method consists of accompanying consumers when they are making their purchases and asking them to describe the thoughts entering their minds. We thus get information gathered *in situ*, the transcription of which constitutes the protocol (or script) of the purchase. An example of a protocol appears in Figure 8.1.

Many variations on this basic procedure exist. If speaking out loud while shopping causes too many problems (not all consumers are comfortable with speaking into a microphone in a shop), then the consumer can be accompanied by someone who prompts the person during prolonged silences. A quasi-conversation thus develops. In other cases, the progress of a shopper is filmed and they are asked to comment later on the video of their trip. Even though most protocols are carried out in self-service shops, others can include an interaction with salespeople.

The protocol method provides a great deal of data which keeps track of the infor-

Figure 8.1   An excerpt from a protocol

> 'Ah yes, chilled products ...'
>
> 'Me, I'm quite special because I look for a fresh cheese with the least amount of fat possible.... So I take ... at 20 percent fat ... it's still within the limit that I allow myself ... and it's still excellent.'
>
> 'The price goes up often, but it's not excessive.'
>
> 'I buy the large size, the 1 kg: it's easier when one buys in large quantities ... because there are many of us in the evenings.'
>
> 'I always take this brand because I know it's good ... I've never had any problems, not with the freshness, nothing ... because it's popular ... it's a good brand.'
>
> 'I hesitate to buy low-fat yoghurts ... because it's only me that eats them. You have to keep everyone happy so I'm going to choose some others ... stirred ones ... just for a change.'
>
> 'A traditional cheese ... some Camembert, for those not on diets ... for the boys who need the calories ... a nice cheese like that will not scare them.'

Source: J. P. Faivre and J. Palmer, 'Protocoles et Arbes de décisions', *Revue Française de Marketing*, July–August–September 1977, pp. 11–30

mation processing going on in the consumer's mind as the decisions are being taken. In contrast to a traditional survey, the dynamics of a purchase are thus preserved. On the other hand, protocols are quite difficult to analyse.[18] The method most commonly used consists of building 'decision trees' (see Figure 8.2) retracing as faithfully as possible the problems consumers are faced with, and the way in which they resolve them, with the help of the information available. Researchers analyse the resulting graphs by looking at their nature, length and structure.

The protocol method is not yet routinely used in commercial research, but it has already provided some interesting results.[19] It has been used, for example, to document the impact of factors linked to the retail environment (product presentation, promotions, etc.) as well as the nature of the interaction with salespeople. It has thus enabled the manufacturer of a cooker to rearrange the control knobs, which were judged as impractical by householders. A European retailer has also used this method to analyse the way in which its staff react to objections from clients. Finally, it has also been used to measure the influence of modifications introduced to improve the atmosphere of a shop; for example, one DIY chain decided to stop making announcements to staff over the PA system after realising, thanks to pro-

Figure 8.2   Protocol data as decision trees

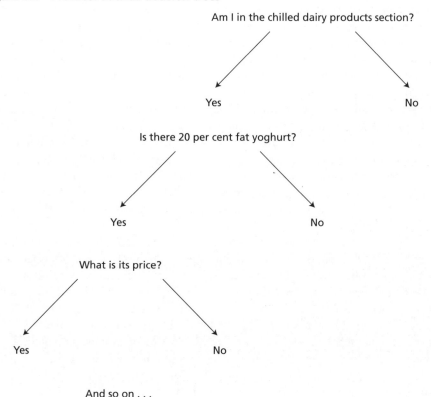

Am I in the chilled dairy products section?

Yes   No

Is there 20 per cent fat yoghurt?

Yes   No

What is its price?

Yes   No

And so on . . .

tocols, that consumers interpreted repeated announcements as a sign of poor organisation in the store.

The information display board method also aims to understand better the information processing strategies used by consumers but is based on a different principle. Instead of observing behaviour in a shop, the method consists of placing consumers in a buying situation and offering them information likely to help them to make a decision. This information is most often presented in the form of an alternative-by-attribute matrix and the data contained in the cells (one row for each alternative and one column for each attribute) are initially covered up with cards. Consumers, simulating a purchasing decision, are thus invited to take account of as much (or as little) information as they wish (by uncovering the appropriate cards) to make their choice. When they have reached a decision they stop. The number, nature and sequence of cards turned over reveals the volume and type of information needed, as well as the strategy followed in its acquisition. For example, in a study carried out for the French Office of Consumers Affairs which was aimed at finding out on which criteria comparative tests published in consumer reports should be based, it was shown – with the help of information display boards – that the sensitivity to different criteria varied greatly according to the nature of the product.[20] For jogging suits, the cut was the most important factor, followed by the fabric; for batteries, it was the price and the lifetime. The sensitivity to brand information could also be quite strong (yoghurts, washing powder) or very weak (curtains, socks). Furthermore, most consumers processed the information in 'columns' (that is, comparing several alternatives against one criterion) rather than by 'rows' (exploring the complete profile of a given alternative). In fact, it would appear that the ability of a consumer to create a mental image of a product or a brand favours the processing of information by row. In many cases, the brand images that consumers maintain are quite precise and enable them, if necessary, to complete a profile from which certain aspects are missing.[21] Such insights are useful to marketers in deciding both the type of information to favour and its mode of presentation.

In contrast to protocols, based upon observation of behaviour at the point of sale, information display boards correspond to a laboratory situation. The buying environment is more artificial but better controlled. New criteria and new product concepts can be introduced, and their acceptability, as well as their informational content, measured.

Whether collected via protocols, information display boards or more traditional research methods, results obtained on information acquisition and treatment strategies have been numerous and rich enough to generate a comprehensive information processing theory of consumer choice.[22] According to this theory, information processing depends equally upon personal characteristics such as cognitive style (see Chapter 2), contextual factors such as time available or other aspects of the environment (see Chapter 10), and the way in which information is presented.[23] Even though specific processes will be used depending upon the individual and the situation, it is possible to offer a few generalisations about certain aspects of information processing which tend to remain unchanged; they are described below.

The magic number seven

Miller showed, in a famous article, the existence of limits to human beings' capacity to process information. Specifically, he estimated the maximum number of units of information which can be analysed simultaneously as being seven (plus or minus two, depending upon the individual). In a commercial context this would mean that a consumer would have difficulty in considering more than seven choice criteria at once (or seven brands). Even if the specific number is debatable, the general conclusion remains valid and it is clear that consumers cannot absorb an unlimited amount of information.[24] How then do people react to an increase in the volume of information made available to them? In a series of experiments, Jacoby and his colleagues showed the existence of 'information overload' effects: the quality of consumers' decisions deteriorates when the available data exceed the capacity to process it. For example, fewer consumers choose a brand of washing powder which they consider the best (the closest to their ideal) as the number of brands and choice criteria available increase.[25] This is an interesting result. For many years it has been considered that the more information consumers have, the better off they are. Under pressure from consumer associations, a 'right to information' has been accepted and has led to an increase in regulation, most notably in the area of packaging labels (nutritional content and additives) or the writing of a contract (guarantee clauses, conditions of sale). Ironically it would seem that beyond a certain threshold, consumers are hindered by such information rather than helped.

When swamped with information, it would appear that many consumers adopt a **psychology of simplification**. Typically, they begin their search from anchor points or levels which they use as a reference.[26] How does a novice fisherman, for example, not get lost in the forest of rods which the large specialist shop offers? He can give priority to one criterion to the detriment of others, for instance select the lowest price, or in a smaller shop take the advice of the salesperson, or even place his confidence in a brand which seems to be better than the rest.[27] By thus reducing the range of alternatives, he can rapidly arrive at a decision without losing confidence in his choice. The price, the salesperson or the brand enable him to avoid making a choice which may otherwise have been a chore. It is also possible to proceed via abstraction (for example, using information relating to the repair cost of a car, a driver can make a judgement about its economic value) or by aggregation, according to one of the models presented in Chapter 4 (lexicographic, linear, etc.). Of course, the identification or even the control of these simplification mechanisms is of great importance to manufacturers and retailers.[28] Years before it became mandatory, the French retailer Carrefour placed comparative information by unit of weight (price per litre, kilogram, etc.) for products such as oil, washing powder and milk. Similarly, Virgin Megastore edits brochures presenting the best price–quality relationships for hi-fi equipment.

Conversely, a **psychology of complication** will lead to the kind of variety-seeking purchase presented in the previous section. Tired of the same biscuit with which they are too familiar, consumers 'flit around' other brands or types.

Generally speaking, many decision theory researchers believe that consumers apply – at least implicitly – the principles of **economics of information**, according to which they stop collecting additional information when they feel its incremental value is less than the cost and the trouble of getting it.[29] But consumer and product-related factors also play a role.[30] It has often been observed that lower-income groups who would benefit most from additional 'rational' information limit their search to their immediate, often biased environment.[31] It would also seem that shoppers search less for utilitarian goods such as durables than for value-expressive products such as clothing.[32]

Beyond its volume, the nature of the information processed has also been the subject of much inquiry and analysis. In marketing, people usually identify four kinds of information **source** depending on whether they are controlled or not by a commercial organisation, and whether they are standardised or customised. A TV advertisement constitutes standardised controlled information, whereas the advice of a friend is customised and, in general, unbiased. The recommendation of a salesperson or the results of a comparative test occupy intermediate positions. Which kind of information is most often used?

In general, the more information is customised and perceived as unbiased, the more likely it is to influence a decision. Independence from a commercial source leads to credibility and customisation brings relevance: the advice of friends is valuable because it is sincere and relevant. Standardised commercial sources should have, in contrast, much less impact but they are much more widespread and because of this, easily available. Is their lesser credibility compensated for by their greater accessibility? It all depends once again on the level of involvement of the consumer. When actively searching for information, involved consumers tend to head towards those sources considered to be most useful. Advice is thus taken from experts, knowledgeable people and often those who have already bought the product being considered – particularly if it is expensive, showy, presents some risk or is infrequently bought. In the case of uninvolved passive reception, advertising (especially media advertising) has a greater chance of reaching the target, as consumers lower their perceptual filters. The level of expertise the consumer has will also affect information search; connoisseurs tend to be more selective and pay more attention to original, first-hand information, while novices will often look to their friends for advice.[33]

More generally, the use of information depends on its 'internal attribution' by the individual, given the image one maintains of oneself. A study made on a programme of post-psychiatric rehabilitation has shown that the rate of participation in discussion groups rose from 90 to 95 per cent when $8 was offered to participate but fell to 75 per cent when the $8 was taken away. In the latter situation, subjects were clearly denied an internal attribution of their behaviour, which was sufficient to generate the initial 90 per cent level of participation.[34]

For or against comparative advertising?

The value of information largely depends on the way in which it is presented and structured. For example, a sequential presentation (first, second, third) often has more influence than a simultaneous one.[35] Furthermore, comparative information (that which enables several alternatives to be compared with each other) seems to carry more weight than stand-alone information (which does not enable a comparison to be made). This issue is at the heart of the current debate over comparative advertising.

In the USA, any brand can highlight aspects of superiority over competitive products in commercial advertising (as long as they can be proven); Pepsi-Cola has used the results of blind tests showing its taste superiority over Coca-Cola for a long time. In most European countries, however, such advertising is only authorised under very restrictive conditions, and a washing powder brand like Ariel, in order to convince potential customers of its performance, can only compare itself with a 'normal detergent' without specifying the name. More direct comparisons may often lead to legal problems, as in most European countries every superiority claim has to be substantiated with strong empirical evidence obtained using scientific methods.

Advocates of comparative advertising, for example consumer organisations, see this form of publicity as being a better way of informing the consumer because it balances commercial superlatives. Opponents, often advertising agencies and their clients, hold that the risk of defamatory statements is substantial and that the information provided is not necessarily improved when brands are compared with each other (for example, if the battle is based on irrelevant criteria). The results of studies carried out on this issue are quite ambiguous: it seems that comparative advertising captures attention better than non-comparative advertising but it introduces a certain confusion in the listener, notably when there are many points of comparison[36] – and therefore a strong risk of information overload exists. More recent studies have also concluded that levels of persuasiveness are similar.[37] Moreover, comparative advertising can lead to a 'boomerang effect' to the detriment of brands using it, reducing the credibility of the attacker by favouring counter-argumentation.[38] Nothing actually guarantees that consumers exposed to a double message will draw the conclusions intended in the advertisement. In fact, when brand attributions are inverted, the message becomes counter-productive! It would seem, however, that people are more likely to remember the names of brands using this form of advertising.[39]

In summary, it seems that certain rules have to be observed when implementing a comparative advertising campaign:[40]

1 there is no point in attacking a competitor if no substantial competitive advantage exists;
2 it is always dangerous to let it be known that a competitor has tricked the consumer;
3 the consumer has to be capable of verifying the declarations made and of taking advantage of them.

Categorisation

The ongoing debate about the merits and drawbacks of comparative advertising[41] highlights our relatively limited understanding of the **categorisation** processes used by individuals.[42] What is known is that, for purposes of comparison, people tend to group objects into categories and do so at different levels of abstraction.[43] For example, a Tropicana orange juice can be classified first as an orange juice, then as a fruit juice, and finally as a drink. The latter level tends to be more abstract, while the first category often includes individual brands.[44] When people are in a situation where they find it difficult to compare alternatives, they tend to rely on higher, superordinate levels.[45] For each level, people tend to select a **prototype** which best expresses the characteristics of the members of the category and thus serves as a standard of comparison.[46]

It is very important that categorisation principles and typicality patterns are understood by marketing managers as their positioning strategies often consist of attempting to convince consumers that their products belong to the appropriate category and that their brands are prototypical. Even though prototypical brands (Scotch, Klaxon, Kleenex, and so on) are more easily remembered, there are sometimes advantages in differentiating a given brand from the prototype (for example, 7-Up promoted as the 'Uncola'). Advertising messages can be made more specific and prices can deviate from market rates.[47]

In many cases, information processing is more or less balanced between external messages and the information that is held in memory.[48] When relevant data are judged to be missing, consumers often rely on mental short cuts called **heuristics** to make inferences based upon elements already memorised[49] (for example, judging quality from the price[50] or from the country of origin,[51] or assessing functional performance from external appearance[52]), halo effects, often reinforced by assessments of co-variations[53] (a brand judged as generally strong will be favourably judged on a new attribute), or by comparison with other brands.[54] Research has also shown that mental images developed by individuals have a significant impact on later phases of the decision-making process. For example, daydreaming about being on holiday while reading a travel agency brochure increases the desire and the probability of a purchase. Similarly, consumers who imagine themselves looking at cable TV programmes are more inclined to subscribe to them.[55] Strong beliefs can also affect information processing. For example, many consumers believe that larger sizes are always cheaper than smaller ones or that new products are always more expensive.[56] More generally, the greater the amount of information held in memory, the more difficult it is to recall one item precisely. However, memory can be easily activated by appropriate cues (for example, the first notes of a jingle or a well-known symbol).[57]

Having a rich bank of memorised data also facilitates external research to the extent that new incremental information is more rapidly processed and better structured. Information is more quickly recognised as irrelevant or redundant and attention is focused on the most important elements.[58]

More recently, researchers have attempted to deepen their understanding of memory processes by turning their attention to the properties and functioning of the brain, as discussed below.

Left side or right side?

We know that the two hemispheres of the brain take on different cognitive activities: on the left side lies logic and abstraction, while the right side is the seat of intuition and imagination. The left side processes textual or semantic elements and the right side visual ones. Normally either the left or the right hemisphere is dominant and certain tests can differentiate the 'rightists' from the 'leftists'. For example, according to the so-called Stroop effect, if you are exposed for a fraction of a second to the word 'red' written in blue and then asked about the colour of the letters, you would tend to say 'red' if you were a 'leftist' but 'blue' if a rightist.

Currently, researchers are trying to understand why certain messages are better processed and remembered by leftists than rightists and vice versa. For example, it has been shown, thanks to electroencephalograms obtained during the visualisation of advertising messages, that leftists respond better to verbal stimuli (text) and rightists to non-verbal ones (music, images).[59] The relationship between text and illustration plays an important role in all communication efforts and much research is going on in this relatively new area of consumer study.[60]

The formulation of decisions

Rapidly or slowly and via a more or less complicated route, the information processing phase usually results in a choice – or rather a series of choices. We refer to plural choices because a consumer who opts to buy a product is confronted with many related decisions: product, brand, model, item, price range, point of sale, time of purchase,[61] volume of purchase and method of payment.

The way people formulate decisions has been studied from many angles and has even given birth to a new discipline known as behavioural decision theory (BDT). BDT researchers often assume that people make decisions on the basis of potential gains or losses for them, a process known as **mental accounting**.[62] For example, suppose you are offered a choice of receiving 10 Euros plus a ticket for a lottery where there is a 50 per cent chance of winning 100 Euros or just a ticket for a lottery where there is a 50 per cent chance of winning 120 Euros. Which option would you choose? Even though the expected gains are the same in both cases, loss aversion will lead most people to go for the first alternative. Similarly, it has been found that when people have already paid for a service, they feel more committed to consume it even though some risk may be involved. For example, compared with those who have not paid yet, people who have already bought their ticket to a football game will be more likely to decide to go to the stadium even if, on the day of the game, a sudden drop in the temperature results in very icy roads making it somewhat unsafe to drive. Generally speaking, people seem more sensitive to losses than to gains and this probably explains the success of full refund policies adopted by many European mass merchandisers. It also explains why people hesitate much less to splurge when they receive unexpected bonuses.

The order in which decisions are taken may seem a minor issue. Yet, it represents one of the most formidable challenges for consumer goods companies as it is at the very heart of the battle which manufacturers and retailers face today. Let us examine it.

> Jim Good has decided to buy the new Philips video camcorder which he saw advertised in a specialist magazine. He goes to Comet, his preferred shop, and discovers that this particular model is not sold there. What will he do? If he decides to leave the shop to look for it in another then his brand loyalty is greater than his loyalty to the store. The opposite is true if he is persuaded by a salesperson to buy another brand.

Store loyalty depends upon many controllable factors, of which the most important are the location, the assortment or stock range offered, the perceived price level, the services provided and the atmosphere.

The location of a sales outlet determines its 'merchandising zone', which can be divided up into concentric circles corresponding to different levels of proximity.[63] Hence, 20 per cent of Sainsbury's customers may live within 5 minutes (by car), 30 per cent within 10 minutes, etc. Such figures are obtained from an analysis of cheques and credit cards, or, in countries where they are meaningful, from the observation of car number plates in car parks. However, consumers do not make all their purchases in the nearest shop. If the product is very important to them, they will take the time and effort to get it. Vuitton, the luxury leather goods company, has less than a dozen boutiques in France but this certainly does not stop affluent women from provincial France visiting the Avenue Montaigne or Champs Elysées store in Paris to buy their handbags. The strategy used by consumers in making their purchases also contributes to de-emphasising distance. A housewife may walk to the marketplace every day and visit the local shops. An employed woman may prefer to make all her purchases at the end of the week and might go to a supermarket perhaps situated a long way from home.

The range of alternatives resulting from the store assortment policy also increases the complexity of the purchasing decision. In London, Harvey Nichols and Harrods have acquired a clientele who come from far beyond Knightsbridge, attracted by the thousands of items on sale. The proximity of these two stores reinforces the image of this area as a major shopping venue. It is worth noting that it is the perceived rather than the real assortment which attracts clients; and, as seen in Chapter 2, their perception depends upon their areas of interest. A beginner may be confused by the range offered in the plumbing section of a DIY store; a professional plumber would perhaps have difficulty in finding exactly what he or she wants.

Another decisive criterion in the choice of a sales outlet is the price level – again as perceived by the customer. One type of shop, known as 'hard discounters' (Lidl, Aldi, Netto, etc.) have based their success on their ability to offer the lowest prices, at least for the most common, and therefore the most visible, items. Others commit to reimburse any price difference for a number of standard products. The recent decision to adopt a common European currency may strongly affect the perception of price discounts, especially when they are expressed in monetary units (as opposed to percentages). In ten of the eleven Euroland countries, price differences expressed in Euros will look smaller, while in Ireland, they will appear larger.

A service-based approach can, however, compensate well for a price difference. Ease of payment, guarantees, reimbursement if dissatisfied, loan of a delivery vehicle and special offers are just a few of the many ways of attracting customers. Certain stores have studied further the needs of their customers and provide services beyond the usual level. In Sweden, Obs for example has anticipated the concerns of families by offering a playing area for small children; in the UK, Tesco and Sainsbury's, by providing an in-store café, are encouraging customers to come in groups and thus transform a chore into an enjoyable outing. Such initiatives find their full development in the policy of creating and selling an 'experience' through managing an **atmosphere** in the store. A 'consumer experience' may be defined as an orchestration of services which fit into a general theme.[64] At IKEA everything – from the flag which welcomes you at the entrance, through the smorgasbord which is offered in the restaurant, to the names of the products sold in the store – conjures up Sweden. Here families, often travelling some distance, are offered an excuse for a trip out in which the purchase of furniture may be only a pretext. The distinction between shopping and entertainment is progressively blurred.

In fact the kind of atmosphere sought can vary from one consumer to another for the same sales outlet.[65] Some people appreciate the structured layout and the choice offered in a supermarket, whereas others prefer the informal atmosphere and human contact of a street market. The atmosphere in a shop also depends on the products presented. The same piece of jewellery may appear more luxurious in a specialist jeweller than in a department store. The services offered make up an integral part of the purchasing experience of the consumer. For example, a woman may take great pleasure in trying on a number of dresses and listening to the flattering comments of the salesperson even if she intends to buy only one – or perhaps none. When customer expectations regarding store atmosphere are very different and specialisation is not an option, the only solution left is to divide up the sales space into areas dedicated to a particular client base. This phenomenon can be seen in many large department stores across Europe.

Once inside the shop, consumers have to select the items they want. Many aspects of the interior arrangement can affect this choice. Among them are the shelf layout, promotional offers, the displays and the way prices are displayed. The shelf layout inside a shop often has a strong influence on purchasing patterns. Knowing that passing by a particular shelf can trigger a purchase decision, many supermarket managers place basic food items at the back of the store in order to give customers a chance to pass by shelves which they would not necessarily go to spontaneously (clothing, household goods). Furthermore, the sales area is reorganised from time to time in order to break shopping habits.

Point-of-sale promotions are also designed to facilitate **impulse buying,** particularly in the case of new brands or products.[66] Depending upon the commercial objective, these promotions can be placed at the ends of the aisles and highlighted by placards pointing out the product, or take the form of demonstrations or tasting stands. Promotional prices share the same objective. Discounts or special sales give the consumer the feeling that they have got a good deal while reducing the risk attached to changing brand or being disloyal to a product.

The specific placing of products on the shelves and the policy of dividing up the space between the shelves also has a strong influence. Many studies have demonstrated the link between the market share held by a product and the number of facings occupied on the shelf.[67] For fashion goods, it seems that many consumers associate the success of an item with the number of them displayed in the shop. Furthermore, products placed right at the top or at the bottom enjoy less success than those placed at eye level (of an adult or child depending on the product category). Finally, the displays at cashiers' desks systematically contain items of low unit value which tend to be forgotten on shopping lists (chewing gum, razor blades, TV magazines).

The way prices are displayed in the shop can similarly influence the choices made by customers. Certain shops indicate two prices, the 'normal' price crossed out and replaced with a lower one specific to the shop. This aims to convince the buyer of the price competitiveness of the shop. Recently, the inclusion of 'display by' and 'use by' dates has revolutionised the chilled dairy products section (milk, yoghurts and desserts). Certain consumers do not hesitate to go through the stock to find a product with a slightly more favourable date.

Finally, in certain kinds of store, the role of the salesperson is to direct customers to the products most appropriate to them (and if possible the most profitable to the store). To implement this, they must of course know their customers very well. Mr Brown the grocer, has learned, over time, the tastes and needs of each of his customers; he asks Mrs Smith about her children while she is choosing because he knows that way she may buy more. On the other hand, he will exchange few words and quickly serve Mr Jones, who is always busy.

The style of the salesperson, of course, must fit with all the other aspects of the shop so that the sales outlet and its customer base are perceived as being in harmony.[68] In the case of jewellers' shops, a French study has resulted in the identification of four kinds of outlet strongly differentiated in the mind of the consumer.[69] First, there is the 'Place Vendôme' type (located around Place Vendôme, rue de la Paix and Faubourg St Honoré in Paris), including the big names: Cartier, Boucheron, Van Cleef. These serve as references and express the great tradition of French jewellery making. The products are perceived to be of top quality (particularly the gems), original, expensive and well presented. However, these are places most consumers never imagine visiting because they do not belong to the traditional customer base, seen as being the very privileged (rich Americans, Arab sheikhs), with whom they do not feel they 'fit'. The welcome there is perceived as rather cold and impersonal – 'the salespeople examine you from head to toe, trying to unmask you, and if you find favour with them, they begin to flatter you in order to make you buy something'. In other words: an impossible dream.

Next the craftsman-jeweller, whom consumers know by reputation or via friends or relatives and who sometimes lives above the shop. It is here that many people imagine making the important purchases; the relationship is often based on trust. Consumers know that they are dealing with a specialist – they could even ask to have something especially designed and made for them.

Then comes the local jeweller. This is often a jeweller/watchmaker functioning as both a shop and workshop for repairs. It is here that consumers say that they go most often to make the smaller jewellery purchases (medals, chains) or for small repairs. However, they rarely go there to browse, first because the door is often shut ('if we ring the bell, we have the impression that we are bothering someone'), and second because the items seem a little old, poorly presented, arranged without much care. Also, the jeweller is not seen as particularly nice, being perceived as a merchant inspiring little confidence and often lacking competence. In brief, visiting this shop is more of a chore than a pleasure.

Finally, the 'new jewellers'. The shops have pleasant-sounding names which create a good impression. The jewels are not too flashy, genuine and well presented. They are original but remain accessible. The welcome and the ambience are warm and consumers feel they can browse without being hassled.

As for the ideal jewellers, consumers describe this as a shop which would offer a good choice without getting too confused, where the staff would be competent but discreet, and above all a shop where they could circulate freely around the cases dedicated to the jewellery. The shops would have flowers in and soft music would be playing. The lighting would be suited to display the jewellery a little like in a museum. Going into the jeweller's would be a bit like going travelling to a dream destination.

Store loyalty thus represents a strong asset which retailers try to protect against their ever-present enemy: **brand loyalty**. What is it that makes consumers so attached to a brand that they will sometimes go elsewhere to find it if it is not in their usual shop? Brand loyalty is much more than just a form of repeat purchasing observed over time.[70] As we saw in the chapter on brand perceptions and images (Chapter 2), it also expresses a preference, a favourable attitude, a particular sensitivity. The sensitivity to a brand varies a lot from one product to another and, for the same product, from one group of consumers to another. Attachment to the brand is thus stronger for champagne or coffee than for biscuits or ice cream.[71] To account for differences between consumers, it is necessary to consider the perceived choice with which the consumer is confronted. According to this perception, brand sensitivity can vary.[72] Six factors are in operation. First, the level of involvement of the consumer in the product category. The more the product interests them, the more the customer is ready to search and process information over the relative characteristics of each brand. This explains why there are so many guides and magazines about buying a car, while comparative studies of batteries are much less frequent.

The belief that differences exist between products' performance also affects brand sensitivity. If Mr Jones thinks that all long-life milk is the same or similar for example, he will attach no significance at all to the brand. The feeling of being competent to make a choice also acts in a similar way. It is one thing to believe that differences between brands exist; it is another to feel sufficiently competent to decipher them.

The feeling that a product category is undergoing rapid change often decreases brand loyalty and sensitivity. In areas such as hi-fi or home computing, reputations are made and lost rapidly, and consumers take more account of what a salesperson may say than the brand name. Production agreements between manufacturers tend to reinforce this phenomenon, at least when consumers know about them. Also, functional problems with the product lead to a distrust which, due to a sort of reverse halo effect, may extend to all brands present on the market. If my digital camcorder is always breaking down, I may be tempted to feel that it's because this kind of technology is still not fully developed and such products are inherently risky purchases.

To all these elements of a psychological nature, we must add an obvious one – the number of brands available. The more the market is concentrated, the greater the sensitivity to brands. The cola market is thus dominated by two major brands (Coca-Cola and Pepsi,) which each have their ardent supporters.[73]

The selection of the sales outlet and the product/brand are not, of course, the only two decisions to be made even if they often are the most visible and important ones. Usually, a consumer also has to choose the purchase volume, the time to buy and the method of payment.

The **purchase volume**, when considered in aggregate, is impressive. In Western Europe alone, 360 million consumers spend more than 200 Euros each week to buy a tremendous variety of products and services. Food items alone represent almost one-fifth of the total. Strong differences can however be observed within Europe: while, on average, food expenditure represents 18 per cent of a European household income, this percentage jumps to 27 per cent in Greece and falls to 14 per cent in the United Kingdom.[74] Of course, the specific needs depend on a number of factors – size of household, age, taste and all the other elements examined in the first part of this book. However, certain trends affect practically the whole population. For example, the proportion of income allocated to food is constantly declining in Europe, from 30 per cent around twenty years ago to less than 20 per cent today.[75] Similarly, yearly penetration rates for products such as ground coffee or heavy-duty washing powder exceed 50 per cent all over Europe (except in Ireland). For other goods, however, strong differences remain: whereas less than 20 per cent of Spanish households consume butter at least once a year, more than 50 per cent of German, French or Austrian households do so. When one compares the structure of household budgets across European countries (see Table 8.1), it is obvious that it is somewhat risky to talk about a Euro-consumer. But trends tend to be similar, when analysed over a long period (twenty years in our table), even though absolute percentages still widely vary, reflecting different economic as well as socio-political environments (affecting such areas as health, education and culture). Let us consider alcoholic beverages, and more specifically the case of beer and wine consumption in Europe.[76] In 1995, among EU countries, beer consumption was highest in Ireland (141 litres per capita) and lowest in Italy (25.4). Conversely, wine consumption was strongest in France (63.5 litres) and lowest in the UK (12.8). However, it can be observed that in beer countries (Ireland, Germany, Denmark, the United Kingdom, Belgium and the Netherlands), where per capita consumption is at least 80 litres, beer consumption is decreasing steadily, while wine consumption is experiencing strong growth. Thus, in 2000, wine consumption has reached 28.8 litres per head in Ireland, 20 in Germany and 33.2 in Denmark as opposed to (respectively) 2.2, 4.7 and 3 litres in 1950. Just the opposite is happening in wine countries (France, Italy, Spain, Portugal and Greece), where wine consumption is decreasing in favour of beer. In the year 2000, beer consumption is 38.3 litres in France, 27.8 in Italy and 74.6 in Spain compared with (respectively) 21.8, 3.4 and 2.2 in 1950. However, and even if a number of managers expect the emergence of Euro-brands,[77] the wine and beer consumption curves are not likely to cross each other in Europe – at least not in the next twenty-five years.

The **moments** of purchasing and consumption are also worth analysing. For products regularly consumed, the time of purchase is determined either by the need

Table 8.1 European household expenditures

Type of expenditure	Date	Bel	Den	Ger	Spa	Gre	Fra	Irl	Ita	Lux	NL	Por	UK
Food, drinks and tobacco	1970	28.0	29.9	23.4	41.4	32.0	26.0	45.0	38.6	28.4	26.0	41.0	26.5
	1990	19.0	21.2	16.8	37.9	21.8	19.1	35.0	20.7	19.4	18.1	37.1	21.5
Clothes and shoes	1970	8.7	7.7	9.6	12.4	8.0	9.5	9.8	8.8	9.4	10.7	9.1	8.8
	1990	7.8	5.3	7.4	8.7	8.9	6.4	6.9	10.1	6.1	6.9	10.3	6.2
Housing, heating and lighting	1970	15.5	18.1	15.2	14.0	18.1	15.3	11.4	12.1	17.5	12.6	6.8	17.1
	1990	16.7	27.8	18.3	11.6	12.6	18.9	10.3	14.8	19.8	18.7	5.0	18.5
Furniture, appliances, etc.	1970	11.7	9.6	9.6	7.4	7.8	10.2	7.6	7.0	9.4	11.6	10.1	7.8
	1990	10.8	6.5	8.4	8.2	6.6	7.8	7.7	9.4	10.8	8.5	8.6	6.7
Health and medical services	1970	6.8	2.0	9.5	4.1	2.9	7.1	2.5	3.8	5.4	8.5	3.9	0.9
	1990	11.2	2.1	14.2	3.8	3.8	9.3	3.8	6.6	7.5	12.5	4.5	1.4
Transport and communication	1970	10.3	14.9	13.3	8.3	10.2	13.4	9.3	10.1	10.9	9.4	12.6	12.6
	1990	13.6	16.3	15.9	14.3	15.4	16.7	12.9	12.2	17.5	11.0	15.4	17.9
Entertainment education and culture	1970	4.7	8.2	9.6	4.8	5.8	6.9	7.8	7.7	4.0	8.4	5.0	8.6
	1990	6.6	9.8	9.2	5.6	6.5	7.6	10.7	9.2	4.3	9.9	5.7	9.7
Other goods and services	1970	14.3	9.6	9.8	7.6	15.2	11.6	6.6	11.9	15.0	12.8	11.5	17.7
	1990	14.3	11.0	9.8	9.9	24.4	14.2	12.7	17.0	14.6	14.4	13.4	18.1

Source: Eurostat

to restock or by the shopping habits of the household. In many families, Saturday morning is traditionally reserved for the weekly shopping. The emergence of large commercial centres and hypermarkets on the edge of towns in most European countries has created a trend towards shopping at weekends. Some shops can achieve as much as 30 per cent of their weekly sales on Sunday, which explains their resistance to constraining legislation on opening hours during weekends. But the consumption and hence the purchase of many products may also be dictated by rites of cultural or religious origin; eating fish on Fridays has been a rule in Roman Catholic households for a long time; turkey and mince pies are a Christmas Day ritual for many British people.

The consumption of many products is also influenced by the **time** available to the consumer.[78] The spread of appliances such as vacuum cleaners, washing machines and microwave ovens; the ability to do more and more things simultaneously[79] (for example, walking and talking on the portable phone at the same time); and the use of external services (fast food, dry-cleaning) have considerably changed the time frames within which households operate.[80] More and more consumers now consider time has become their most valuable resource. According to certain economists, due to a relatively stable amount of time spent working and a growing number of consumer activities (because of increasing income levels), there even exists a tendency to reduce the time spent on each activity as well as to reduce time-consuming activities.[81] For example, the time spent in preparing a meal has fallen from nearly two hours in the 1950s to about twenty minutes today, while medicines and vitamins are replacing activities (sports, eating out) leading to similar effects. For the same reasons, the amount of time that certain goods are being used (household electrical, hi-fi, video) is becoming less and less in relation to their lifetime. Furthermore, many people feel they are more and more pressed for time and such a perception affects their behaviour.[82] As a result, such innovations as one-hour photo processing, thirty-minute home pizza delivery and no-appointment, no-delay car exhaust replacement have been very successful all over Europe. Individuals are also less tolerant of activities which imply a delay and inhibit their use of time, for example administrative slowness and airline delays.[83] The more consumers feel a product benefits them, the less they tolerate delay.[84]

Finally, the selection of a **method of payment** sometimes represents an important area for reflection and decision making. Not always significant for frequently bought items, it takes on a major role for durable goods, essentially due to the role of **credit**.

Consider the case of savings. According to OECD statistics, European households save between 5 per cent (Finland) and 19 per cent (Belgium) of their income. Strong variations also exist among savings patterns. A recent comparison of such patterns in Hungary and France has revealed that Hungarian households tended to prefer tangible investments such as real estate, while the French were increasingly buying shares and bonds, which, considered together, represented more than 40 per cent of their savings.[85] Currently, even if savings rates have to a large degree stabilised in Europe, the amount of savings available remains considerable and constitutes a basic element in the financing of many durable goods purchases. By anticipating the moment of purchase, credit has enabled a number of people to own goods which they would not have otherwise been able to. Studies have shown that consumers are much more sensitive to the monthly repayment amount than the number of payments. This explains the practice of certain furniture retailers (zero per cent interest rate, first payment deferred one year) as well as the difference in the size of the characters indicating the monthly amount and those detailing the number of repayments in car advertisements. Credit has become one of the key factors in today's markets.

Post-purchase phenomena

The decision-making process is not completed by taking possession of the object acquired. The **consumption** phase leads to a series of reactions which, in turn, can affect later purchase decisions.

We described in the previous section how the time available interacts with consumption. In fact a consumer most often experiences a feeling of either satisfaction or discontent when in contact with the product.[86] **Satisfaction** may be defined as a psychological state induced by an absence of difference between expectations and the product's actual performance.[87] For example, if consumers expect a bank to be friendly, they will be satisfied if they discover that such is in fact the case. The previous definition implies that satisfaction is a relative concept. Two consumers to whom the same meal has been served in the same restaurant can have very different reactions depending upon their level of expectation or appreciation of the menu and service. The way in which expectations are formed is not fully understood.[88] Some analysts feel that modifications brought by companies to the offer play a significant part in shaping expectations.[89] In such circumstances, consumer decisions are easier to influence by manufacturers. More generally, past experience, available information (advertising and brochures but also friends' advice) and the sociocultural environment (which tends to define standards of comparison) have been identified as important factors. In fact, many researchers distinguish between two kinds of expectation – *normative* expectations, which specify the way in which the product should behave, and *predictive* expectations, which indicate the way in which people think that it will behave.[90] For most people, the latter has probably a greater impact on satisfaction than does the former. To the extent that a satisfied customer often decides to repurchase the same product or brand, understanding the nature and amount of satisfaction has become a critical issue in many businesses.[91] However, the relationship between satisfaction and loyalty is not always direct.[92]

For measuring satisfaction, there exist a wide range of techniques which differ as to their objectives, nature and structure. Certain scales have been developed directly to measure consumers' global and attribute-specific impressions. For example, France Telecom uses two indices (ISC1 and ISC2) which measure the welcome received in the shops and the welcome received over the telephone. In 1992 these dissatisfaction indices were 10.1 and 13.3 per cent against their targets of 10 per cent. Other techniques rely on 'objective' indicators of quality, for example flight delays or the breakdowns of household appliances. Of course, quality has first to be defined and operationalised.[93] Certain measures are immediate (such as questionnaires placed in hotel rooms), while others are used a long time after the purchase or even consumption.[94] Satisfaction can also be measured via a hotline, that is a free telephone line placed at the disposal of the customer (for example the 'games counselling' line opened by Nintendo).

If satisfaction often (but not always) leads to loyalty, **dissatisfaction**, usually due to performance below expectations, leads to a feeling of deception provoking in turn complaints, which can go as far as a boycott.[95] In general, the higher the level of income and education, the more a consumer tends to complain when dissatisfied. For a long time it has been thought that dissatisfaction was proportional to the difference between expectation and performance.[96] However, others think the opposite: if the product is very important for the consumer, the smallest difference can take on the form of a catastrophe. Both reactions can be observed among guests little used to luxury hotels. Some minimise all problems in order to enjoy their experience fully, while others dramatise every incident because of their extremely high levels of expectation. Generally speaking, it would seem that the more consumers are involved in the purchase and consumption of a product, the greater the risk of disappointment.[97] The psychological state of satisfaction or dissatisfaction can be more or less transient, depending on the nature of the situation encountered. The main scenarios are summarised in Figure 8.3. A lot also depends on the origin of the discontent. If consumers attribute it to an external cause (for example, a

Figure 8.3   Satisfaction and dissatisfaction

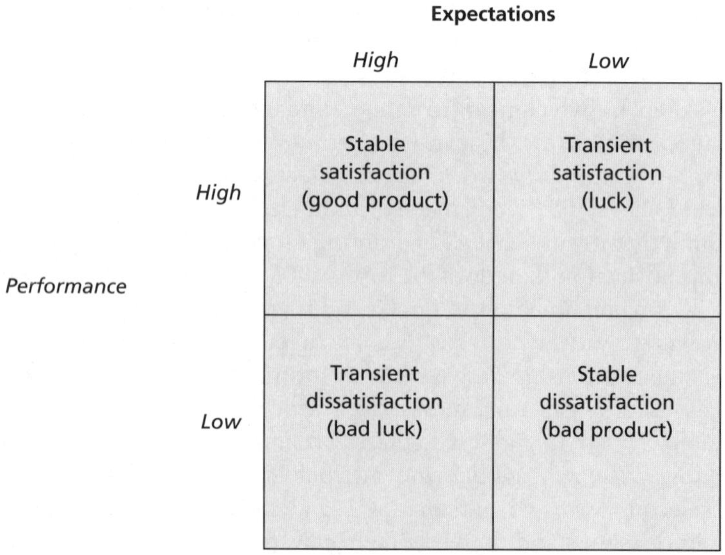

	Expectations	
	High	*Low*
Performance **High**	Stable satisfaction (good product)	Transient satisfaction (luck)
Performance **Low**	Transient dissatisfaction (bad luck)	Stable dissatisfaction (bad product)

manufacturing defect), they are more inclined to complain than if it was a fault of their own (for instance, a mistake in using it).

A sequence of purchases generated by continuous satisfaction creates loyalty, which, in the case of frequently bought products, may take the form of a **reflex**. Consumers place their preferred brand of coffee in their trolley without even thinking about it; we can thus speak about routine purchases. The process of becoming loyal to a brand or to a product does not differ fundamentally from the more basic learning mechanisms discussed in Chapter 3. Generalisation and discrimination phenomena in particular strongly affect buying behaviour, especially in the case of commodities.

Marking products with bar codes and reading them by scanner (as is common today) enables an extremely detailed and accurate recording of purchases made in supermarkets.[98] Coupled with media exposure data obtained for the same households (that is, the so-called 'single source' approach),[99] such information will enable researchers to refine considerably their understanding of the mechanisms underlying purchasing and consumption in the future.

Notes

[1] For a critical assessment of such an assumption, see R. W. Olshavsky and D. H. Granbois, 'Consumer Decision Making – Fact or Fiction', *Journal of Consumer Research*, September 1989, pp. 93–100.

[2] See W. D. Hoyer and N. M. Ridgeway, 'Variety Seeking as an Explanation for Exploratory Purchase Behaviour: A Theoretical Model', *Advances in Consumer Research* (ACR, 1984), pp. 114–19; L. McAlister, 'Choosing Multiple Items From a Product Class', *Journal of Consumer Research*, December 1979, pp. 213–24; L. McAlister and E. Pessemier, 'Variety Seeking Behaviour: An Interdisciplinary Review', *Journal of Consumer Research*, December 1982, pp. 311–22; I. Simonson, 'The Effect of Purchase Quantity and Timing on Variety Seeking Behaviour', *Journal of Marketing Research*, May 1990, pp. 150–62; F. M. Feinberg, B. E. Kahn and L. McAlister, 'Market Share Response When Consumers Seek Variety', *Journal of Marketing Research*, May 1992, pp. 228–37; and B. Kahn and A. M. Isen, 'The Influence of Positive Affect on Variety Seeking Among Safe, Enjoyable Products', *Journal of Consumer Research*, September 1993, pp. 257–70.

[3] E. Rogers, *Diffusion of Innovations,* 3rd edition (Free Press, 1983).

[4] See, however, G. C. Bruner III and R. J. Pomazal, 'Problem Recognition: The Crucial First Stage of the Consumer Decision Process', *Journal of Consumer Marketing*, 1988, 1, pp. 53–63.

[5] A. McFall, 'Priority Patterns and Consumer Behaviour', *Journal of Marketing*, October 1969, pp. 50–5.

[6] See for example R. Elliott, 'How Do the Unemployed Maintain Their Identity in a Culture of Consumption?', *European Advances in Consumer Research*, 1995, pp. 1–4.

[7] See 'Boomer Bucks', *American Demographics,* May 1992, pp. 10–12.

[8] The Henley Centre, *Frontiers: Planning for Consumer Change in Europe,* 1996/1997.

[9] P. Bloch, D. L. Sherrell and N. M. Ridgway, 'Consumer Search: An Extended Framework', *Journal of Consumer Research*, June 1986, pp. 119–26.

[10] M. Zollinger, *Marketing et Stratégies Bancaires: La Métamorphose* (Dunod, 1992).

[11] M. Alba and W. Hutchinson, 'Dimensions of Consumer Expertise', *Journal of Consumer Research*, March 1987, pp. 411–54.

[12] P. H. Bloch, D. Sherrell and N. Ridgway, 'Consumer Search: An Extended Framework', *Journal of Consumer Research*, June 1986, pp. 119–26.

[13] I. Simonson, J. Huber and J. Payne, 'The Relationship Between Prior Brand Knowledge and Information Acquisition Order', *Journal of Consumer Research*, March 1988, pp. 566–78.

[14] M. Bucks, 'The Effects of Product Class Knowledge on Information Search Behavior', *Journal of Consumer Research*, June 1985, pp. 1–16.

[15] J. Urbany, P. R. Dickson and W. L. Wilkie, 'Buyer Uncertainty and Information Search', *Journal of Consumer Research*, September 1989, pp. 208–15.

[16] J. Jacoby and L. B. Kaplan, 'The Components of Perceived Risk', *Advances in Consumer Research*, 1972, pp. 382–92.

[17] K. Gronhaug, 'Risk Indicators, Perceived Risk and Consumers' Choice of Information Sources', *Swedish Journal of Economics*, 1972, pp. 246–62.

[18] J. P. Faivre and D. Duguest, 'L'Étude des Décisions d'Achat par la Méthode des Protocoles', *Cahiers de Recherche du Centre HEC-ISA*, 1981, No. 175.

[19] J. R. Bettman and C. W. Park, 'Effects of Prior Knowledge and Experience and Phase of the Choice Process on Consumer Decision Processes: A Protocol Analysis', *Journal of Consumer Research*, December 1980, pp. 234–48.

[20] B. Dubois, 'Information Display Boards: A Critical Review', *ESOMAR Conference Proceedings*, 1982, pp. 87–102.

[21] D. McGinnis and L. Price, 'The Role of Imagery in Information Processing: Review and Extensions', *Journal of Consumer Research*, March 1987, pp. 473–90.

[22] See J. Bettman, *An Information Processing Theory of Consumer Choice* (Addison-Wesley, 1979).

[23] J. R. Bettman and P. Kakkar, 'Effects of Information Presentation Format on Consumer Information Acquisition Strategies', *Journal of Consumer Research*, March 1977, pp. 233–40; and S. Painton and J. W. Gentry, 'Another Look at the Impact of Information Presentation Format', *Journal of Consumer Research*, September 1985, pp. 240–4.

[24] G. Miller, 'The Magical Number Seven Plus or Minus Two: Some Limits on our Capacity for Processing Information', *Psychological Review*, March 1956, pp. 81–97.

[25] J. Jacoby, D. Speller and G. K. Berning, 'Brand Choice Behaviour as a Function of Information Load: Replication and Extensions', *Journal of Consumer Research*, June 1974, pp. 33–42; also see J. Jacoby, 'Perspectives on Information Overload', *Journal of Consumer Research*, March 1984, pp. 432–5.

[26] See D. Gensch and S. Ghose, 'Elimination by Dimension', *Journal of Marketing Research*, November 1992, pp. 417–29.

[27] J. Huber and N. M. Klein, 'Adapting Cut-offs to the Choice Environment: The Effects of Attribute Correlation and Reliability', *Journal of Consumer Research*, December 1991, pp. 346–57.

[28] I. Simonson and A. Tversky, 'Choice in Context: Trade-off Contrast and Extremeness Aversion', *Journal of Marketing Research*, August 1992, pp. 281–95.

[29] J. R. Hauser, G. L. Urban and B. D. Weinberg, 'How Consumers Allocate Their Time When Searching for Information', *Journal of Marketing Research*, November 1993, pp. 452–66.

[30] W. L. Moore and D. R. Lehmann, 'Individual Differences in Search Behavior for a Nondurable', *Journal of Consumer Research*, December 1980, pp. 296–307.

[31] S. E. Beatty and S. Smith, 'External Search Effort: An Investigation Across Several Product Categories', *Journal of Consumer Research*, June 1987, pp. 83–95. See also G. C. Kiel and R. Layton, 'Dimensions of Consumer Information Seeking Behavior', *Journal of Marketing Research*, May 1981, pp. 255–9.

[32] N. Srinivasan and B. Ratchford, 'An Empirical Test of a Model of External Search for Automobiles', *Journal of Consumer Research*, September 1991, pp. 233–42; and D. Midgley, 'Patterns of Interpersonal Information Seeking for the Purchase of a Symbolic Product', *Journal of Marketing Research*, February 1983, pp. 74–83.

[33] J. E. Urbany, P. R. Dickson and W. L. Wilkie, 'Buyer Uncertainty and Information Search', *Journal of Consumer Research*, September 1989, pp. 208–15.

34 See A. Tybout *et al.*, 'Information Availability as a Determinant of Multiple Request Effectiveness', *Journal of Marketing Research*, August 1983, pp. 280–90.

35 J. Jacoby, R. Chestnut and W. Silberman, 'Consumer Use and Comprehension of Nutrition Information', *Journal of Consumer Research*, September 1977, pp. 119–28.

36 N. Giges, 'Comparative Ads: Better than ...', *Advertising Age*, 22 September 1980, pp. 59–62.

37 P. W. Miniard *et al.*, 'A Re-examination of the Relative Persuasiveness of Comparative and Non-comparative Advertising', *Advances in Consumer Research*, 1994, pp. 299–313.

38 L. Golden, 'Consumer Reactions to Explicit Brand Comparisons in Advertisements', *Journal of Marketing Research*, November 1979, pp. 517–32.

39 D. J. Lincoln and A. Coskun Samli, 'Empirical Evidence of Comparative Advertising's Effects: A Review and Synthesis', in N. Beckwith *et al.* (eds), *Proceedings of the 1979 Educators Conference* (American Marketing Association, 1979) pp. 361–6.

40 See G. E. Belch, 'An Examination of Comparative and Non-comparative Ads', *Journal of Marketing Research*, 1981, pp. 333–49.

41 For additional reading on the topic of comparative advertising, see T. E. Barry, 'Comparative Advertising: What Have We Learned in Two Decades?', *Journal of Advertising Research*, March–April 1993, pp. 19–29; C. Pechmann and S. Ratheshwar, 'The Use of Comparative Advertising for Brand Positioning: Association versus Differentiation', *Journal of Consumer Research*, September 1991, pp. 145–60; and S. Demirdijian, 'Sales Effectiveness of Comparative Advertising', *Journal of Consumer Research*, December 1987, pp. 372–8.

42 M. Sujan and C. Dekleva, 'Product Categorisation and Inference Making: Some Implications for Comparative Advertising', *Journal of Consumer Research*, 1987, pp. 372–8.

43 J. B. Cohen and K. Basu, 'Alternative Models of Categorisation: Toward a Contingent Processing Framework', *Journal of Consumer Research*, March 1990, pp. 393–408.

44 See E. Rosch, 'Principles of Categorisation', in E. Rosch and B. B. Lloyd (eds), *Recognition and Categorization* (Lawrence Erlbaum, 1978).

45 M. D. Johnson, 'The Differential Processing of Product Category and Non-comparable Choice Alternatives', *Journal of Consumer Research*, December 1989, pp. 300–9.

46 M. Sujan, 'Consumer Knowledge: Effects on Evaluation Strategies Mediating Consumer Judgements', *Journal of Consumer Research*, June 1985, pp. 31–46.

47 J. Meyers-Levy and A. M. Tybout, 'Schema Congruity as a Basis for Product Evaluation', *Journal of Consumer Research*, June 1989, pp. 39–55. See also M. Sujan and J. R. Bettman, 'The Effects of Brand Positioning Strategies on Consumers' Brand and Category Perceptions: Some Insights from Schema Research', *Journal of Marketing Research*, November 1989, pp. 454–67.

48 G. Sperling, 'The Information Available in Brief Visual Presentations', *Psychological Monographs*, 1960, 11–74.

49 V. S. Folkes, 'The Availability Heuristic and Perceived Risk', *Journal of Consumer Research*, June 1989, pp. 12–23.

50 On the price–quality relationship, see D. M. Gardner, 'Is There a Generalized Price–Quality Relationship?' *Journal of Marketing Research*, May 1971, pp. 241–3; and K. B. Monroe, 'Buyers' Subjective Perceptions of Price', *Journal of Marketing Research*, 1973, pp. 70–80.

51 D. Maheshwaran, 'Country of Origin as a Stereotype: Effects of Consumer Expertise and Attribute Strength on Product Evaluations', *Journal of Consumer Research*, September 1994, pp. 354–65; and S. T. Hong and R. S. Wyer, Jr, 'Effects of Country-of-Origin and Product-Attribute Information and Product Evaluation: An Information Processing Perspective', *Journal of Consumer Research*, September 1989, pp. 175–87. For an application on luxury goods, see B. Dubois and C. Paternault, 'Does Luxury Have a Home Country?' *Marketing and Research Today*, May 1997, pp. 79–85.

52 H. Beales *et al.*, 'Consumer Search and Public Policy', *Journal of Consumer Research*, June 1981, pp. 11–22.

53 D. Roedder-John, C. A. Scott and J. R. Bettman, 'Sampling Data for Covariation Assessments: The Effects of Prior Beliefs on Search Patterns', *Journal of Consumer Research*, June 1986, pp. 38–47.

54 A. Dick *et al.*, 'Memory Based Inferences During Consumer Choice', *Journal of Consumer Research*, June 1990, pp. 82–93.

55 L. Gregory *et al.*, 'Self-Relevance Scenarios as Mediators of Likelihood Estimates and Compliance: Does Imagining Make it So?' *Journal of Personality and Social Psychology*, 1982, pp. 88–99.

56 C. P. Duncan, 'Consumer Market Beliefs: A Review of the Literature and an Agenda for Future Research', *Advances in Consumer Research*, 1990, pp. 729–35. See also G. T. Ford and R. A. Smith, 'Inferential Beliefs in Consumer Evaluations: An Assessment of Alternative Processing Strategies', *Journal of Consumer Research*, December 1987, pp. 363–71.

57 G. L. Sullivan and K. J. Berger, 'An Investigation of the Determinants of Cue Utilization', *Psychology and Marketing*, Spring 1987, pp. 63–74.

58 M. Burcks, *op. cit.*

59 M. Rotschild *et al.*, 'Hemispherically Lateralized EEG as a Response to Television Commercials', *Journal of Consumer Research*, September 1988, pp. 185–98.

60 See for example C. Janiszewski, 'The Influence of Non-attended Material on the Processing of Advertising Claims', *Journal of Marketing Research*, August 1990, pp. 263–78; and M. L. Rotschild and Y. J. Huyn, 'Predicting Memory for Components of TV Commercials from EEG', *Journal of Consumer Research*, March 1990, pp. 472–8.

61 V. S. Folkes *et al.*, 'When to Say When: Effects of Supply on Usage', *Journal of Consumer Research*, December 1993, pp. 467–77.

62 R. Thaler, 'Mental Accounting and Consumer Choice', *Marketing Science*, Summer 1985, pp. 199–205. See also T. B. Heath, S. Chatterjee and K. Russo France, 'Mental Accounting and Changes in Price: The Frame Dependence of Reference Dependence', *Journal of Consumer Research*, June 1995, pp. 90–7.

63 For a recent example of how such areas are measured, see C. Phillips, 'Guardian Properties: The Management of a Local and an International Shopping Centre', in H. H. Larsen (ed.), *Cases in Marketing* (Sage, 1997), pp. 142–69.

64 P. Kotler, Professor Honoris Causa Address, HEC, France, 16 September 1998.

65 P. Kotler, 'Atmospherics as a Marketing Tool', *Journal of Retailing*, Winter 1973/1974, pp. 48–64. See also K. Spies, F. Hesse and K. Loesch, 'Store Atmosphere, Mood, and Purchasing Behaviour', *International Journal of Research in Marketing*, February 1997, pp. 1–18.

66 For more reading on impulse buying, see D. T. Kollat and R. P. Willett, 'Customer Impulse Purchasing Behavior', *Journal of Marketing Research*, February 1967, pp. 21–31; and D. Rook, 'The Buying Impulse', *Journal of Consumer Research*, September 1982, pp. 189–99.

67 Ronald Curhan, 'The Relationship between Shelf Space and Unit Sales in Supermarkets' (Marketing Science Institute: December 1971).

68 A. G. Woodside and J. W. Davenport, 'The Effect of Salesman Similarity and Expertise on Consumer Behavior', *Journal of Marketing Research*, 1974, pp. 433–6; and M. L. Rischins, 'An Analysis of Consumer Interaction Styles in the Marketplace', *Journal of Consumer Research*, June 1983, pp. 73–82.

69 'A Study of Jewellers', unpublished report, J. Walter Thompson.

70 See M. Uncles and G. Laurent, editorial to the special issue on brand loyalty of the *International Journal of Research in Marketing*, 1997, 14, pp. 399–404; J. Jacoby and R. W. Chestnut, *Brand Loyalty, Measurement and Management* (John Wiley, 1978); M. Mellens, M. G. Dekimpe and J. B. Steenkamp, 'A Review of Brand-loyalty Measures in Marketing', *Tijdschrift voor Economie en Management*, 1996, pp. 507–33; and P. Hawkes, 'Building Brand Loyalty and Commitment', *Journal of Brand Management*, 1994, pp. 337–47. For a different view, see A. S. C. Ehrenberg, *Repeat-Buying: Facts, Theory and Applications* (Griffin, 1988).

71 B. Dubois and G. Laurent, 'A Situational Approach to Brand Loyalty', in E. Arnold and L. Scott (eds), *Advances in Consumer Research*, 1999, Vol. 26, pp. 657–63.

72 J. N. Kapferer and G. Laurent, *op. cit.*

73 R. Enrico, *Cola Wars* (Intereditions, 1986), preface by B. Dubois.

74 *Marketing Bulletin*, Europanel 1996, pp. 1–24; see also *Trends in Europe*, Food Marketing Institute, 1995.

75 For more on food habits, see S. Askegaard and T. K. Madsen, 'The Local and the Global: Exploring Traits of Homogeneity and Heterogeneity in European Food Cultures', *International Business Review*, 1998, Vol. 7.

76 D. Smith and H. S. Solgaard, 'Is There a Global Convergence in Consumer Tastes?' *CEMS Business Review*, 1997, 2, pp. 73–85. See also D. Smith and J. R. Skalnik, 'Changing Patterns in the Consumption of Alcoholic Beverages in Europe and in the United States', *European Advances in Consumer Research*, Vol. 2 (Provo: ACR, 1995), pp. 343–55.

77 M. Saghafi and D. Sciglimpaglia, 'Marketing in an Integrated Europe', in M. Bergadaà (ed.), *Marketing Today and for the 21st Century*, Vol. 2, Essec: Proceedings of the 24th EMAC Conference, (1995), pp. 1221–41.

78 M. M. Bergadaà, 'The Role of Time in the Action of the Consumer', *Journal of Consumer Research*, December 1990, pp. 289–302. See also L. P. Feldman and J. Hornik, 'The Use of Time: An Integrated Conceptual Model', *Journal of Consumer Research*, March 1981, pp. 407–19.

79 C. Felker Kaufman, P. M. Lane and J. D. Linquist, 'Exploring More than 24 Hours a Day: A Preliminary Investigation of Polychronic Time', *Journal of Consumer Research*, December 1991, pp. 392–401.

80 J. Voss and R. Blackwell, 'Market for Leisure Time', in M. J. Schlinger (ed.), *Advances in Consumer Research*, Vol. 2, 1975, pp. 837–45.

81 S. R. Linder, *The Married Leisure Class* (Columbia University Press).

82 R. J. Graham, 'The Role of Perception of Time in Consumer Research', *Journal of Consumer Research*, March 1981, pp. 335–42.

83 P. E. Hendrix, T. C. Kinnear and J. R. Taylor, 'The Allocation of Time by Consumers', in W. L. Wilkie (ed.), *Advances in Consumer Research*, 1979, Vol. 6, pp. 38–44.

84 W. Mischel, 'Processes in Delay of Gratification', in L. Berkowitz (ed.), *Advances in Experimental Social Psychology*, Vol. 7 (Academic Press, 1974) pp. 238–92.

85 B. Dubois, 'Financial Investment Choices in Developed and Emerging Countries: A Cross-National Comparison', *Proceedings of the Fifth International Conference on Marketing and Development*, Beijing, June 1995.

86 Y. Evrard, 'Consumer Satisfaction as a Social Indicator', *ESOMAR Congress Proceedings*, Social Change Analysis, 1980. Also see C. Drige and D. Halstead, 'Post-purchase Hierarchies of Effects: The Antecedents and Consequences of Satisfaction for Complainers and Non-Complainers', *International Journal of Research in Marketing*, 1991, pp. 315–28.

87 In the marketing literature, this is known as the disconfirmation model. See R. Oliver, *Satisfaction: A Behavioral Perspective on the Consumer* (McGraw-Hill, 1996). See also P. C. Wilton and D. K. Tse, 'Models of Consumer Satisfaction: An Extension', *Journal of Marketing Research*, May 1988, pp. 204–12; and J. E. Swan and I. F. Trawick, 'Disconfirmation of Expectations and Satisfaction with a Retail Service', *Journal of Retailing*, Fall 1981, pp. 49–67.

88 See however G. A. Churchill and C. Surprenant, 'An Investigation into the Determinants of Customer Satisfaction', 1982, University of Wisconsin Working Paper, pp. 1–82.

89 R. N. Bolton and J. H. Dieuw, 'A Longitudinal Analysis of the Impact of Service Change on Consumer Attitudes', *Journal of Marketing*, January 1991, pp. 1–9.

90 T. R. Wotruba and P. L. Duncan, 'Are Consumers Really Satisfied?' *Business Horizons*, February 1975, pp. 85–90.

91 See F. F. Reicheld, *The Loyalty Effect: The Hidden Force Behind Growth, Profits, and Lasting Value* (Harvard Business School Press, 1996).

92 See J. M. M. Blomer and H. D. P. Kasper, 'The Complex Relationship between Consumer Satisfaction and Brand Loyalty', *Journal of Economic Psychology*, 1995, 16, pp. 311–29. See

also R. T. Rust and A. J. Zahorik, 'Customer Satisfaction, Customer Retention, and Market Share', *Journal of Retailing*, 1993, pp. 193–215.

[93] J. Cronin, Jr and S. A. Taylor, 'Measuring Service Quality: A Reexamination and Extension', *Journal of Marketing*, July 1992, pp. 351–7. Also see M. B. Holbrook and K. P. Corfman, 'Quality and Value in the Consumption Experience: Phaedrus Rides Again', in J. Jacoby and J. C. Olson (eds), *Perceived Quality: How Consumers View Stores and Merchandise* (Lexington Books, 1985), pp. 31–58.

[94] A. Andreasen, 'A Taxonomy of Consumer Satisfaction/Dissatisfaction Measures' (University of Illinois Research Papers, 1976).

[95] J. Singh, 'Consumer Complaint Intentions and Behavior: Definitional and Taxonomical Issues', *Journal of Marketing*, January 1988, pp. 93–107.

[96] R. N. Cardozo, 'An Experimental Study of Customer Effort, Expectation, and Satisfaction', *Journal of Marketing Research*, August 1965, pp. 244–9.

[97] J. Anderson, 'Arguments Concerning Representations for Mental Imagery', *Psychological Review*, 1978, pp. 249–77. See also J. W. Gamble, 'The Expectations Paradox: The More You Offer Customer, Closer You are to Failure', *Marketing News*, 14 March 1988, p. 38.

[98] G. Allenby, 'A Unified Approach to Identifying, Estimating and Testing Demand Structures with Aggregate Scanner Data', *Marketing Science*, Summer 1989, pp. 265–80. See also the special issue of the *International Journal of Research in Marketing* (1991) dedicated to an analysis of panel data.

[99] See R. C. Blattberg *et al.*, *The Marketing Information Revolution* (Harvard Business School Press, 1995).

9

The decision-making unit

Learning objectives

After reading this chapter, you will understand:

1 the nature of the family as a decision-making unit and the various roles played by its members;

2 the variety of methods which have been used to measure relative influence within the family;

3 the many factors which explain why members' relative influence varies across families;

4 the concept of the family life-cycle;

5 the functions played by family structures;

6 the type of conflicts which may exist within the family and their modes of resolution.

Key words

decision-making unit	syncratic	relative contribution
initiator	autonomous and	theory
influencer	autocratic decisions	family life-cycle
decision maker	autocratic and	consumer socialisation
buyer	democratic families	conflict
user	patriarchal and	conflict management
relative influence	matriarchal	
influence triangle	structures	

Until now we have defined and analysed the consumer as if he or she were a single physical person. We have also assumed that the buyer and the consumer were one and the same. For everyday products (a packet of cigarettes, a pair of tights), it is often true that the buyer and the consumer are the same person. Most men buy their cigarettes themselves and most women buy their own tights. On the other hand, for many products (food, home equipment, financial services) such an assumption is inaccurate as many people intervene in the purchase and consumption process and decisions are often 'muddled through'.[1] In such cases, one can talk about collective decision making and the notion of the consumer as an individual must be abandoned in favour of that of a **decision-making unit**.

For relatively complex purchases, we can imagine up to five roles linked to a purchase decision. First there is the **initiator**, the person who is at the origin of the idea. In a company, for a fax machine this could be a secretary, a manager, a member of the purchasing department, or even someone from outside such as a sales representative. Next there is the **influencer**, anyone who either directly or indirectly plays a part in somebody's purchase decision. For important purchases the list of people influencing the decision can be quite long, from the author of a comparative test published in a consumers' review to a star using her popularity to recommend a product on television. We come next to the **decision maker(s)**, often involved in information search. It is they who make the evaluation and select from among all the various options: brand, model, place, time, and so on. The **buyer** makes the transaction itself by taking possession of the product in exchange for money. Finally, the **user** makes use of the product to get the required performance corresponding to its functions. Sometimes, the product is destroyed on its first use (this is often the case for food products), and other times it is reused many times (durable goods).

In some cases, all these roles are filled by one and the same person and we thus talk about the consumer. If, noticing that my biro has broken, I go to the local stationer's shop to buy a new one, I am at once initiator, influencer, decision maker, buyer and consumer. However, if I buy some dog food recommended by a vet which was put on the shopping list by my wife, who then should be considered as the target of a marketing effort? In general, however, purchasing decisions are rarely made by one individual; they almost always involve a decision-making unit. For example, one study showed that 70 per cent of teenagers choose their parents' bank as their first bank.[2] In the world of domestic consumption, our main area of interest in this book, the most prevalent decision-making unit is undoubtedly the family unit.

In Europe, the 360 million individual consumers represent about 160 million households (defined by the European Community Household Panel as 'shared residence and common housekeeping arrangements') with an average number of 2.2 members per unit. A recent study concluded that the 'traditional family' (usually defined as a man and a woman with or without unmarried children) is largely predominant in Europe – representing about 72 per cent of the population – though different patterns such as living alone or unmarried cohabitation are becoming more popular.[3] Within Europe, however, strong variations exist. Multigenerational living arrangements are still common in Greece, Spain and Portugal. While the number of marriages is decreasing and the number of divorces is increasing almost everywhere in Europe, couples marry much younger in Portugal than in Denmark and the greatest age difference between married couples is observed in Greece. The average household size also varies significantly with 3.1 members in Poland and 3.0

in Portugal but only 2.2 in Germany and 2.1 in Sweden. Even if the growing trend towards households composed of only one person – bachelors, divorcees, the widowed – is more pronounced in northern than southern Europe (34 per cent of all households in Germany and 34 per cent in Denmark, but only 16 per cent in Greece and 14 per cent in Portugal), 90 per cent of respondents to a recent survey indicated that 'family life was one of the most important things to them'.[4] As far as shopping is concerned, the family purchase remains the rule rather than the exception.

Who does what?

The problem of role identification within a family has been the subject of much research and insight, arising partly from home economics and partly from family sociology. To discover the relative influences of household members, certain methodological difficulties have to be resolved.[5] Is it best to proceed via survey questioning or observation? Who and how many people must be interviewed? Together or separately? Which measure of influence should be used?

Most results obtained to date have been based on studies carried out with only one member of the household (in general the mother, as she has often been easier to contact). When both spouses are questioned separately, a reasonable agreement between responses is usually observed;[6] this agreement is better still when the questions refer to specific products rather than general situations, and when results are combined rather than analysed individually.[7] When divergence appears, this is in general due to a tendency on the part of the partners (more often the husband than the wife) to enlarge their role.[8] To corroborate the responses, an interesting but relatively expensive technique can be used called the crossed interview – the husband describes his wife's role and vice versa. Of course, for purchases in their areas of interest (such as toys or holidays), the sample surveyed must be enlarged to cover children[9] as well as teenagers,[10] even though interviewing them raises many methodological as well as ethical problems.[11] For example, it has been found that children have difficulties in generalising about their own behaviour and find it difficult to answer abstract questions.

As for the relative influence measuring instrument, a bipolar scale is commonly used: woman decides – man decides. Less frequently, a number of 'points' are proposed which are divided up based on the self-reported influence; Figure 9.1 presents the results of a study carried out using this method. Twelve electronic consumer goods are positioned on an 'influence triangle' which takes account of the relative influence of the mother, the father and the children.[12] Of course, all family members may have different perceptions and this may explain why somewhat contradictory results have sometimes been found in the literature, depending upon which particular interviewing method was used.[13]

Also worth noting is the ingenious technique of controlled observation, which consists of proposing to each family member a simulated purchase and inferring from their behaviour the way in which they use their relative decision-making

Figure 9.1 The influence triangle

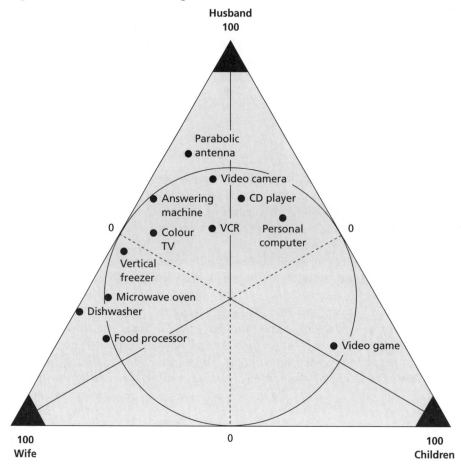

power.[14] The results obtained indicate a wide range of processes taking place. The division of roles varies:

1 according to the product category;

2 for the same product, by the different phases of the purchasing process; and

3 by certain household characteristics.[15]

A Sofres (Taylor Nelson) study carried out among French couples resulted in the results presented in Table 9.1. These figures, which sometimes challenge intuition (how many of us knew that women decide on the brand of beer bought in one out of two cases, for example?), clearly establish the effect of the product category. Based on this evidence, cleaning products appear to be feminine territory, while wine is chosen primarily by men. For men's underwear, the consumer and the decision maker are clearly different: it is the woman who buys in two out of three cases.

Table 9.1 Relative influence of husbands and wives on brand choice for fast-moving goods

	Husbands (%)	*Wives (%)*
Food products		
Mineral water	25	75
Beer	53	47
Wine	63	37
Aperitif	49	51
Instant coffee	20	80
Table oil	12	88
Yoghurt	13	87
Cheese	32	68
Hygiene products		
Shampoo	17	83
Soap	13	87
Toothpaste	23	77
Shaving cream	64	36
Cleaning products		
Floor cleaning	7	93
Heavy-duty washing powder	5	95
Aluminium paper	6	94
Other		
Pet food	22	78
Men's underwear	34	66

Source: Sofres

The distribution of influence observed corresponds to a division of tasks within the family.[16] In fact, products and services fall into specific spheres of influence. The way a product is used appears to be more revealing than its nature; for example, it is generally the female of the household who buys cleaning products, except perhaps those used for washing the car. In a sense, a family can be compared to a corporation with members taking on different responsibilities such as procurement, accounting, general management, and so on. To account for the resulting spheres of influence, triangular representations are often used such as that shown in Figure 9.2, arising from an INSEE study carried out among 5000 households.[17] On this triangle, six zones appear corresponding to specific functional areas. First, the major decisions. These concern the choice of friends, where to go on holiday, where to live and children-related issues. For most couples, these decisions – known as **syncratic** decisions – are reached jointly. They relate to the big issues of family life. If the family was a corporation, this area would be the responsibility of the board of directors. Decisions regarding major items, which include furnishings for the home and electrical goods, are also mainly shared – these are investment decisions. Most often, the decision-making process involves accommodation rather than consensus. For provisions (clothes, ordinary purchases) we enter the daily management area, more tactical, culminating in household purchases (food, cleaning products,

Figure 9.2   The division of tasks within the family

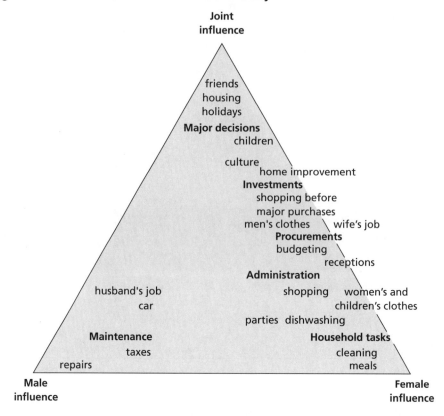

etc.) largely under female control. The administration (budget management, financial matters) occupies a separate position; it is either the man or the woman who deals with it but rarely both – decisions are, therefore, **autonomous** ones. Finally, occasional household maintenance is male territory. This concerns minor repair work or even washing the car (**autocratic** decision).

Some variation is observed in Europe regarding the allocation of tasks within the household. Table 9.2 opposite compares the percentage of men who 'do something' in each of the following areas: shopping, washing the dishes, taking children to school, dressing them, cooking and housekeeping. A useful feature of this Euro-barometer survey is that, in most cases, questions were asked to both adult members of the family, allowing some cross-validation of results. Interestingly enough, 'southern' husbands tend to participate more in 'socially visible' activities such as shopping but seem minimally involved in more domestic chores such as washing the dishes or housekeeping.

Of course, for certain products, the decision-making unit enlarges to include the children. According to one study, they influence toy purchases in only 5 per cent of cases when they are less than six years old. However, their influence increases with

Table 9.2 What do husbands do in Europe?

	According to wives						According to husbands					
	Shopping	Washing dishes	Taking children to school	Dressing children	Cooking	House keeping	Shopping	Washing dishes	Taking children to school	Dressing them	Cooking	House keeping
	(%)	(%)	(%)	(%)	(%)	(%)	(%)	(%)	(%)	(%)	(%)	(%)
Germany	70*	46	30	21	22	34	72	50	28	24	23	33
Belgium	49	55	35	26	29	29	45	58	37	24	34	33
Denmark	39	55	23	32	36	26	42	53	26	32	26	26
Spain	48	25	42	57	30	29	NA	NA	NA	NA	NA	NA
France	48	48	49	38	37	35	54	44	49	31	27	24
UK	51	72	26	37	48	42	NA	NA	NA	NA	NA	NA
Greece	91	16	16	22	20	13	88	13	23	25	17	12
Ireland	16	18	72	14	10	7	NA	NA	NA	NA	NA	NA
Italy	69	5	39	30	23	12	58	10	45	19	17	11
Netherlands	53	66	6	28	28	34	59	65	8	22	31	38
Portugal	75	37	36	55	39	26	NA	NA	NA	NA	NA	NA

* Read: According to their wives, 70% of husbands participate in shopping activities.
NA: Not available

age: 30 per cent for 6–8-year-olds, 55 per cent for 8–10-year-olds and 70 per cent above ten years. Other studies have found that children tend to convince their parents to choose environmentally friendly products[18] or brands they have seen advertised on television – even when such brands were not aimed at them.[19]

Actually, the situation is more complicated given that the role played by family members evolves according to the different stages in the decision-making process (examined in detail in Chapter 8). The same Sofres study reveals, in the case of household equipment, the modifications shown in Table 9.3. All situations are represented in this table. The influence of the dominant member (male or female, depending upon the product) can be stronger (colour TV) or weaker (carpet) to trigger the purchase than in selecting the brand. Information search, which can be carried out together or separately, seems on the other hand to be more balanced.[20]

Finally, with the evolution of lifestyles, roles change over time. An American study, carried out over a twenty-year period for the same products, showed that food supplies are more often bought by the wife alone today. However, insurance products, particularly life assurance, have become more 'masculine'. Car purchases, the choice of where to live or where to go on holiday are decided jointly much more often than was the case in the past.[21]

How can we explain these results? Also, how do we explain the numerous deviations from the average figures presented in the preceding tables? To take account of the range of family decision-making processes, many factors have been identified. Among the socio-economic variables, whether the wife works or not clearly plays a part. According to one study, in families where the wife does not work, the influence of the husband is four times stronger: the wife has an influence over 20 per cent of purchasing decisions if working but only 5 per cent if she stays at home. This is easy to understand. The husband, sole provider of household resources, enjoys greater economic power, even if it is the wife who actually makes most of the purchases. Another study has revealed that working wives manage the budget in 88 per cent of cases against 66 per cent for housewives; they are also less likely to do the washing up on their own (38 per cent versus 62 per cent) but are more involved in the choice of friends (74 per cent versus 64 per cent). In Europe, only one woman out of three describes herself as a 'housewife' but this jumps to 60 per

Table 9.3 Evolution of influences according to decision stages (percentage of influence)

	Initiator		Information search		Brand choice	
	Husband	Wife	Husband	Wife	Husband	Wife
Washing machine	35	65	45	55	40	60
Linen	5	95	29	71	8	92
Carpets	44	56	44	56	36	64
Colour TV	64	36	57	43	61	39
Camera	55	45	51	49	56	44
Car	76	24	65	35	69	31

Source: Sofres

cent in Ireland and drops to 4 per cent in Denmark.[22] When both partners are working, joint decision making is most common. There even exists a theory known as **relative contribution theory**, according to which the participation of each spouse in household decisions is a function of their relative economic resources.[23] Thus in homes where the husband brings in the major part of the revenue, he tends to take charge of all the important decisions, particularly those relating to the budget. While such a theory is not completely unfounded, a strict proportionality between income and power is observed very rarely.[24]

Socio-professional norms tend to complicate things. Among the working classes, it is often the wife who holds the purse strings, whereas for farm workers, the husband is more dominant. People employed in commerce, craftspeople and the liberal professions divide up tasks more evenly.[25] Where people live also has an impact; in the country, role specialisation is more pronounced than in cities.[26] A higher level of education also increases the percentage of decisions made jointly.

Such influences also rely on cultural influences, illustrated via dominant values as well as religious and national affiliations. A key value in understanding relative influence patterns is the **sex role stereotype** prevailing in the family.[27] Families where sex roles are defined according to very traditional norms (the husband is at work while the wife stays at home) will make decisions taking into account the 'masculine' or 'feminine' character associated with given products or activities. In Japan for example, it is customary for a wife to stay awake, even late at night, to welcome home her husband; she will also avoid interfering with his professional life.[28] In European Protestant households, the husband's influence is traditionally very strong, while it is much less so in Jewish households. An interesting study compared the separation of roles for seven products in five countries: Venezuela, the United States, France, the Netherlands and Gabon (see Figure 9.3).[29] If grocery purchases are made mostly by women everywhere and car purchases by men, other products reveal important differences. For example, the Gabonese husband is much more involved in furniture purchases than the American or even the Venezuelan, while in the Netherlands and France, decisions are made jointly.

Other characteristics also play a part. For example, a limited number of children (one or two) or a small age difference between the parents (less than a few years) tends to increase the proportion of decisions taken together. However, the length of the marriage seems to favour specialisation.[30] When older, each spouse has more clearly marked out their 'turf'[31] even though a few researchers have argued that retired people tend to shop more together given their increased time resources.[32] To integrate all these aspects, a useful notion is that of the **family life-cycle**.

The family life-cycle

A family evolves over time. The notion of a 'family life-cycle' aims to structure this evolution by identifying a number of key stages. Even though various models exist,[33] the most readily accepted arises from family sociology and comprises nine

Figure 9.3   Purchasing decisions in five countries

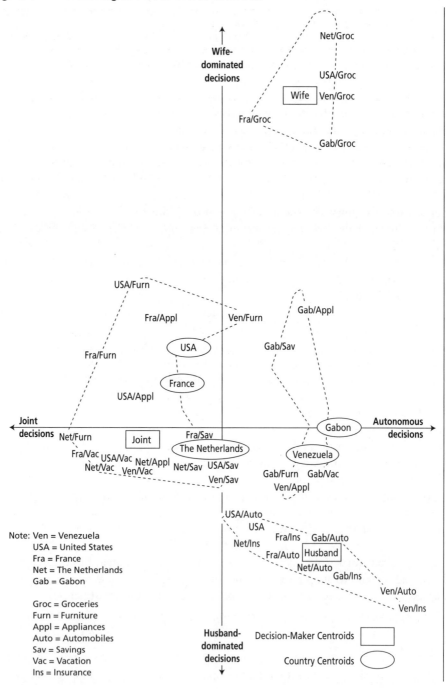

Note: Ven = Venezuela
      USA = United States
      Fra = France
      Net = The Netherlands
      Gab = Gabon

      Groc = Groceries
      Furn = Furniture
      Appl = Appliances
      Auto = Automobiles
      Sav = Savings
      Vac = Vacation
      Ins = Insurance

Figure 9.4 The family life-cycle

---

1 Young singles no longer living with parents
A limited income but a large latitude in using it. Beyond the necessary durable goods to equip the first home outside the family, discretionary spending enables fashions to be followed (clothes, eating out) and is used for entertainment (trips, holidays).

2 Young married couple without children
They enjoy growing revenues, mainly thanks to the woman working. Durable goods (furniture, white goods) and leisure represent an important part of spending.

3 Married couple with children under six
The arrival of the first child often means the mother has to give up work and the available resources decline while the family needs increase: larger house, better equipment (dishwasher, washing machine) as well as everything needed for the children. It becomes more difficult to save.

4 Married couple with children over six
The financial situation improves thanks to the husband's job progression and the wife's return to work. The needs of the children remain significant but diversify – it is the age for bicycles, school spending and piano lessons.

5 Older couples with children
Financially at ease, the family moves house, buys a second car and finalises household goods. Health and education may absorb a large part of the budget.

6 Older couples without children, head of family working
The financial situation reaches its peak. As fundamental needs are satisfied, the level of resources enables the purchase of luxury products and the couple to devote more resources to travelling, leisure and saving for retirement.

7 Older couples without children, head of the family retired
Income declines quickly, while health spending increases. Sometimes the house is exchanged for something smaller.

8 Older single working person
Income is still quite high, certainly meeting needs. Travel, leisure and health spending occupy a major place, depending on the situation.

9 Older single retired person
Income is declining. Primary needs are for attention, affection and security.

---

steps identified and explained in Figure 9.4,[34] while Figure 9.5 presents another similar classification used in the UK. Given their impact over purchasing and consumption behaviour, such classifications are widely used in marketing.[35]

Beyond studies of budgetary responsibility and product-specific monographs,[36] research has shown that:

1 mature mothers of large families, very familiar with everyday products, tend to be more sceptical about innovations;[37]

2 sensitivity to advertising is inversely linked to the phase in the life-cycle – the older we get, the less we consider it;[38]

Figure 9.5   Life-cycle stages in Great Britain

1 Granny Power	14%	People aged 55 to 70. Neither the head of the family nor the partner are in full-time work. Children have left home
2 Grey Power	12%	People aged 45 to 60. The head of the family and/or the partner are working. Children have left home.
3 Silver Power	18%	Married couples with children (aged 5 to 15 years)
4 Younger Silver Power	16%	Young couples with young children (0–4 years)
5 Platinum Power	7%	Married couples under 40 without children
6 Golden Power	15%	Single people under 40.

Source: System 'Life Stages' cited in S. O'Brien and R. Ford, 'Can We at Last Say Goodbye to Social Class?' *Journal of Market Research Society*, July 1988, pp. 289–331

3 the joint nature of family decisions decreases as children are born[39] and with the length of the marriage;[40]

4 the family life-cycle is a good indicator of participation in sports.[41]

Other studies have compared the predictive power of the life-cycle with other variables. For example, it has been shown that the family life-cycle: (a) better accounts for the purchase of durable goods than age;[42] (b) better predicts the degree of agreement between the spouses when buying a car than the length of the marriage;[43] and (c) is a better indicator of leisure activities than age or social class[44] but is less precise than income in explaining clothing purchases.[45]

Of course, the demographic evolution has had a profound impact on the family. Since the 1960s, in France as in all other European countries, the number of households has grown much faster than the overall population. From 1970 to 1995 it has gone from 16 to 23 million, an increase of more than 30 per cent, while the population has grown by only 8 per cent over the same period. In Germany, the number of households is now 37 million for a population of 81 million; similar figures are 22 and 57 million for Great Britain, 12.5 and 40 million for Spain, and 20 and 57 million for Italy. Naturally, the fall in the number of household members accounts for this change. In Western Europe, nearly one family in ten had four or more children just after the Second World War; nowadays there is less than one in twenty. On the other hand, the number of single-person households, which represented less than one-fifth of the total at the end of the 1940s, is close to one-third today (27 per cent in France, 28 per cent in Belgium, 30 per cent in Austria and the Netherlands, 34 per cent in Germany and 40 per cent in Sweden). The decrease in household size itself is the result of many factors, among which are:

• **A lower birth rate** linked to the increase in female employment. No country in Europe (except Ireland) has a fertility rate which is high enough to maintain its population. The European average is now 1.45 children per woman, while 2.1 would be necessary.

- **A decline in marriage** In Western Europe, after Sweden, France is the country where the marriage rate is the lowest. From 417 000 in 1982, the number of French marriages has stabilised at around 280 000 today. The increase in cohabitation in a large part explains this tendency.[46] It directly affects many markets – those for engagement rings, wedding dresses and marriage agencies. The disaffection with marriage is perhaps also explained by hesitation in the face of a decision which demands a longer and longer commitment (fifty years when people get married at 25) in a world which changes ever more quickly. If it remains an important value, it is no longer considered an institution. According to a recent study, less than one person in four considers marriage as an 'indissoluble union'. The new 'pact' (called PACS in France and adopted in late 1998) offers a legal alternative to couples (of all sexual orientations) who do not wish to marry.

- **Marrying later** Throughout Europe people are marrying later; however, the French are delaying marriage longer and longer. The average is 29 years old for men (24 in 1970) and 27 for women (22 in 1970). There are three reasons for this: (a) single people marry later; (b) older single people are more likely to marry; and (c) the age for remarriage increases. There follows from this a whole series of delays in the acquisition of goods such as furniture and electrical appliances.

- **The increase in divorce** In Europe, the UK has the highest divorce rate with 3 divorces per 1000 inhabitants. This is twice as high as in Japan but only two-thirds of the US rate. But strong differences exist between European countries. In Finland and Sweden the rates are comparable with the UK, but they fall to 0.7 in Greece and Spain, 0.4 in Italy and almost zero in Ireland (where divorce has been prohibited for a long time). In fifteen years, the likelihood that couples will divorce has more than doubled, from 14 to 30 per cent. The markets for housing, work and leisure have of course been altered by such developments.[47] Almost half of Club Med clients are people who travel alone.

For marketing managers, modifications in the structure of the family are both an opportunity and a threat.[48] If it has caused problems in a number of traditional markets, it has also given rise to new niche markets, for example the singles market.

Derogatorily termed 'bachelors' and 'spinsters' in the past, the single people of today comprises a wider group including the unmarried, divorced and widowed. Estimated at almost 100 million in Europe, these 'mono-households' have a growing potential for consumption. Single people go twice as often to restaurants, nine times more often to the cinema and buy three times as many books as couples. If they are less well supplied with washing machines and dishwashers, they possess more video recorders, hi-fi equipment and photographic equipment. Their spending at weekends is ten times higher than that of larger households. Many products and services have been designed especially for them: home-delivered food, deep-frozen single portions, launderettes showing videos as well as many leisure clubs, introduction agencies and marriage bureaux. In the future, it would seem that under the combined effects of urbanisation, professional mobility and a change of mentality, this parcelling up of society will continue, resulting in an ever-increasing fall in the proportion of large families.

All this change has made necessary a re-examination of the initial concepts.[49] For example, Management Horizons, an American consulting firm, has constructed a grid of life-cycle against income. There are five stages:

1 young single people;
2 young couples (without children);
3 young parents;
4 mature families;
5 older households (including single people).

For each category, a distinction is made according to whether income is greater or less than the group median.[50] Murphy and Staples have proposed a new cycle also consisting of five major stages and thirteen inter-linked sub-categories[51] (Figure 9.6). Whatever the model adopted, the family life-cycle is a very fruitful notion since it enables the identification of homogeneous groups which can be reached with the help of specifically adapted commercial policies.

Figure 9.6   A modernised family life-cycle

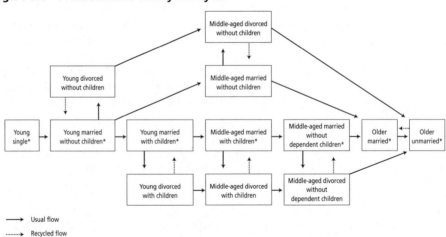

→ Usual flow
┈┈▸ Recycled flow
∗ Traditional family flow

The three roles of the family

Research has also been undertaken focusing on the role of the family in today's society. It has been argued that its three main functions are:

1 to facilitate social life;
2 to provide psychological support; and
3 to provide for the well-being of its members.[52]

Accordingly, the family unit can be understood as a social cell, as a way of organising daily life and as a unit of consumption.

As a **social cell**, the family represents the main mechanism enabling a society to survive. The nature and composition of the family unit relates to the social and cultural environment to provide a framework and a means of sharing power and prestige among its different members. Researchers have thus been led to oppose **autocratic families**, in which the main power is concentrated in a single person, with **democratic families**, where decisions are made jointly.[53] Among the first type, a distinction is made between the **patriarchal** and **matriarchal** mode depending on the dominant sex, the matriarchal mode being less common but still present in certain societies. The second group is classified into several types according to the role of the children. In certain cases such a role is restricted, with the children largely submitting to parental influence, whereas in others the child (or children) takes control and the family organises itself, consciously or unconsciously, around him or her.[54]

Of course, the way family members interact with each other exerts a strong influence over the purchase and consumption of household products. In a patriarchal system, the decision of the 'head of the family' to save more results immediately in a reduction of discretionary spending. Democratic families in contrast are characterised by being predisposed to negotiate. It follows that many purchasing and consumption decisions, whether concerning a single member or the whole unit, are taken together. Additionally, along with the cultural heritage of which they are part, preferences for brands and purchasing strategies are transmitted between generations of the same family. Thus mothers advise their daughters about which make-up products to use and, in certain families, both father and son are Ford or Rover lovers. The process by which children learn how to behave as consumers is known as 'consumer socialisation'.[55]

As an organisational **structure for daily life**, the family defines the use of time as well as the ways in which the various household tasks will be shared out. Studies of time budgets have thus revealed that, on average, a Western European married man spends fourteen and a half hours per day in the home and his wife nearly nineteen. The implications of this structure go far beyond marketing as they concern all family activities, particularly those relating to saving, investment, work and leisure. The family structure and evolution thus define the context in which purchasing and consumption decisions are made. For example, the decision to move from the centre of town to the suburbs can be the reason that the daily visit to the street market is abandoned in favour of a weekly trip to the suburban shopping centre. Purchasing strategies are also affected by changes in family life structure. For example, an enlargement of the family often leads to the need to buy a larger apartment or even a house. Several studies have shown that the order in which the children are born in particular plays a role in triggering certain purchases. Hence the first-born requires an outlay of about 1200 Euros during the first year against 500 Euros for the others. People buy a camcorder for their first child and record on tape all of the baby's first moves, but the next child seldom receives the same level of attention.

As a **unit of consumption**, finally, the family represents the focal point for many purchasing decisions. Meals are consumed together and this influences the kind of food consumed, just as the need to live under the same roof leads to the use of various hygiene and cleaning products. Hence a comparative analysis of spend on the same items depending on the composition of the family reveals clear differences. For example, single people spend less on their housing and clothing than all the other categories. On the other hand, their spend on meals taken outside the home is among the highest.

The collective nature of family consumption almost always implies the design and implementation of an evolving strategy for purchasing the corresponding products and services. Let's take an example. The Smith family has decided, either explicitly or implicitly, to delegate to Mrs Smith the responsibility for buying all the food, and it is her job to understand the preferences and reactions of each person and to take these into account when doing the shopping. Mrs Smith is thus in the role of a 'supplier', having exclusive contact with the sales outlets. Nothing prevents her gradually extending her responsibilities and playing the role of a 'change agent' for the family. Supposing that Mr Smith has run out of razor blades and asks his wife to buy some more the next time she goes shopping. Not finding her husband's usual brand, she buys another and thus triggers a change in her husband's habits and preferences. Similarly, children exposed to a commercial about a particular brand of cornflakes while watching their favourite TV programme may develop a strong preference for this brand and decide to accompany their mother on her next shopping trip to make sure she selects and puts in the trolley the appropriate brand.[56]

In summary, it seems quite artificial and dangerous to analyse purchasing and consumption decisions independently of the environment in which they arise. Buying and consuming are activities which are based upon the household lifestyle, the definition of which they also contribute to. To be thoroughly understood, these activities require a solid knowledge of the way in which tasks are identified and responsibilities shared out within the family.

Conflict and conflict management

Up to this point, we have presented family purchasing decisions as if they were always harmonious. In fact, disagreements often occur in households. The study of conflicts and how they are resolved is important because it clarifies both the dynamics of the purchase and the real nature of decision-making power.[57]

According to research carried out on this topic, it would seem that conflict is relatively common in family purchasing and consumption decisions, the probability of a conflict increasing with the importance of the purchase.[58] An American study revealed that, for the purchase of a home there is disagreement over the location in almost one out of four cases, while an English study led to a slightly lower figure (one out of five).[59] Not all decisions present the same risk of a conflict. The sources of disagreement arising from these two studies appear in Table 9.4. According to these results, it would appear that the time a house is purchased or the moment when it is built are seldom sources of conflict but consensus is more difficult to obtain when it comes to the interior decoration or even the price.

Based on a range of studies, a typology of conflicts may be developed.[60] Conflicts that are hardest to resolve concern the actual objectives behind the purchase. In this case, family members disagree over the need to buy an item at all. In general, such conflicts arise from a different perception of the problem or even of its urgency. Mr Jones wants to change his car because he finds the new models very interesting; Mrs Jones sees this expense as unnecessary, their current car being perfectly satisfactory in her opinion. On the other hand, she feels that the front of the house needs repainting urgently, but her husband thinks it can wait for a while. Coming next are conflicts over the choice of product or brand, where the protagonists agree about the problem, but not its solution. The disagreement could rest on a preference for a particular product over another (for example, a couple both want to go on holiday but he prefers the sea and she the mountains); or the desire for a specific brand rather than another: the son is dying to have the latest Levi 501s but his mother thinks that a less expensive pair of jeans will be perfectly suitable. Conflict could also arise over the point of sale.

Finally, the conflict may be linked to the respective roles of the members of the decision-making unit: there is agreement over the product to buy but not over the

Table 9.4 Conflicts in the choice of a home (percentage of families mentioning a disagreement)

Type of decision	USA (%)	Great Britain (%)
Location	24	20
Interior decoration	24	17
Price	15	12
Style	11	13
Room layout	7	18
Date of construction	4	5
Time of purchase	2	2

Source: S. Douglas, unpublished HEC study

Figure 9.7   Role attribution in decisions made by couples

		Wife thinks the decision will be made:		
		by her husband	jointly	by herself
Husband thinks the	by himself	1	4	2
decision will be	jointly	4	1	4
made:	by his wife	3	4	1

1 = no conflict
2 = conflict by excess: each spouse expects to make the decision
3 = conflict by default: each spouse expects the other to make the decision
4 = partial conflict: only one spouse expects a joint decision

way to acquire it, and particularly over the question of who will go and buy it. For couples, we can identify three kinds of conflict depending on the expectations of each spouse (see Figure 9.7). The 'conflict by excess' (cell 2) arises mostly over products used by both spouses, while the 'conflict by default' (cell 3) is often encountered when the purchase is judged to be a chore, undesirable or not worthwhile. Finally, partial conflicts (cell 4) are more easily resolved to the extent that the territory is claimed by only one partner. If one of the spouses decides alone, the other will feel only surprised or disappointed but not cheated, because he or she was not expecting to take a decision by him or herself.

The analysis of conflict resolution techniques as they apply to purchasing behaviour is an area which has not been explored a great deal. The tactics employed seem to be quite numerous and vary in relation to the nature of the conflict. They have often been grouped around two major strategies, the first based on the search for mutual agreement and the second on confrontation (Figure 9.8).[61] *Role specialisation* belongs to the first group: strategies of agreement. This is a very common and apparently useful mechanism in the case of conflicts related to the objectives of the purchase or the way to proceed. What does it consist of? From the beginning of the marriage or gradually over time, each partner – usually with the agreement of the other – takes care of a certain number of tasks over which their authority is never challenged. For example, in many countries it is the husband who fills in the tax return, the wife rarely being consulted even if her signature is sometimes required at the bottom of the form. In contrast, it is often the wife who controls the children's education and manages the relationship with the school. She takes the children to school, meets the teachers and goes to parents' meetings. For the husband, it is enough to look at the end-of-term reports.

Of course, the 'natural' competence recognised in each spouse and often transferred from cultural models of the societies in which they live can be challenged in the case of failure. It can also evolve over time, for example under the influence of professional changes (for example, the wife giving up work for the birth of their first child) or alterations in the health of one of the spouses (such as illness or disability).

The '*family meeting*' consists of reaching an agreement – not by separating the

Figure 9.8 A typology of modes of family conflict resolution

```
1 Strategies of agreement
        • Role specialisation
        • Family meeting
2 Strategies of confrontation
    2.1 Persuasion strategies
            • Harassment
            • Alertness
            • The 'fait accompli'
            • The involvement of the other
            • The alliance
    2.2 Negotiation strategies
            • Exchange
            • Multiple purchase
            • Postponement
            • The next time
```

roles but by considering each point of view in order to arrive at a final decision (possibly with the aid of a vote). This is the way certain families resolve the problem of place and duration of holiday. Each person states their preference and then they decide together. To a certain extent, the meeting is an adaptation of democratic government at a family level. It is often employed in households where the children have reached an age where they can use reasonable arguments.

Confrontation strategies comprise two types of approach depending on whether persuasion or negotiation is favoured. Among the persuasive tactics, *harassment* seems to be used a lot by children. It consists of continually returning to the issue until satisfaction is provided because the parents give in. *Alertness* is more subtle – it relies on taking advantage of a moment of weakness or fatigue on the part of the partner to gain agreement to the plan. An immediate purchase – or *fait accompli –* is also widely practised, especially when family disagreement is anticipated by the buyer and the choice is irreversible. Alternatively, spouses can *involve their partners* in a shopping trip to try to 'seduce' them. Hence many women ask their husbands to accompany them for important purchases in order to avoid reproach later. Studies carried out on purchases of garments and jewellery also indicate that when made together these tend to be larger. Finally, the *alliance* strategy implies at least three people in the household. The person interested in the acquisition tries to convince one of the other two in order to put pressure on the third. Many children are past masters of this technique, convincing one or other of parents depending on circumstances.

The most common tactic of negotiation is *exchange*. This relies on offering the partner some concessions in order to obtain satisfaction. If Mr Jones buys the latest electronically controlled drill, then Mrs Jones asks for a new coat. In families with children, a form of bargaining or reward system is often negotiated relating to school results in return for pocket money. The *multiple pur-*

chase also relies on this approach; unable to reach agreement, something is bought for everybody. Of course, the kind of product must be suitable – clothes, shoes etc.

'*Postponement*' and '*the next time*' enable the process to be managed over time. The first is used for important purchases where there is a lot of indecision – 'We are not ready, we will have to think, weigh the pros and cons' are familiar statements to the ears of a car salesman. The 'next time' purchase also allows time to be gained against a future promise. When used with their offspring, some parents secretly hope that children will forget or that their tastes will change.

Several attempts have been made to assess how often these various techniques for conflict resolution are used.[62] In Canada for example, it was discovered that for television purchases, the techniques of seeking agreement were used more frequently than negotiation or persuasion tactics.[63] However, each family member had their own preference, for instance family discussion for the husband and a search for extra information by the wife. In Europe, studies have confirmed the use of the multiple-purchase strategy for the choice of holidays (fifteen days by the sea, fifteen in the mountains; or even two weeks in a hotel, two weeks self-catering). Of course these studies are not easy to conduct as families do not always admit to the existence of conflicts in front of strangers and the results obtained perhaps overestimate the degree of a consensus to be found. Also, it appears that each family member overestimates their own influence. Many variables affect the techniques chosen – presence, number and age of the children, educational level of the partners, age, income, and position in the life-cycle. Hence, the tactic of role separation increases in importance with age (and the length of the marriage).

Most results concerning family decision making have been obtained in Western society and are based on the dominant model of the nuclear family (married couple with or without children). Not much is known about how families in other societies function. In Africa, for example, the concept of family is much larger (including cousins, friends and so on) and it would be interesting to carry out comparative studies.[64] Even in the West, few studies have tried to establish the role of grandparents or siblings. For certain purchases (presents offered for birthdays and ceremonies, children's clothes) their impact may well be substantial.

Furthermore, most of what is currently known has arisen from cross-sectional research, conducted at one point in time – like a snapshot. A longitudinal approach aimed at showing how certain family events (birth of a child, children starting school, change of job location, etc.) change the attribution of roles in purchasing, and the styles of consumption of a panel of families would certainly enrich our understanding and provide some useful insights.

Finally, the emergence of new family models (single parents, cohabitation, etc.) has come at the right time to enrich the range of structures observed up until now and will contribute to enhancing the knowledge needed to understand many aspects of collective purchasing and consumption.

Notes

[1] C. W. Park, 'Joint Decisions in Home Purchasing: A Muddling-Through Process', *Journal of Consumer Research*, September 1982, pp. 151–62.

[2] L. Arnaud, 'Le Marché Bancaire des Particuliers', *Revue Banque*, 1983, 432, pp. 1143–8.

[3] 'Statistics in Focus: Population and Social Conditions', *Eurostat* (Office for Official Publications of the European Communities, 1996).

[4] 'Women and Men in the European Union: A Statistical Portrait', *Eurostat* (Office for Official Publications of the European Communities, 1996).

[5] See A. Burns and J. A. Hopper, 'An Analysis of the Presence, Stability, and Antecedents of Husband and Wife Purchase Decision Making Influence: Assessment, Agreement and Disagreement', *Journal of Consumer Research*, 1986, pp. 175–80; K. Corfman, 'Perceptions of Relative Influence, Formation, and Measurement, *Journal of Marketing Research*, 1991, pp. 125–36.

[6] See C. W. Park and E. Iyer, 'An Examination of the Response Pattern in Family Decision Making', in K. Bernhardt *et al.* (eds), *Proceedings of the American Marketing Association Educators Conference*, 1981, p. 148; and H. L. Davis and B. P. Rigaux, 'Perception of Marital Roles in Decision Processes', *Journal of Consumer Research*, June 1974, pp. 51–62.

[7] H. Davis, 'Measurement of Husband–Wife Influence in Consumer Purchase Decisions', *Journal of Marketing Research*, August 1971, pp. 305–12. See R. Peterson *et al.*, 'Husband–Wife Report Disagreement', *International Journal of Research in Marketing*, 1988, pp. 125–36.

[8] H. Davis, S. Douglas and A. Silk, 'Measure Unreliability: A Hidden Threat to Cross National Marketing Research? *Journal of Marketing Research*, Spring 1987, pp. 98–109.

[9] P. Filiatraut and J. R. Brent-Ritchie, 'Joint Purchasing Decisions: A Comparison of Influence Structure in Family and Couple Decision Making', *Journal of Consumer Research*, September 1980, pp. 131–40.

[10] S. E. Beatty and S. Talpade, 'Adolescent Influence in Family Decision-Making: A Replication with Extension', *Journal of Consumer Research*, September 1994, pp. 332–41; and E. Foxman, P. Tansuhaj and K. Ekstrom, 'Family Members' Perceptions of Adolescents' Influence in Family Decision Making', *Journal of Consumer Research*, March 1989, pp. 482–91.

[11] See L. Perrachio, 'Designing Research to Reveal the Young Child's Emerging Competence', *Psychology and Marketing*, Winter 1990, pp. 257–76; and B. Reece, 'Children and Shopping: Some Public Policy Questions', *Journal of Public Policy and Marketing*, 1986, pp. 185–94.

[12] For a complete exposition of the method, see B. Dubois and R. Z. Marchetti, 'The Influence Triangle: A New Methodology for Identifying the Influence Process in Family Buying Decisions', in M. J. Baker (ed.), *Perspectives in Marketing Management*, Vol. 3, Chap. 18 (Wiley, 1992).

[13] J. F. Grashof and D. F. Dixon, 'The Household: The "Proper" Model for Research into Purchasing and Consumption Behavior', *Advances in Consumer Research*, 1980, pp. 486–91; R. A. Peterson, D. L. Alden, M. O. Attir and A. Jolibert, 'Husband–Wife Report Disagreement', *International Journal of Research in Marketing*, 1988, pp. 125–36.

[14] W. Kenkel, 'Family Interaction in Decision Making on Spending', in N. Foote (ed.), *Household Decision Making* (New York University Press, 1961), p. 152.

[15] For an overall review, see H. Davis, 'Decision Making within the Household', *Journal of Consumer Research*, March 1976, pp. 241–60.

[16] See H. Davis, 'Decision-Making Within the Household', *Journal of Consumer Research*, March 1976, pp. 241–60; M. Menasco and D. J. Curry, 'Utility and Choice: An Empirical Study of Wife/Husband Decision-Making', *Journal of Consumer Research*, June 1989, pp. 87–97.

[17] M. Claude and F. de Singly, 'L'Organisation Domestique: Pouvoir et Négotiation', *Economie et Statistique*, 1986, pp. 3–30.

[18] See H. Schlossberg, 'Kids Teach Parents How to Change Their Buying Habit', *Marketing News*, 1992, p. 8.

[19] G. J. Gorn and R. Florsheim, 'The Effects of Commercials for Adult Products on Children', *Journal of Consumer Research*, March 1985, pp. 962–7.

[20] For other similar results, see H. L. Davis and B. P. Rigaux, 'Perception of Marital Roles in Decision Processes', *Journal of Consumer Research*, March 1975, pp. 60–6.

[21] I. C. M. Cunningham and R. T. Green, 'Purchasing Roles in the US Family', *Journal of Marketing Research*, October 1974, p. 63.

[22] *Key Figures: Bulletin of Economic Trends in Europe and Summaries* (Office for Official Publications of the European Communities, July 1997).

[23] See J. Pahl, *Money and Marriage* (Macmillan, 1990).

[24] C. B. Burgoyne, 'Money in Marriage: How Patterns of Allocation both Reflect and Conceal Power', *Sociological Review*, 1990, pp. 634–65.

[25] M. Komarovsky, 'Class Influences in Family Decision Making and Expenditures', in N. Foote (ed.), *Household Decision Making* (New York University Press, 1961), pp. 255–65.

[26] N. Touzard, *Sociologie Familiale* (PUF, 1960).

[27] W. Qualls, 'Household Decision Behaviour: The Impact of Husbands' and Wives' Sex Role Orientation', *Journal of Consumer Research*, September 1987, pp. 264–79.

[28] For other examples, see C. Webster, 'Effects of Hispanic Ethnic Identification on Marital Roles in the Purchase Decision Process', *Journal of Consumer Research*, September 1994, pp. 319–31; R. J. Baran, 'Patterns of Decision Making Influence for Selected Products and Services Among Husbands and Wives Living in the Czech Republic'; and J. B. Ford, M. S. LaTour and T. Henthorne, 'Perception of Marital Roles in Purchase Decision Processes: A Cross-Cultural Study', *Journal of the Academy of Marketing Science*, Spring 1995, pp. 120–31.

[29] See R. T. Green, J. P. Leonardi, J. L. Chandon, I. Cunningham, B. Verhage and A. Strazzieri, 'Societal Development and Family Purchasing Roles: A Cross National Study', *Journal of Consumer Research*, March 1983, p. 436. Also see D. Hempel, 'Family Buying Decisions: A Cross-Cultural Perspective', *Journal of Marketing Research*, August 1974, pp. 295–302.

[30] J. L. McGhee, 'The Vulnerability of Elderly Consumers', *International Journal of Aging and Human Development*, 1983, pp. 223–46.

[31] R. Ferber and L. Lee, 'Husband–Wife Influence in Family Purchasing Behavior', *Journal of Consumer Research*, June 1974, pp. 44–50.

[32] N. Keating, 'What Do I Do With Him 24 Hours a Day? Changes in the Housewife Role at Retirement', *The Gerontologist*, 1980, pp. 437–43.

[33] For a history of the concept, see P. Murphy and W. Staples, 'A Modernised Family Life Cycle', *Journal of Consumer Research*, June 1979, pp. 12–22.

[34] See J. B. Lansing and J. Morgan, 'Consumer Finances Over the Life Cycle', in L. Clark (ed.), *Consumer Behaviour*, Vol. 2 (New York University Press, 1955) adapted by W. Wells and G. Gubar, 'Life Cycle Concept in Marketing Research', *Journal of Marketing Research*, November 1966, pp. 355–63.

[35] A. R. Andreasen, 'Life Status Changes and Changes in Consumer Preferences and Satisfaction', *Journal of Consumer Research*, December 1984, pp. 784–94.

[36] For an example relating to energy consumption, see D. Fritzche, 'An Analysis of Energy Consumption Patterns by State of Family Life Cycle', *Journal of Marketing Research*, May 1981, pp. 227–9.

[37] G. Barton, 'The Life Cycle and Buying Pattern', in L. Clark, *op. cit.*

[38] N. Miller, 'The Life Cycle and the Impact of Advertising', in L. Clark, *op. cit.*

[39] W. Kenkel, 'Family Interaction in Decision Making on Spending', in N. Foote *Household Decision Making* (New York University Press, 1961).

[40] D. Blood and D. Wolfe, *Husbands and Wives: The Dynamics of Married Living* (Free Press, 1960); and D. Granbois, 'The Role of Communication in the Family Decision Making Process', in S. Greyser (ed.), *Proceedings of the American Marketing Association*, 1963.

[41] E. Laird Landon Jr and W. Locander, 'Family Life Cycle and Leisure Behavior Research', *Advances in Consumer Research* (ACR, 1983), pp. 133–8.

[42] *Ibid.*

[43] E. P. Cox III, 'Family Purchase Decision Making and the Process of Adjustment', *Journal of Marketing Research*, May 1975, pp. 189–95.

[44] R. Hisrich and M. Peters, 'Selecting the Superior Segmentation Correlate', *Journal of Marketing Research*, July 1974, pp. 60–3.

[45] J. Wagner and S. Hanna, 'The Effectiveness of Family Life Cycle Variables in Consumer Expenditure Research', *Journal of Consumer Research*, December 1983, pp. 281–91.

[46] See A. Audirac, 'La Cohabitation: Un Million de Couple Non-Mariés', *Economie et Statistiques*, March 1985, pp. 13–35.

[47] J. H. McAlexander, J. W. Schouten and S. D. Roberts, 'Consumer Behavior and Divorce', in *Research in Consumer Behavior* (JAI Press, 1992).

[48] M. Martin Young, 'Disposition of Possession During Role Transitions', *Advances in Consumer Research*, 1991, pp. 33–9.

[49] See C. Schaninger and W. Danko, 'A Conceptual and Empirical Comparison of Alternative Household Life Cycle Models', *Journal of Consumer Research*, March 1993, pp. 580–94; R. Wilkes, 'Housesomd Life-Cycle Stages: Transitions, and Product Expenditures', *Journal of Consumer Research*, June 1995, pp. 27–42; and S. D. Roberts, P. K. Voli and K. A. Johnson, 'Beyond the Family Cycle: An Inventory of Variables for Defining the Family as Consumption Unit', *Developments in Marketing Science*, 15 (Academy of Marketing Science, 1992), pp. 71–5.

[50] T. Murrane, *Consumer Market Matrix: A Segmentation Strategy* (Management Horizons, 1984).

[51] P. Murphy and W. Staples, *op. cit.* See also M. Gilly and B. Enis, 'Recycling the Family Life Cycle: A Proposal for Redefinition', *Advances in Consumer Research* (ACR, 1981), pp. 271–6.

[52] G. Allan, *Family Life* (Blackwell, 1985); G. S. Becker, *A Treatise of the Family* (Harvard University Press, 1991); A. Grossbard-Schechtman, 'Gary Becker's Theory of the Family: Some Interdisciplinary Considerations', *Sociology and Sociological Research*, 1981, 1, pp. 1–11; and Y. Castellan, *Psychologie de la Famille* (Privat, 1993). It is worth noting that depending upon culture, one aspect of the family unit may prevail over the other two. For example, in China the family is primarily considered as a micro-model of society, while in the USA it is rather viewed as an extension of the self. See Y. Pan and W. Vanhonacker, 'Chinese Ethnicity: Value Structure and Family Orientation. A Comparison with American Culture', *European Advances in Consumer Research*, 1993, pp. 222–5.

[53] For different classifications based on family value orientations and their evolution, see P. Laslett and R. Wall (eds), *Household and Family in Past Time* (Cambridge University Press, 1972); E. Todd, 'Le poids des structures familiales', *Sciences Humaines*, February 1996, p. 37; D. Olson and M. L. McCubbin, *Families: What Makes Them Work* (Sage, 1993); and G. S. Becker, *op. cit.*

[54] See W. Becker, 'Consequences of Different Kinds of Parental Discipline', in M. L. Hoffman and L. W. Hoffman (eds), *Review of Child Development Research*, 1964, pp. 169–204. For illustrations of child influence or parental yielding in consumer research, see L. Isler, E. T. Popper and S. Ward, 'Children's Purchase Requests and Parental Responses: Results from a Diary Study', *Journal of Advertising Research*, October/November 1987, pp. 28–39.

[55] S. Ward, 'Consumer Socialization', in H. Kassarjian and T. Robertson (eds), *Perspectives in Consumer Behavior*, (Scott, Foresman, 1980), p. 380; see also G. P. Moschis, 'The Role of Family Communication in Consumer Socialization of Children and Adolescents', *Journal of Consumer Research*, March 1985, pp. 898–913; and R. L. Moore and G. P. Moschis, 'The Role of Family Communication in Consumer Learning', *Journal of Communication*, Autumn 1981, pp. 42–51.

[56] See C. Atkin, 'Observation of Parent–Child Interaction in Supermarket Decision-making', *Journal of Marketing*, October 1978, pp. 41–5. See also H. H. Stipp, 'Children as Consumers', *American Demographics*, February 1988, pp. 78–82.

[57] See W. J. Qualls and F. Jafffe, 'Measuring Conflict in Household Decision Behavior: Read My Lips and Read My Mind', *Advances in Consumer Research*, 1992, pp. 522–31.

[58] See K. Corfman and D. Lehmann, 'Models of Cooperative Group Decision-Making and Relative Influence: An Experimental Investigation of Family Purchase Decisions', *Journal of Consumer Research*, June 1987, pp. 1–13.

[59] S. Douglas, HEC unpublished manuscript.

[60] See M. C. Nelson, 'The Resolution of Conflict in Joint Purchase Decisions by Husbands and Wives: A Review and Empirical Test', *Advances in Consumer Research*, 1988, pp. 436–41.

[61] See H. Davis, *op. cit.* Also see L. Krishnamurthi, 'Conjoint Models of Family Decision Making', *International Journal of Research in Marketing*, 1988, pp. 185–98; and F. Boecker, 'La Formulation des Préférences au sein des Familles dans le Cas des Biens Durables', *Recherche et Applications en Marketing*, 1992, 7, pp. 51–66.

[62] See, for example, R. Spiro, 'Persuasion in Family Decision Making', *Journal of Consumer Research*, March 1983, pp. 393–401.

[63] P. Filiatraut and J. R. Brent Ritchie, *op. cit.*

[64] See, by way of example, P. H. Coffi, 'Alimentation et Valeurs: Le Cas du Changement des Habitudes Alimentaires dans les Foyers Abidjanais', unpublished doctoral dissertation, HEC 1991.

10

Purchase and consumption situations

Learning objectives

After reading this chapter, you will understand:

1 the concept of a purchase and consumption situation;

2 how situations are identified and measured;

3 the impact of situational factors on consumer behaviour;

4 the implications attached to situational variables for marketing strategy and action.

Key words

situation	situational inventories	situational segmentation
context	attribution theory	situational positioning

'What is your favourite drink? Which brand of biscuit do you buy? What jewellery do you like to wear?' How many times have we heard or even asked this type of question? How many times have you given or received the response: 'It depends!' But what does it depend on? Less on permanent consumer or product characteristics, it seems, than on the circumstances surrounding purchase and consumption. Whether it is a hot or cold day, whether you are buying something for yourself or someone else, or whether it's a special occasion modifies your purchase decision and in some cases may even reverse it. It all depends on the **situation**.

Consumer research has traditionally focused on product attributes or consumer profiles, which are relatively easy to measure, and has until recently paid less attention to situational factors. Even today many studies measure 'habitual' purchasing behaviour while treating situational factors as an undesirable bias that interferes with results. Recent developments in numerous markets challenge this approach. As a result of increased purchasing power, the explosion of the product offering and the reduced impact of social norms on their lives, consumers are continually adapting their behaviour and reassessing their expectations and intentions.[1] More and more companies admit that they are finding it increasingly difficult to understand this ever more inconsistent and unpredictable consumer[2] with traditional techniques. In the era of the 'chameleon' consumer, the situational approach offers a fresh perspective which places it alongside the great traditions of consumer research.

Taking the situation into consideration requires a different approach to those presented until now in this book. Instead of analysing the influence of consumer characteristics on purchasing decisions, the situational approach sees the **context** of the buy as the essential variable. The impact of situational factors is probably best demonstrated when comparing gift purchases with personal purchases.[3] For many product categories, the gift is an essential dimension of the purchase. One study, for example, showed that 40 per cent of all cameras and 80 per cent of those owned by women are purchased as gifts.[4] Gift purchases represent 4.3 per cent of annual household spending in the UK and 13 per cent in the USA.[5]

According to the situational approach, the consumer is one of a number of equally important parameters, such as the product or the environment. Inspired by studies of field theory in psychology[6] and ecological research,[7] this approach considers that the purchase act is a result of certain forces (atmospheric conditions, for example) which are beyond the control of individual determinism. The situational approach is more descriptive and predictive than truly explicative. It examines co-variation rather than causal relationships. It considers the buying and consuming situation as a lived-in and observable phenomenon, one which results from a complex chemistry of contingent factors.

In this last chapter we present both the dimensions and the results derived from this approach, as well as identifying its limits and likely evolution.

Situating the situation

Despite common use in everyday language, the word 'situation' is not easy to define and remains difficult to apply.[8] In essence, a situation is a configuration of elements which stand out in time and space. For example, a Sunday family picnic or queuing at the supermarket checkout on a Saturday afternoon. The two types of situation of particular interest here are, of course, purchase and consumption situations.[9] How can these be characterised?

Belk, one of the first to address this question, refers to the situation as 'all those factors particular to a time and place of observation which do not follow from a knowledge of personal (intra-individual) and stimulus (choice alternative) attributes, and which have a demonstrable and systematic effect on current behaviour'.[10] Since it restricts the situational field solely to those elements which are supposed to have an impact on behaviour, this definition poses a problem because it tends to confuse the determinants of a situation – that is, its attributes and their effect.[11] Nevertheless, it provides us with a basis from which we can organise the unlimited number of stimuli which characterise a given environment. The personal traits of a consumer (sex, age, personality) and the stable properties of objects (for example, their texture, colour and size) are explicitly excluded since they do not vary from one situation to another. Almost everything else is situational.

Generally speaking, a situation can be described in terms of five elements:[12]

1 the physical environment (space, light, temperature, sound);

2 the social environment (for example, the absence or presence of others);

3 time (the time of day, the season, the time elapsed since the last purchase);

4 the role context (for example, a business trip or a holiday); and

5 the conditions determining the mental state of the individual in the situation, for example his or her mood or emotions at a given moment.[13]

There has been much debate over whether it is more appropriate to analyse a situation from an 'objective' perspective, such that an external observer can understand it, or from a 'subjective' perspective, meaning as it is viewed and perceived by the consumer.[14] The difference is important because measurement methods and selected variables will not be the same. For example, if one wishes to study consumer behaviour in a crowd situation, the first approach will favour objective measures of 'density' such as the number of people per square foot, whereas the second method will lead researchers to study the psychological feel of the situation, which may be open to diverse interpretations.[15] A crowd situation is often positively interpreted when choosing a popular restaurant; however, it is negatively perceived (given the frustration connected with waiting) when going to a post office or bank, for instance.[16] Similarly, sixty furious students crammed into a lecture theatre which normally seats only half this number will feel perfectly at ease at a popular disco which has exactly the same capacity.

Those who prefer the objective perspective point out that if a researcher wants to modify the situation later, which is often the case in marketing, it is essential to measure the initial situation on the basis of factors which are independent from those perceived by consumers. For example, a store manager will be more interested to discover that customer dissatisfaction is generated by an excessive music level than he would be if customers simply said they found the store too noisy. Those who advocate the subjective approach believe it is impossible to diagnose the mechanism of influence if limited to observations which exclude the psychological state of the individual.

In reality, everything depends on the objective of the study. If one is primarily interested in predicting the most likely outcome in a given situation, the objective approach may suffice. If, however, the aim is to explain the specific processes at work, the perception of that situation can be more important than the situation itself.

Numerous studies vouch for the role played by situational factors in the purchase and consumption of products and services. For example, the choice of a fast-food restaurant depends on the day and the time of day (time perspective), as well as whether one is alone or accompanied (social environment): a consumer is unlikely to choose the same venue for a family outing on a Saturday night as for lunch during the week. The criteria for satisfaction are also modified by the situation: the consumer may appreciate the promptness of the service less and the variety of the menu more in the second case than in the first.[17] Equally, a recent study revealed that 75 per cent of the clients of the French hotel chain Novotel are on expense accounts, while only 10 per cent of Formula One (another no-star chain belonging to the same group) clients are in the same situation. The same study showed that a client company can easily alter the behaviour of its salesforce in this respect simply by modifying the way in which they are reimbursed for expenses (if expenses are allowed on an item-by-item basis, Novotel is chosen; if paid according to a daily expense allowance, Formula One would be favoured). Another study found that consumers buy different brands of athletic shoe for different purposes: Adidas was preferred to Reebok for daily use but was less in demand for sports training. The comfort of a shoe was found to be less important for a gift purchase than its looks, while exactly the opposite was true of personal purchases.[18]

Behaviour in a store also depends upon the situation. A rushed consumer tends to (a) postpone purchases to a later date; (b) reduce impulse buying; and (c) change brands if he or she doesn't find their usual product.[19] Other studies have shown:

1 that consumers are more dependent on the advice of sales staff when purchasing gifts;[20]

2 that the gift-buying criteria for hairdryers and dinner services vary according to the perceived profile of the recipient; and

3 that more shops are visited when shopping with other people.[21]

From these results and others of a similar nature,[22] we can conceptualise the influence of the situation as indicated in Figure 10.1. As this figure illustrates, the product or service – beyond its functional properties (for example the memory capacity of a personal computer) and symbolic attributes (its brand and the reputation which is attached to it[23]) – is 'staged in the situation' before it is acquired and consumed. As a result, there are hardly any intrinsic product factors which alone determine the consumer's consumption or perception of a product. The glass of champagne served graciously by the air hostess seems very expensive to the holidaymaker who couldn't get a ticket in economy class and was forced to pay for a business class ticket. The same person travelling business class on expenses would probably enjoy the same drink without a second thought for the price paid for the ticket.

A situation thus corresponds to a particular configuration (partial or complete) from the five base ingredients identified earlier. To say, for example, 'I was quietly watching television at home when some friends dropped by unexpectedly and I had to run out immediately and buy drinks to offer them' makes explicit reference to the physical environment (at home), the social environment (friends), the time perspective (immediately, unexpectedly), the role context (offer) and preceding conditions (quietly watching television).

Depending on the orientation, the light shed on the situational context can be

Figure 10.1   The influence of the situation on consumer behaviour

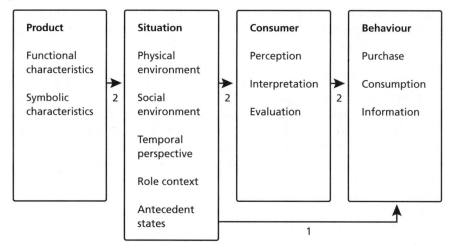

visualised in Figure 10.1. Those who prefer the objective approach are mainly interested in the direct relation (arrow 1) between the components of the observable situation and purchasing or consumption behaviour.[24] Those who prefer to study the impact of the situation as it is perceived, interpreted and evaluated pay more attention to measures of the subjective state of the consumer (arrow 2).[25] The first process illustrates a 'behaviourist' approach based on the analysis of the mechanism relating stimuli (the situational elements) and responses (the purchase and consumption behaviour), while the second is allied to the 'cognitivist' tradition concerned with images and feeling. The difference in perspective exercises a profound influence on the selection of measurement methods.

How is a situation measured?

The most commonly used method for empirical studies consists of designing lists of situations and then presenting them to consumers. This method, based on the cognitive approach, comprises three steps. In the first, a group of consumers spontaneously describe the circumstances in which they typically buy and consume a particular product. (Alternatively, a sample of consumers can be asked to keep a diary of buying and consumption activity over a predetermined period of time.)[26] The rough data are then 'reduced' to a structured repertory of the situations most frequently encountered. For example, an American study found seven typical situations for beer consumption:[27]

- entertaining friends
- in a restaurant or coffee shop
- watching television (particularly sports)

- during a physical activity, either sports or DIY
- picnicking or during a weekend outing
- working at home
- relaxing

Using psychometric techniques similar to those developed by trait personality researchers[28] (see the last section of Chapter 1), the final step involves the construction of inventories such as those presented in Figures 10.2 (for buying situations) and 10.3 (for consumption situations). It is also possible to use the 'ready-made' inventories developed by environmental psychologists,[29] but they are often too broad to capture buying behaviour that is necessarily of a local nature.

Situational inventories, though fairly easy to use, nevertheless present two major difficulties. The first problem has to do with the development of a universal set of potential situations: how does one reduce the number of categories to a manageable list while retaining the level of complexity required to explain a significant variety of consumption contexts? Psychologists, recognising this difficulty, have tried to build nomenclatures of situations that go beyond specific characteristics of

Figure 10.2 Example of buying situation categories (meat-based purchases)

Here is a list of products: hot dogs, steak, chicken, hamburgers, casserole, spaghetti, fish, pork chops, roast beef, ham, bacon. I will describe some situations in which you might buy one of these products. Place an 'x' in the position which, on the following scale, indicates the likelihood that you would decide to buy each product:

Extremely   *Not at all*
likely   *likely*

1 You are planning a party for a few friends and are wondering what to serve for dinner.
2 You are at home on a weekday evening wondering what to have for supper.
3 You are at the supermarket to pick up some meat for a picnic and are trying to decide what to buy.
4 You are about to order dinner at a reasonably good restaurant where you are eating with friends.
5 About 9 o'clock in the evening you are getting hungry, even though you had dinner a few hours ago.
6 After inviting some guests for dinner tonight you realise that there is nothing thawed to serve them; so you run to the supermarket to pick up some meat.
7 You thought you would stop at a fast-food takeaway for a quick bite.
8 No one at home has been very excited by your cooking recently and you are wondering what you might try on them for supper this weekend.
9 You are at the supermarket in front of the meat counter and are wondering what to buy in case friends or relatives drop by this weekend.

Source: Adapted from Russell Belk, 'An Explanatory Assessment of Situational Effects in Buyer Behaviour', *Journal of Marketing Research*, May 1974, pp. 156–63. For another example (supermarket coffee purchases), see Bernard Dubois, 'Un autre aspect dans l'étude du consommateur: l'approche situationnelle,' *Revue Française de Marketing*, no. 129, pp. 73–81

Figure 10.3   Example of a situational inventory of consumption (beverages)

When really thirsty	I drink	Corn or potato brandy
Smoking after dinner		Coffee
When alone		Liqueur
Feeling sleepy in the afternoon		Mineral water
Reading the paper in the morning		Squash
Before sitting down at the table		Tea
With a really delicious piece of meat		Wine
		Whisky
		Beer

Source: From a Swedish study on beverage consumption occasions. See Rolf Gunnar Sandell, 'Effect of Attitudinal and Situational Factors on Reported Choice Behaviour', *Journal of Marketing Research*, November 1968, pp. 405–8

objects and people.[30] In theory, it should be possible to identify general dimensions of classification such as those that exist for individuals (for example socio-demographic characteristics or personality traits) or for products (as in the traditional distinction made between consumer goods, industrial products and services). Sherif and Sherif, for example, propose a four-factor approach to developing situation inventories:

1 factors associated with the people involved in the situation (number, nature, previous relationships, etc.);

2 aspects characterising the task or the problem to be solved (newness, complexity);

3 dimensions of the physical environment (site, space, facilities);

4 the factors which bring together the three preceding elements, such as the extent of the individual's involvement in the task.[31]

In commercial studies, no satisfactory solution to the problems of classification has yet been found.[32] For example, in comparing the situational choice dimensions for two types of food product (snacks and meat products), using the same sample of consumers, Belk found that the underlying factors did not overlap.[33] When these results were analysed in conjunction with another study addressing restaurant selection, he discovered only one common dimension: variety seeking.[34] This lack of overlap in situational choice factors is perhaps due to the diversity of study objectives. In certain studies, the nature of the behaviour elicited by the situation is measured, while in others the study concentrates on the mechanisms that explain the purchase decision.

In the first case it is probably more interesting to analyse situations from the standpoint of the consumer's response to it, for example a feeling of ease or frustration. If, however, one is interested in explaining buying behaviour, the situation is perhaps best understood through its attributes (for example, social visibility). In analysing ten situations for choice of aperitif, Lutz and Kakkar noted three factors explaining the choices made: (a) the relationships to others (presence of other people, visibility to others, importance to others); (b) the personal implications (level of consumption, importance to self); and (c) the temporal relationship (length of the act of consumption and the interval between two purchases).[35]

In practice, it therefore seems preferable to describe a nomenclature of situations specific to a product category, rather than to rely on generic lists.[36] The quality of the resulting taxonomy depends above all on the care given to the collection of scenarios, although techniques used for data reduction can greatly help in the presentation of results. For example, a systematic analysis of situations of jewellery purchases identified the following four categories:

1 the 'emotional' self-purchase, highly impulsive;

2 the planned personal purchase, for example to celebrate a professional achievement;

3 the purchase of a gift for an 'official' occasion (such as a baptism ceremony);

4 the purchase of a gift for an 'intimate' occasion (for example, the anniversary of a first meeting, the first holiday as a couple, etc.).

If the frequency of these four jewellery-buying situations were monitored over an extended period of time, this would allow manufacturers and retailers to anticipate trends in this market.[37] Similarly, three situations were identified for the purchase of flowers: (a) buying for personal enjoyment; (b) the purchase for 'obligatory occasions'; and (c) the gift purchase.[38] Through a careful analysis of information related to consumers, products and situations, new perspectives on market segmentation may emerge.

The second problem, linked to the use of inventories, has to do with the hypothetical nature of survey questions. Normally, the consumer is asked what he or she would do if they found themselves in a particular situation. Nothing, however, indicates whether or not the consumer would actually behave in such a way should the situation in fact arise; furthermore, one must also be aware of the risk of obtaining responses that are prompted, or, at the very least, influenced by the specific wording of the questions.[39] In line with the behaviourist perspective, others have proposed that (particularly as far as the time perspective is concerned) analysis should be based on 'real' situations rather than simulated ones.[40] Leaving aside the direct observation, which is difficult to interpret and apply at a more general level,[41] two approaches are feasible: laboratory tests and field tests. The nature of laboratory settings enables a greater degree of control over the parameters of a situation. By reproducing in a commercial context the well-known experiment by Asch on group conformity to norms (see Chapter 5), for example, one researcher showed that the choice between different suits (which were in fact identical but not presented as such) was not independent of the presence or absence of others. When a few people (behaving according to instructions given by the researcher) expressed a strong preference for one of the suits, the subject followed the norm they had created by agreeing with them. Similarly, it is relatively easy to manipulate situational variables, and to measure their impact on buyer behaviour, in the mini-markets and 'store laboratories' often used in new product development research. For example, the time allotted to shoppers to make their selections can be reduced; stockouts can be simulated; or elements of 'distraction' can be introduced (promotional activities, interruptions by salespeople, etc.). The major limiting factor of the laboratory is, clearly, its confined nature. This is what 'field' situations aim to overcome.

Because of their contingent and often unexpected character, situational factors are not easily examined in natural purchase and consumption settings. Certain methodologies can nevertheless be helpful. For example, three American researchers developed an ingenious study to analyse the differences between habitual consumption, expected consumption and effective consumption. They used three instruments:

1 pre-surveys regarding planned food purchases;

2 follow-up questionnaires regarding what was actually bought; and

3 an analysis of the contents of the dustbins of the households being studied.

Using the data obtained during each of the three stages of the study, the researchers analysed the differences between everyday consumption, planned consumption and actual consumption. Interestingly, they showed that taking into account unexpected situations greatly improved the prediction of consumption volume. For example, when several people (rather than just one person) were involved in shopping for food, the choice of breakfast cereal changed; similarly, when a family member fell sick, the purchases of oranges increased.[42]

Clearly, given that situational research is still in the early stages of development, it is difficult to recommend one approach over another. The results summarised above were obtained using different methods, each of which shed light on both already established and original findings. It is true that a multi-modal approach is often expensive; however, until more research is available, a multi-modal methodology can provide a safety net for the bias implicit in using a single approach.

What is known today about the impact of situations on purchase and consumption?

Some findings have already been presented in the introductory part of this chapter. A comparative analysis of a few dozen studies conducted explicitly on this subject leads to three conclusions.

The isolated impact of situational factors is limited but significant[43]

In the Swedish study on beverage consumption already cited, for example, differences in situation could not explain more than individual differences in decision making.[44] This is an understandable result. If this were not the case it would suggest that, regardless of the characteristics of the product or consumer, there are fundamental situational factors which dictate behaviour. The situational approach was developed largely in response to excessive focus on product attributes and consumer profiles; it would be ironic if, in turn, it had fallen into the same trap as other highly focused research approaches.

One may wonder, however, what indirect impact one given situation has on the choice between a set of possible solutions to the same problem: for example, if I have little time for lunch, my options may be limited to (a) a sandwich at the corner cafe; (b) a snack from a vending machine; or (c) a takeaway. At the same time, other possibilities may be excluded (restaurants or a home-cooked meal), options which in other circumstances may have been preferred.[45] In this way, the situation can determine the suitability of certain products relative to others.[46]

The interaction between product and situation has a powerful influence on behaviour

The impact of situational factors varies according to the product category being studied.[47] In the 'garbology' study already mentioned, for example, the situation had more of an impact on purchases of meat than on those of cheese, fruit juice, vegetables or beer. Similarly, another study has shown that taking situational variables into account – such as the circumstances relating to consumption – improves the performance of decision-making models for certain brands.[48] For example, even if a consumer prefers 7-Up, he or she may chose to drink a caffeinated drink such as Coca-Cola while preparing for an examination. Similarly, product differences are more important to teenagers when buying for themselves than when they are buying for someone else in the family.[49]

More broadly, certain product characteristics may magnify or reduce the impact of the situation. Brand awareness is one of them. A product with a strong brand name reduces the potential impact of situational factors, which is one of the reasons why so many companies are concerned today about investing in brand equity.[50] At the same time, a product with multiple applications reduces the level of decision making required for a given situation and therefore tends to stabilise choices; you do not need two different CD players to listen to classical and pop music. On the other hand, people do not go to work in sportswear.

It is equally important to know at which level the situational factors exert the strongest influence: at the product, brands or attribute level? **Attribution theory**, according to which an individual always attributes the causes of his or her behaviour to specific factors, considers the conditions in which a particular behaviour is linked to a given situation rather than a given product.[51] These conditions depend on the interaction of situations and products.[52] Some products (sugar soap, for example) are used only in very specific situations (for cleaning walls), whereas others which belong to the same category (household detergents) have a more diversified use. Companies launching new products are confronted by a real dilemma. In order to develop a reputation and clear image, it is important to establish a distinctive market position – if possible, one not occupied by a competitor. On the other hand, there is a risk in overemphasising the link between a product and particular purchase situations at an early stage, especially if these situations are not commonplace. For example, in Western Europe, the market for engagement rings has declined in line with the number of couples getting married.

The importance of the situation varies greatly from one consumer to another

Psychologists have shown that all individuals are not equally sensitive to elements in their environment;[53] it is, therefore, not surprising to find individual differences in the way in which the situation affects consumption and purchase behaviour.[54] The concept of involvement has often been used to illustrate this fact.[55] The greater a consumer's level of involvement in a product category, the less situational factors affect decision making.[56] An informed classical music fan will be less sensitive to a promotion on a disc recorded by a second-rate performer than would be the average buyer, who may see the same offer as a bargain.

Equally, the personal features of an individual may be more or less significant depending on the environment. For example, the feeling of belonging to an ethnic or cultural group strengthens or fades depending on the geographical environment (the British, for instance, probably feel more British abroad than at home), the temporal environment (national sentiment is particularly strong during events such as the World Cup) or the social environment (for example, at home with the family). In the same vein, 'good country cooking' may be ideal for a family reunion but inappropriate for a business lunch.[57]

Managerial implications

The situational approach offers managers a fresh perspective in understanding market structure (strategic view), as well as presenting new insights into how to reach target audiences (tactical view). At the strategic level, understanding the situation provides new opportunities for segmentation and a new language with which to position the brands and communicate with the consumer.

Marketing executives traditionally segment markets by real or perceived product attributes and/or consumers' objective or subjective characteristics. There are two problems with this approach: the variables selected are often of little relevance (this is often the case for a product's technical characteristics) or difficult to use (for example, lifestyle). By addressing situational factors in purchase and consumption, these problems can be overcome. The 'nibbling' market can be segmented based on specific consumption situations.[58] The 'nutritional' nibbler (22 per cent of the European population) considers nibbling as equivalent to having a meal; in contrast, the 'guilty' nibbler (9 per cent) sees nibbling as something done between meals; the 'social setting' nibbler (15 per cent) only consumes with friends; and for the 'unconditionals' (15 per cent) no situation is inappropriate if it means satisfying their appetite. These groups consume neither the same quality nor the same volume of product. In business-to-business marketing, segmentation by purchasing situation is becoming quite popular.[59]

By offering a new way of structuring markets, the situational approach also enriches thinking on the actual and desired positioning of products. Using this approach, one study has identified thirty-two positioning platforms for suntan lotion by cross-referencing six personal characteristics (man, woman, adolescent, child, light complexion, dark complexion) with four consumption situations (on the beach, at the pool, under a sun lamp, during winter sports).[60] The most important product attributes to highlight vary in each case; for example, a lotion containing an antifreeze is suitable for winter use, while a floating plastic bottle reduces the risk of losing the product while on the beach. In the same way, consumer benefits linked to the positioning of the product also change. For example, product safety (medical positioning) is more important under a sun lamp than beside a swimming pool. In Europe, many advertising campaigns strive to reposition their products and brands in consumption situations other than those with which they are traditionally associated; for example, Cointreau is now positioned more as an ingredient for cocktails than an after-dinner liqueur. The success of theme restaurants and theme parks[61] also demonstrates the possibility of increasing the perceived added value of an otherwise banal service by judicious management of the situational aspects.

At a more tactical level, the situational approach concerns both product and promotion decisions. If a company discovers that its products are more often associated with certain purchase or consumption situations than others, it can try to discover the reasons for this: is it due to intrinsic features of the product itself (such as its formulation, conditions of use, packaging)? Is it due, perhaps, to an image which is too limiting, or to its price? The answer to these questions often leads to the relaunch of existing products or to the creation of new ones – for example, perfume in a travel-size atomiser or the portable computer (the laptop).

In advertising, a clear understanding of purchase and consumption situations warns creative departments about the risk of putting a product in a 'staged' context that will be judged inadequate or inappropriate by the target audience. Several years ago, Playtex created a television advert showing a housewife who, while disembarking from an aeroplane, thought that she had forgotten her girdle. This approach was less successful in Europe than in the United States because European housewives find it more difficult to picture themselves flying regularly. Multiple consumption occasions can also be created for a product by varying the situations depicted in advertisements. Figure 10.4 illustrates one such approach in the case of cognac, which is presented as suitable for any hour of the day. Obviously, this approach presumes that one knows not only the situations in which the product is used but also the factors which predispose consumers to enter these situations. This is relatively under-researched territory: up to now, research has considered the individual more as a 'victim' than as a 'creator' of situations.[62] However, certain researchers have shown that the frequency with which consumers are involved in

Figure 10.4 A situational advert

different types of shopping can be predicted from their socio-demographic characteristics: emergency purchases, weekly shopping, and so on.[63]

Finally, promotional tools provide companies with possibilities for experimentation that are particularly effective in creating 'climates' or 'atmospheres' likely to affect perceptions of a product or service.[64] For example, companies try to understand what makes a consumer consider a product as being 'upmarket' or, on the contrary, as run-of-the-mill.[65] A carpet that is a little softer, a brochure that is slightly glossier or a welcome that is a little more respectful are all indicators which endow a point of sale with touches of elegance and refinement which it might not otherwise have gained. Alternatively, direct marketing can increase the awareness of the different roles that can be assumed by the consumer: head of the household, manager, spouse, etc. The concept of a 'situational self-image', which describes an individual's self-perception at a given moment and in a given context, merits further exploration.[66] For example, an individual will generally feel somewhat more patriotic on the nation's commemorative day, whether it be Bastille Day for the French, St Andrew's Day for the Scots or St Patrick's Day for the Irish.

Giving explicit recognition of purchase and consumption situations in the study of consumer behaviour opens new horizons. Even if the methodological problems are still not fully resolved, the extension of current work and the development of new lines of investigation appear justified by the potential benefits. At the moment, research into person–situation–product interactions seems to offer the most hope of obtaining results sufficiently convergent to provide practical classifications and recommendations. By incorporating purchase and consumption situations in surveys and databases traditionally centred on consumer–product interactions, a particularly useful body of knowledge will be built up, accurate in its representation and operational in its application.

Notes

[1] B. Dubois, 'Le Consommateur Cameleon', *Harvard L'Expansion*, Summer 1991, pp. 7–13.

[2] 'L'Impossible Mr Consommateur', *Enjeux-Les Echos*, January 1993, pp. 50–7.

[3] See, for example, D. G. Mick and C. Faure, 'Consumer Self-Gifts in Achievement Contexts: The Role of Outcomes, Attributions, Emotions, and Deservingness', *International Journal of Research in Marketing*, October 1998, pp. 293–308.

[4] Yves Negro, 'Achat de Cadeau et Image du Magasin', Université de Rennes, Working Paper 1975, No. 5.

[5] T. Garner and J. Wagner, 'Gift-Giving: An Economic Perspective', paper presented at Allied Social Sciences Association, Chicago, 1987.

[6] K. Lewin, 'Field Theory and Experiment in Social Psychology: Concepts and Methods', *American Journal of Sociology*, 1939, 44, pp. 868–96.

[7] R. G. Barker, 'Explorations in Ecological Psychology', *American Psychologist*, 1965, 20, pp. 1–14.

[8] W. Thomas, 'The Behavioural Pattern and the Situation', *Proceedings, 22nd Annual Meeting, American Sociological Society*, 1927, 22, pp. 1–13.

[9] Hansen also proposes to isolate exposition situations to one communication but, in the analysis, these do not constitute a particular case of a consumption situation. Refer to F. Hansen, *Consumer Choice Behaviour* (New York, 1972).

[10] R. W. Belk, 'An Exploratory Assessment of Situational Effects in Buyer Behaviour', *Journal of Marketing Research*, May 1974, pp. 156–63.

[11] S. Troye, 'Situationist Theory and Consumer Behaviour', *Research in Consumer Behaviour*, 1985, 1, pp. 285–321.

[12] R. W. Belk, 'Situational Variables and Consumer Behaviour', *Journal of Consumer Research*, December 1975, pp. 157–64.

[13] Originally, Belk proposed that the psychological state of the consumer before the purchase be directly taken into consideration. But it then becomes almost impossible to distinguish the individual from the situation. This subject is discussed in the two articles by A. Wicker and R. G. Barker, 'Commentaries on Belk's Situational Variables and Consumer Behaviour', *Journal of Consumer Research*, December 1975, pp. 164–5; and by J. A. Russell and A. Mehrabian, 'Environmental Variables in Consumer Research', *Journal of Consumer Research*, December 1975, pp. 62–3. In the end, it seems better to limit oneself to the psychological states that the individual himself brings to the situation. For example, the disappointment of a consumer by his previous purchase can be an integral part of the present situation.

[14] R. W. Belk, 'The Objective Situation as a Determinant of Consumer Behaviour', *Advances in Consumer Research* (ACR, 1975), pp. 427–37; and R. Lutz and P. Kakkar, 'The Psychological Situation as a Determinant of Consumer Behaviour', *Advances in Consumer Research* (ACR, 1975), pp. 439–53.

[15] M. K. Hui and J. G. Bateson, 'Perceived Control and the Effects of Crowding and Consumer Choice on the Service Experience', *Journal of Consumer Research*, September 1991, pp. 174–82.

[16] D. Stokols, 'On the Distinction between Density and Crowding: Some Implications for Future Research', *Psychological Review*, 1972, 79, pp. 275–7.

[17] K. Miller and J. Ginter, 'An Investigation of Situational Variation in Brand Choice Behaviour and Attitude', *Journal of Marketing Research*, 1979, pp. 111–23.

[18] G. Mouallen *et al.*, 'Les Attitudes et les Preferences: L'Importance des Criteres de Choix et des Situations d'Achat', study at HEC under the supervision of the author (HEC, December 1992).

[19] C. W. Park, E. S. Iyer and D. C. Smith, 'The Effects of Situational Factors on In-store Grocery Shopping Behaviour: The Role of Store Environment and Time Available for Shopping', *Journal of Consumer Research*, May 1989, pp. 422–33.

[20] A. B. Ryans, 'Consumer Gift Buying Behaviour: An Exploratory Analysis', in P. Barnett, A. Greenberg and D. N. Bellenger (eds), *Proceedings of the American Marketing Association Educator's Conference* (AMA), 1977.

[21] D. H. Granbois, 'Improving the Study of Customer In-store Behaviour', *Journal of Marketing*, October 1968, pp. 28–33.

[22] P. Kakkar and R. Lutz, 'Situational Influence on Consumer Behaviour: A Review', in H. Kassarjian and T. Robertson (eds), *Perspectives in Consumer Behaviour*, 3rd edition (Dryden Press, 1981), pp. 204–14.

[23] R. H. Holman, 'Product Use as Communication: A Fresh Appraisal of Venerable Topic', *Review of Marketing* (American Marketing Association, 1981), pp. 106–19.

[24] R. W. Belk, 'The Objective Situation as a Determinant of Consumer Behaviour', *Advances in Consumer Research*, 2 (ACR, 1975), pp. 427–37.

[25] R. Lutz and P. Kakkar, 'The Psychological Situation as a Determinant of Consumer Behaviour', *Advances in Consumer Research* (ACR, 1975), pp. 439–53.

[26] See for example Gilles Laurent, 'A study of Multiple Variant Consumption for Frequently Purchased Consumer Products', unpublished PhD dissertation, Sloan School of Management, Massachusetts Institute of Technology (Cambridge, Mass., 1978)

[27] W. O. Bearden and A. G. Woodside, 'Interactions of Consumer Situations and Brand Attitudes', *Journal of Applied Psychology*, 1976, pp. 176–96. Also see 'Consumption Occasion Influences on Consumer Brand Choice', *Decision Sciences*, 1978, pp. 273–84 and E. H. Demby, 'The Creative Consumer: A Report on Psychographics', *AMA*, 1968.

28 H. Triandis, 'Exploratory Analyses of the Behavioural Components of Social Attitudes', *Journal of Abnormal and Social Psychology*, April 1964, pp. 420–30; also see E. Norman, S. McHunt and J. McHunt, 'Sources of Behavioural Variance as Measured by the S-R Inventory of Anxiousness', *Psychological Bulletin*, 1966, pp. 336–46.

29 A. Mehrabian and J. A. Russell, *An Approach to Environmental Psychology* (MIT Press, 1974). Also see K. S. Bowers, 'Situationism in Psychology: An Analysis and Critique', *Psychological Review*, 1973, pp. 307–36.

30 R. Bellows, 'Toward a Taxonomy of Social Situations', in S. B. Sells (ed.), *Stimulus Determinants of Behaviour* (Ronald Press, 1963), pp. 197–212.

31 M. Sherif and C. Sherif, *An Outline of Social Psychology* (Harper & Row, 1956), pp. 121–2.

32 S. Troye, *op. cit.*

33 R. W. Belk, 'An Exploratory Assessment of Situational Effects in Buyer Behaviour', *Journal of Marketing Research*, May 1974, pp. 156–63.

34 R. W. Belk, 'The Objective Situation as a Determinant of Consumer Behaviour', *Advances in Consumer Research*, 2 (ACR, 1975), pp. 427–37. On the notion of variety seeking, see L. McAlister and E. Pessemier, 'Variety-Seeking Behavior', *Journal of Consumer Research*, December 1982, pp. 311–22; and L. McAlister, 'A Dynamic Attribute Satiation Model of Variety-Seeking Behavior', *Journal of Consumer Research*, September 1982, pp. 141–50. See also P. Aurier, 'Recherche en Variété: Un Concept Majeur de la Théorie en Marketing', *Recherche et Applications en Marketing*, 1991, 6(1), pp. 85–106.

35 P. Kakkar and R. Lutz, 'Towards a Taxonomy of Consumption Situations', *AMA Conference Proceedings*, 1975, pp. 206–210.

36 See regarding this idea R. K. Srivastasa *et al.*, 'A Customer-Oriented Approach for Determining Market Structures', *Journal of Marketing*, 1984, Winter, pp. 32–45. For an example mixing the two approaches, see B. Dubois and G. Laurent, 'The Functions of Luxury: A Situational Approach to Excursionism', *Advances in Consumer Research*, 1996, pp. 470–7.

37 B. Dubois, *1977–87: Dix Ans d'Evolution du Marché des Bijoux* (Étude Bijhorca/Or Information, 1988).

38 See D. L. Scammon *et al.*, 'Is a Gift Always a Gift? An Investigation of Flower Purchasing Behaviour Across Situations', *Advances in Consumer Research* (ACR, 1981), pp. 531–6.

39 P. Reingen, 'Demand Bias in the Assessment of Situational Effect on Consumer Behaviour', *Advances in Consumer Research*, 1976, pp. 130–6.

40 J. Hornik, 'Situational Effect on the Consumption of Time', *Journal of Marketing Research*, 1982, pp. 44–5. On the temporal element of the situation, see L. Feldman and J. Hornik, 'The Use of Time: An Integrated Conceptual Model', *Journal of Consumer Research*, March 1981, pp. 407–19. Also see M. Bergadaà, 'The Role of Time in the Action of the Consumer', *Journal of Consumer Research*, December 1990, pp. 289–302; For cross-cultural comparisons on this topic, see J. Schroeder *et al.*, 'Social Time Perspective and Cross-Cultural Consumer Behaviour: A Framework and Some Results', *European Advances in Consumer Research* (ACR, 1993), pp. 18–23; J. C. Chebat and M. V. Venkatesan, 'Time-Orientation and Canadian Consumer Behaviour: Case of French and English Speaking Canadians', *European Advances in Consumer Research* (ACR, 1993), pp. 24–7; and G. Morello, 'Attitudes Towards Time in European, USA and Japanese Companies', *European Advances in Consumer Research* (ACR, 1993), pp. 28–38.

41 W. E. Wells and L. A. Lo Sciuto, 'Direct Observation of Purchasing Behaviour', *Journal of Marketing Research*, 1966, pp. 227–33.

42 J. A. Cote, J. McCullough and M. Reily, 'Effects of Unexpected Situations on Behaviour–Intention Differences: A Garbology Analysis', *Journal of Consumer Research*, September 1985, pp. 188–94.

43 See K. Bowers, 'Situationism in Pyschology: An Analysis and A Critique', *Psychological Review*, 1973, pp. 307–36; see also J. A. Cote, 'The Person by Situation Interaction Myth: Implications for the Definition of Situations', *Advances in Consumer Research* (ACR, 1986), pp. 37–41.

44 R. G. Sandell, 'Effects of Attitudinal and Situational Factors on Reported Choice Behaviour', *Journal of Marketing Research*, 1968, pp. 405–8.

45 See I. Sinha, 'A Conceptual Model of the Role of Situational Type on Consumer Choice Behaviour and Consideration Sets', *Advances in Consumer Research*, 1994, pp. 477–82.

46 See R. V. Skivastava, 'Usage-Situational Influences on Perceptions of Product Markets: Theoretical and Empirical Issues', *Advances in Consumer Research*, 1981, pp. 106, 111.

47 S. B. Sells, 'Dimensions of Stimulus Situations which Account for Behaviour Variance', in S. B. Sells (ed.), *Stimulus Determinants of Behaviour* (Ronald Press, 1963), pp. 3–15.

48 U. N. Umesh and J. A. Cote, 'Influence of Situational Variables on Brand Choice Models', *Journal of Business Research*, 1988, pp. 91–9. See also on the same subject W. O. Bearden and A. G. Woodside, 'Interactions of Consumer Situations and Brand Attitudes', *Journal of Applied Psychology*, 1976, pp. 764–9.

49 S. E. Beatty and S. Talpade, 'Adolescent Influence in Family Decision Making: A Replication With Extension', *Journal of Consumer Research*, September 1994, pp. 332–41.

50 D. Aaker, *Managing Brand Equity* (Free Press, 1991). See also J. N. Kapferer, *Strategic Brand Management: Creating and Sustaining Brand Equity Long Term*, 2nd edition (Kogan Page, 1997).

51 See E. E. Jones, D. E. Kanouse, H. H. Kelley, R. N. Nisbett, S. Valins and B. Weiner, *Attribution: Perceiving the Causes of Behavior* (General Learning Corporation, 1972).

52 R. W. Mizerski, L. L. Goden and J. B. Kernan, 'The Attribution Process in Consumer Decision Making', *Journal of Consumer Research*, September 1979, pp. 123–40.

53 I. G. Sarason, R. E. Smith and E. Diener, 'Personality Research: Components of Variance Attributable to the Person and the Situation', *Journal of Personality and Social Psychology*, 1975, pp. 199–204.

54 R. Becherer, F. Morgan and L. M. Richard, 'Person–Situation Interaction Within a Consumer Behaviour Context', *Journal of Psychology*, July 1979, pp. 235–42, and J. A. Cote, 'The Person by Situation Interaction Myth: Implication for the Definition of Situations', *Advances in Consumer Research* (ACR, 1986), pp. 37–41.

55 J. L. Zaichhkowsky, 'Measuring the Involvement Construct', *Journal of Consumer Research*, December 1985, pp. 341–52.

56 R. Clarke and R. W. Belk, 'The Effect of Product Involvement and Task Definition on Anticipated Consumer Effort', *Advances in Consumer Research* (ACR, 1979), pp. 313–18.

57 D. Stayman and R. Deshpandé, 'Situational Ethnicity in Consumer Behaviour', *Journal of Consumer Research*, December 1989, pp. 361–71.

58 H. Assael, *Consumer Behaviour and Marketing Action*, 3rd edition (Kent, 1987), p. 273.

59 For example, J. Berrigan and C. Finkbeiner, *Segmentation Marketing* (Harper Business, 1993).

60 P. Dickson, 'Person–Situation: Segmentation's Missing Link', *Journal of Marketing*, 1982, pp. 56–64.

61 J. Browne and A. Church, 'Theme Parks in Europe', *Travel and Tourism Analyst*, February 1987, pp. 35–46.

62 J. H. Leigh and C. Martin Jr, 'A Review of Situational Influence Paradigms and Research', *Review of Marketing* (American Marketing Association, 1981), pp. 57–74.

63 R. Holman and R. W. Dale, 'The Availability of Discretionary Time: Influences on Interactive Patterns of Consumer Shopping Behaviour', *Advances in Consumer Research* (ACR, 1980), pp. 431–8.

64 P. Kotler, 'Atmospherics as a Marketing Tool', *Journal of Retailing*, Winter 1973–74, pp. 48–64. See also K. Spies, F. Hesse and K. Loesch, 'Store Atmosphere, Mood and Purchasing Behaviour', *International Journal of Research in Marketing*, February 1997, pp. 1–18.

65 See B. Dubois and G. Laurent, 'Product Upscale Proneness: A Situational Approach', 1994 HEC working paper.

66 C. T. Schenk and R. Holman, 'A Sociological Approach to Brand Choice: The Concept of Situational Self Image', *Advances in Consumer Research* (ACR, 1980), pp. 610–17.

11

Conclusion

Through the first ten chapters of this book we have shown how a number of concepts and theories, originating in the social sciences, help us to understand many static and dynamic aspects of purchase and consumption behaviour. But just as a blind person will imagine an elephant differently depending upon which part of the animal he or she touches, a variety of partial approaches does not make a whole and the reader may now be tempted to put together all the pieces of the puzzle.

In this ultimate chapter, we try to help in this endeavour by describing and evaluating some of the contributions which have attempted to describe, explain and predict consumer behaviour taken in its entirety.

The complexity of consumer behaviour, and the variety and number of factors to be taken into account, have obliged researchers interested in integrated frameworks to present their synthetic efforts as simplified conceptual structures usually referred to as **models**. We examine three of the most significant ones, presenting them in growing order of complexity, based on the number of selected variables as well as their relationships.

The Nicosia model

More than thirty years ago, Francesco Nicosia was among the first authors to develop a consumer behaviour model which, in its structure, was patterned after a computer program. The simplified (and never since updated) version of his model is presented in Figure 11.1.[1] Nicosia's idea was to analyse consumer decisions as resulting from a process which can be structured in terms of four 'fields', themselves subdivided into sub-fields (in the same way as an overall computer program can be dissected into sub-programs). Thus, the purchase field (field three) emerges from an information search and evaluation field (field two), resulting in its turn from a message exposure field (field one). More specifically, the firm's attributes (sub-field one) produce a message which, if received by consumers, interacts with their own attributes (sub-field two) to give rise to an attitude towards the company, its products and brands. This attitude is then integrated into a means–ends information search and evaluation process (pre-action field), which may or may not result in the

Figure 11.1   The Nicosia model

Field one: From the source of a message to the consumer's attitude

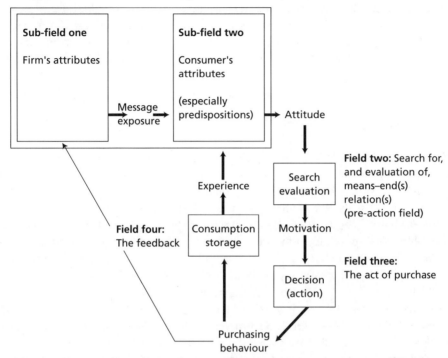

formation of a product or brand-specific motivation, eventually transformed into a purchase act (depending upon situational factors). Consumption (or storage) activities finally lead to the emergence of an experience that, in turn, becomes itself a consumer attribute – thus closing the loop.

Let us illustrate how the model is intended to work. Mr Smith, a well-off consumer interested in high-tech products, reads an advertisement one day for a new digital camcorder (message exposure). He persuades himself that he should buy such a product (attitude). After comparing alternative brands, he develops a favourable intention towards the Sony model (motivation). In the store, however, the salesperson suggests he should rather buy another, better-performing camcorder, which he buys (purchase). A week later, during a dinner with friends, he details all the wonderful features of his new camcorder (feedback).

Today, the value of the model developed by Nicosia is primarily historical. Nicosia was among the very first consumer researchers to develop an integrated framework, building on what others had discovered in a number of different disciplines. The structure of his model highlights the process nature of consumer decisions. Variables are clearly defined and their relationships made explicit.[2] However, and despite the suggestions made by Nicosia himself, the model has never been completely and empirically tested and, therefore, its predictive power is unknown. Furthermore, the distinctions made between certain constructs (for example, the idea of generic attitudes underlying specific motivations) are not really in line with the way these concepts have been approached in the literature (and discussed in this book). Also, purchase acts are presented as individual decisions and social and family influences are left implicit. Finally, it would appear that the step-by-step progression towards purchase primarily applies to durable products and fails to account for impulse buying. Nicosia's contribution remains a very useful start.

The Howard–Sheth model

The model developed by J. Howard and J. Sheth is often considered as the most significant attempt to integrate knowledge about consumer purchase and behaviour. Published in 1969, it exerted (and to some extent continues to exert) a profound influence on subsequent work in this area. Its basic orientation is 'behaviourist' in nature in that the model basically attempts to explain how, through learning, certain inputs corresponding to marketing stimuli are transformed into outputs such as purchase or other behavioural responses. The structure of the model is presented in Figure 11.2 and is illustrated by the following mini-case:[3]

My most recent purchase was a box of La Paz cigars, the green variety. I used to smoke Meccarillos. They are good little cigars but I had found them a little dry recently, even though they are not very expensive. After lunch the other day, one of my colleagues offered me a Green La Paz and I liked it. I asked him about the price of a box, which although a bit expensive was still affordable. Other colleagues do not find them strong enough but I disagree. The Green La Paz have a nice aroma and are always fresh in their metal box. They also look nice and really like freshly rolled tobacco leaves; they correspond well to their image of 'Brazilian type'. I did not find them immediately. The first tobacconist I went to had La Paz cigars, but the Brown variety. I bought them and was disappointed. I should not have trusted the salesman. I did not know these brown La Paz and I was unsure about their quality. I was hesitating but, unfortunately, the salesman influenced my judgement. Yesterday, I found them and made sure they were the Green La Paz.

   The box is a bit expensive but that does not worry me too much because they last longer than the Meccarillos. Besides, they are much cheaper than the little Davidoffs. My wife offered me a box of Davidoffs once but it's exorbitant because I smoke them like cigarettes. At the moment, the only brands I smoke are the La Paz, sometimes the Meccarillos, and sometimes the Davidoffs. But when someone offers me something else, I don't refuse. I like to change from time to time when I discover a good brand.

Figure 11.2 exhibits four types of variable:[4] Input variables, hypothetical constructs (all located inside the central rectangular box), output variables and exogenous variables.

Input variables correspond to stimuli from the commercial and social environment. Commercial stimuli include both objects 'such as the products themselves' and their symbolic representations (for example, names and logos). In our mini-case, the green metal box illustrates the former and the 'Brazilian type' name the latter. Social stimuli refer to word-of-mouth and other influence processes such as, in our example, colleagues' recommendations. Inputs are then processed and stored through their interaction with a series of hypothetical contructs corresponding to internal state variables, which, not being directly observable, have to be inferred by the researcher. These constructs fall into two categories depending upon whether they rely on learning or perception mechanisms. The first group, central to the formation of decisions, include motives (for example, the pleasure of smoking cigars), alternatives available in the 'evoked set' (La Paz Green, La Paz Brown, Meccarillos, Davidoff), mediators (decision rules), predispositions such as attitudes towards products and brands (Davidoff is exhorbitant, Meccarillos are a little dry), inhibitors (such as the unavailability of La Paz Green on a given purchase occasion), and satisfaction.

Whether specific (that is, limited to a given product category) or generic, **motives** provide impetus to action and arouse the buyer's attention, making him or her aware of environmental stimuli. The **evoked set** corresponds to the various brands which, in the buyer's mind, could satisfy his or her needs. **Decision mediators** refer to the mental rules for matching alternatives with motives and ranking them in

Figure 11.2 The Howard–Sheth model

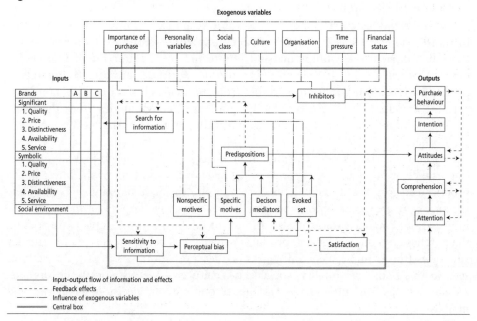

Source: Adapted from J. Howard and J. Sheth, *The Theory of Buying Behavior* (Wiley, 1969)

terms of their want-satisfying capacity. **Predispositions** are the preferences resulting from the interplay between the previous three factors. **Inhibitors** are all the factors, such as lack of availability but also including time pressure and other situational variables, which create a disruption between preferences and actual purchases (such as, in our example, buying La Paz Brown instead of La Paz Green when the chosen item was not available). Finally, **satisfaction** has to do with the perceived degree of congruence between expectations and the purchase and consumption experience. In a routine situation, predispositions are well established and therefore difficult to change. Much so-called impulse behaviour is really the outcome of strong predispositions and a facilitating commercial stimulus such as a store display. Conversely, in a new purchase situation, the buyer does not have well-developed decision mediators and his or her evoked set is not well formed. The buyer is therefore highly sensitive to information.

Perceptual constructs include **sensitivity to information** (in our example, the willingness to try new cigars), **perceptual bias** ('it's expensive but that does not worry me too much'), and **information search** (such as the questions asked about La Paz Green).

Sensitivity to information regulates the intake of information by sensory receptors. It depends both upon the degree of stimulus complexity and the buyer's predispositions (for example, attitudes towards advertising). Information entering the buyer's mental processing system is then filtered by perceptual mechanisms, which not only select what information will be attended to but may also distort it, usually to make it congruent with the pre-existing frame of reference. Finally, the search for information will be active when the buyer sees ambiguity in his or her motives, evoked set or mediators.

Output variables correspond to observable responses from the buyer. Most of them are related to specific hypothetical constructs. **Attention** thus reveals sensitivity to information. **Comprehension** is affected by the amount of knowledge that the consumer has at a given point in time. **Attitudes** are directly related to predispositions. **Intentions,** too, result from predispositions but also take into account anticipated inhibitors. Finally, **purchase behaviour** describes the overt manifestation of one's predispositions; naturally, all these variables interact with each other.

Exogenous variables refer to external influences on the decision-making process. **Importance of purchase** corresponds to the level of involvement of the buyer in the product category (as measured, in our example, through smoking habits). **Time pressure** may create inhibition and usually has a negative impact on the search for information. **Financial status** is also a frequent inhibitor, for example by restricting the purchase or consumption of products perceived as being expensive in particular situations (for example, Davidoff cigars are acceptable only as a gift). As we have seen in this book, **personality, social class, culture** as well as **social and organisational settings** will often have an impact on motives, decision mediators and inhibitors.

The dynamics of buyer behaviour are regulated by learning processes. In the early phases, buyers have changeable alternatives and unstable mediators. Their motives are strong, their sensitivity high and their information search activities intense. After a number of purchases, decision processes tend to stabilise. The evoked set is more precisely defined, as are the decision rules. Sensitivity to information is reduced to a minimum and perceptual biases are fully operating. The consumer has entered a 'simplification' stage. Perfect loyalty, however, tends to erode over time and variety seeking may occur ('I like to change from time to time when I discover a good brand'). Consumers then reactivate the decision-making process: new motives emerge and the information search reappears. They now enter a stage of complication until processes become stabilised again. Throughout their lives, consumers go back and forth between routine and discovery in this way.

The Howard and Sheth model is a very comprehensive one. Most of the factors considered in this book find a place in their theory and the hypothesised relationships between them adequately portray basic human processes. Variables are clearly defined and their links, established on the basis of an extensive review of prior work, suggest many avenues for further research. For example, many studies have been conducted on the nature, size and structure of evoked sets since their theory was published. Furthermore, their model has been adapted to account for business-to-business situations as well as family purchases. Finally, their work has been subject to at least two empirical tests. The first one, conducted in the USA, has confirmed most of the relationships delineated in the model,[5] while the second, conducted in Argentina, led to similar conclusions.[6]

At the same time, it is clear that these two tests are not enough to establish the predictive power of the model. Today, the Howard and Sheth model is primarily used as a frame of reference to generate hypotheses about consumer behaviour rather than to predict specific behaviour related to products or brands.

The Engel *et al.* model

Contrary to the two previous models, the Engel *et al.* model has been regularly updated since its first version was published in 1968, the main reason being that its major purpose was to serve as an integrative framework for the corresponding textbook. Figure 11.3 presents the latest available version, corresponding to the eighth edition of their manual.[7]

As explained by Engel and his colleagues, the purpose of their model is to provide (a) explanations for behaviour; (b) a frame of reference for organising and stimulating research; and (c) a foundation for management information systems. Like Nicosia, Engel *et al.* put the emphasis on decision processes. Purchasing is primarily understood as a problem-solving task which can be analysed in terms of a sequence of successive stages. The five key steps are identified as (a) need recognition, (b) search, (c) pre-purchase alternative evaluation, (d) purchase and (e) post-purchase phenomena such as satisfaction or dissatisfaction. The sequence is rather similar to Howard and Sheth's with, however, more explicit recognition given to

Figure 11.3   The Engel *et al.* model

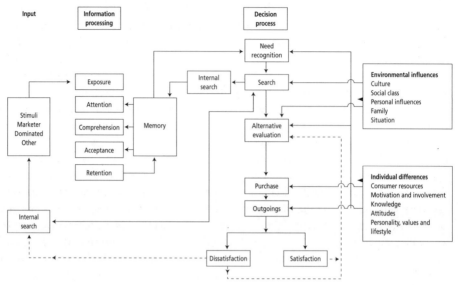

Source: J. E. Engel, R. D. Blackwell and P. W. Miniard, *Consumer Behavior*, 8th edition (New York: Dryden Press, 1995)

the first two stages. As we did in Chapter 8, a need is defined as resulting from a gap between the ideal and the actual state. Search includes acquisition of external information but also an internal search into the memory, a variable left implicit in Howard and Sheth's model. Memory, in turn, affects all the information processes characterising (as in Nicosia's model) the way in which external messages are selected, comprehended, accepted and remembered. Finally, as Howard and Sheth, Engel and his colleagues distinguish variables which exert an external influence over all these factors. Such exogenous variables include both environmental and individual differences. The former are identical to Howard and Sheth's, while the latter explicitly include consumer resources (not only money – or financial status – but also time and information processing abilities), motivation and involvement, knowledge, attitudes, personality, values and lifestyle. As can be seen, the Engel *et al.* model can be considered as 'halfway' between Nicosia's and Howard and Sheth's. Less behavioural in orientation than the latter, it pays more attention than the former to external influences. Its distinctive feature is its strong emphasis on cognitive phenomena, particularly information processing and memory factors. It seems more appropriate to describe situations in which consumers do a lot of thinking rather than react emotionally or automatically (reflexes). However, it has never been subjected to empirical testing and has sometimes been criticised for being 'too cognitive'.[8] Critics point out that for many purchases, a decision never occurs and behaviour is largely influenced by habits or cued by features of the consumer's situation which pre-empt decision making.[9]

Towards a final model?

It should be clear from the above discussion that no model, however sophisticated, will ever account for all the facets of purchase and consumption behaviour. Decisions made by consumers are too diversified and too contingent to be accounted for by a single explanatory scheme. Thus, in concluding this book, the aim is not to present yet another model but rather to offer a simple framework which is not intended to predict the behaviour of any particular consumer but to put into perspective all the major factors which have been presented and discussed here.

Understanding consumers is a two-step process. First one has to document and structure purchase and consumption activities. Then one has to provide explanations, sometimes predictions. Recording behaviour requires the identification of an appropriate unit of analysis, which is necessary to define what to observe and how to observe it. As shown in Figure 11.4, the notion of situation provides the most logical starting point, as situations establish a natural bridge between people and purchase or consumption activities. Depending upon the situation, the same individual may acquire a wide variety of products in totally different ways, from

Figure 11.4   A final model?

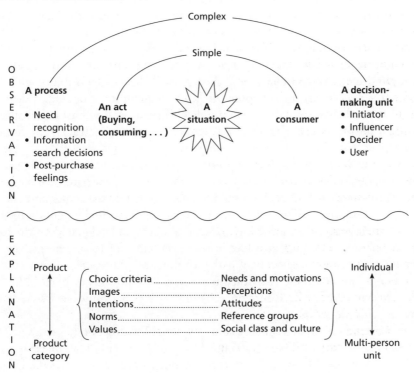

the routine purchase of a pack of cigarettes to the complex and prolonged acquisition of a second home.

For calibrating situations, we have already identified the key parameters: the physical environment (for example, at home, in the store), the social context (alone, with family, with friends) and the time perspective (immediately, within a month, within a year). But it all depends, of course, upon the type of behaviour being investigated. To structure the field of observation, the concept of a process is useful insofar as it allows the recognition and analysis of stages and progression facilitators as well as obstacles.

Need recognition, information search and processing, decisions to purchase and consume, and post-purchase feelings are all important moments for consumers but, contrary to the previously discussed models, they need not follow each other in a logical sequence. In a **simple** situation, almost everything is internalised and appears as a reflex. I leave home to go to work, I buy a newspaper, I read it. There is no real deliberation or evaluation. At best, one remembers the last purchase. Apparent brand loyalty may actually be a habit, not a conscious psychological commitment. Advertising is not there to convince but simply to provide a reminder.

By contrast, a **complex** situation involves a process. Need recognition is explicit and articulate. It usually but not always leads to an external information search. Data collected from commercial (advertising, salesforce, and so on) and non-commercial (word-of-mouth) sources are classified, compared and evaluated. Their role is to facilitate a choice and contribute to a decision. After the product is purchased, its use generates – depending upon expectations – satisfaction or dissatisfaction, which will serve as an input into the next round of decisions.

Contrary to routine situations, which normally involve only one person, a complex purchase is usually made by a **decision-making unit**. The initiator, the influencer, the decider, the purchaser and the user will share responsibility within their respective roles. Divergent viewpoints will be frequent and sometimes degenerate into overt conflicts, especially when goods and services are consumed collectively (holidays, furniture, etc.). There is no real consumer but instead a community of users.

If now one wishes to **explain** and not simply describe behaviour, the preferred level of analysis will influence the nature of the most appropriate variables to consider. At the simplest level, the situation involves only one consumer and one product. His or her motivations, involvement and personality direct attention to specific product attributes, as recognised by perceptual filters and evaluated on the basis of prior experience. Resulting attitudes in turn generate preferences, eventually transformed into purchase intentions. Whether or not a purchase will actually take place depends not only upon the individual but also on the norms prevalent in his or her social environment, as derived from existing reference groups, social class affiliations and cultural values.

Less rigid than Nicosia's but less complex than Howard–Sheth's or Engel et al.'s, the structure put forward here is intended to be a compact but flexible frame of reference. As explained before, the objective is not to predict any specific behaviour but rather to help identify the variables most likely to play an important role in a given type of situation.

Having reached the end of our exploration of consumer behaviour, it is perhaps time to look back and reflect upon the journey. We would like to suggest to the reader a last exercise. This book began by describing the story of the Martins looking for their new car. Let us read again that story. In doing so, the reader will have no trouble identifying the contribution of all the major concepts presented in this book to reaching a better understanding of the Martins' behaviour. Mr Martin's professional occupation largely determines his **motivations** and his degree of **involvement**. Living in a suburb and working in Paris, he uses his car daily to go to work. His poised and reflective **personality** makes him an attentive and cautious consumer, who takes time and ponders his decisions. The favourable **perception** he has of Ford as well as his past **experience** lead him to stay loyal to this make when his car breaks down. Holding managerial responsibilities in a company, he pays a lot of attention to price and other economic criteria, which play an important part in the development of his **attitudes** and **preferences**. But he is not alone to decide. For his son, a future engineer, technical characteristics predominate, while aesthetic considerations are more important for his wife. Each member of the family is influenced by their social environment. Discussions with neighbours, colleagues and their friends, the Vidals, reveal the existence of strong **reference groups** and **opinion leaders**.

Over the years, the Martins have adopted a **lifestyle** influenced by their **social class** affiliations and **cultural** milieu: they prefer to pay cash and buy new cars. The car breaking down, the systematic exposure to automotive magazines and the several visits paid to dealers are but a few of the moments characterising their **purchase process**, while family discussions and the father–son alliance illustrate the dynamics of the **decision-making unit**. Finally, the unfriendly welcome at Central Auto and the dirtiness of the place attest the impact of **situational factors**.

The difference between our first and second reading of the Martins' story lies in the ability we now have to refer to concepts, schemes and theories to account for an otherwise anecdotal episode. Such concepts and theories allow us to elucidate the Martins' decisions but could have served equally well for other families, including our own. The various constructs presented in this book constitute our conceptual toolbox. Suddenly, the billions of purchase and consumption decisions made every second all over the world begin to lose some of their opacity. We now possess the keys allowing us to decipher their meanings. We finally begin to *understand the consumer*.

Notes

[1] For a full description, see F. M. Nicosia, *Consumer Decision Processes* (Englewood Cliffs, NJ: Prentice Hall, 1966).

[2] For a comprehensive evaluation, see G. Zaltman, C. R. A. Pinson and R. Angelmar, *Metatheory and Consumer Research* (Holt, Rinehart & Winston, 1973).

[3] Adapted from B. Pras and J. P. Tarondeau, *Comportement de l'Acheteur* (Sirey, 1981).

[4] For a compact presentation of the model, see J. Howard and J. Sheth, *A Theory of Buying Behavior*, in H. H. Kassarjian and T. S. Roberston (eds), *Perspectives in Consumer Behavior* (Scott, Foresman: 1968), pp. 467–87. For a detailed presentation, see J. Howard and J. Sheth, *The Theory of Buying Behavior* (Wiley, 1969).

[5] J. U. Farley and L. W. Ring, 'An Empirical Test of the Howard–Sheth Model of Buyer Behavior', *Journal of Marketing Research*, November 1970, 427–38.

[6] D. R. Lehmann, J. U. Farley and J. A. Howard, 'Testing of Buyer Behavior Models', *ACR Proceedings*, 1971, 232–42.

[7] J. E. Engel, R. D. Blackwell and P. W. Miniard, *Consumer Behavior*, 8th edition (New York, Dryden Press, 1995).

[8] A. Ehrenberg, *Repeat Buying: Theory and Applications*, 2nd edition (London: Griffin and Co. 1988).

[9] R. W. Oslshavsky and D. H. Granbois, 'Consumer Decision-making: Fact or Fiction?' *Journal of Consumer Research*, September 1979, 93–100.

Index

Note: Page numbers in **bold** indicate keywords emboldened in text; those in *italics* indicate chapters. Most references are to Europe unless otherwise indicated.

Index